The equivalence of direct and semi-direct speaking tests

Two week
loan

STUDIES IN LANGUAGE TESTING . . . 13
Series editor: Michael Milanovic and Cyril J. Weir

Also in this series:

An investigation into the comparability of two tests of English as a Foreign Language: The Cambridge–TOEFL comparability study
Lyle F. Bachman, F. Davidson, K. Ryan, I-C Choi

Test taker characteristics and performance: A structural modelling approach
Antony John Kunnan

Performance testing, cognition and assessment: Selected papers from the 15th Language Testing Research Colloquium, Cambridge and Arnhem
Michael Milanovic, Nick Saville

The development of IELTS: A study of the effect of background knowledge on reading comprehension
Caroline Margaret Clapham

Verbal protocol analysis in language testing research: A handbook
Alison Green

A multilingual glossary of language testing terms
prepared by ALTE members

Dictionary of language testing
Alan Davies, Annie Brown, Cathie Elder, Kathryn Hill, Tom Lumley, Tim McNamara

Learner strategy use and performance on language tests
James Enos Purpura

Fairness and validation in language assessment: Selected papers from the 19th Language Testing Research Colloquium, Orlando, Florida
Antony John Kunnan

Issues in Computer-adaptive testing of reading proficiency
Micheline Chalhoub-Deville

Experimenting with uncertainty: Essays in honour of Alan Davies
A. Brown, C. Elder, N. Iwashita, E. Grove, K. Hill, T. Lumley, K.O'Loughlin, T. McNamara

An Emperical investigation of the componentiality of L2 Reading in English for academic purposes
Cyril J. Weir, Yang Huizhong, Jin Yan

The equivalence of direct and semi-direct speaking tests

Kieran J. O'Loughlin

CAMBRIDGE
UNIVERSITY PRESS

PUBLISHED BY THE PRESS SYNDICATE OF THE UNIVERSITY OF CAMBRIDGE
The Pitt Building, Trumpington Street, Cambridge, United Kingdom

CAMBRIDGE UNIVERSITY PRESS
The Edinburgh Building, Cambridge CB2 2RU, UK
40 West 20th Street, New York, NY 10011–4211, USA
10 Stamford Road, Oakleigh, VIC 3166, Australia
Ruiz de Alarcón 13, 28014 Madrid, Spain
Dock House, The Waterfront, Cape Town 8001, South Africa

http://www.cambridge.org

First published 2001

Printed in Great Britain at the University Press, Cambridge

Typeface Times 10/12pt.   *System* QuarkXPress®   [UCLES]

British Library cataloguing in publication data

University of Cambridge, Local Examinations Syndicate
The equivalence of direct and semi-direct speaking tests

Author: Kieran J. O'Loughlin

1. Education. Assessment 2. Education. Tests. Setting

ISBN   0521 66098X   hardback
        0521 667933   paperback

Contents

Series Editor's note   **vii**

Preface   **ix**

Acknowledgements   **xi**

Chapter One

Introduction   **1**

Rationale   1

Methodological approach   2

Structure of the book   3

Direct, semi-direct and indirect speaking tests   4

Establishing the equivalence of direct and semi-direct tests   6

Research findings   12

Conclusion   31

Chapter Two

The *access:* test   **33**

Background to the test   33

Development of the test   34

The oral interaction sub-test   35

Conclusion   45

Chapter Three

Methodology   **47**

The instrumental case study approach   47

Research design of the study   55

Summary   61

Chapter Four

Trial 1: The analysis of test scores   **62**

Overview   62

The December 1992 trial   62

A preliminary study   65

The current study   69

Conclusion   79

Chapter Five
Trial 1: The analysis of candidate language output   **80**
    Overview   80
    Rationale   80
    Methodology   81
    Discourse Study A: The qualitative analysis   84
    Discourse Study B: Lexical density   100
    Conclusion   115

Chapter Six
Trial 2: The study of test processes   **117**
    Introduction   117
    The June 1994 trial   117
    Method   121
    Findings   125
    Conclusion   143

Chapter Seven
Trial 2: The analysis of test scores   **145**
    Introduction   145
    Analysis with anchored item difficulty estimates   145
    Analysis with unanchored item difficulty estimates   150
    Bias analysis   157
    Conclusion   161

Chapter Eight
Summary and conclusions   **163**
    Overview   163
    Summary of findings   163
    Implications of findings   169

References   **173**
Appendices   **180**
Subject index   **276**
Author index   **278**

Series Editor's note

This volume addresses the issue of spoken language assessment looking in particular at the equivalence of direct and semi-direct oral interviews. Kieran O'Loughlin's work is based on the development and validation of the spoken language component of the *access:* test designed in the early 1990s for migrants to Australia. It is an important language testing project in the Australian context and was funded by the Commonwealth Department of Immigration and Ethnic Affairs. While the project as a whole brought together experts from a number of Australian universities, the oral test was developed by a team at the University of Melbourne. This volume is of particular significance and interest to the language testing community because it takes a multi-faceted view of the investigation of test comparability. While much research of this sort has tended to look only at quantitative data, largely correlational analyses, O'Loughlin taps into a range of different types of evidence and attempts to explore the process of construct validation in oral assessment to a depth that is rarely found.

The assessment of spoken language ability is a topic of enduring importance in the work of the University of Cambridge Local Examinations Syndicate (UCLES) given that UCLES assesses the spoken language ability of about 800,000 candidates around the world every year. The issue of semi-direct versus direct assessment of speaking has continued to be a topic of interest at UCLES and we have found that O'Loughlin's work makes a valuable contribution to our understanding. His work closely reflects our own interests particularly in the area of the qualitative analysis of oral interview interaction.

The importance of oral assessment and the need to better understand the complex issues and interactions that underlie performance in this particular context have long been a topic of debate at UCLES. As early as 1945, Jack Roach, an Assistant Secretary at UCLES at the time, was writing on the topic in his internal report entitled 'Some Problems of Oral Examinations in Modern Languages: An Experimental Approach Based on the Cambridge Examinations in English for Foreign Students.' Indeed, in his book Measured Words (1995), Bernard Spolsky considers Roach's work to be 'probably still one of the best treatments in print of the way that non-psychometric examiners attempted to ensure fairness in subjective traditional examinations'. Roach's work is addressed in more detail by Cyril Weir in a volume currently being prepared for this series that focuses on the revision of the Certificate of Proficiency in English (CPE).

Over the last ten years or so, a considerable amount of work has taken place at UCLES in order to gain a better understanding of oral interview interactions, processes and rating scales both in quantitative and qualitative studies. Working internally or with colleagues at universities in the UK, USA and Australia, numerous studies have been carried out. Amongst other things, projects have looked at:

discourse variation in oral interviews;

rating scale validation;

interlocutor frames and how their use by examiners can be described and monitored;

interlocutor language behaviour;

a methodology to allow test designers to evaluate oral assessment procedures and tasks in real time;

comparisons of one-to-one and paired oral assessment formats;

test takers' language output;

the development and validation of assessment criteria.

In 1998 UCLES EFL established, within its Validation Department, a dedicated unit to drive research in the area of performance testing, which essentially covers the assessment of speaking and writing.

It should also be noted that the next volume in this series, *A qualitative approach to the validation of oral language tests*, by Anne Lazaraton also makes a valuable contribution to the assessment of spoken language ability. Both O'Loughlin's and Lazaraton's volumes underline UCLES commitment to furthering understanding of the dimensions of spoken language assessment.

Preface

This study investigates the equivalence of direct (live) and semi-direct (tape-mediated) speaking tests. The issue is explored through a comparison of live and tape-based versions of the speaking component of the *access:* test, a four-skill English language test designed for prospective non-English speaking background (NESB) skilled migrants to Australia. The *access:* test was developed between 1992 and 1994 by a consortium of Australian universities and Adult Migrant Education Program (AMES) providers under the aegis of the National Centre for English Language Teaching and Research (NCELTR), Macquarie University. The project was funded by the Commonwealth Department of Immigration and Ethnic Affairs (DIEA). The *access:* test was used in overseas test centres from January 1993 until May 1998 when it was replaced by the International English Language Testing System (IELTS). The oral interaction sub-test was designed by the Language Testing Research Centre (LTRC) at the University of Melbourne, Australia in 1992. The two versions of the speaking sub-test were used interchangeably in overseas test centres and candidates normally had no choice about the version which they would undertake. It was important, therefore, that candidates' final results should not be adversely affected by the particular method used to assess their oral proficiency.

Much previous comparability research in language testing has relied primarily on *concurrent validation* which focuses on the equivalence between test scores. However, in this book, it is argued that examining the relationship between test scores provides necessary but insufficient evidence as to whether the same language constructs are being tapped in different tests. This provided the rationale for a study which employed a wide range of very different types of evidence (including test taker language output, feedback from the various 'players' in the test process such as test developers, interviewers, test takers and raters as well as test scores) and analyses (both qualitative and quantitative) in order to investigate the equivalence of the direct and semi-direct versions of the *access:* oral interaction sub-test. In so doing, it demonstrates the need to examine language tests from multiple perspectives in order to obtain deeper insights into what they appear to measure and thus provide richer, more comprehensive evidence for *construct validity* of which concurrent validity is only one (albeit important) component. In turn, it is argued, this approach provides a more solid and therefore more valid basis from which to draw conclusions about test equivalence.

The various types of data used in the study were gathered from two separate trials conducted in Melbourne, Australia (December 1992 and June 1994) where test takers undertook both the live and tape-based versions of the oral component of the *access:* test.

The statistical analysis of test scores from the two versions in the December 1992 trial were contradictory insofar as conflicting results were obtained from the different measures used to measure their equivalence. However, the most rigorous measure indicated a lack of equivalence.

A comparative study of test taker language output under the two test conditions was then undertaken using audio recordings obtained from the December 1992 trial. While broad qualitative analyses of a range of discourse features suggested that there were important similarities between nearly all of the tasks on the two versions, a more detailed quantitative analysis of lexical density suggested that all tasks on the live version were characterised by a significantly higher level of interactivity than on the tape version. This result suggested the possibility that different oral skills were being tapped in the live and tape versions despite the attempt to equate them at the design stage, i.e. interactive versus monologic speaking ability.

The examination of test processes in the June 1994 trial provided further evidence in support of this conclusion but suggested that the apparent lack of equivalence between test scores obtained in the two versions could also partly be explained by the impact of a number of contaminating factors other than oral proficiency on the measurement process. These factors included the quality of the interaction between candidate and interlocutor on the live version, the adequacy of preparation and response times on the tape version, candidates' level of comfort with the two versions as test environments and the existence of rater bias in relation to individual candidates on both versions.

Finally, the analysis of test scores and especially the band levels obtained by candidates in the June 1994 trial confirmed the apparent lack of equivalence between test scores reported in the December 1992 trial.

Overall, these findings suggested that the live and tape-based versions of the oral interaction sub-test could not be safely substituted for each other primarily because they were drawing on different components of the oral proficiency construct but also because the measurement process appeared to have been insufficiently constrained so as to yield a satisfactory level of reliability across the two formats.

Acknowledgements

I am grateful to the following organisations for permission to reproduce previously published material in this book: firstly, Arnold Publishers for an article entitled 'Lexical density in candidate output on direct and semi-direct versions of an oral proficiency test' appearing in *Language Testing* (1995) 12, 2: pp. 217–37 (see Chapter 5) and secondly, NCELTR publications, Macquarie University, for a chapter entitled 'Test taker performance on direct and semi-direct versions of the oral interaction module' published in *access: issues in language test design and delivery* (1997): pp. 117–46 (see Chapters 6 and 7).

I dedicate this book to Don Hay, and to all of the other unsung heroes of the AIDS pandemic – the living and the dead.

J'ai toujours pensé que j'étais étranger à cette ville et que je n'avais rien à faire avec vous. Mais maintenant j'ai vu ce que j'ai vu, je sais que je suis d'ici, que je le veuille ou non. Cette histoire nous concerne tous.

La Peste, Albert Camus

1 Introduction

Rationale

This study explores the equivalence of direct (live) and semi-direct (tape-mediated) speaking tests. This has become an important issue in language testing with the recent advent of semi-direct tests which claim to represent firstly, a valid and reliable substitute for direct procedures in many contexts and secondly, a more standardised and cost-efficient approach to the assessment of oral language proficiency than their direct counterparts. The key question examined in this study is whether or not the two test formats can be considered equivalent in both theoretical and practical terms. This equivalence issue is examined here in the context of the oral interaction component of the *access:* test (the Australian Assessment of Communicative English Skills), a 'high stakes' English language test targeted at prospective skilled migrants from non-English speaking backgrounds (NESB).

The *access:* oral interaction sub-test was developed in two versions – direct (live) and semi-direct (tape-mediated) – and administered in test centres around the world between 1993 and 1998. The direct version was designed to be used on an individual face-to-face basis (i.e. a single candidate speaking with a trained interlocutor) while the semi-direct version was developed for use in a language laboratory setting where groups of test takers undertake the test simultaneously. Administrators at the overseas test centres were therefore able to make a choice between the two versions based on the human and/or technical resources available to them at any given time. Specifically, this decision depended on first, the number of candidates being tested at each centre; secondly, the technological facilities available (including language laboratories); and thirdly, the availability of suitable interlocutors for the live version.

Since test takers were assigned arbitrarily to either version depending on the location where they undertook the test, it was important that their performance should not be adversely affected by the particular format to which they were allocated. This issue provided the practical motivation for the investigation into the interchangeability of the two versions of the *access:* oral interaction sub-test undertaken in this study.

Given the constraints placed on overseas test centres it is important to note at this point that the central validation question did not involve determining which version of this speaking test was *preferable* but, instead, to what extent the two versions could be considered *equivalent* on the basis of data drawn from test trials. The development of the test is described in more detail in Chapter 2.

Methodological approach

From a theoretical perspective it should be noted that much previous comparability research in language testing has been based on *concurrent validation,* which focuses on the degree of equivalence between test scores. Traditionally, this validation procedure has examined the strength of correlation between scores derived from two tests. High correlations are taken to indicate that the two tests measure the same language abilities while low correlations suggest this is not the case. Many of the empirical studies reported later in this chapter attempt to establish the equivalence of direct and semi-direct speaking tests in this way. However, as Shohamy (1994) convincingly argues, investigating the relationship between test scores provides necessary but insufficient evidence as to whether the same language abilities are being tapped in different tests. She suggests that this issue can only be answered through the more complex process of *construct validation* in which concurrent validation plays an important but nevertheless partial role.

This study therefore attempts to go beyond concurrent validation in order to examine the comparability or equivalence of the direct and semi-direct versions of the **access:** oral interaction sub-test. A *case study approach* (Merriam 1988; Yin 1989; Johnson 1992; Nunan 1992) was adopted to carry out the investigation because of first, its holistic focus on the 'bounded system' (i.e. the **access:** oral interaction sub-test); secondly, its exploratory, iterative orientation; and thirdly, its capacity to accommodate different philosophical perspectives and research methods (both quantitative and qualitative). This research project was conceived as an *instrumental* case study (Stake 1994) because, in examining the comparability of the live and tape-based versions of this speaking test, it aimed to shed light on the potential equivalence of this and other pairs of direct and semi-direct oral proficiency tests.

In philosophical terms, (as outlined in Chapter 3), an accommodationist stance (Cherryholmes 1992; Lynch 1996) was used to address the research question. This stance enabled the equivalence issue to be investigated from within both the *positivistic* and *naturalistic* research paradigms. Because of its dual emphasis on both product and process and its reliance on both quantitative and qualitative research methods, this strategy eventually allowed for more solidly grounded, valid conclusions than would have been the case if only one paradigm had been used.

The data for the study were collected from two separate trials of this test (December 1992 and June 1994) where candidates undertook both the live and tape-based versions of the *access:* oral interaction sub-test.

In the first 'case', the December 1992 trial, the comparability issue was addressed from within a positivistic framework and the focus was on different kinds of *products*, test scores and test taker language output. Firstly, the equivalence of scores obtained by the trial candidates who had completed both versions was examined using multi-faceted Rasch measurement. Secondly, in order to investigate whether the language produced under the two test conditions was comparable, the discourse features of sample audiorecordings from the December 1992 trial were analysed both qualitatively and quantitatively using a framework developed by Shohamy (1994). The focus on test scores and test taker output in this trial yielded important but contradictory evidence in relation to the equivalence issue. This subsequently led to the adoption of another very different perspective from which to address the research question in a subsequent trial.

In the second 'case', the June 1994 trial, the comparability issue was first examined from a naturalistic perspective and the investigation focused on test *processes* including the processes of test design, test taking and rating. This involved tracking the various stages of the trial and gathering a variety of data using observation, interviews and questionnaires. In this case both the data and methods of analysis were mainly qualitative. The test scores from this trial were then analysed quantitatively again using multi-faceted Rasch analyses and the results of selected candidates interpreted using the findings from the previous study of test taking processes. This led to additional quantitative analyses of the test scores from this trial.

By moving back and forward between the positivistic and naturalistic perspectives, therefore, the researcher was able to gather a wide range of evidence to support the conclusions reached in the study. The necessity for this dual perspective will become clearer as the evidence on the validity of the live and tape-based tests unfolds in later chapters.

Structure of the book

The rest of this chapter reviews the literature comparing direct and semi-direct tests of oral language proficiency. After introducing direct, semi-direct and indirect tests of oral proficiency, it discusses the most important theoretical claims made about direct and semi-direct tests and then examines the findings reported in a range of empirical studies comparing the two kinds of tests. Chapter 2 introduces the *access:* test in general and the oral interaction sub-test in particular. The comparability of the two versions of the oral interaction sub-test is also briefly examined from the perspective of the relevant test specifications. Chapter 3 describes the methodology used to empirically investigate the equivalence of the direct and semi-direct versions of the *access:* oral interaction sub-test. Chapter 4 examines this issue in relation to the test scores obtained from the first trial held in December 1992 using multi-faceted Rasch measurement. Chapter 5 looks at the comparability question from the perspective of test taker language output on the two versions in the same trial. Chapter 6 explores the test design, test taking and rating processes in a later trial (June 1994) in order to provide a very different perspective on the equivalence of the two versions. Chapter 7 examines the test scores from this second trial again using multi-faceted Rasch analyses. Chapter 8 summarises the findings of the research and then evaluates the usefulness of the various methodologies used in the study to address the main research question and the significance of the findings based on these techniques.

Direct, semi-direct and indirect speaking tests

Clark (1979) provides the basis for distinguishing three distinct types of speaking tests, namely, indirect, semi-direct and direct tests. *Indirect* tests generally refer to those procedures where the test taker is not actually required to speak and belong to the 'precommunicative' era in language testing. Examples of this kind of procedure are the pronunciation tests of Lado (1961) in which the candidate is asked to indicate which of a series of printed words is pronounced differently from others. *Direct* speaking tests, on the other hand, according to Clark (1979: 36) are

> *... procedures in which the examinee is asked to engage in a face-to-face communicative exchange with one or more human interlocutors.*

Direct tests first came into use in the 1950s when the Oral Proficiency Interview (OPI) was developed by the US Foreign Services Institute (FSI). The OPI, as it was originally conceived, is a relatively flexible, unstructured oral interview which is conducted with individual test takers by a trained interviewer who also assesses the candidate using a global band scale. This model has been widely adopted around the world since the 1970s as the most appropriate method for measuring general speaking proficiency in a second language. The Australian Second Language Proficiency Ratings (ASLPR) oral interview developed by Ingram and Wylie (1984) is modelled closely on the original OPI.

In the last decade or so different models of the OPI have evolved. In response to criticisms about the validity and reliability of the original OPI there has been a growing trend towards greater standardisation of the procedure using a range of specified tasks which vary in terms of such characteristics as topic, stimulus, participant roles and functional demands.

An important example of this kind of test is the speaking component of the International English Language Testing System (IELTS), which has been developed by the University of Cambridge Local Examinations Syndicate (UCLES) and is used to assess the readiness of candidates to study or train in the medium of English. The IELTS test can presently be taken in 105 different countries around the world each year. The current speaking sub-test takes the form of a structured interview consisting of five distinct sections which systematically vary the communicative demands made on candidates. These include an introduction where the candidate and interviewer introduce themselves, an extended discourse task in which the candidate speaks at length about a familiar topic, an elicitation task where the candidate is required either to elicit information from the interviewer or to solve a problem, a speculation and attitudes task where the candidate is encouraged to talk about his/her future plans and proposed course of study, and finally a conclusion where the interview is brought to a close (UCLES 1999). UCLES has developed other similar types of speaking tests including the Preliminary English Test, Cambridge First Certificate in English and Certificate of Proficiency in English oral interviews. This more structured, task-based approach to the direct testing of speaking has grown considerably in popularity around the world in recent years. It was also adopted in the development of the direct version of the *access:* speaking sub-test (see Chapter 2).

The term *semi-direct* is employed by Clark (1979: 36) to describe those tests which elicit active speech from the test taker

> ... *by means of tape recordings, printed test booklets, or other 'non-human' elicitation procedures, rather than through face-to-face conversation with a live interlocutor.*

Normally an audio-recording of the test taker's performance is made and later rated by one or more trained assessors.

Semi-direct tests first appeared during the 1970s and have grown considerably in popularity over the last 25 years, especially in the United States. They represented an early attempt to standardise the assessment of speaking while retaining the communicative basis of the OPI (Shohamy 1994: 101). In addition, they are clearly more cost efficient than direct tests, particularly when administered to groups in a language laboratory, and provide a practical solution in situations where it is not possible to deliver a direct test e.g. where the training and/or deployment of interlocutors is a problem. In recent years they have come under close scrutiny in relation to their validity in particular as we shall see later in this chapter.

Examples of semi-direct procedures used in the US include the Test of Spoken English (TSE) (Clark and Swinton 1979), the Recorded Oral

Proficiency Examination (ROPE) (Lowe and Clifford 1980) and the Simulated Oral Proficiency Interview (SOPI) (Stansfield *et al.* 1990). Examples of semi-direct tests designed in the United Kingdom include the Test in English for Educational Purposes (TEEP) (James 1988) and the Oxford-ARELS Examinations (ARELS Examinations Trust 1989).

Of the three procedures – direct, semi-direct and indirect tests of oral proficiency – indirect tests are generally viewed as the least valid measure of the ability to speak a language precisely because the test taker is not required to speak at all in the course of the test.

Establishing the equivalence of direct and semi-direct tests

This section reviews the most important theoretical arguments and empirical findings to date about the potential equivalence of direct and semi-direct speaking tests in relation to their relative validity, reliability and practicality.

Theoretical claims

Validity

In opening the debate on the equivalence issue Clark (1979) argued that direct tests are the most valid procedures as measures of global speaking proficiency because of the close relationship between the test context and 'real life'. In other words, direct tests more authentically reflect the conditions of the most common form of 'real world' communication, face-to-face interaction. Yet, Clark (1979: 38) also acknowledges that the OPI, the most widely used direct procedure, fails to meet these conditions in two important respects. First, there is the problem of the interviewer:

> *In the interview situation, the examinee is certainly aware that he or she is talking to a language assessor and not to a waiter, taxi driver, or personal friend.*

Secondly, the language elicited in an interview is unlikely to reflect the discourse of 'real-life' conversation. In particular, the fact that the interviewer controls the interview means that the candidate is normally not required to ask questions.

Hughes (1989) and van Lier (1989) also challenge the validity of the oral interview in terms of this asymmetry which exists between the interviewer and the candidate. Hughes (1989: 104) points out that in an oral interview 'the candidate speaks as to a superior and is unwilling to take the initiative'. Consequently, only one style of speech is elicited, and certain functions (such as asking for information) are not represented in the candidate's performance.

Hughes recommends the inclusion of tasks such as role plays and discussions as ways of varying the type of interaction, although the underlying asymmetry between interviewer and candidate may not be automatically removed by simply incorporating other tasks in which the participants seem more equal.

Van Lier pursues a stronger version of this argument. He questions whether an interview can validly serve the purpose of assessing oral proficiency by contrasting the essential features of conversations and interviews. An interview, in van Lier's (1989: 496) terms, is distinguished by 'asymmetrical contingency':

> *The interviewer has a plan and conducts and controls the interview largely according to that plan.*

On the other hand, a conversation, van Lier (1989: 495) contends, is characterised by

> *face-to-face interaction, unplannedness (locally assembled), unpredictability of sequence and outcome, potentially equal distribution of rights and duties in talk, and manifestation of features of reactive and mutual contingency.*

The emphasis in an interview is on the successful elicitation of language rather than on successful conversation. Van Lier (1989: 505) calls for research into whether or not conversation is the most appropriate vehicle to test oral proficiency. If so, he argues,

> *we must learn to understand the OPI, find out how to allow a truly conversational expression of oral proficiency to take place, and reassess our entire ideology and practice regarding the design of rating scales and procedures.*

If direct tests, particularly oral interviews, can be criticised for their lack of authenticity then, at face value, semi-direct tests are even more open to this charge. Clark (1979: 38), for instance, argues that they

> *require the examinee to carry out considerably less realistic speaking tasks (than direct tests) – such as responding to tape-recorded questions, imitating a voice model, or describing pictures aloud – which, although they do involve active speaking, represent rather artificial language use – situations which the examinee is not likely to encounter in a real-life (i.e. non-test) setting.*

However, it should be noted that such 'artificial' tasks as 'describing pictures aloud' have also been used in some direct tests including the live version of *access:* oral interaction sub-test (see Chapter 2).

Underhill (1987: 35) is also strongly critical of the lack of authenticity in semi-direct tests:

> *There are few situations in the real world in which what the learner says has absolutely no effect on what he hears next.*

Secondly, he suggests, there is the problem that the assessor misses visual aspects of the candidate's communication in a semi-direct test since their judgement is normally based on an audio-recording of the test performance. Thirdly, while a direct test can be lengthened or directed more carefully if the interviewer considers the speech sample produced by the candidate to be inadequate for assessment purposes, this is not the case in a semi-direct test where the amount of response time allowed is 'set' in advance. Lastly, speaking to a microphone rather than another person may be unduly stressful for some candidates, especially if they are unused to a language laboratory setting. Possible means of reducing their anxiety include giving instructions in the native language, or in written form, or by ensuring that all test takers are familiar with the system in advance.

Both Clark (1979) and Underhill (1987) therefore clearly favour the use of direct tests over their semi-direct counterparts, at least for measuring general speaking proficiency. Clark (1979: 38) contends that

> *the face-to-face interview appears to possess the greatest degree of validity as a measure of global speaking proficiency and is clearly superior in this regard to both the indirect (non-speaking) and semi-direct approaches.*

Clark (1979: 39) suggests that semi-direct tests lend themselves better to what he calls 'diagnostic achievement tests' which measure discrete aspects of speaking performance such as vocabulary items and syntactic patterns, (although this seems a rather reductive view of the potential use of this kind of test). In general, he argues against using either test type for 'cross purposes', i.e. for either obtaining detailed achievement information using a direct test or measuring global proficiency using a semi-direct test. However, Clark (1979: 48) also suggests that:

> *semi-direct tests may be proposed as second-order substitutes for direct techniques when general proficiency measurement is at issue but it is not operationally possible to administer a direct test. In these*

instances, it is considered highly important to determine – through appropriate experimental means – a high level of correlation between the two types of instruments when used with representative examinee groups.

In accordance with the traditional requirements for concurrent validation (Alderson *et al.*, 1995: 178) a correlation of 0.9 or higher is argued to be the appropriate level of agreement at which test users could consider 'the semi-direct testing results closely indicative of probable examinee performance on the more direct measures' (Clark 1979: 40). However, a high correlation between scores obtained from direct and semi-direct tests of oral proficiency does not in itself constitute sufficient evidence that a semi-direct test can be validly substituted for a direct one: the two kinds of tests may not be measuring the same construct. In other words, they could be assessing different components of the oral proficiency trait. The inadequacy of concurrent validation is a central issue in this study and its limitations will be examined more closely later in this chapter in relation to empirical studies previously carried out on the equivalence of direct and semi-direct tests.

Finally, while Clark's (1979) suggestion that direct tests are preferable because they generally approximate 'real-life' communication more closely than semi-direct tests is reasonable (albeit perhaps rather simplistic – see the discussion of the study by Hoejke and Linnell (1994) later in this chapter), he fails to articulate precisely which speaking skills are tapped in the two test formats. In a later publication Clark (1986: 2) is more explicit about what is lacking in semi-direct tests:

interactive discourse-management aspects of the student's overall speaking proficiency cannot be readily elicited (or by the same token, effectively assured) through semi-direct techniques.

This limitation notwithstanding, Clark (1986: 2) is now more optimistic that the semi-direct format

can serve to validly and efficiently measure many of the other performance aspects that constitute overall speaking proficiency.

He argues that this is particularly true of 'proficiency-oriented semi-direct tests' which attempt to approximate as closely as possible the '... linguistic content and manner of operation' as well as the scoring procedures of a live interview.

Van Lier (1989: 493) adopts a less equivocal position than Clark (1986). He considers face-to-face direct tests to be, in principle, more valid than other test formats including semi-direct tests in most circumstances since

*face-to-face talk is to be regarded as the unmarked form of interaction,
and communicating by telephone or speaking into a microphone as
marked forms of interaction.*

He argues that proficiency in these marked forms of communication is an
advanced skill which should only be tested in special instances:

*Hence, although remote interaction may be part of performance
testing for specific groups of learners, it would appear to be an unfair,
that is invalid, measure of general oral proficiency.*

While 'remote communication' may be more difficult for some test takers,
this may not necessarily be the case for other people unaccustomed to face-
to-face interaction. However, if different speaking abilities do underlie these
two kinds of communication then the interchangeability of direct and semi-
direct tests of oral proficiency is left in doubt.

Reliability
While semi-direct tests have been typically viewed as inferior to direct tests
in relation to validity they are often seen as possessing potentially stronger
reliability. Hughes (1989) argues that the chief advantages of semi-direct
procedures are the uniformity of their elicitation procedures and the increased
reliability which is likely to flow from such standardisation. This uniformity
is inevitably placed under threat in direct tests because of interviewer
variability. As Lazaraton (1996: 154) suggests,

*[t]he potential for uneven interviewer performance in a face-to-face
interview is one reason that [semi-direct tests] are so appealing i.e.
they remove the variability that a live interlocutor introduces.*

This is particularly true of the relatively unstandardised OPI where the
content and form of the questions posed to the test taker can vary considerably
from one interview to another.
This lack of standardisation can then have adverse effects on test
performance and reliability of scoring. Underhill (1987: 31), for example,
points out that, in an oral interview, the lack of script or set tasks gives this
procedure its flexibility and yet

*this flexibility means that there will be a considerable divergence
between what different learners say, which makes a test more difficult
to assess with consistency and reliability.*

Underhill also contends that the more predictable content of candidate output in semi-directs tests means that the scoring criteria can be more easily and accurately constructed. This, he claims, is likely to yield more reliable results. In direct tests where the interviewer also acts as the rater (such as the OPI) there is also some doubt cast over whose performance is actually being assessed. James (1988: 116) suggests that the situation

> *... can develop into a catechesis often with examiners' marks reflecting their satisfaction with their own performances rather than those of the candidates.*

In general, therefore, semi-direct tests are believed to provide a more reliable measure of oral proficiency than their direct counterparts.

Practicality

It is frequently claimed that semi-direct tests offer a more practical alternative to the assessment of speaking proficiency than direct tests. Underhill (1987) lists several important advantages which semi-direct tests possess in this regard. First, since groups of candidates can be tested simultaneously in language laboratories using this format, a semi-direct test can be conducted more economically and efficiently. Secondly, the marking does not have to be done in real time since the candidate's performance is audio-recorded and can take place whenever and wherever it is convenient to do so (although it should be noted that the same provision could be built into a direct test). Thirdly, its fixed structure allows assessors to listen to the tapes more quickly by fast-forwarding past instructions and longer task stimuli. Fourthly, tape-mediated tests can be useful where there are logistical problems in obtaining suitable interviewers. Finally, it is undeniable that most forms of direct procedures are more expensive than their semi-direct counterparts because of the higher costs incurred in the selection and training of interviewers and assessors and the administration of the test.

On the other hand, Underhill notes that technical problems can result in poor quality recordings or even no recording at all when a semi-direct format is adopted. Of course, either of these eventualities can occur when direct tests are being recorded for later assessment by raters other than the interviewer. However, live tests where the interviewer carries out the assessment obviously avoid this problem.

At this point it is important to note that in much of the preceding discussion the term 'direct test' is defined solely in relation to the OPI no doubt because of its dominance in the world of proficiency testing until very recently. The prototypical OPI is very different from most semi-direct procedures not simply in terms of whether the candidates speak to a microphone or another person but also in terms of its structure and its degree of standardisation. Taken together these differences make it extremely difficult to compare the two kinds of tests.

Research findings

This section reviews the empirical research literature on the comparability of direct and semi-direct tests of oral proficiency.

Concurrent validation

Following Clark (1979), attempts to establish the equivalence of these two types of speaking test have relied primarily on concurrent validation, at least until very recently. This form of validation involves correlating the test scores obtained from the same group of test takers, who have undertaken two different tests. If the correlation between the scores is strong then it has been traditionally inferred (often prematurely) that the two tests are measuring the same ability. Concurrent validation also assumes that one of the tests is a valid measure of the language ability in question and can therefore serve as the 'criterion behaviour' (Bachman 1990: 249). In most of the research reported to date the direct test – normally the OPI – fulfils this function. It is assumed that it is the semi-direct test whose validity needs to be established in this process.

The OPI and the scale which is used to rate it have been in use in various forms since the 1950s. The OPI was originally developed by the US Foreign Service Institute which is responsible for the training of diplomats and foreign service officers in foreign languages. It was adapted by the American Council for the Teaching of Foreign Languages (ACTFL), the Educational Testing Service (ETS) and the Interagency Language Roundtable (ILR) in the 1970s and became known therefore as the main assessment tool of the 'AEI' proficiency movement (Lowe 1988). The OPI, and the scale on which it is scored, have been widely accepted as a standard for assessing oral proficiency in a foreign language in the US and other countries (Bachman 1991). It is also the precursor of the Australian Second Language Proficiency Ratings (ASLPR) (Ingram and Wylie 1984).

The prototypical OPI consists of a face-to-face interview conducted in the target language by a trained interlocutor (who usually also carries out the assessment) and can include a role play segment. The topics, language input and timing of the interview are adjusted according to the candidate's perceived proficiency which is probed using questions requiring increasingly more complex responses. The topics are chosen by the interlocutor from a range of possible options as specified in the test manual. The OPI usually ends with a 'wind down' phase consisting of one or more easy questions designed to put the examinee at ease and to facilitate the ending of the test. The candidate's performance is scored holistically using either the ILR or ACTFL/ETS scales. The ILR scale consists of 11 levels of general oral proficiency ranging from '0' (no ability to communicate effectively in the language) to '5' (functioning as an educated native speaker). It includes five mid-points (i.e. 0+, 1+, 2+, 3+, 4+) for performances that surpass the requirements for a given level but which fail to reach the next level. However, these mid-points are not defined. The ACTFL/ETS scale, which is derived from the ILR scale, describes different proficiency levels beginning at 'Novice', which consists of three sub-levels, moving up to 'Intermediate', also comprising three sub-levels, 'Advanced', with two sub-levels and finally 'Superior'. Tables 1.1 and 1.2 provide the headings from the official descriptions of proficiency at the various levels on the ILR and ACTFL/ETS scales respectively. Table 1.3 shows the relationship between the ILR scale and the ACTFL/ETS scale (Lowe 1987; Clark and Clifford 1988).

Table 1.1

The ILR scale

LEVEL 1
Elementary proficiency: able to satisfy routine travel needs and minimum courtesy requirements.

LEVEL 2
Limited working proficiency: able to satisfy routine social demands and limited work requirements.

LEVEL 3
Minimum professional proficiency: able to speak the language with sufficient structural accuracy and vocabulary to participate effectively in most formal and informal conversations on practical, social and professional topics.

LEVEL 4
Full professional proficiency: able to use the language fluently and accurately at all levels normally pertinent to professional needs.

LEVEL 5
Native or bilingual proficiency: speaking proficiency equivalent to that of an educated native speaker.

Table 1.2

The ACTFL/ETS scale

NOVICE
The novice level is characterised by an ability to communicate minimally with learned material.

INTERMEDIATE
The intermediate level is characterised by an ability to create with the language by combining and recombining learned elements, though primarily in a reactive mode; initiate, minimally sustain, and close in a simple way basic communicative tasks; and ask and answer questions.

ADVANCED
The advanced level is characterised by an ability to converse in a clearly participatory fashion; initiate, sustain, and bring to closure a wide variety of communicative tasks, including those that require an increased ability to convey meaning with diverse language strategies due to a complication or an unforeseen turn of events; satisfy the requirements of school and work situations; and narrate and describe with paragraph-length connected discourse.

SUPERIOR
The superior level is characterised by the ability to participate effectively in most formal and informal conversations on practical, social, professional, and abstract topics; and support opinions and hypothesise using native-like discourse strategies.

Table 1.3

Relationship between the ILR scale and the ACTFL/ETS scale

ILR	ACTFL/ETS
3 and above	Superior
2+	Advanced Plus
2	Advanced
1+	Intermediate-High
1	Intermediate-Mid & Low
0+	Novice-High, Mid & Low
0	0

The OPI and its immediate successors have dominated the landscape of speaking tests for the last 25 years. And yet, periodically, there have been attempts to find a more standardised, cost-effective but still sufficiently valid and reliable assessment instrument to replace it. Semi-direct tests appeared to many language testing experts to have the potential to provide such an alternative.

The earliest attempt to devise a semi-direct test in the US was the TSE (Clark and Swinton 1979). The TSE was introduced by the Educational Testing Service (ETS) in 1980 to meet a general need for an international standardised test of oral English proficiency. It is now used in over 80 countries around the world, often as an adjunct to the Test of English as a Foreign Language (TOEFL), which does not have a speaking component. The TSE has also been widely used by universities in the US to assess the oral proficiency of NESB international teaching assistants (ITAs). The test is tape-based, conducted entirely in English and of approximately 20 minutes' duration. It consists of six discrete tasks including answering simple personal questions, reading aloud, sentence completion, narration using a sequence of pictures, description and discussion of a topical issue. The test is scored for pronunciation, grammar, fluency and an overall category, comprehensibility, which represents a more general assessment of the test taker's oral proficiency.

In an early study Clark and Swinton (1980: 18) found that scores on the TSE and OPI obtained by a group of foreign teaching assistants (N = 134) correlated at $r = 0.80$. This result suggested to them that the TSE was 'a reasonable alternative to the FSI interview when it is not possible to carry out face-to-face testing' even though it is lower than the figure of 0.9 originally proposed by Clark (1979) to be the acceptable level of agreement at which a semi-direct test might be substituted for a direct test.

In a more recent study Southard and Sheorey (1992: 54) attempted to establish whether a rated interview 'could serve as a substitute for a standardised measure such as the TSE'. This study is unusual insofar as it uses a semi-direct measure of oral proficiency as the 'criterion behaviour' (Bachman 1990: 249) against which the concurrent validity of the direct interview procedure is investigated.

In Southard and Sheorey's study the TSE results of 19 ITAs in the department of English at Oklahoma State University were compared with their performance on a direct interview test. The interview consisted of a structured conversation between individual ITAs and a panel of five judges including two experienced ESL professionals and three 'naïve' assessors (the director of the English department's freshman composition program and two undergraduate students). Candidates were then rated by each member of the panel on a five point scale in the following categories: pronunciation, grammar, vocabulary, auditory comprehension and overall communicative competence.

On the basis of statistically significant (in most cases) but still relatively low correlations between scores on the various criteria used in the two tests (ranging from 0.19 to 0.89) Southard and Sheorey (1992: 62) suggest that *a well-designed, on-campus interview conducted by experienced ESL teachers who are given structured training in evaluating oral proficiency can be used as an alternative instrument if a standardised test like the TSE is not readily available.*

However, given the mainly modest correlation figures reported and the limitations of using such evidence to infer that the two tests are measuring the same abilities, this conclusion appears rather dubious. It is also surprising to note here, unlike in most other recent studies, that a semi-direct procedure is assumed to be valid from the outset and that at no stage of this study is this assumption about the TSE seriously called into question. In the literature generally, it is normally the validity of direct measures of oral proficiency which is taken for granted and that of semi-direct alternatives which needs to be established.

Another early semi-direct test developed in the US, this time designed to assess foreign language oral proficiency, was the ROPE (Lowe and Clifford 1980). The ROPE test more closely resembled the OPI than did the TSE in several important ways. In the ROPE test candidates listen to a series of tape-recorded questions in the target language and provide responses ranging from 'yes/no' to detailed expressions of opinion. Unlike the TSE, there are no written or visual stimuli in this test. The ROPE is scored on the ILR scale from 0+ to 5 (see Table 1.1 above). While the ROPE more closely approximated to the OPI in terms of the kinds of questions used and the method of scoring than the TSE, an important limitation was that not all candidates could understand the questions since they were presented in the target language (Stansfield *et al.* 1990). Lowe and Clifford report a correlation of $r = 0.90$ between scores on the OPI and ROPE across several languages including French, German and Spanish, which meets the level of agreement stipulated by Clark (1979) for test substitution. However, this result should be viewed cautiously given that the total number of subjects was only 27. More importantly, as suggested above, this result alone may not be sufficient to conclude that the two kinds of tests are equivalent.

These studies therefore clearly illustrate the exclusive reliance which has been placed on concurrent validation to establish the equivalence of direct and semi-direct assessment procedures until very recently. As we shall see, this approach was also favoured, at least initially, in comparing the OPI with a more recently developed semi-direct foreign language test, the Simulated Oral Proficiency Interview test (SOPI).

The impetus for the development of the SOPI in the late 1980s was created by problems relating to the testing of less commonly taught languages in the US such as Chinese and Portuguese. In these instances the prohibitive costs and practical difficulties involved in training and deploying suitable interviewers for the OPI meant that a different test format needed to be created, one that could be administered on a one-off basis to individual candidates as well as to large groups throughout the country where required. A semi-direct test seemed to have the potential to meet these needs.

The first SOPI was developed by Clark and Li (1986) (although not labelled as such) at the Center for Applied Linguistics (CAL), Washington, DC to assess oral proficiency in Chinese. Stansfield and Kenyon (1988) later used this model (formally naming it the simulated oral proficiency interview or SOPI) to create a similar test in Portuguese. This was followed by the development of tests in other less commonly taught languages including Hebrew (Shohamy *et al.* 1989), Hausa and Indonesian (Stansfield and Kenyon 1989). All of these tests were developed at CAL.

Interestingly, the development of the SOPI also reflected in its design increasing concerns emanating from language testing research about the validity and reliability of the OPI. In terms of its validity Shohamy (1983), for instance, queried whether a single type of interaction (i.e. an interview) was sufficient to assess oral proficiency. Perrett (1987) argued that while the oral interview may enable assessment of the candidate's phonological and lexico-grammatical skills and some aspects of discourse competence, it does not provide sufficient information about the candidate's control over an adequate range of text types, speech functions and exchange structures. Raffaldani (1988) suggested that the interview format is the main reason why the OPI fails to elicit some important aspects of communication: a limited number of speech functions are sampled and so candidates have little opportunity to display either discourse or sociolinguistic competence. As noted earlier in this chapter, van Lier (1989) also questioned whether an interview was the most suitable vehicle for the measurement of oral proficiency since it largely fails to tap the test taker's conversational ability. In terms of reliability, Shohamy (1983) suggested that OPI scores were affected by a range of contextual variables including topic, type of interaction and interviewer behaviour. Each interview is therefore different because these variables are not tightly controlled.

There was growing interest, therefore, amongst language testing experts in exploring the potential of semi-direct tests to enhance the reliability and validity of speaking tests by controlling such variables and including a range of task types (Shohamy 1994). Thus, by the mid-1980s, they were no longer necessarily conceived as merely 'second order substitutes for direct techniques' (Clark 1979: 48) but as potentially more valid and reliable than their direct counterparts.

The SOPI differed from the OPI in several important respects. As in the OPI, there is an initial 'warm up' phase where the candidate is asked a number of simple personal background questions. The rest of the test consists of a series of set tasks (in contrast to the more open-ended question and answer structure of the OPI) which elicit oral discourse through the use of both aural and visual stimuli. These tasks include giving directions using a map, describing a picture, narrating a story based on a picture sequence, talking about topical subjects and lastly, responding to situations in which the communicative tasks and the audience are specified. In addition, all tasks on the SOPI (with the exception of the 'warm up' phase) are normally read aloud in English on tape and written in English in a test booklet as well as in the target language. As in the OPI, the test becomes progressively more demanding as the test continues: each task is intended to probe or verify a higher level of proficiency until the final 'wind down' stage where candidates are asked one or more simple questions. Unlike the OPI, the SOPI is assessed retrospectively by trained raters using the audio-taped recording of the candidate's test performance. Like the OPI, however, the SOPI is assessed holistically using the ACTFL/ILR scale, which is grounded in a view of language proficiency as a unitary ability. In other words, the components associated with the various points on the rating scale are considered together rather than individually (Stansfield 1991; Stansfield and Kenyon 1992a; Stansfield and Kenyon 1992b).

On the basis of research carried out at CAL in Washington, DC, Stansfield (1991) suggested that the SOPI had shown itself to be a valid and reliable substitute for the OPI. In relation to a comparison of scores on the two kinds of tests, Stansfield reported high Pearson correlations *(r)* in the range of 0.89–0.95 on the OPI and SOPI in Chinese, Portuguese, Hebrew and Indonesian. On the basis of these findings Stansfield (1991: 206) argued that

> ... *the SOPI correlates so highly with the OPI that it seems safe to say that both measures test the same abilities.*

However, it should be noted that the numbers of test takers under investigation in each case were again relatively small, ranging from 10 to 30, and the correlation figures should therefore be regarded with some caution.

A more fundamental problem with Stanfield's conclusion is that, as previously suggested, high correlations between scores on the two kinds of tests provide necessary but insufficient evidence that they measure the same ability: it would also be desirable, for instance, to show that the OPI and SOPI scores in these studies were not consistently related to measures of other language or non-language abilities in order to provide a sounder basis for this conclusion (Bachman 1990: 250). Where high correlations exist between the two tests, it may be possible to safely predict OPI scores from SOPI scores but this does not necessarily imply that the same ability is being measured. Another difficulty with concurrent validation as noted previously is that it assumes that one of the tests is a valid measure of the language ability in question and can therefore serve as the 'criterion behavior'. However, as Bachman (1990: 249) suggests:

> *without independent evidence supporting the interpretation of the criterion as an indicator of the ability in question, there is no basis for interpreting a correlation with that criterion as evidence of validity.*

Given the widespread controversy about the validity of the OPI (see above) it would appear unwise to draw any conclusion about the validity of the SOPI simply on the basis of high correlations between scores on the two tests.

At the statistical level, another limitation of most correlation co-efficients (including the Pearson correlation used in Stansfield's (1991) study), is that they provide a measure of *linearity* rather than equivalence between two sets of scores. It is still possible, therefore, that candidates may have performed systematically better on either the OPI or the SOPI despite the strength of the relationship between the scores. The high correlations, therefore, may allow the score of a candidate on either test to be fairly confidently predicted from the other but do not necessarily indicate that the two tests were equally difficult. The inclusion of descriptive statistics in Stansfield's study, particularly the means, variances and standard deviations of the OPI and SOPI scores for each language, would have assisted in providing this information.

There is an additional problem with the interpretation of high correlations between the scores on the two tests. Unless the correlation is perfect in the positive sense (i.e. +1), there will be candidates for whom the level of performance differed from one test to the other. A correlation of 0.9 indicates that this is the case for approximately 20% of test takers. Thus, in Stansfield's study, it appears that the results for a significant minority of candidates in each of the four languages could not be predicted from one test to the other. It may be that the performance of these people was affected by the two different test formats (i.e. live or tape-mediated), although there may have been other factors influencing them as well, such as a positive or negative practice effect resulting from taking the two tests within a short space of time.

In a later study, Stansfield and Kenyon (1992b) used generalisability theory (also known as G-theory) to further explore the issue of score comparability using the same data as in Stansfield's (1991) study. Generally low levels of subject by test interaction were found for candidates who had undertaken the two kinds of tests in all four languages. However, the results of this analysis did suggest a tendency for some candidates to perform differentially on the two test formats in three of the five studies undertaken, a finding which supports the criticism of the correlational results in the earlier study (see above). Unfortunately, Stansfield and Kenyon (1992b: 356) were unable to confirm from their analysis using G-theory whether this indicated that 'many examinees deviated a little in their performance on the two tests or whether a few examinees deviated a lot, or some combination in-between'.

Stansfield also examines the comparative characteristics of the OPI and SOPI tests in the light of his empirical findings based on test scores. He argues that the SOPI may be more reliable than the OPI first because 'the OPI requires that each examinee be given a unique interview, whereas the format and questions on a SOPI are invariant' (Stansfield 1991: 202). As a result, raters reported that it was often easier to arrive at a decision on a score in the case of the SOPI. Secondly, the greater length of speech sample produced in the SOPI (typically 20–23 minutes versus 15 minutes on the OPI) may make for more accurate judgements about a candidate's proficiency level. Thirdly, the fact that the SOPI is recorded means that it can be assessed by the most reliable rater while the OPI is sometimes rated by interviewers who may not always be the most accurate judges.

In relation to the issue of validity, Stansfield (1991: 203) suggests that one important problem with the OPI is that the candidate's performance may be significantly affected by the skill of the interviewer whereas the SOPI offers the same quality of language input to each candidate. This has since been identified as an important source of measurement error in speaking tests.

In addition, Stansfield (1991: 204) argues that the reason the OPI and SOPI correlate so highly may be because 'neither format produces a "natural" or "real-life" conversation'. Even in the OPI, he contends, both interviewer and candidate understand that 'it is the examinee's responsibility to perform. Little true interaction takes place' (Stansfield 1991: 205). However, such a conclusion needs to be empirically investigated by examining data other than test scores (such as the discourse produced under the two test conditions) to discover whether, in fact, this is indeed the case.

Notwithstanding his concerns about the reliability and validity of the OPI, Stansfield (1991: 207) still views it as 'potentially the more valid and reliable measure when carefully administered by a skilled interviewer and rated by an accurate rater'. On the other hand, given that both of these conditions are not always met in the case of the OPI, Stansfield considers that the OPI may be more suitable for placement and program evaluation purposes and the SOPI more appropriate when important decisions are to be based on test scores given the high degree of 'quality control' it offers. However, this line of reasoning is suspect since it may not always be possible to gauge in advance the importance of the results from any assessment procedure for the life chances of test takers in the short or long term.

From a different perspective, Stansfield appears not to have considered possible sources of variability arising from the semi-direct test format. For instance, candidates may vary considerably in their experience with language laboratories, particularly in a test context. Some test takers may also require greater preparation and response times than are provided on such an inflexible format. These kinds of factors could have an impact on candidate performance as much as the sources of variability in the OPI suggested by Stansfield. Total 'quality control', therefore, may not be guaranteed using either a direct or semi-direct format: the candidate may be advantaged or disadvantaged by features of the test method under either condition. The aim in both cases, as Bachman (1990: 161) suggests, is 1) to minimise the effect of such factors and 2) to maximise the effects of the language abilities which the test intends to measure, thereby enhancing the reliability and validity of the test scores.

On the basis of their research focusing on test scores, Stansfield and Kenyon (1992b: 359) conclude that the OPI and SOPI are highly comparable as measures of oral language proficiency: they may be viewed, it is asserted, as 'parallel tests delivered in two different formats' with the important caveat that

> ... the SOPI may be better suited to elicit and measure extended speech involving longer turns than short responses that are more typical of interaction between two people. In this sense, the SOPI format may be somewhat more friendly for the examinee at the Advanced level or above on the ACTFL scale than for the Intermediate level examinee, because Advanced level speakers (by definition) are able to use paragraph length discourse. It may also be the case that the kind of interaction provided by the face-to-face interview is most appropriate for the Novice and Intermediate examinee.

Furthermore, Stansfield (1991: 207) claims that the SOPI does not provide the extensive probing that may be necessary to discriminate between candidates at the highest level of proficiency, i.e. Superior. These qualifications suggest that the choice of test format needs to be carefully guided by the level(s) at which the test is attempting to reliably discriminate.

Beyond concurrent validation

More recently, the issue of equivalence between direct and semi-direct speaking tests has begun to be addressed from different angles as researchers have become increasingly aware of the limitations of relying primarily on concurrent validation to establish test comparability. This has led, for instance, to careful analyses of both the test instruments used in these comparisons and of the test taker language produced under the two conditions.

Shohamy (1994) was one of the first researchers to question the over-reliance on concurrent validation in exploring test equivalence. Adopting a sceptical view of the studies by Stansfield (1991) and Stansfield and Kenyon (1992b), she argued convincingly that high correlations between scores on the Hebrew OPI and SOPI (ranging from $r = 0.89 - 0.95$, N = 40) provided necessary but insufficient evidence for test substitution, since the two tests may not have necessarily been measuring the same trait. This provided her with the impetus for a detailed study of both the elicitation tasks used and the language produced in the Hebrew OPI and SOPI.

In comparing the elicitation tasks as described in the test specifications for the Hebrew OPI and SOPI, Shohamy found important differences in the expected range of language functions and topics featuring in the two tests. While in the SOPI it was anticipated that candidates would use 14 different functions ranging from describing and narrating to hypothesising and apologising, in the OPI the range was from approximately 5 functions for low and middle proficiency candidates to about 12 for high level candidates. The same pattern was reflected for the range of topics. Fifteen topics of a personal, social and political nature were required for the SOPI compared to 14 topics of a similar range on the OPI for middle and high proficiency candidates but only 9 topics focusing exclusively on personal information for low level candidates. Potentially, therefore, in the case of lower level candidates, the OPI may be realised as a test which elicits very restricted language in terms of the number and variety of functions and topics.

In the a posteriori analysis of test taker language output in the Hebrew OPI and SOPI, Shohamy found no significant differences in the number of errors made in the domains of morphology, syntax and lexicon. However, there was a significantly larger number of self-corrections used on the SOPI and shifts to the candidate's first language on the OPI. SOPI candidates also paraphrased or restated the stimulus questions more often in their responses.

Furthermore, qualitative analysis of the language samples showed the two tests to be quite different in terms of their genres and rhetorical structures. The OPI turned out to be a 'conversational interview' and the SOPI a 'reporting monologue'. The structure of the OPI was question – answer – question while the structure of the SOPI was performance – new task – performance. In the OPI the boundaries between topics were more fluid and the shifts from one topic to the next much smoother than in the SOPI.

Contrary to the descriptions in the test specifications, the SOPI elicited a more limited range of speech functions than the OPI. The tasks on the SOPI which attempted to elicit varied functions, in fact, produced language that consisted mainly of simple, restricted functions such as description, narration and reporting. On the other hand, the more limited types of elicitation tasks on the OPI (mainly direct questions) in fact produced language which included a wide range of functions including requesting clarification, disagreeing and criticising.

These findings suggest that the two-way interaction in the OPI produces a richer, more varied language sample, although Shohamy provides insufficient information about whether this difference was equally marked amongst candidates performing at varying proficiency levels on the two tests. It is conceivable, for instance, that the weaker candidates were able to use only a limited number of functions on both tests. More importantly, perhaps, the limited range of functions on the SOPI may have been a result of the way in which the tasks were constructed.

In Shohamy's study the SOPI answers also included more self-correction, repetition of phrases in the eliciting questions and paraphrasing than in the OPI. There was also a more restricted range of prosodic and paralinguistic features in the SOPI responses: first, less variation in both intonation and voice range and secondly, mainly hesitations and silence when no answer was available. The discourse produced in the SOPI was also generally more formal and had greater cohesion.

Furthermore, Shohamy found in the OPI that the relationship between the amount of lexicon (i.e. content items) and grammar (i.e. function items) was approximately 40% lexicon and 60% grammar, while these figures were reversed for the SOPI i.e. 60% lexicon and 40% grammar. This relationship is known as a measure of lexical density (usually expressed simply as the percentage of lexicon) and has been mainly used to date as an index of the degree of 'orality' versus 'literacy' in both spoken and written discourse. It is argued that texts which are more literate – and these include both written texts and spoken texts such as speeches – are characterised by a higher degree of *lexical density* (i.e. contain a higher percentage of lexical items) than more oral texts which again include both spoken texts and written texts such as highly informal letters (Ure 1971; Halliday 1985). On the basis of the lexical density figures reported in her study, therefore, Shohamy argues that the SOPI produced language which was significantly more 'literate' than the OPI. However, it is argued in Chapter 5 of this book that lexical density in spoken discourse may be more clearly understood as an index of the degree of *interactivity* in spoken discourse.

Shohamy's (1994: 118) interpretation of the various differences which emerge in this study between the OPI and the SOPI is that the test context or format (i.e. face-to-face or tape-mediated), rather than the elicitation tasks, is the most powerful determinant of the type of language produced:

> *The different oral discourses that are produced by the two tests are a result of the different contexts in which the language is elicited. Context alone seems to be more powerful than the elicitation tasks themselves.*

However, in another study, Shohamy *et al.* (1993) concede that, since the tasks on the two tests were not identical, some of the observed differences in candidate output may also have resulted from differences in the elicitation tasks themselves, although they do not specify which features. It is conceivable that there are a range of test method factors which have an impact on the type of language produced in tests of oral proficiency, including the format, (i.e. direct or semi-direct) but also characteristics of the tasks (e.g. topic structure), the degree of interactivity as well as the amount of preparation and response time given to candidates.

The general implication in Shohamy's (1994) study is that the OPI and SOPI do not appear to measure the same language construct and are therefore not necessarily interchangeable as tests of oral proficiency, even where a high correlation exists between scores on the two tests. Shohamy concludes that while different discourse samples are obtained in the two tests, it is difficult to determine which language sample, or test from which it is produced, is in fact more valid as new developments in communication technology (e.g. answering machines, dictaphones, e-mail) challenge the primacy of face-to-face talk. She suggests that, while the OPI appears to have higher validity than the SOPI because of the centrality of conversation in oral interaction, the assessment of oral language proficiency in the future may require the use of both direct and semi-direct tests. Where a choice between the two test formats needs to be made, she suggests, a variety of factors should be considered including the context and purpose of the test.

In another recent study Hoejke and Linnell (1994) examined the equivalence issue from a more theoretical standpoint. They compared three speaking tests used to assess the oral proficiency of NESB teaching assistants (ITAs) in US universities: firstly, the semi-direct SPEAK test (the institutional version of the TSE), secondly, the OPI and finally, another direct test, the Interactive Performance (IP) test, a direct specific purposes performance test.

The SPEAK test is a retired form of the TSE available to institutions wishing to administer and score the test on-site. The IP test requires candidates to give a 10-minute videotaped presentation on a topic in their prospective teaching fields and answer questions from a panel of evaluators comprising three ESL specialists and, in some cases, an undergraduate student. The format of the IP necessitates the use of certain language functions required in the instructional contexts in which ITAs work. The test also attempts to simulate the classroom situation by giving the audience some control of the topic. The assessment focuses on language performance within a communicative competence framework.

Hoejke and Linnell compared the three tests from several related perspectives: first, Bachman's (1990, 1991) conceptualisation of 'authenticity' in language testing; secondly, his framework of test methods facets; and thirdly, the discourse elicited in the three tests. They focused particularly on Bachman's 'interactional/ability' approach to the notion of authenticity. This approach identifies the fundamental characteristics of language use in target and test settings through focusing on the interaction of language user, task and context. It examines the extent to which a test engages the candidate's language ability in comparison to the tasks of the target-use setting without attempting to mirror 'real life', a goal which has been criticised as naïve since no test setting exactly resembles its real-life counterpart (Spolsky 1985; Stevenson 1985; Bachman 1990, 1991). In the context of assessing ITA language performance, Hoejke and Linnell conclude that the IP test is the most satisfactory from this perspective, not so much because it resembles the 'real-life' task of teaching, but because its tasks engage the speaker's competence in ways similar to the tasks of the target-use context more comprehensively than the other two tests. The SPEAK test, on the other hand, is found to be the least satisfactory, not simply because of its semi-direct format *per se*, but, more precisely, because it does not adequately tap the candidate's discourse, interactional and sociolinguistic competences, all crucial to the role of language assistant. The OPI more closely resembles 'authentic' language use in this context. However, the interaction on the OPI still differs considerably from that of the classroom setting as it occurs only between two speakers and it is the interviewer who guides the discussion.

The study by Hoejke and Linnell underscores the importance of content validity or the need to demonstrate the extent to which test performance reflects the specific language abilities in question. It also highlights the fact that 'authenticity' is not necessarily guaranteed in oral proficiency testing, irrespective of whether a direct or semi-direct format is adopted. In essence, the study demonstrates the extent to which '... the test must be "authentic" as well as statistically viable' (Hoejke and Linnell 1994: 122).

Face validity

Another perspective from which the equivalence of direct and semi-direct speaking tests has traditionally been examined is face validity, in particular, test taker feedback. However, to date, this type of validity has been viewed as having only a subsidiary role to play in establishing test comparability.

Face validity or 'test appeal' is still largely regarded by many theorists in language testing as having a useful, albeit limited role in making tests acceptable and 'user friendly' to test takers and test users but not as having implications for construct validation (see, for example, the range of views presented in Bachman 1990: 285–9). In particular, research into test taker feedback is often seen as marginal to the main task of test validation. Where test developers, test takers and test users disagree about which form of a test is preferable it is most often the preference of the test 'experts' which holds sway. However, there has been some disagreement on this question. Shohamy (1982: 17), for instance, argues that

... knowing that attitude and anxiety are significant factors in test performance should lead to careful deliberation before applying an evaluation procedure that may have a negative emotional impact no matter how statistically reliable and valid it is.

More recently, Alderson *et al.* (1995: 173) suggest

... face validity is important in language testing. For one thing, tests that do not appear to be valid to users may not be taken seriously for their given purpose. For another, if test takers consider a test to be valid ... they are more likely to perform to the best of their ability on that test and to respond appropriately to items.

Questionnaire feedback from test takers on the OPI and SOPI has been gathered in a number of studies. Shohamy (1982: 15–16), for instance, reports highly favourable test taker reactions to the OPI considered separately and provides the following explanation for this state of affairs:

Students seem to feel that the oral interview reflected their actual knowledge of the language since they could see the direct relationship between the testing procedure and their performance ... They perceived the oral interview as a low anxiety test and some even thought that it was a fun test which made them feel comfortable and created a relaxing atmosphere. Many perceived it as a pleasant experience.

The SOPI has consistently proved to be less popular than the OPI since its introduction. Clark (1988) compared the reactions of 27 candidates after they had undertaken both the OPI and the first SOPI (although not labelled as such) in Chinese. Notwithstanding the strong equivalence between test scores, 63% of candidates reported feeling more nervous on the tape test, 19% on the interview and 18% equally nervous on both tests. 78% found the tape test more difficult, 7% the live and 15% found them equally difficult. On the other hand, a similar percentage of respondents (74% on the live and 70% on the tape) felt that their speaking ability in Chinese had been adequately probed on the two tests. 96% of candidates thought the live questions were fair while 70% felt the tape questions were fair. Individual comments indicated that the main problem on the tape format was the difficulty of some tasks for a number of weaker test takers. Finally, 89% of candidates expressed a preference for the live test compared to 4% for the tape test and 7% no preference. Clark's (1988: 197) conclusion is that:

From an administrative viewpoint, implications of the questionnaire data would seem to be that face-to-face interviewing is preferable whenever the necessary resources can be made available, but that when an alternative approach is required, the examinees involved will generally consider themselves adequately tested through semi-direct means, albeit as a 'second-choice' procedure.

In developing the next form of the SOPI in Portuguese, Stansfield *et al.* (1990) similarly found test takers strongly favoured the live interview despite an average correlation of $r = 0.93$ between scores on the two tests. Of the 30 test takers who completed a questionnaire after undertaking the OPI and SOPI in Portuguese, 69% felt more nervous on the tape test, 24% more nervous on the live test and 7% equally nervous on the two formats. 90% of them found the tape test more difficult and 10% found the two tests equally difficult. Individual comments suggested that the tape format was felt to be an 'unnatural' context in which to be tested. Overall, 86% of test takers expressed a preference for the live interview, 7% for the tape condition and 7% no preference. However, respondents were generally positive about the fairness of both tests: all of the candidates felt the questions on the live test were fair and 83% felt similarly about the tape test. In addition, 73% of test takers believed that their maximum level of Portuguese had been probed under both conditions.

In a subsequent study, examining feedback from OPI and SOPI test takers in a range of languages, Stansfield (1991) reports that while most preferred the live format because of the human contact it provided as in the earlier studies, about a quarter either preferred the tape format or had felt there was no difference. Where the semi-direct version was preferred it was because test takers were not so nervous talking to a tape-recorder as to an unfamiliar and highly competent speaker of the target language. In general, however, Stansfield (1991: 204) concedes that:

Since speaking into a tape recorder is admittedly a less natural situation than talking to someone directly it is possible that the SOPI format will cause undue stress.

A number of studies have examined test taker reactions to direct and semi-direct tests apart from the OPI and SOPI. In a report to the Australian Council of Overseas Qualifications (COPQ), McNamara (1987) investigated the reactions of 56 former and intending candidates to the then-existing tape-mediated format of the speaking component of the Occupational English test (OET), a test for overseas trained health professionals in Australia. The original speaking test consisted of a three-minute impromptu talk on a non-professional subject, delivered into a tape-recorder. McNamara found that

52% advocated changing the test (of which more than half expressed a strong preference for a face-to-face format), 30% found the tape-based format acceptable and 18% offered no opinion. Specific comments included the following:

No more talking into a tape recorder, please!

Candidates are not used to talking to a recording machine and voices from a tape can be very hard to listen to. Anyway doctors are dealing with patients and people mainly.

I would like to change the part played by the tape ... It is quite easy to talk to a person rather than speaking to a tape, something which is inanimate.

I didn't like speaking to a tape. I would have preferred to speak to someone.

The tape-mediated procedure was subsequently changed to a direct procedure in which candidates were required to participate in face-to-face role plays (based on situations relevant to their professional practice) with a trained interlocutor who normally also carried out the assessment. The new form of the OET speaking sub-test is more fully described in McNamara (1988, 1990a and 1990b).

However, test taker preference for a direct format should not be assumed. After piloting the semi-direct speaking component of the Test in English for Educational Purposes (TEEP) test for prospective students entering tertiary courses, James (1988:116) reported that

in many cases, students stated in the post-test questionnaires that they preferred a test in a language laboratory because they felt more secure than in a face to face situation.

Most negative responses focused on procedural matters (such as insufficient response time) rather than on the test format itself. This apparent preference on the part of most test takers for a semi-direct format (although it is unclear what percentage of test takers 'many cases' represents in the above quotation) could be at least partly explained by the fact that they were all thoroughly briefed and trained in this format before the trial.

It should be noted that the results of James' (1988) study are atypical. In a more recent study comparing test taker performance and attitudes across a range of direct and semi-direct elicitation modes including face-to-face interaction, the telephone, videotape and audiotape, Shohamy *et al.* (1993) once again found a strong preference for the direct format: 96% of candidates (N = 10) favoured either the live face-to-face or telephone modes while only 4% opted for the two modes using recorded input, the video and audiotapes.

It appears therefore, if asked to choose between the two formats, test takers generally prefer the direct format for speaking tests. On the other hand, this finding does not necessarily imply that their reactions to the tape-based format *per se* will always be negative. In a study of test taker feedback in the development of the Occupational Foreign Language Test (Japanese), a tape-mediated test of spoken Japanese for the tourism and hospitality industry in Australia, Brown (1993) found that 57% of trial candidates (N = 53) liked the tape-based format, 25% disliked it and 18% were neutral. This result was somewhat surprising given that many of these candidates indicated they had had little or no exposure to recording their voice in a language laboratory, especially in a test situation. However, the results might not have been so favourable had the respondents been given the opportunity to compare their reactions to this tape-mediated test with another live test. Negative reactions to the test appeared to be largely the result of inadequate response time despite the fact that the assessor used in the trial felt the responses were generally sufficient to rate the candidates' levels accurately. The response time was subsequently increased in order to reduce test taker frustration and anxiety.

In more general terms, Hamp-Lyons and Lynch (1995) have urged language testing researchers to pay greater attention to the voices of test takers, test personnel (including interviewers and raters), test users and other interested groups in the validation process (i.e. face validity), rather than simply listening to themselves. From these perspectives, test taker feedback becomes a legitimate, indeed valuable source of evidence for test validity. The debate on the importance of 'test appeal' exemplifies the current controversy surrounding the conceptualisation of validity which is taken up in Chapter 3.

Towards the adoption of multiple perspectives

More recently, research undertaken by Luoma (1997) into the speaking component of the Intermediate level English test (which forms part of the National Certificate of Language Proficiency in Finland) uses an even broader range of methods than had hitherto been the case to address the issue of equivalence of direct and semi-direct tests. In this context, the semi-direct test consisted of a warm up reading aloud task then three other set tasks: Simulated conversation where test takers were required to to express fairly simple functions e.g. greeting, making appointments, apologising for being late to a business appointment, reacting in situations where they were required to read a description of a situation and then say what might be said in such a situation at greater length than in the previous task and finally, presenting views and opinions where they gave two mini-presentations of about two minutes each. While the tape was monolingually English the test booklet was written in both English and Finnish to ensure test takers understood the instructions. The live test, on the other hand, was conducted entirely in English. It consisted of a short warm up phase and two test tasks: first, a peer discussion among two or three candidates and secondly, a more interview-like discussion between the interlocutor and each individual candidate. In both tasks the topics were unkown to the test takers prior to the test.

In Luoma's study a total of 37 candidates undertook both the live and tape-mediated versions of the test. A wide variety of quantitative and qualitative data including test scores, audio and video recordings, transcripts of language output, questionnaire feedback and interviews with both test takers and raters were gathered and examined to investigate the comparability of the two versions.

While the test scores in Luoma's study correlated strongly ($r = 0.89$), test takers once again overwhelmingly preferred the live test. The tape test was found to provide the same level of quality control for all candidates, sampled a wider range of situations and, contrary to Shohamy's (1994) study, elicited a broader variety of functions than the live version. On the other hand, the live test was clearly more interactive but only two topics were covered and the quality of interlocutor input was found to be highly variable. Differences were discovered in both test taker language output from the two tests and what the raters were paying attention to in their assessments in each instance.

In general, Luoma's findings underscored the centrality of interaction in the live test and its absence in the tape-mediated test. While the underlying constructs of the two versions were shown to be different in some senses, the strength of the relationship between test scores indicated that scores from one version could be safely used to predict scores from the other. Luoma (1997: 136) posits two alternative explanations for the high correlation between test scores. First, it may be that 'where different aspects of language ability were tested, these aspects develop simultaneously in individual language learners'. Secondly, it is possible that raters were not 'assessing the performances [on the two versions] as such, but what the performances indicated to them of the candidates' ability to use language outside the test context'. In this way, the raters 'buffer the possible variability in performances through compensating for the effects of test tasks [across the two versions]'. Because of the conflicting evidence, Luoma (1997: 132) concludes that there is no simple answer to the comparability question but rather 'it depends on how important the differences are to the one asking the question.'

Luoma's study demonstrates the potential of combining investigations into test outcomes and processes to obtain a richer, more complex picture of test comparability. Yet, like most of the previous studies reported in this chapter, her findings are based on a comparison of two tests which differ not only in terms of format but also in relation to the type of tasks used in each case. This makes it difficult to draw clear conclusions about their equivalence.

Conclusion

The literature on the comparability of direct and semi-direct speaking tests is fairly substantial. The main emphasis in the empirical research reported in this literature has been on concurrent validation focusing on the degree of equivalence between test scores. There has also been a limited amount of quantitatively oriented research into test taker feedback on the two kinds of tests. More recent studies, however, have begun to explore alternative forms of comparison such as detailed examinations of the different test instruments and test taker language output. While these new directions have already provided important insights into the comparability issue, there is a need to complement them with other perspectives as well. In particular, with the exception of Luoma (1997), very limited attention has been given to the examination of test design, test taking and rating *processes* and how an understanding of these components of assessment procedures may provide the basis for a more complex comparison between the two kinds of tests, especially when combined with the analysis of test *products* (such as test scores and test taker language output). This is the methodogical approach adopted in this study.

Research in language testing has only recently begun to take up such a dual perspective. In oral proficiency testing there have been a number of recent studies investigating the interaction between candidate and interlocutor on direct speaking tests the impact on test scores (e.g. Neeson 1985; Lazaraton 1991; Ross and Berwick 1993; Lazaraton and Saville 1994; Morton and Wigglesworth 1994; Filipi 1995; Morton, Wigglesworth and Williams 1997). Another notable example of research combining a focus on process and product in testing speaking is a study of how raters interpret rating scales (Pollitt and Murray 1993). To date, however, such an approach has seldom been adopted in comparability studies. Attending to both process and product has the potential to provide greater insight into construct validity or what test scores actually mean, and thus a stronger basis from which to compare them. In the present study, the necessity for this more complex perspective will become clearer as the evidence on the validity of the ***access:*** live and tape-based versions of the oral interaction sub-test unfolds.

The other important issue which emerges from this chapter is that in most studies to date the two tests being compared differ not only in terms of format (i.e. whether they are direct or semi-direct) but also in relation to such important features as their overall rhetorical structure, the nature of the tasks, the type of stimuli and the scoring criteria. This makes investigations into their equivalence problematic in some senses. In Shohamy's (1994) ground-breaking study, for instance, it is clear that no real attempt was made by test developers to match the SOPI with the OPI (apart from incorporating questions of gradually increasing difficulty and adopting the same rating scale to score the two tests). This is also true of most of the other studies reviewed in this chapter. Conversely, the research which will be described in this book allowed for a more controlled investigation into the equivalence of direct and semi-direct tests since the two versions of the *access:* oral interaction sub-test were carefully matched from the outset of the development process. As a result, the findings in this study are likely to be clearer and therefore potentially more authoritative – hence its value and importance.

This chapter has briefly outlined the focus of the study and reviewed the literature on the comparability of direct and semi-direct tests of oral proficiency. Chapter 2 will describe the development of the *access:* test in general and the oral interaction sub-test in particular.

2 The *access:* test

This chapter introduces the *access:* test in general and the oral interaction sub-test in particular. The comparability of the two versions of the oral interaction sub-test is also briefly examined from the perspective of the relevant test specifications.

Background to the test

The late 1980s witnessed an unprecedented expansion of the skilled migration program in Australia. However, many skilled immigrants continued to arrive in Australia with minimal competence in English. While, in theory, all skilled non-English speaking background (NESB) migration applicants were required to have their English language proficiency tested as part of the selection process, in practice, this requirement was waived for some categories of applicants. Nor was it consistently applied to applicants in the other skilled categories, the majority of whom were permitted to self-assess given the lack of an adequate testing system in place at overseas posts (Hawthorne 1997).

By 1992, with Australia in recession and unemployment mounting, there was increasing evidence to suggest that skilled migrants with limited English language proficiency faced a disproportionate labour market disadvantage (Hawthorne 1997). The Federal Government was also seeking ways of reducing the costs of English language training in the adult migrant sector. It was against this background that the then Commonwealth Department of Immigration and Ethnic Affairs (DIEA) developed a new English language testing policy as part of an overhaul of its skilled migration program. It subsequently invested AUD$ 1.9 million in the development of a new testing system by a consortium directed by the National Centre for English Language Teaching and Research (NCELTR), Macquarie University, who would report to a DIEA management committee. The NLLIA Language Testing Research Centre (LTRC) at the University of Melbourne was given principal responsibility for the development of the oral interaction sub-test, Adult Migrant Education Services (AMES) in NSW for the reading and writing sub-tests and NCELTR for the listening sub-test. AMES, Victoria and the NLLIA Language Testing and Curriculum Centre (LTCC), Griffith University would also participate in an advisory capacity. Work on the development of the four sub-tests began in September 1992.

While NCELTR co-ordinated the creation of the new testing system, DIEA continued to develop and refine its new testing policy. In a leaflet entitled *Migrating to Australia: English Language Assessment* issued in January 1993, DIEA set out its new regulations for verification of claims made by migration applicants about their English language proficiency. Four levels of proficiency (see Table 2.1 below) were distinguished for the purpose at this time.

Table 2.1

General English language proficiency levels, DIEA, January 1993

VOCATIONAL
This means that you have a good command of English in a wide range of social and work situations and can communicate with a fairly high degree of fluency.

FUNCTIONAL
This means that you can use English well enough to deal with most common social situations and some work situations, but you do not have thorough or confident control of the language.

BASIC (SURVIVAL)
This means that you know enough English to deal with familiar, everyday situations.

LIMITED (BASIC)
This means that you have some knowledge of English, but only enough to understand and make yourself understood in a very limited way.

Development of the test

Originally, DIEA and NCELTR agreed that there would be one test to assess Vocational English language proficiency and another to assess Functional proficiency. Thus, a Vocational level test was initially developed with plans to begin work on its Functional level counterpart immediately after this process had been completed. However, in early 1993 (after the first form of the Vocational test had been developed), DIEA requested NCELTR to design a single test which would reliably identify candidates at both the Vocational and Functional levels in all four macro-skills (listening, reading, speaking and writing).

The *access:* test was first trialled in Australia during December 1992 and administered in six overseas test centres in March 1993 with test papers and recordings being returned to Australia to be marked by trained raters. Candidates were guaranteed a six week turnaround in results. By October 1994 the test was available in 27 locations around the world and wider global coverage was anticipated in future years. It was envisaged that the scoring of performance would eventually be carried out in overseas centres where possible to increase administrative efficiency. Although the test was offered on a user-pays basis, fees were scaled in line with specific location expenses. These fees were designed to cover local administration and some test development costs.

In May 1994 the *access:* contract was put out to tender and, at the end of the year, awarded to a new partnership between Griffith University and the International Development Program (IDP). This partnership continued to manage the development and administration of the *access:* test until May 1998 when the Federal government unexpectedly abandoned it in favour of the IELTS, primarily, it would appear, on the grounds of cost-efficiency.

The oral interaction sub-test

Choice of formats

Initially, it was envisaged that the oral interaction sub-test would be developed in a direct format only. However, it soon became apparent that overseas test centres would need to be able to opt for a semi-direct format as well since adequate numbers of suitably qualified native speakers of English to act as interlocutors on the live version could not be guaranteed in all locations.

While trial candidates would undertake both versions of the test in order to establish their equivalence, overseas test centres were to be given the choice of format depending on the number of candidates presenting for the test as well as the availability of appropriately qualified interviewers and language laboratories. Thus, from the outset it was the local administrators of the test rather than the candidates who made this selection.

Given these constraints on overseas test centres, the crucial comparability issue explored in this study is not which version of the oral interaction sub-test was *preferable*, but rather whether the two versions were *equivalent* in the context of the test trials.

Development of the two formats

Draft test specifications for the direct and semi-direct formats of the oral interaction sub-test, targeted at the Vocational level only, were drawn up by a test development team from the LTRC, University of Melbourne in

September 1992. They were then vetted and given provisional approval by the Test Development Committee (TDC) at NCELTR during the following month. The discussion which follows draws heavily on these draft specifications.

The draft specifications stated that the live version of the oral interaction sub-test was designed for use with individual candidates and a trained interlocutor in a face-to-face context while the tape version was designed to be administered to a group of candidates in a language laboratory. The live version would not exceed 20 minutes in duration and the tape version 30 minutes when administered overseas, although it was anticipated that the trial versions would be up to 15 minutes longer in both cases for the purpose of trialling a greater number of tasks. Both versions were designed to be conducted entirely in English.

The two versions of the oral interaction sub-test consisted of a range of tasks which were derived from the current literature on oral language testing and designed to 'reflect the variety of situations in which adult Australians might find themselves in the everyday course of their work, social and educational pursuits' (Brindley and Wigglesworth 1997: 45). In particular, the test development process was informed by the findings of Shohamy (1994) which were reported previously in conference papers in 1991 and 1992. As outlined in Chapter 1, Shohamy's results suggested that two widely used speaking tests, the Oral Proficiency Interview (OPI) and the Simulated Oral Proficiency Interview (SOPI), were not interchangeable, since the elicitation tasks and language samples obtained from candidates who had undertaken the two tests differed in important ways. Mindful of these results, the test developers attempted to construct the two versions of the oral interaction sub-test in such a way that both the elicitation tasks and candidate responses would match each other as closely as possible:

Tasks in the direct and semi-direct formats of the test are developed in tandem in an attempt to ensure the comparability of the two formats. Before administration of a test, a trialling procedure is carried out in which candidates undertake direct and semi-direct formats of the test. Subsequent statistical analyses of the trial results allow for concurrent validation of the two types of tests.

Test specifications, September 1992

It is worth noting the assumption here that concurrent validation would provide sufficient evidence that the two versions were equivalent. However, as suggested in the previous chapter, statistical comparisons of test scores provide necessary but insufficient evidence that two tests measure the same language abilities and that other kinds of evidence, including test documents, test taker language output and test processes, need to be examined in order to establish their comparability.

The draft specifications also stated that both versions would consist mainly of tasks involving 'one-way' (monologic) exchange where the candidate is required to communicate information in response to prompts from the 'interlocutor' in order to secure their equivalence. However, in order to exploit the possibilities of face-to-face interaction, a role play allowing for 'a more "authentic" information gap activity in which meaning is negotiated between candidate and interviewer' was also included on the live version.

A key element in designing the 'monologic' tasks was that they would not require interlocutor input once the candidate had begun to speak in response to the prompt. The prompts themselves would be carefully scripted to provide control over the input of interlocutors with varying levels of experience and expertise in this role, particularly in the overseas centres. Limiting the potential variability in their input on most of the tasks in the interest of reliability was therefore considered highly desirable by the test developers in the process of designing the live version.

The decision to reduce interactivity on the live version was made reluctantly given its centrality in most 'real world' communication and indeed most direct speaking tests. However, at the time the specifications were developed this appeared to the test developers to be the most reasonable way first, to ensure comparable language output on the two versions following Shohamy's (1994) findings and secondly, to provide greater quality control in the live version at overseas test centres. The two-way live role play represented a concession to the reduced interaction of the other live tasks by the test developers. Its inclusion therefore reflects a degree of ambivalence on their part about the role of interaction in the live version.

Most of the tasks would also be designed to share important characteristics across the two versions, including task structure and expected range of language functions as shown in Tables 2.2 and 2.3 below. In terms of their structure tasks were characterised according to a model developed by Gardner (1992) and derived from research in second language acquisition. First, tasks were classified as either *planned* (allowing preparation time) or *unplanned* (designed to elicit spontaneous language). Secondly, they were distinguished as either *open* (allowing a range of possible solutions) or *closed* (allowing a restricted set of possible responses).

Table 2.2

Test tasks: live version, oral interaction sub-test, September 1992

	Discourse form	Stimulus	Language functions	Task type
1	WARM UP			
2	a) Description	three set questions	describing	unplanned, open, monologic
	b) Narration	sequence of cartoons	narrating, explaining	planned, closed, monologic
3	Role play	role play cards	explaining, apologising, making excuses	planned, closed, dialogic, convergent
4	Exposition	percentage table	describing, comparing, analysing, explaining, speculating	planned, closed, monologic
5	Discussion	four set questions	describing, narrating, explaining, giving opinions, speculating	unplanned, open, monologic

Gardner's model also makes a distinction between two-way exchange tasks which are convergent (involving problem solving in which the aim is to arrive at a particular goal) and those which are divergent (without specific goal, involving decision making, opinion and argument). The only two-way task, the live role play, was designed to be convergent.

The tasks would require test takers to use a wide range of language functions including describing, comparing, interpreting, narrating, explaining, summarising, apologising, analysing, speculating, discussing and giving opinions on both versions. The range of topics to be covered on the two versions was the same involving contexts encountered by adults in Australia in the course of their everyday life, work or study.

Table 2.3

Test tasks: tape version, oral interaction sub-test, September 1992

	Discourse form	Stimulus	Language functions	Task type
1	WARM UP			
2	a) Description	three set questions	describing	unplanned, open, monologic
	b) Narration	sequence of cartoons	narrating, explaining	planned, closed, monologic
	c) Summary	recorded dialogue	summarising	planned, closed, monologic
3	Role play	telephone message	apologising, explaining, making excuses	planned closed, monologic
4	Exposition	percentage table	describing, comparing, analysing, explaining, speculating	planned, closed, monologic
5	Discussion	four set questions	describing, narrating, explaining, giving opinions, speculating	unplanned, open, monologic

Both formats would include an unassessed 'warm up' period where candidates were asked three or four general questions about themselves to reduce their anxiety and help them feel comfortable with either the interlocutor on the live version or the recorded voice on the tape version. In the description task on each of the two formats candidates would be asked three questions about a setting with which they were familiar, such as a school or work environment. The narration task on both formats would require them to re-tell a story based on a sequence of eight pictures. In the summary task (tape version only) candidates would listen to a dialogue and then summarise its contents for another person. The role play task on the live version would consist of a two-way exchange where the candidate and interviewer were given written prompts to guide them in performing their respective roles. The role play on the tape version, by contrast, would require candidates to leave a telephone answering machine message in response to a written prompt. In the exposition task on both formats candidates would be asked to describe, explain, analyse and interpret information in the form of tables, graphs or diagrams. Finally, the discussion task on the two formats would require candidates to answer three or four set questions on subjects of general or vocational interest. For the purpose of trialling, more than one example of a particular task type would be included in some cases. A choice would then be made between the alternatives following analysis of the test scores from the trial. Finally, in both versions the amount of preparation time for each task would be set in advance; however, only on the tape version was the amount of response time fixed beforehand.

The scoring criteria chosen by the test development team to rate the test tasks on the two formats were also matched, generally focusing on fluency and accuracy. These criteria included *Fluency, Resources of grammar, Vocabulary, Coherence and cohesion, Appropriacy, Intelligibility* and *Overall communicative effectiveness*. Different combinations of these criteria were used to rate particular tasks as deemed appropriate by the test development team after listening to sample audio recordings of performances on both the live and tape-based versions of the oral interaction sub-test from the first trial held in December 1992.

At this point a technical distinction needs to be made between a 'task', a 'criterion' and an 'item'. The term 'task' refers to the whole activity the candidate is required to undertake (e.g. role play) and the term 'criterion' denotes a rating category (e.g. *Fluency, Vocabulary*). An 'item', on the other hand, refers to either an individual scoring criterion on a particular task (e.g. description: *Resources of grammar*) or a global criterion (e.g. *Communicative effectiveness*). In the first trial form of the test there were 23 items on the live version and 24 on the tape version, all equally weighted in the subsequent statistical analyses of test scores. The one salient difference was that an additional global criterion, *Comprehension*, was included on the live version (but not the tape) in order to assess the candidate's interactive listening ability. The complete list of scoring criteria used to rate individual tasks on the two versions is included in Chapter 4 (Table 4.1).

Each of the scoring criteria was assessed on a six-point Likert scale with descriptors (these were identical for the two versions of the test). The full list of descriptors for the scoring criteria initially used to rate candidates on both versions of the test is included in Appendix 4.1. These descriptors were derived empirically using the sample audio recordings of candidate performance referred to above. This process involved members of the test development team formulating and eventually agreeing on definitions of proficiency at six levels for each criterion. For example, levels 6 and 4 under the category *Fluency* were characterised as follows:

6 Speech is as fluent as, and of a speed similar to, an educated native speaker.
4 Speaks more slowly than native speakers, with some hesitations and groping for words though without impeding communication.

The same levels under the category *Resources of grammar* were described as:

6 Range and control of a native speaker.
4 Generally demonstrates control of a variety of structures. Errors are noticeable but not systematic and do not interfere with communication.

The one category which did not have descriptors was the overall criterion *Communicative effectiveness.*

The first set of tasks for the oral interaction sub-test was developed by the LTRC in early November 1992. They were subsequently revised in the light of feedback from the Test Development Committee (TDC) at NCELTR. Following construction of the tasks, booklets were developed for candidates to be used in both the live and tape-based versions. Both booklets included the stimuli for the test tasks. In addition, in the tape version, the instructions for the tasks were written, as well as spoken on the tape, since the candidate would not have the advantage of clarifying misunderstandings with the interlocutor. A tapescript and sound recording were also produced for the tape version and an interlocutor's booklet for the live version.

For both the test trials and overseas administrations the interlocutors were required to be native speakers, with formal training in the teaching of English to speakers of other languages (TESOL), and with at least two years experience teaching at a range of proficiency levels. The test booklet for interlocutors provided them with detailed instructions concerning language input to be used with candidates as well as the requirements for each task. In addition, with the exception of the role play, interlocutors were instructed not to intervene once the candidate was clear about the task requirements. As previously suggested, it was anticipated that the highly scripted nature of the interlocutor's input would provide greater 'quality control' on the live version.

The first direct and semi-direct versions of the oral interaction sub-test

(Form A) were trialled in Melbourne in December 1992 on a total of 94 candidates recruited from several local tertiary institutions and language centres. This initial trial is the focus of Chapters 4 and 5 of this book. The 12 interlocutors and 13 raters employed in the trial were all qualified and experienced teachers of adult ESL.

A half-day training session for interlocutors was conducted prior to the trial where a volunteer ESL student undertook the live version with one of the interlocutors. This led to discussion about appropriate interlocutor behaviour in both the more 'monologic' tasks and the more 'dialogic' role play as well as further practice where pairs of teachers acted out the roles of interlocutor and candidate on selected tasks. While this was the model used for training sessions prior to the test trials conducted in Australia, video and print materials were also developed for preparing interlocutors at the overseas test centres where the *access:* test was administered.

Following the first trial administration a full-day training session for raters was conducted in January 1993. Like the interlocutors they were required to be native speakers, with formal training in TESOL, and with at least two years experience teaching at a range of proficiency levels. In the training session raters first listened to a sample of tasks selected from a range of audio recordings from the live and tape versions and practised using the rating scales for the criteria relevant to each task. Their scores were then collated and individual raters asked to justify their assessments, particularly when they were very different from the rest of the group. Thus, the aims of this initial training session were first, to acquaint raters with the test tasks and rating scales and secondly, to encourage them to compare and critically reflect on their scoring. After their ratings from the trial had been examined using multi-faceted Rasch analysis (Linacre 1989–95), raters were also given individual feedback on the internal consistency or intra-rater reliability of their scoring. Wigglesworth (1993) provides a detailed account of this aspect of the training process. Follow-up training for experienced raters consisted of shorter group calibration sessions immediately prior to carrying out scoring of audio recordings from other trial and overseas administrations together with continued individual feedback. Further whole-day training sessions were only held for the purposes of inducting new raters and for re-training others who had not rated for some time.

The oral interaction sub-test was first administered overseas together with the other sub-tests in listening, reading and writing in March 1993. All four sub-tests were targeted at the Vocational level only. One centre, Hong Kong, administered the semi-direct version of the oral interaction sub-test to 51 intending immigrants. Five centres, Moscow, Warsaw, Beirut, New Delhi and Amman, administered the direct version to a total of 80 candidates.

In April 1993 work began on a revised oral interaction sub-test which would reliably identify candidates at both the Vocational and Functional levels in accordance with DIEA's wishes at this time. By May 1994 a number of revisions to the original test specifications for the oral interaction sub-test, including the tasks and the scoring criteria, had been completed. Chapters 6 and 7 of this book focus on a trial, based on the revised test specifications (see Appendix 1.1), which was held in Melbourne in June 1994.

The only important modification to the test tasks was in section 2a, the description task. On both formats the structure of this task had previously been unplanned and open. Its structure was now planned and closed. The new task consisted of two or three questions in which candidates would be shown some visual material, such as cartoon pictures or photos, and required to describe, compare and discuss them. The test development team considered that providing stimulus material for this question would offset the risk of candidates remembering little or nothing about a specified past environment with which they were supposedly familiar and also made their responses more comparable for the purpose of rating. One further alteration was made in section 4, the exposition task. An additional possibility now was that candidates could be asked to give a set of instructions about a procedure outlined in diagrammatic or point form. The summary task on the tape version was still included despite the lack of counterpart on the live version.

The scoring criteria were now assessed on a seven-point scale with appropriately modified descriptors. This modification was made by the test developers to encourage raters to use more points on the scale: previous analyses of test scores had revealed that raters were reluctant to use the highest point on the scale for all of the scoring criteria. In addition, references to native speaker levels of performance in the descriptors for each of the scoring criteria were removed. As suggested by a number of authors, including Alderson (1980), Bachman and Savignon (1986), Bachman (1988, 1990), Davies (1991) and Hamilton *et al.* (1993), native speakers, like non native speakers, vary in their ability to handle the performance demands of communicative tasks. It is therefore extremely difficult to appeal to such a slippery criterion in trying to describe levels of performance on language tests. It is also worth noting that the criterion, *Appropriacy*, was no longer in use on either version, following analysis of the first trial administration, as it appeared to be measuring a separate skill from the other criteria. The complete list of scoring criteria used to rate individual tasks on both versions of the revised test is included in Chapter 6 (Table 6.2). The revised set of descriptors for each of the scoring criteria is included in Appendix 6.1.

Six general levels of performance on the oral interaction sub-test were distinguished by May 1994 for the purpose of candidate classification. These levels of performance and their descriptors (where applicable) are shown in Table 2.4.

Table 2.4

Proficiency levels: oral interaction sub-test, June 1994

LEVEL 6 [Undefined]

LEVEL 5
Can communicate effectively in spoken English in a range of social, educational and work situations. Communication is appropriate with a high degree of fluency. Language is grammatically accurate most of the time with a wide range of vocabulary which is used effectively in most situations.

LEVEL 4
Can communicate in spoken English to handle everyday communication in social, educational and work situations. Can communicate with a fair degree of fluency despite some grammatical inaccuracies. Vocabulary is wide enough to express most ideas, particularly in familiar situations.

LEVEL 3
Can communicate general information in spoken English in most everyday social situations. Can use basic grammatical structures although inaccuracies are frequent. Although vocabulary is limited at this level most common concepts can be expressed.

LEVEL 2
Can communicate in spoken English well enough to hold a very simple conversation. Limited control of basic grammatical structures. Vocabulary is limited to common words and phrases.

LEVEL 1
No practical speaking ability in English.

In terms of its reliability of measurement the test was designed to discriminate most clearly between the three upper levels, i.e. Level 4, Level 5 and Level 6. Level 4 corresponded to Functional proficiency and Level 5 (and above) to Vocational proficiency. The cut-off points for these three levels were derived from a trial in September 1993 where the entire cohort of test takers (N = 121) undertook the Australian Second Language Proficiency Ratings (ASLPR) interview procedure as well as both the live and tape-based versions of the *access:* oral interaction sub-test.

The ASLPR (Ingram and Wylie 1984) is designed to measure language ability in the four macro-skills (speaking, listening, reading and writing) using nine levels from zero to native-like proficiency (i.e. 0, 0+, 1-, 1, 1+, 2, 3, 4 and 5). Each of these levels is accompanied by detailed descriptions of what individuals can typically do at each level. An additional level between 2 and 3 (i.e. 2+) is also widely used although it has not yet been formally described.

The ASLPR interview is used to assess speaking and listening skills and is conducted in the target language by a trained interviewer who normally scores the candidate as well. In each case, the topics, questions and timing of the interview are chosen according to the candidate's perceived level of proficiency which is probed using questions requiring increasingly more complex responses. Reading and writing skills are normally assessed concurrently using appropriate tasks. As the ASLPR was the instrument most widely used to assess the English language proficiency of adult immigrants in Australia at this time, it was deemed by DIEA to be the most appropriate source of information on which to draw in order to establish benchmark levels of performance on the *access:* test.

In the September 1993 trial candidates' ASLPR scores were used to benchmark results obtained from the two versions of the oral interaction sub-test. This process seldom enabled these results to be aligned with the proficiency levels shown in Table 2.4 above by equating Level 4 with ASLPR 2 (minimum social proficiency), Level 5 with ASLPR 2+ and Level 6 with ASLPR 3 (minimum vocational proficiency). The cut-off scores were then carried over to subsequent trial and overseas administrations using previously trialled tasks as 'anchors' in the statistical analyses of the test raw scores. This procedure enabled candidate performance on any given form of the oral interaction sub-test to be related directly to performance on earlier forms of the same test (see Chapter 7 for further details).

Although the ASLPR ratings were the primary means of establishing cut-off levels in this process, other information (such as test developers' views of what constituted typical performances at the various overall levels and analysis of samples of candidates' performances in relation to these levels) was also considered in order to offset over reliance on this procedure. The issue of cut-off scores will be further discussed in relation to the findings in this study in Chapter 7.

Finally, it is worth noting that the paragraph in the draft specifications (September 1992) cited earlier in this chapter, which refers only to concurrent validation as a means of establishing equivalence between the live and tape versions of the test, remains unchanged in the revised specifications of May 1994. It is therefore clear that other methods of demonstrating the comparability of the two versions were still not envisaged at this stage of developing the test.

Conclusion

This chapter has outlined the development of the *access:* test in general and the oral interaction sub-test in particular. In briefly comparing the two versions of the oral interaction sub-test in relation to the test specifications, the careful attempt by test developers to establish equivalence between them has been underlined. In general, it appears that the two versions were fairly well matched in their design in terms of the tasks and scoring criteria used in each case. Perhaps the most distinctive – and contentious – feature of the design of the oral interaction sub-test raised in the discussion was the attempted minimisation of interaction on the live version (with the exception of the role play task) in order to maximise its comparability in terms of language output with the tape version and to ensure quality control in overseas test centres.

What is original about this study, therefore, is that, unlike previous research, it examines the comparability of direct and semi-direct tests which were carefully matched in design in a bid to secure their equivalence. Whether or not this was actually achieved in practice, however, is the central issue explored in subsequent chapters of this book.

Chapter 3 will describe the methodology used to compare the direct and semi-direct versions of the ***access:*** oral interaction sub-test in the current study.

3 Methodology

This chapter describes the methodology used to examine the equivalence or interchangeability of the direct and semi-direct versions of the *access:* oral interaction sub-test in this study. First, it introduces the *instrumental case study* approach, outlines the philosophical perspectives underpinning the investigation and explores relevant issues of validity and reliability. Secondly, the chapter provides a rationale for the approach taken in the study and then outlines the research design, including the procedures and methods of data analysis adopted in the study. The chapter concludes with a discussion of the role of the researcher in the various phases of the investigation.

The instrumental case study approach

This section introduces the case study in general and the instrumental case study in particular, discusses the philosophical perspectives underpinning the study as well as relevant notions of validity and reliability and examines key methodological principles.

The case study defined

Strictly speaking, the case study approach is not a method. Instead, it is normally defined in terms of its unit of analysis. Merriam (1988: 9–10) provides the following definition:

> a case study is an examination of a specific phenomenon such as a program, an event, a person, an institution or a social group. The bounded system, or case, might be selected because it is an instance of some concern, issue, or hypothesis.

In a sense, of course, this could be a description of any form of empirical research and yet what is distinctive about the case study is its holistic focus on the 'bounded system' in context. Thus, for Yin (1989: 23)

> *a case study is an empirical inquiry that investigates a contemporary phenomenon within its real-life context; when the boundaries between phenomenon and context are not clearly evident; and in which multiple sources of evidence are used.*

As Yin suggests, the other main distinguishing feature of case study research is its use of a variety of evidence (both qualitative and quantitative) to explore the issue(s) under investigation.

The case study is sometimes construed as a limited type of ethnography, a research method derived from anthropology and firmly grounded in the naturalistic paradigm. Ethnography, like other forms of naturalistic inquiry, is based on the assumption that human behaviour cannot be understood without incorporating into the research the perceptions and insights of those involved in the study, not simply the researcher. It mainly employs observation, interviews and other sources of qualitative data as methods of data collection. However, while a case study can share the same naturalistic philosophical assumptions as an ethnography (although, as discussed below, this is not always true), case studies are generally more limited in scope than ethnographies, focus less on cultural interpretation and more frequently use both qualitative *and* quantitative data and analyses (Nunan 1992).

Johnson (1992) provides the basis for distinguishing most case studies in terms of design and methods. In developing a working design the researcher may start by delineating the research questions and the unit selected for study and then choose initial data collection and analysis techniques. As the study progresses new perspectives on the 'bounded system' may emerge requiring different methods to be utilised.

There are relatively few methodological rules for case studies. As Johnson (1992: 83) suggests, case study methodology is highly flexible and is devised in response to the purpose of the study. The type of data gathered and the methods of data analysis employed in the study, as noted above, may be of a quantitative and/or qualitative nature.

The case study approach was adopted to carry out the research for this investigation because of first, its holistic focus on the case or 'bounded system' (i.e. the *access:* oral interaction sub-test); secondly, its exploratory, iterative orientation; and thirdly, its capacity to accommodate different philosophical perspectives and research methods (both quantitative and qualitative).

The intrinsic versus instrumental case study

Stake (1994: 237) distinguishes between *intrinsic* and *instrumental* case studies. In the intrinsic case study the researcher is focused entirely on the particular case:

> *It is not undertaken primarily because the case represents other cases or because it illustrates a particular trait or problem, but because, in all its particularity and ordinariness, this case itself is of interest.*

In the instrumental case study, on the other hand, a particular case is investigated to throw light on an issue or theory. In this instance, Stake (1994: 237) suggests

> *a particular case is examined to provide insight into an issue or refinement of theory. The case is of secondary interest; it plays a supportive role, facilitating our understanding of something else. The case is looked at in depth, its contexts scrutinised, its ordinary activities detailed, but because this helps us pursue the external interest.*

While the distinction between intrinsic and instrumental case studies is an important one, Stake (1994: 237) points out that there is not always a clear line distinguishing them. Instead, 'a zone of combined purpose separates them' since the researcher may 'simultaneously have several interests, often changing'.

The research reported here is an example of an instrumental case study. In focusing on whether the live and tape-based versions of the ***access:*** oral interaction sub-test were interchangeable in the test trials conducted in Australia (two of which became the 'cases' here), the study aims to shed light on the *potential* equivalence of this and other pairs of direct and semi-direct speaking tests. The implications of the findings in this study are discussed in Chapter 8.

Philosophical assumptions

This section outlines the philosophical assumptions underpinning the case study approach adopted here. The case study has been employed in the field of applied linguistics to date by researchers working within both the *positivistic* tradition of research (see, for example, Sato 1985) and the *naturalistic* tradition (see, for example, Benson 1989). However, in recent discussion of research methods (cf. Merriam 1988; Yin 1989; Johnson 1992; Nunan 1992) it is normally located in the second of these traditions.

The positivistic paradigm continues to dominate research in language testing. This is perhaps not surprising given the importance of the measurement dimension in this enterprise. The positivistic position basically asserts that reality is objective, that facts can be separated from values and that the researcher's task is to arrive, as far as possible, at 'context free' conclusions about what is produced in the study. It typically relies exclusively on the expert knowledge of the researcher, who normally employs mainly quantitative data and methods of data analysis to test tightly framed hypotheses formulated at the outset of the study (Guba 1990b; Lynch 1996).

In more recent years this traditional form of positivism has been superseded by *postpositivism*. This viewpoint asserts that while external reality exists it can never be fully comprehended. Moreover, while objectivity remains a regulatory ideal in social inquiry it can only be approximated. Postpositivism embraces the use of multiple methods of inquiry (although the quantitative variety is still generally favoured) to enhance reliability and to offset the bias inherent in any one source of evidence. It also displays a willingness to consider the insights and feedback from the people participating in the research about the issue(s) at hand, not simply those of the researcher(s), albeit to a limited extent. Despite these concessions, postpositivism remains fundamentally tied to the positivist paradigm in terms of its underlying philosophical assumptions. Indeed, it is questionable whether postpositivism actually represents an entirely separate paradigm at all (Guba 1990b; Phillips 1990; Lynch 1996).

Both positivism and postpositivism stand in sharp contrast to the other main paradigm in social science research, the naturalistic or constructivist perspective. Naturalistic inquiry assumes that reality is not objective, that facts and values cannot be meaningfully distinguished and that phenomena are best understood within the context in which they are explored. It primarily uses qualitative data (such as observation and interviews) and qualitative methods of analysis. In contrast to research based on positivistic principles, the research is exploratory and process-oriented. Naturalistic research therefore demands an emergent as opposed to a pre-formulated design (Guba 1990b; Lynch 1996; Merriam 1988: 17).

Most significantly, perhaps, as a logical extension of its view of reality, the naturalistic paradigm rejects the notion of external, objective truth which underlies the positivistic paradigm. Instead, the naturalistic position asserts that

> *truth is a negotiable commodity contingent upon the historical context within which phenomena are observed and interpreted.*
>
> (Nunan 1992: xii)

The idea that truth is a 'negotiable commodity' also implies that researchers need to seriously take into account the views of the people who participate in their studies in order to arrive at an understanding of what is being investigated, as well as their own observations and insights.

These diametrically opposed perspectives on the nature of 'truth' underpin very different views of the nature, purpose and significance of social research.

As a result, the positivistic and naturalistic research paradigms, and thus the quantitative and qualitative methods they respectively each favour, are seen by some scholars, (e.g. Guba and Lincoln 1989), as fundamentally incompatible. From this perspective, these two different kinds of methods can only provide information that counts as evidence within the paradigm to which they belong.

However, as writers such as Cherryholmes (1992) and Lynch (1996) have suggested, it is possible to find a way out of this potential stalemate by adopting an *accommodationist* (i.e. compatabilist) stance. In support of this perspective Howe (1988) argues that social science research need not employ only one kind of understanding. He claims that both the 'scientific' understanding derived from positivistically oriented research and the 'interpretive' understanding stemming from naturalistic research should be admitted as legitimate forms of knowledge. From this viewpoint, it is permissible, even desirable, to mix the methods of the two paradigms (including their research designs, data gathering techniques and types of data and analysis) in order to allow the different kinds of understanding which result from the use of both methods to inform each other. The accommodationist stance derives from pragmatic philosophy and represents a middle ground between the positivistic and naturalistic paradigms. It is essentially according to Lynch (1996: 20)

> *[a] non-paradigm allowing for methods to change and develop our notion of paradigm and vice-versa ... the pragmatist stance puts paradigm and method at the service of practice in order to be able to have something rational and convincing to say about the object of inquiry.*

Adopting an accommodationist position does not mean that both qualitative and quantitative methods will always be employed in any given study – the appropriate choice of methods will hinge on the nature and purpose of the research. Nor will a mixing of these methods necessarily lead to consistent or complementary findings. In fact, it may be that such a combination will result in conflicting and even contradictory perspectives about a given issue. This situation may then lead the researcher to further considerations about the relative merits of the different methods in the particular research context.

The accommodationist stance is the theoretical position underlying the instrumental case study approach used in this study. In the first instance, investigating the equivalence of test products (namely, test scores and test taker language output) from the live and tape versions of the oral interaction sub-test necessitated a positivist orientation. Later, the naturalistic perspective was adopted as the most suitable model for an 'inside' exploration of the two tests, looking at such issues as how they are produced, what happens in the two test events and how they are rated.

Thus, adopting an accommodationist stance enabled the researcher to move between two very different research perspectives. In so doing, the researcher was able to gather a wide range of evidence and use a variety of methods (both quantitative and qualitative) to support the conclusions reached in the study. The necessity for this dual perspective will become clearer as the evidence on the validity of the live and tape-based versions of the oral interaction test unfolds.

The preceding discussion has attempted to outline the philosophical issues and problems associated with combining quantitative and qualitative methods in conducting empirical research. Too often, as Lynch (1996: 21) suggests, such a mixing of methods is used in applied linguistics research as if the philosophical assumptions associated with these methods were necessarily the same. The accommodationist stance allows the researcher to work within both the positivistic and naturalistic research paradigms while acknowledging their differences especially in relation to what counts as evidence in any given inquiry.

Validity and reliability

The case study, particularly when undertaken from within the naturalistic paradigm, has been criticised in relation to issues of reliability and validity, both internal and external. Much of this criticism, as Nunan (1992: 58) notes, stems from the fact that it is based on a detailed examination of a particular context or situation.

Reliability in research relates to the consistency of the findings. A study has internal reliability if its conclusions are or can be independently ratified by more than one researcher, or, at least that they seem reasonable in the light of the data collected. External reliability refers to whether the study can be replicated. Given that published accounts of naturalistic case studies generally report only a limited proportion of a large quantity of qualitative data, it is often difficult, as Nunan (1992) points out, for other researchers either to analyse the data themselves or to attempt replication of the study. This is not normally the case with more positivistically oriented research. In discussing ethnographic research, LeCompte and Goetz (1982) suggest methods of enhancing the reliability and validity which would appear to apply equally well to most case studies. In relation to internal reliability, they recommend the use of low inference descriptors which describe behaviour on which it is easy to agree, multiple researchers, participant researchers, peer examination and mechanically recorded data to guard against threats to internal reliability. LeCompte and Goetz claim that external reliability can be safeguarded by carefully detailing the status of the researcher(s), the choice of subject(s), the context and conditions under which the research is undertaken, the analytic constructs and premises of the study and the methods of data collection and analysis.

Validity relates to the 'truth' of research findings. Internal validity relates to whether the observed relationship between variables could be inferred as causal. This may, however, not be a crucial issue, particularly in naturalistically oriented studies. As Nunan (1992: 59) suggests,

> *if the researcher is not attempting to establish a causal relationship between variables, the issue of internal validity will be less problematic than if such a relationship is being sought.*

In any case, internal validity cannot be automatically guaranteed where positivistic methods are employed. Thus, in both positivistic and naturalistic research the apparent relationship between key variables needs to be closely scrutinised before causality can be deduced.

Finally, external validity primarily concerns the issue of generalisability or to what extent can the research findings be generalised to other groups. Because of the case study's concentrated focus on the particular instance, however, the ultimate goal may not necessarily be to arrive at a generalisation about the whole population of instances as in many other kinds of research. Stake (1988: 256) underscores this feature of the approach:

> *In the case study, there may or may not be an ultimate interest in the generalisable. For the time being, the search is for an understanding of the particular case, in its idiosyncrasy, in its complexity.*

Nunan (1992: 59) suggests that

> *if the researcher is not interested in the issue of generalisation, then the issue of external validity is not a concern.*

However, the issue remains vexed for contexts in which there may be a motivation to extend the findings beyond the limits of the 'bounded system' of the case as in the instrumental case study.

While generalising can be problematic in any empirical study, whether positivistically or naturalistically oriented, this does appear to be particularly true for the case study. LeCompte and Goetz (1982) suggest that the case study's external validity can be enhanced, if necessary, by paying close attention to particularity issues including the uniqueness of the phenomena under investigation to a particular site, the influence of the researcher on the outcomes, historical effects and the extent to which abstract terms and constructs are shared across different groups and sites. Merriam (1988: 177) advocates first, providing a rich, thick description so that readers can make their own judgements about the generalisability of the findings; secondly, attempting to discuss the typicality of the case compared to others in the same class; and thirdly, conducting a cross-case analysis in order to strengthen the study's external validity. However, none of these recommendations provides a clear answer to the question of whether the case study can lead to explicit conclusions which go beyond the particular instance being examined.

More recently, Stake (1994) suggests that the case study can be oriented to broader issues or theories beyond the specific instance being examined. The instrumental case study, in particular, generally aims to take the reader beyond the specific instance under investigation. Its methods, according to Stake (1994: 242–3),

> *draw the researcher towards illustrating how the concerns of [other] researchers and theorists are manifest in the case.*

This could involve, for instance, using a previously developed design or method of data analysis. While acknowledging its potential for linking in with these broader concerns, Stake (1994: 238) also cautions against allowing the quest for generalisations to dominate the instrumental case study:

> *Damage occurs when the commitment to generalise or create theory runs so strong that the researcher's attention is drawn away from features important for understanding the case itself.*

Provided the researcher does justice to the particularity of the case, the instrumental case study, as Stake (1994: 245) suggests, can be 'of value in refining theory and suggesting complexities for further investigation, as well as helping to establish the limits of generalisability'.

As suggested previously, the research reported here is an example of an instrumental case study. In examining the comparability of the live and tape-based versions of the *access:* oral interaction sub-test in two different test trials, the study has *potential* implications for the equivalence of this and other pairs of direct and semi-direct speaking tests, either presently in use or yet to be developed. These implications are discussed in Chapter 8.

Because of what they see as a positivistic bias in the meaning of the terms 'validity' and 'reliability', Guba and Lincoln (1989) have proposed an alternative set of criteria for evaluating naturalistic research which they refer to as *trustworthiness* criteria. Instead of internal validity they refer to *credibility,* which is enhanced by procedures such as prolonged engagement, persistent observation and triangulation. Instead of external validity (or generalisability) the notion of *transferability* is proposed. This notion refers to the degree to which working hypotheses derived from the study in question can be transferred to other contexts. The researcher is required to provide a sufficiently thick description of the study to allow the reader to determine whether such a transfer is possible. Rather than ensuring reliability, the naturalistic inquirer attempts to achieve *dependability* by way of continually testing working hypotheses through prolonged engagement. Peer *debriefing* leading to feedback from 'disinterested' colleagues, *member checking* with participants in the research about conclusions drawn by the researcher and *inquiry audits* focusing on the degree of consistency achieved in the study are examples of other means of enhancing dependability. This typology appears to offer a more appropriate basis for strengthening the findings of naturalistic research.

Guba and Lincoln have also developed a further set of considerations which they call *authenticity criteria* (i.e. *fairness, ontological authenticity, educative authenticity, catalytic authenticity and tactical authenticity*) which do not attempt to parallel the traditional notions of validity and reliability. These criteria emphasise the representativeness of the views gathered in the research process, the degree to which participants' understanding of the key issues is increased in this process and finally, the extent to which something is actually done as a result of the research.

The different perspective cast by Guba and Lincoln on judging the merits of naturalistically oriented research has important significance for the way in which this kind of research is carried out in the current study. Equally, however, the more traditional ways in which validity and reliability are understood and safeguarded are relevant to the positivistically oriented research which also forms part of this study. Adopting an accommodationist position (see above) meant that care needed to be exercised in adopting the most appropriate procedures for strengthening the findings according to which types of research methods were employed at any given stage of the study.

Research design of the study

Rationale

As suggested earlier in this chapter, the case study approach was adopted to carry out the research reported here because of first, its holistic focus on the case or 'bounded system'; secondly, its exploratory, iterative orientation; and thirdly, its capacity to accommodate different philosophical perspectives and research methods (both quantitative and qualitative). The study should be understood as an *instrumental case study* because, in examining the comparability of the live and tape-based versions of the ***access:*** oral interaction sub-test in the context of the test trials, it aims to shed light on the potential equivalence of this and (with suitable caveats) other direct and semi-direct pairs of oral proficiency tests.

The accommodationist stance, outlined in the previous section, is the theoretical position underlying this study. This strategy enabled the research question to be addressed from both positivistic and naturalistic perspectives. Because of its emphasis on both product and process and its reliance on both quantitative and qualitative research methods, this strategy eventually allowed for more solidly grounded, valid conclusions than would have been the case if only one paradigm had been used.

Procedure

The data for the study was collected from two separate trials of this test (December 1992 and June 1994) where candidates undertook both the live and tape-based versions.

In the first 'case', the December 1992 trial, the comparability issue was addressed from within a positivistic framework and the focus was on two different kinds of *products*: (a) test scores and (b) test taker language output.

The first question to be examined was whether the *scores* obtained from candidate performance on the two versions were equivalent. In order to do this, the raw scores obtained from this trial were analysed using multi-faceted Rasch measurement (see Chapter 4).

However, as Shohamy (1994) suggests, even when the equivalence of test scores can be established, this does not provide sufficient evidence that two tests measure identical language abilities. She argues that more convincing evidence includes examination of the *test taker language output* produced under the two test conditions using the tools of discourse analysis. Accordingly, sample audio recordings from the December 1992 trial were examined in relation to the discourse features of test taker output on the two test versions using a framework developed by Shohamy (1994). Two different kinds of analyses were conducted at this stage. First, a broad qualitative discourse analysis of the language samples was carried out. Secondly, a detailed quantitative comparison of these samples was conducted (see Chapter 5). While the analyses of test scores and test taker language output provided some important initial answers to the equivalence question, they were still tentative and even partially contradictory. This led to the adoption of another very different perspective from which to address the research question in a subsequent trial.

In the second 'case', the June 1994 trial, the comparability issue was first examined from a naturalistic perspective and the investigation focused on test *processes,* including the processes of test design, test taking and rating. This change of perspective was motivated by the inconclusiveness of the findings based on test products in the December 1992 trial. In this part of the study the various stages of the trial were tracked (see Table 6.1 in Chapter 6). The data gathered at this time included observation notes based on the performances of two candidates on both the live and tape versions, video and audio recordings of these performances, audio-taped interviews with test developers, candidates, interlocutors and raters and, finally, written questionnaires and feedback sheets from candidates and raters. In this case both the data and methods of analysis were mainly qualitative (Chapter 6). The test scores from this trial were then analysed quantitatively again from within a positivistic perspective and the results of selected candidates interpreted using the findings from the previous study of test taking processes. This led to additional quantitative analyses of the test scores from this trial (Chapter 7). The type of data gathered and techniques of analyses used in each phase of the research are summarised in Table 3.1 below.

Table 3.1

**Summary of types of data gathered and techniques
of analyses used in the study**

Phase	Data	Data type	Method of analysis
A Trial 1	test scores	quantitative	quantitative
B Trial 1	language output	qualitative	qualitative
C Trial 1	language output	qualitative	quantitative
D Trial 2	test processes	qualitative	qualitative
E Trial 2	test scores	quantitative	quantitative

By moving back and forward between the positivistic and naturalistic perspectives, therefore, the researcher was able to gather a wide range of evidence to support the conclusions reached in the study. As suggested earlier in this chapter, the necessity for this dual perspective will become clearer as the evidence on the validity of the live and tape-based tests unfolds in the next few chapters.

Methods of data analysis

In this section the methods of analysis used to analyse the data collected from the two trials of the *access:* oral interaction sub-test are outlined.

Multi-faceted Rasch measurement

In both trials test scores were analysed quantitatively using multi-faceted Rasch measurement to address the research question (see Chapters 4 and 7).

Rasch measurement (a version of Item Response Theory based on a one-parameter model) calibrates item difficulty and person ability and calculates a probabilistic estimate of candidate ability based on modelled predictions of person-to-item response behaviour (McNamara 1996a). Given its probabilistic orientation, Rasch measurement appears to be based on the modified positivistic perspective discussed earlier in this chapter.

The computer program FACETS (Linacre 1989–95) extends this approach to include rater characteristics as another facet. In this analysis each candidate receives a *logit* score which expresses the ability of the candidate in terms of his/her probability of obtaining a particular score (or above) on any item, given the difficulty of the item and the harshness of the rater. Thus, the program compensates for differences across facets. Other facets such as the test version (i.e. live or tape-based) or interlocutor may also be included in the analysis and contribute to the ability measure of each candidate. In addition to the ability measures for the candidates, the analysis provides a set of measures (also in logits) for each facet, including the difficulty of items and the harshness of raters. Because the program FACETS compensates for differences in severity between raters, the main focus of their training and subsequent assessment of test candidates is on establishing and maintaining intra- (as opposed to inter-) rater reliability, i.e. self-consistency rather than absolute agreement with other raters.

Following the use of the FACETS program to analyse the test score data in both the December 1992 and June 1994 trials the equivalence of test scores from the live and tape-based versions of the oral interaction sub-test was examined from two perspectives: first, the psychometric unidimensionality of the two versions (based on the degree of correspondence between candidate ability estimates) and secondly, their relative difficulty. For the June 1994 trial test scores were also compared using 'anchored' item ability estimates, i.e. the difficult estimates of previously trialled tasks were preset into the FACETS analysis. The anchoring process enabled results from one form of the test to be meaningfully compared with earlier forms of the test. It also allowed previously established cut-off points for overall levels of performance to be carried forward from one administration to the next. A comparison of candidates' performance in terms of the overall proficiency levels they achieved on each of the two versions could then be made.

Further FACETS analyses, known as 'bias analysis' in multi-faceted Rasch measurement, identify unexpected but consistent patterns of behaviour which may occur from an interaction of a particular rater with respect to some component or 'facet' of the rating situation such as, in this test, a particular candidate, format or item. The output of these analyses shows first, whether individual raters are scoring, say, a particular person or item more harshly or leniently relative to how they assess other people or items, and secondly, whether they are behaving consistently towards each individual person or item. It is important that these follow-up analyses be carried out since the candidate ability estimates produced by the main analysis in the FACETS program do not take account of these interactions which are, therefore, a potential source of measurement error. Bias analysis was used in the study of the December 1992 trial to explore the interactions between rater and format. In the study of the June 1994 trial the interactions between first, rater and person and second, rater and format were investigated.

Discourse analysis

Following the analysis of test scores in the December 1992 trial a selection of the audio recordings of 20 candidates on both the live and tape-based versions of the oral interaction sub-test were transcribed and their discourse features compared using the framework adopted by Shohamy (1994) in her study of the Hebrew OPI and SOPI (see Chapter 1 for a discussion of her findings). These features included lexical density, rhetorical functions and structure, genre, speech moves, communicative properties, discourse strategies, content and topic of discourse, prosodic/paralinguistic features and contextualisation, type of speech functions, discourse markers and register. With the exception of lexical density, all of these features were analysed qualitatively (see Study A, Chapter 5). The analysis of lexical density is reported separately (see Study B, Chapter 5) because it involved a more detailed, quantitative examination of test taker language output and yielded different results in relation to the equivalence of the two versions than the other categories.

Qualitative data analysis

The analysis of the qualitative data gathered in the June 1994 trial followed a set of procedures described by Lynch (1996) in the context of language program evaluation. The first step in this process involved establishing the initial thematic framework following the data gathering process. Next, the data for each stage was organised for analysis and coded using abbreviated labels for the themes and patterns which were beginning to emerge. The coding was provisional until all of the data had been carefully scrutinised. Coding marked the beginning of the process of classification and reduction of the data so that the most significant themes were isolated. Tentative interpretations and conclusions were then drawn from the classified and reduced data. Even at this stage, however, the researcher worked back and forth between the 'raw' data, the classification of the data and whatever preliminary interpretations were formed before reaching any final conclusions. This stage also included the search for alternative explanations to those that were initially established in the process. The main focus throughout this process was the issue of the equivalence between the two versions of the oral interaction sub-test and this is reflected in the reporting of the results in Chapter 6.

Each of these three methods of data analysis provided a distinctly different perspective on the issue of comparability between the direct and semi-direct versions of the *access:* oral interaction sub-test. Using a range of perspectives eventually yielded richer, more complex insights into this issue than would have been the case if only a single method had been employed.

The role of the researcher

The researcher in the positivist tradition is often construed as a disinterested, external and 'objective' analyst of the phenomena under investigation. From the naturalistic perspective, however, the researcher not only makes 'subjective' judgements throughout the duration of any given study (including what to investigate and how it should be done as well as whatever conclusions are drawn), but may also actively influence the outcomes of the study. It is therefore important, especially where naturalistic methods such as observation and interviewing are used (see Chapter 6), to identify the stake held by researchers in order to evaluate the results of their work critically.

The author of this study co-ordinated the initial stages of the development of the *access:* oral interaction sub-test from September 1992 to March 1993. He was involved in all aspects of this process including the creation of test specifications and setting up the first trial in December 1992 as well as the first overseas administration in March 1993. He was not, however, consulted in the original decision to adopt the two different formats for the test. As explained in Chapter 1 this represented a practical solution to the problems of administering a speaking test in overseas centres and was initiated by senior managers of the *access:* test development project team before the researcher was appointed to work on the test.

In April 1993 when the author began work on this study he was no longer formally working on the test. Naturally, however, particularly given the nature of this research project, he maintained a strong interest in its development and continued to be consulted by members of the project team until December 1994 when the *access:* test was transferred to the Language Testing and Curriculum Centre (LTCC) at Griffith University.

It is perhaps unsurprising that, in the initial stages of this project at least, the author was cautiously optimistic that the direct and semi-direct versions of the oral interaction sub-test would emerge as essentially interchangeable, given that he had played a major role in attempting to design the two versions accordingly. It was only as he began to compare the two versions from the range of perspectives outlined above that he began to critically re-evaluate this belief. The findings in this study, particularly in the investigation into test processes in Chapter 6, should be interpreted in the light of the author's evolving stance on the interchangeability question.

Summary

To re-cap, a case study approach was adopted to investigate the research question because of first, its holistic focus on the case or 'bounded system'; secondly, its exploratory, iterative orientation; and thirdly, its capacity to accommodate different philosophical perspectives and research methods (both quantitative and qualitative). The research was conceived as an *instrumental* case study because, in examining the comparability of the live and tape-based versions of the *access:* oral interaction sub-test in the context of the test trials, it aimed to shed light on the potential equivalence of this and other pairs of direct and semi-direct oral proficiency tests.

In philosophical terms an *accommodationist* stance was used to address the research question. This stance enabled the equivalence issue to be addressed from within both the *positivistic* and *naturalistic* research paradigms. Because of its dual emphasis on both product and process and its reliance on both quantitative and qualitative research methods, this strategy eventually allowed for more solidly grounded, valid conclusions than would have been the case if only one paradigm had been used.

This chapter has outlined the general approach and research methods used in this study to investigate the comparability of the direct and semi-direct versions of the *access:* oral interaction sub-test in the context of the test trials. The next four chapters describe each phase of the study in detail and report the relevant findings.

4 Trial 1: The analysis of test scores

Overview

This chapter examines the equivalence of the direct and semi-direct versions of the *access:* oral interaction sub-test in relation to the test scores obtained from the first trial administration held in Melbourne in December 1992. First, the tasks, scoring criteria and rating procedures used in this trial are described. Secondly, the results of a preliminary study undertaken by Wigglesworth and O'Loughlin (1993) based on the test score data are critically examined. Thirdly, the findings from subsequent analyses of the same test score data are reported. In both cases the equivalence issue was addressed using multi-faceted Rasch analyses.

The December 1992 trial

Table 4.1 details the full range of tasks and scoring criteria used in the December 1992 trial of Form A of the *access:* oral interaction sub-test. This first form of the test aimed to reliably identify candidates at the Vocational level only (at this initial stage seen as corresponding to Level 3 on the ASLPR scale. Level 3 in speaking on the ASLPR scale is defined as 'able to speak the language with sufficient accuracy and vocabulary to participate effectively in most formal and informal conversations on practical, social and vocational topics' (Ingram and Wylie 1984)).

Each of the scoring criteria was assessed on a six-point scale with descriptors. (These were identical for the two versions of the test.) The descriptors were derived empirically by the test development team following the first trial administration using audio recordings of a sample of candidate performances from both the direct and semi-direct versions. A full list of the descriptors adopted for each level of the individual scoring criteria is provided in Appendix 4.1.

In this trial 94 volunteer NESB candidates recruited from several local English language centres and tertiary institutions in Melbourne attempted both versions of the test. Each test taker was paid AUD$20 upon completion of the trial oral interaction sub-test and a post-test questionnaire.

Table 4.1

Test tasks and scoring criteria Form A (trial), December 1992

	LIVE		TAPE
1.	Warm up (unassessed)	1.	Warm up (unassessed)

2.	A) Description
	    – fluency
	    – grammar
	    – vocabulary
	B) Narration
	    – fluency
	    – grammar
	    – vocabulary
	    – coherence and cohesion
	C) Exposition (1)
	    – fluency
	    – grammar
		2.	A) Description
			    – fluency
			    – grammar
			    – vocabulary
			B) Narration
			    – fluency
			    – grammar
			    – vocabulary
			    – coherence and cohesion
			C) Exposition (1)
			    – fluency
			    – grammar
			D) Summary
			    – fluency
			    – grammar

3.	Role play (1)
	    – fluency
	    – grammar
	    – appropriacy
	Role play (2)
	    – fluency
	    – grammar
	    – appropriacy
		3.	Role play (1)
			    – fluency
			    – grammar
			    – appropriacy
			Role play (2)
			    – fluency
			    – grammar
			    – appropriacy

4.	Exposition (2)
	    – fluency
	    – grammar
		4.	Exposition (2)
			    – fluency
			    – grammar

5.	Discussion
	    – fluency
	    – grammar
	    – vocabulary
	Global criteria
	    – intelligibility
	    – communicative effectiveness
	    – comprehension
		5.	Discussion
			    – fluency
			    – grammar
			    – vocabulary
			Global criteria
			    – intelligibility
			    – communicative
			      effectiveness

For the purpose of providing an overview of the composition of this trial test cohort, candidates can be divided into two broad groups on the basis of how closely they resembled the target overseas test population using data obtained from questionnaires completed by them on the day of the trial administration. The more 'non-target-like' group (i.e. NESB students, generally under twenty-five years of age and living in Australia on a temporary basis while completing their tertiary studies) comprised 32% of the group. The remaining 68% belonged to the more 'target-like' group which was composed of NESB professionals who were generally over 25 years of age and qualified in a wide range of fields including engineering, medicine, teaching, administration, computing, librarianship and architecture. However, given that they had mostly already obtained permanent residence, had been in Australia for more than 18 months and were undertaking the test here, it should be acknowledged that even this group did not entirely fit the profile of the target test taker population. Given these differences between the trial and operational test populations the findings reported here cannot be directly applied to the operational context. Nevertheless, as suggested previously, they do have potential implications for any group of people undertaking the test and indeed for the interchangeability of other direct and semi-direct speaking tests.

Of these 94 trial candidates in the December 1992 trial, approximately half were administered the live version first, and half were administered the tape version first. Their performances on both versions were all audio taped so that they could be rated retrospectively. Ten tape-based recordings were unsuccessful due to technical faults in the recording equipment in the language laboratory, and these candidates were therefore excluded. One additional candidate was excluded because the live version recording became unintelligible after only one rating. Thus, the analysis was based on the scores from a total of 83 candidates on both the direct and semi-direct versions of the test.

Thirteen teachers were recruited for the purpose of rating the tapes. They were all trained TESOL teachers and had at least five years' experience teaching a range of levels. Prior to rating the tapes, each rater participated in a comprehensive whole-day training session. The rating process was conducted in two phases. Initially each tape was rated by two raters. Thus, for the first stage, eight raters each scored 37 tapes and one rater scored 36 tapes at home over a period of one week. The rating design was such that no rater assessed any particular candidate on either version more than once. This meant that each candidate was assessed by four different raters.

In the second stage of the rating, the other four raters rated every audio recording (83 x 2=166). Two of this group of raters rated the tape version first, and two rated the live version first. The purpose of these multiple ratings was to reduce to the greatest possible extent the degree of measurement error so that the ability estimates obtained for each of the candidates were as reliable as possible.

A preliminary study

In a study of the test score data obtained from this trial administration, Wigglesworth and O'Loughlin (1993) undertook a preliminary investigation into the issue of comparability between the two versions of the test using the multi-faceted Rasch program, FACETS (Linacre 1989–95), which was introduced in Chapter 3. Three FACETS analyses were conducted: one for the live data, one for the tape-based data and one for the combined data. For the live and tape data taken separately four facets of the test situation were included in the analysis: (1) candidate, (2) rater, (3) item and (4) order (i.e. the order in which each version was undertaken by candidates). In the analysis using the combined data another facet was added: (5) version, i.e. live or tape. All of the test items were equally weighted in the three analyses. The output for each of the facets from these analyses is given in Appendix 4.2. These facets are related to each other as increasing or reducing. Figure 4.1 below shows a graphical summary of the results from the analysis using the combined data only in this study. This kind of summary is routinely produced by the FACETS program as part of the output of the analysis.

Figure 4.1

**All facet summary, oral interaction sub-test, FACETS analysis (1)
December 1992 trial.**

Measr	+ Candidate	- Rater	- Version	- Order	- Item
5 +		+	+	+	+
	24 40				
	94				
	90				
4 +		+	+	+	+
	28 37				
	46 53				
	77				
	1				
	93				
3 +	78	+	+	+	+
	62 68 89				
	9				
	11 20 27				
	60 61 86				
	82				
2 +	4 56 6	+	+	+	+
	7				
	31 32				
	70 83	2			
	17 29 39				
	19 45				
	12 50 55				Exp1G I
	67 72 85				
1 +	22 30 48	+	+	+	+
	71				
	15 74 79	11			RP1G NarG
	80				
	34 36 63	1 10			IDisG RP2G NarV
	64 92				TExp1G TNarG Exp2G
	49 5 69	7			DesG TNarV
	75 81				
					CommEff RP1A TSumG
					TExp2G
	13 52 8		Tape	First	Exp1F DesV DisV
					TAns2G TDesG TDesV
					TDisG
0 *	*	*	*	*	Int RP1F RP2A *
					NarC TAns1G TDisV
	10 26 33	6	Live	Second	TAns2A TComm TExp1F
	54 84				TStoC
	58 87	3 8 9			RP2F NarF Exp1F
		4			
	2				DesF DisF TInt
					TStoF
	16	13			TAns2F TSumF TExp2Fl
		12			Comp TDesF TDisF
-1 +	51	+	+	+	+ TAns1F
					TAns1A
	57				
	25	5			
-2 +	38 47	+	+	+	+
	35				
	43 88				
	18				
-3 +		+	+	+	+

In Figure 4.1, the facets are positioned horizontally. The '+' or '-' before the facet name (e.g. '-Item') indicates whether the facet measures are positively or negatively oriented. The first column represents the logit scale which is the same for all facets. The remaining five columns show an overview of the results for each of the five facets used in the analysis. In this output candidates are ordered with the most able people at the top and the least able at the bottom. The other facets are ordered so that the most difficult element of each facet is towards the top and the least difficult towards the bottom. The most severe rater therefore was rater 2. The tape version is shown here to have been slightly more difficult than the live version overall. Furthermore, the version candidates undertook first emerged as slightly more difficult than the one they did second. Finally, the most difficult item proved to be exposition 1 – *Grammar* (live version) and the easiest item role play 1 – *Appropriacy* (tape version).

Table 4.2 below provides summary statistics for candidates in each of the three analyses.

Table 4.2

Summary statistics, oral interaction sub-test, FACETS analysis (1), December 1992 trial (N = 83)

	LIVE	TAPE	COMBINED
Number of items	23	24	47
Candidates:			
Mean logit score	0.90	1.09	1.19
SD (logits)	2.00	1.92	1.70
Mean standard error (logits)	0.13	0.14	0.09
Person separation reliability (like K-R 20)	1.00	0.99	1.00

The candidates' scores obtained from the FACETS analysis are probablistic estimates (expressed as logits) of their ability which take into account the difficulty of each of the test items, the relative severity of the raters who scored their peformances and other facets which included here the difficulty associated with the order in which the two versions were undertaken and, for the combined data, the relative difficulty of each version.

Wigglesworth and O'Loughlin (1993) found that the ability estimates of candidates obtained from the analyses of the live and tape data taken separately were strongly correlated at $r = 0.92$, a result very similar to those reported in the OPI/SOPI studies surveyed in Chapter 1. The concurrent validity of both versions of the test was also investigated in relation to ASLPR ratings assigned to test takers by their interlocutors and an observer (all trained and experienced users of this procedure) on the basis of their performance in the live version of the *access:* test. Reasonably strong Spearman correlations of *rho* = 0.89 for the live version and *rho* = 0.87 for the tape version were obtained, although the validity of these ASLPR ratings may have been jeopardised, given that they were not obtained using the interview method designated for this assessment procedure.

Finally, the comparability of the test scores was investigated in relation to cut-off scores. The cut-off scores for Vocational level were calculated by entering the ASLPR scores into the FACETS program as separate items for each candidate on the two versions of the test. This provided a logit value equivalent to ASLPR 3 (i.e., the Vocational level) for each version. The cut-off levels differed slightly for the two versions and were a function of the overall item difficulty in each case. Thus, the cut-off scores were 0.10 for the live version and -0.10 for the tape version. 53 candidates achieved Vocational level on both versions while 20 failed to reach this level. There were seven candidates who reached this level on the live version but not the tape version compared to three candidates who achieved Vocational level on the tape version but not on the live version.

Thus, despite the strength of the correlation between the candidate ability estimates (r = 0.92), 12% of candidates were found to have achieved Vocational level on one version but not on the other. Wigglesworth and O'Loughlin (1993) attributed this result to the effect of order as an intervening variable insofar as in all ten of these cases the candidate failed the version of the test they had completed first. Thus, there appeared to be a positive practice effect operating on their second performance.

However, following the publication of the study by Wigglesworth and O'Loughlin (1993), it was discovered that the above inference was erroneous since it ignored the fact that 'order' was one of the facets of the test situation included in each of the FACETS analyses. This meant that, in producing the candidate ability estimates for each version, the FACETS analysis had compensated for any significant effect arising from the order in which candidates undertook the two versions. Thus, the source of band level differences obtained for a significant minority of candidates on the two versions remains obscure from this study. What the examination of band levels in this study does confirm, however, even from a purely psychometric perspective, is that high correlations between test scores provide insufficient evidence for test equivalence.

There are two final criticisms to be made of the initial study of the December 1992 trial by Wigglesworth and O'Loughlin (1993). First, including five facets of the test situation in the analyses may have been excessive given the relatively small number of candidates and items. McNamara (1996a:140) points out that designs incorporating a greater number of facets require larger data sets than used here to ensure stability of estimate of facets. In retrospect, therefore, it would probably have been more prudent to limit the number to a maximum of three facets in each analysis. While the facets included in the initial analyses would need to have been candidate, rater and item, the effect of the order in which the two versions were undertaken could have been compensated for by carrying out subsequent analyses with the live and tape data taken separately, this time incorporating candidate, rater and order as facets. It should be noted, however, that the overall effect of order was not great. The output for this facet from the analysis of the combined data (see Appendix 4.2) indicates that the version undertaken first was only 0.2 of a logit or 4% more difficult than the version completed second. This difference is sufficiently small to suggest, in practical terms, that the effect of order on candidate performance was minimal, at least in this trial, and that, therefore, it did not need to be included as a facet in the test score analyses.

Secondly, the use of multi-faceted Rasch analysis in Wigglesworth and O'Loughlin's (1993) study could have led to other, more appropriate and rigorous measures of test equivalence than were employed in this study. The remainder of this chapter will be devoted to reporting the results of the application of such techniques. Similar procedures will also be used to examine the equivalence of test scores from another later trial in Chapter 7.

The current study

Following the preliminary study by Wigglesworth and O'Loughlin (1993) the same data set from the December 1992 trial was re-examined to investigate the comparability of the direct and semi-direct versions of the *access:* oral interaction sub-test from two alternative perspectives more appropriate to Rasch measurement: first, the psychometric unidimensionality (based on the degree of correspondence between candidate ability estimates) and, secondly, the relative difficulty of the two versions of the test.

Psychometric unidimensionality of the oral interaction sub-test

The key issue here involved addressing the following question: is it possible to construct a single measurement dimension of speaking ability for the combined data from the two versions of the test? In other words, can the oral interaction sub-test, when the data from the two versions are combined, be considered psychometrically 'unidimensional'? It should be emphasised that what is being examined here is not whether the two tests are measuring the same underlying psychological *construct* or *ability* but rather whether there is *a single underlying pattern of scores* in the data matrix. In other words, as McNamara (1996a: 273) suggests, psychometric unidimensionality does not necessarily imply psychological unidimensionality.

The issue of psychometric unidimensionality was addressed using a series of procedures adapted from McNamara's (1991) study of the application of Rasch Item Response Theory to the validation of the listening sub-test of the Occupational English Test. The first step in addressing this issue was to identify any misfitting candidates from the original FACETS analyses of the live and tape versions taken separately. Misfitting candidates are those test takers whose pattern of scoring is inconsistent with the general pattern of scoring for the test cohort overall. Where this is the case, it suggests that the individual's abilities are not being measured appropriately by the test instrument (McNamara 1996a: 178). Similarly, an item is said to be misfitting where performance on the item is inconsistent with the pattern of performance on the test overall. Misfitting items may be interpreted as items which were either interpreted inconsistently by raters, or else did not form part of a set of items which together define a single measurement trait. Finally, raters are said to be misfitting if their overall scoring lacks self-consistency. Throughout this study 'misfit' will be defined in terms of candidates, raters or items whose infit mean-square value given in the FACETS output is more than 2 standard deviations above the average figure for the relevant set of candidates, raters and items.

Table 4.3 below provides a summary of misfitting items and persons in the original FACETS analysis using the live, tape and combined data sets. The output for each of these analyses is given in Appendix 4.2. The misfitting items in this initial set of analyses were *Appropriacy* on both role plays for the live data taken separately, *Appropriacy* on the second role play for the tape data taken separately and finally, *Appropriacy* on both the first live role play and second tape role play and *Comprehension* on the live version for the combined data.

There are two points to be made on the basis of the findings here. Firstly, it is hardly surprising that *Comprehension* emerges in the combined analysis as misfitting, given that it is a measure of listening and not speaking ability. Its inclusion as an item on the live version only may therefore have undermined full test score equivalence between the two versions.

Table 4.3

Misfitting items and persons, FACETS analysis (1), December 1992 trial (N = 83)

	LIVE		TAPE		COMBINED	
	Mean	SD	Mean	SD	Mean	SD
Item infit	1.0	0.3	1.0	0.2	1.0	0.2
Person infit	1.0	0.2	1.0	0.3	1.0	0.2
Misfitting items and persons						
Items	2		1		3	
	(#12,15)		(#38)		(#12, 23, 38)	
Persons	5		2		4	
	(#17,20,38,84,87)		(#49,75)		(#58,60,68,98)	

Secondly, on the basis of these results, it appears that *Appropriacy* may have been interpreted inconsistently by raters. Because of its strong tendency to misfit this category was subsequently excluded from the scoring criteria employed in this test. However, given that *Appropriacy* was the only measure of sociolinguistic competence included, its omission represented a narrowing of the range of speaking skills being assessed. A preferable solution would have been for the level descriptors to have been revised and for raters to have been more carefully trained and monitored in scoring this category. If *Appropriacy* still proved to be consistently misfitting following this process, then its relation to the other categories used in the test might have needed to be re-examined i.e. it may have been assessing a different ability from the one measured by the other categories. Even if this was the case, the subsequent decision to exclude *Appropriacy* as a rating category does not appear to have been soundly based. A better solution would have been to retain the category and to report *Appropriacy* scores separately from the other scores.

For the next stage of the analysis, the seven misfitting candidates from the live and tape versions taken separately (see Table 4.3 above) were then removed from the data files. Given that their pattern of scoring was inconsistent with the general pattern of scoring for the test cohort overall, it was decided to exclude these candidates from the analysis in the interests of obtaining a clearer picture of the overall equivalence of test scores from the two versions. The edited data were then re-entered into the FACETS program now using only three facets i.e. (1) candidate, (2) rater and (3) item. Three different analyses were then undertaken: one for the live data, one for the tape data and one for the combined data. The output for each of the facets from these analyses is given in Appendix 4.3. Table 4.4 provides summary statistics for candidates in each of the three analyses.

Table 4.4

Summary statistics, oral interaction sub-test, FACETS analysis (2), December 1992 trial (N = 76)

	LIVE	TAPE	COMBINED
Number of items	23	24	47
Candidates:			
Mean logit score	0.86	1.11	1.25
SD (logits)	2.16	1.98	1.77
Mean standard			
error (logits)	0.14	0.14	0.09
Person separation			
reliability			
(like K-R 20)	1.00	1.00	1.00

Table 4.5 below provides information on misfitting items and persons obtained from the FACETS analyses using the edited live, tape and combined data sets. These results suggested (initially, at least) that when the edited live and tape test data were treated as a single test all items except three combined to define a single measurement dimension, and the overwhelming majority of candidates (with only one exception) had been measured meaningfully and reliably in terms of the dimension of ability so constructed. The three misfitting items were the same ones as those in the initial combined analysis i.e. *Comprehension* in the live version, and *Appropriacy* for both the first role play on the live version and second role play on the tape version.

Table 4.5

Misfitting items and persons, FACETS analysis (2), December 1992 trial (N = 76)

	LIVE		TAPE		COMBINED	
	Mean	SD	Mean	SD	Mean	SD
Item infit	1.0	0.3	1.0	0.2	1.0	0.2
Person infit	1.0	0.1	1.0	0.2	1.0	0.2
Misfitting items and persons						
Items	1(#12)		1 (#38)		3(#12,23,38)	
Persons	1(#6)		3(#40,43,85)		1(#47)	

However, if the two versions of the oral interaction sub-test taken together satisfy the psychometric unidimensionality assumption, then the person ability estimates derived from each version taken separately should be independent of the particular condition under which they were obtained. Two statistical tests were used to address this issue.

The first test to be used was a Pearson correlation between the ability estimates obtained from the two versions of the test. The correlation between the two sets of ability estimates uncorrected for attenuation was $r = 0.92$ (the same as when all 83 candidates were included in Wigglesworth and O'Loughlin's (1993) study). The result, when corrected for attenuation (i.e. taking into account the observed reliability of the two versions), using a procedure outlined in Henning (1987: 85–6) was $r = 0.94$. This result suggested a strong relationship between the ability estimates of candidates on the two versions. Figure 4.2 below graphically illustrates this relationship.

Figure 4.2

Scattergram of candidate ability estimates (logits) on the live and tape versions of the oral interaction sub-test, FACETS analysis (2) December 1992 trial (N = 76)

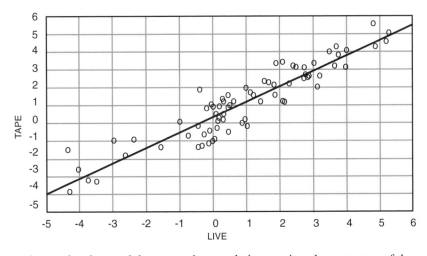

As previously noted, however, the correlation test is only a measure of the linearity of this relationship. McNamara (1991: 153–54) suggests employing an additional, more rigorous test of the equality of ability estimates, a chi-squared (χ^2) test, in order to overcome the limitations of the correlation test. For each candidate a z-score is calculated. The z-score is based on the difference between the candidate's ability estimates (i.e. logit scores) from both the live and tape versions taking into account first, the relative difficulty of each version of the test and secondly, the standard error of these estimates.

The z-score is then squared to get a value of (χ^2) for each candidate and then totalled to yield a statistic which provides a measure of the equivalence between the two sets of scores. This procedure was followed and the resulting value of (χ^2) = 1347.71, df = 75, p< 0.001 suggested that the null hypothesis of equality between the two sets of ability estimates can be rejected, a finding which conflicts with the results of the other tests reported above.

Thus, the results of this statistical procedure (which is more rigorous than standard correlation techniques) indicate that the assumption of unidimensionality has not been met i.e. it is not possible to construct a single measurement dimension of 'speaking ability' from the data obtained from the two versions of the oral interaction sub-test. In other words, this final procedure indicated an overall lack of equivalence between the test scores from the two versions. Possible reasons for this difference will be explored in subsequent chapters.

Test difficulty

The next stage of the investigation concerned the question of comparative difficulty on the two versions of the test. The first step in this process was to map the 'item' difficulty estimates obtained from the FACETS analysis using the combined (live and tape) edited data. (See Appendix 4.3 for a full report of these results.) The term *item* refers to individual scoring criteria on any given task. Thus, 'Description: *Grammar*' constitutes one item. In this map items are abbreviated according to task and criterion. Thus, for example, 'DisV' stands for 'Discussion: *Vocabulary*' and 'NarF' for 'Narration: *Fluency*'. Figure 4.3 below suggests that, in general, the two versions closely mirrored each other in terms of the difficulty of individual matching items. The one notable exception was that the item 'Role play 1: *Appropriacy*' on the tape version was markedly easier than either of its counterparts on the live version. However, the fact that 'Role play 2: *Appropriacy*' on the tape version was of a similar level of difficulty to the matching items on the live version suggests that this could have been a function of the particular task rather than the format to which it belonged. On the other hand, as argued in Chapter 1, it may not be possible to make any direct comparisons about the relative difficulty of items from the live and tape role plays since these tasks were only superficially matched anyway. As outlined in Chapter 1, the live task consisted of a two-way exchange between interlocutor and candidate based on an information gap, and the tape task required candidates to leave a telephone answering machine message.

Figure 4.3

Item difficulty map, FACETS analysis (2) of the oral interaction sub-test using the combined live and tape data sets, December 1992 trial (N = 76)

Item difficulty (logits)	LIVE	TAPE
1.2		
1.1	Exp1G	
1.0		
0.9		NarG, Exp1G
0.8	RP1G	NarV
0.7	NarG	
0.6	RP2G, DisG, Exp2G, NarV	Exp2G
0.5		SumG
0.4		DisG
0.3	DesG	DesG, RP2G
0.2	RP1A	DesV, RP1G
0.1	DesV, ComEff	DisV
0.0	Exp1F	Exp2F
-0.1	RP1F, DisV	ComEff,RP1F,RP2A
-0.2	NarC, RP2A	NarC
-0.3	Int	NarF
-0.4		Int
-0.5	RP2F, Exp2F	Exp1F
-0.6	NarF	RP2F, SumF
-0.7	DesF, DisF	DesF, DisF
-0.8		
-0.9		
-1.0		RP1A
-1.1	Comp	

An additional FACETS analysis including the three facets candidate, rater and format was later carried out using the combined data set to determine the overall relative difficulty of the two formats. Table 4.6 below shows that the live version was marginally (0.06 of a logit or 2%) more difficult than the tape version overall. While this result contradicts the finding in the output from Wigglesworth and O'Loughlin's (1993) study (see Figure 4.1 above) it should be remembered that the result here is likely to be the more accurate first, because all misfitting candidates had been removed from the original data set but, secondly and more important, because the number of facets used to investigate the question of relative test difficulty was reduced from five facets in the original analysis to three facets here. As previously suggested, designs incorporating more than three facets require larger data sets than used in this study to ensure stability of estimate of facets.

Table 4.6

Relative difficulty of the live and tape versions of the oral interaction sub-test, FACETS analysis (2), December 1992 (N = 76)

Obs score Mean	Obs count sq	Obs avrge	Fair avrge	Measure (logits)	Model SE	Infit	
47624	11702	4.1	3.5	0.03	0.01	1.0	*Live*
44683	10894	4.1	3.5	-0.03	0.01	1.0	*Tape*

In practical terms, this analysis, together with the earlier one comparing the individual items on the two formats, suggested that the live and tape versions were highly comparable in terms of difficulty, at least in this trial. However, these findings on their own do not offer support for the psychometric unidimensionality of the two versions. As suggested previously, the more appropriate measure of test score equivalence was the chi-squared (χ^2) test which compared the candidate ability estimates obtained from the scores on the live and tape versions of the test, taking into account the relative difficulty of the two formats. This procedure indicated that the two sets of ability estimates were not equivalent and thus pointed to the existence of a test method effect.

On the basis of the results illustrated in Figure 4.3 above, it appears that Grammar was the most harshly scored criterion, followed by Vocabulary, Communicative Effectiveness, Appropriacy, Intelligibility, Fluency and finally, Comprehension (live version only). This order of harshness is very similar to that obtained in McNamara's (1990a) study of the speaking component of the Occupational English Test (with the exception of Vocabulary, which was not included on that test). Furthermore, given that Comprehension was the most leniently scored item, its use on the live test, but not the tape test, may have contributed to reducing the gap in overall difficulty between the two versions (see Table 4.6 above), i.e. it is likely that excluding this criterion may have resulted in a sharper overall difference in difficulty in favour of the live version.

Bias analysis

In examining the equivalence of test scores from the two versions of the oral interaction sub-test, a further important issue is the effect of format on the scoring of raters. In the analysis of test difficulty reported earlier in this chapter, the effect of format over all raters, candidates and items was found not to be large, i.e. the live version was marginally (0.06 of a logit or 2%) more difficult than the tape version overall. However, it is still possible that individual raters judged performances on one format significantly more harshly or leniently than the other. This hypothesis was investigated using an additional facility within the FACETS program known as *bias analysis*.

Bias analysis in multi-faceted Rasch measurement identifies unexpected but consistent patterns of behaviour which may occur from an interaction of a particular rater with respect to some component of the rating situation such as, in this test, a particular candidate, format or item. The candidate ability estimates produced by the main analysis in the FACETS program do not take account of these interactions which are, therefore, a potential source of measurement error. Bias analysis has been previously employed by McNamara *et al.* (1993) and Wigglesworth (1993) to investigate such threats to reliability in the *access:* oral interaction sub-test.

The focus here is on the interaction between rater and format. Table 4.7 below shows the results from the bias analysis using the edited combined data set for all 13 raters who scored the test. Recall that raters 1–9 marked approximately 20 live and 20 tape-based performances and raters 10–13 all 166 (83 live and 83 tape) performances.

In Table 4.7 column 3 provides the total observed score of each rater for the live and tape versions of the test. Column 4 provides an estimate of each rater's total expected score for the two versions. These predictions are based on the results of the main analysis (using the edited data set) summarised previously in this chapter (see Appendix 4.3 for full details). Column 5 then provides the average difference between the expected and observed score. A bias logit, based on this difference, is then calculated together with its standard error (columns 6 and 7). The bias score is then converted into a standardised Z-score by dividing it by its standard error (column 8). Where the Z-score values fall between -2.0 and +2.0, the rater may be considered to be scoring that version without significant bias. Where the value falls below -2.0 the rater is marking the specified format significantly more leniently in relation to the other format. On the other hand, where the value is greater than +2.0 the rater is scoring the format significantly more harshly compared to the way that rater treats the other one. Furthermore, in this analysis the infit mean square value (column 9) indicates how similar the rater's scoring is for the format overall. Where the value is less than 0.7 the rater's scoring on that version lacks variation, i.e. it is too predictable. Conversely, where this value is greater than 1.3 the rater's scoring lacks consistency.

These figures indicate that raters 1 and 11 were significantly more severe on the live version while raters 2, 3, 4, 5, 6, 8 and 10 were significantly more harsh on the tape version. Rater 5 (live version only) and rater 8 (tape version only) also showed a significant tendency to be inconsistent with an infit mean square value of 1.4 in both cases. In practical terms, however, the overall effects of rater bias in relation to the average difference it made to the raw scores allocated by all of these raters were not substantial, with the exception of raters 1 and 11 who were, on average, half a score point (on a six-point scale) more severe on the live version than the tape version. This suggests that, for the majority of raters, the overall lack of equivalence between the candidate ability estimates obtained from the two versions (see χ^2 test results above) cannot be ascribed to the interaction between format and rater in the scoring process. The scoring of raters 1 and 11, however, does appear to be contributing to this difference. Further details about the interaction between all 13 raters and the individual *items* from each version in this trial are reported in two studies by Wigglesworth (1993; 1994).

Table 4.7

**Bias calibration report, December 1992 trial,
rater – format interactions**

Rater	Format	Obs score	Exp score	Obs-Exp average	Bias (logit)	Error	Z-score	Infit mn sq
1	live	1489	1666	-0.39	0.83	0.07	12.2	1.1
2	live	1423	1379	0.10	-0.21	0.07	-3.1	1.1
3	live	2009	1952	0.12	-0.26	0.07	-3.8	0.9
4	live	2006	1947	0.12	-0.27	0.07	-4.0	0.9
5	live	2209	2165	0.10	-0.24	0.07	-3.2	1.4
6	live	2077	2036	0.08	-0.18	0.07	-2.7	0.9
7	live	1828	1849	-0.04	0.10	0.07	1.4	0.8
8	live	1955	1921	0.07	-0.17	0.07	-2.4	1.2
9	live	2026	2036	-0.02	0.05	0.07	0.7	0.8
10	live	8385	8102	0.13	-0.29	0.03	-9.0	1.0
11	live	7506	7853	-0.16	0.35	0.03	11.0	1.1
12	live	9921	9896	0.01	-0.03	0.03	-0.9	1.1
13	live	9148	9180	-0.02	0.03	0.03	1.1	0.8
1	tape	1616	1439	0.44	-0.94	0.07	-12.8	0.9
2	tape	1524	1569	-0.09	0.19	0.07	2.9	0.8
3	tape	1938	1995	-0.12	0.26	0.07	3.9	0.9
4	tape	1953	2012	-0.12	0.27	0.07	4.0	1.0
5	tape	2101	2145	-0.10	0.24	0.07	3.3	1.1
6	tape	1754	1795	-0.09	0.21	0.07	2.9	0.9
7	tape	1688	1667	0.05	-0.10	0.07	-1.5	0.9
8	tape	1438	1472	-0.10	0.21	0.08	2.7	1.4
9	tape	1920	1908	0.02	-0.05	0.07	-0.7	0.8
10	tape	7350	7634	-0.14	0.31	0.03	9.3	1.0
11	tape	7634	7288	0.18	-0.38	0.03	-11.5	0.9
12	tape	9246	9271	-0.01	0.03	0.03	0.9	0.9
13	tape	8680	8647	0.02	-0.04	0.03	-1.1	0.8

Conclusion

The standard analyses of the FACETS output from the December 1992 trial (including the study of misfitting persons and items and also the strength of correlation between the candidate ability estimates) appeared to provide support for the assumption of psychometric unidimensionality in relation to the two versions of the test. However, a more rigorous measure of the relationship between the ability estimates from the FACETS output (the chi-squared procedure) failed to confirm that a single measurement dimension of speaking ability could be constructed for the combined data obtained from the live and tape versions. In other words, contrary to the more standard measures of unidimensionality, this procedure indicated that the candidate ability estimates obtained from the two versions were not equivalent. Finally, bias analyses indicated that, for most raters, this apparent lack of equivalence could not be ascribed to the interaction between format and rater in the scoring process.

While the lack of equivalence between test scores obtained from the more rigorous test of unidimensionality was compelling, this finding appeared somewhat puzzling at this point, given the discrepancy between the different measures used to address this question. Furthermore, even if this conclusion was accurate, it was unclear from the statistical analyses alone *why* this might be so.

The next stage in the study was to examine the comparability of the two versions in the December 1992 trial from a very different perspective, that of candidate language output.

5 Trial 1: The analysis of candidate language output

Overview

The previous chapter examined the equivalence issue from the perspective of test scores obtained from the December 1992 trial. This chapter focuses on the comparability of the direct and semi-direct versions of the *access:* oral interaction test from the perspective of candidate language output. Specifically, it compares the discourse features of language samples collected in the December 1992 trial using a framework developed by Shohamy (1994). Because the data consisted of audio recordings of candidate performance only vocal output was examined. The results are analysed in relation to the equivalence of the two versions of the test.

Rationale

The motivation for this phase of the study comes from Shohamy (1994), who argues that concurrent validation studies examining the relationship between test scores (such as the one reported in Chapter 4) provide necessary but insufficient evidence about whether two tests measure the same language abilities. She argues convincingly that further evidence about the equivalence of the language produced in both tests is required in order to address this issue more comprehensively. Recall from Chapter 1 that, despite high correlations between the Hebrew OPI and SOPI ($r = 0.89 - 0.92$), Shohamy (1994) found important differences between the discourse features of language samples obtained from the two tests. These results, together with differences found between the nature of the elicitation tasks and the communicative strategies used by test takers, suggested that different speaking abilities were being tapped by the two tests.

In the present study, while the two versions of the oral interaction sub-test were closely matched in terms of design, the most rigorous (and thus more reliable) measure of psychometric unidimensionality used in Chapter 4 (the chi-squared procedure) suggested a lack of equivalence between test scores obtained from the December 1992 trial. However, following Shohamy (1994), an examination of the language produced under the two test conditions was needed to confirm whether the direct and semi-direct versions of the oral interaction sub-test were therefore measuring different language abilities. The next step in this study, therefore, was to examine the equivalence of test taker output from the two versions.

Methodology

Following the analysis of test scores in the December 1992 trial, a selection of the audio recordings obtained from both the live and tape-based versions of the oral interaction sub-test was transcribed and their discourse features compared using the framework adopted by Shohamy (1994) in her study of the Hebrew OPI and SOPI (see Chapter 1 for a discussion of her findings). These features included lexical density, rhetorical structure and functions, genre, speech moves, communicative properties, discourse strategies, content and topic of discourse, prosodic/paralinguistic features and contextualisation, type of speech functions, discourse markers and register. The analysis of language output was carried out in two separate studies. In the first study (Discourse Study A), qualitative discourse analyses of the data were undertaken focusing on all of the above features with the exception of lexical density. In the second study (Discourse Study B), a quantitative examination of test taker language output was carried out focusing solely on lexical density. The analysis of lexical density is reported separately because of its quantitative nature but, more importantly, because it also yielded different results in relation to the equivalence of the two versions than the other categories. Using Shohamy's (1994) categories enabled a direct comparison to be drawn between her findings and the results of this study.

In order to ensure appropriate sample selection, a stratified random sample of 20 test takers from the December 1992 trial was obtained. This process involved selecting ten candidates who had completed the live version first and ten who had completed the tape-mediated version first by drawing candidate numbers at random from each of these two groups. This group of 20 candidates formed an approximately normally distributed range of ability levels using the ability estimates derived from the FACETS program and, as such, was a reasonably representative sample of the whole cohort of 83 candidates.

Four alternate tasks were chosen from the complete list of test tasks (see Tables 2.2 and 2.3, Chapter 2) as the focus of analysis – the description, narration, discussion and role play tasks. The key features of these tasks are shown in Tables 5.1 and 5.2 below.

The first three tasks were closely matched in terms of design across the live and tape versions. Like all of the test tasks (except the live role play) they were intended to be 'monologic' in character on both versions i.e. during the response only the test taker was required to speak in order to successfully fulfil the requirements of the tasks successfully. (See Chapter 2 for further information about these tasks.) The live and tape role play tasks were the most different in terms of their requirements for candidates: the live role play consisted of a two-way exchange based on an information gap while the tape role play required test takers to leave a telephone answering machine message.

Table 5.1

Key features of selected tasks, live version, December 1992 trial

Task	Description	Narration	Discussion	Role play
Topic	educational settings	car breakdown	work	lunch engagement
Type	unplanned open monologic	planned closed monologic	unplanned open monologic	planned open dialogic convergent
No. of questions	3	1	4	1
Language functions expected	describing, explaining, making excuses	narrating narrating, giving opinions	describing, explaining	apologising, explaining, speculating
Preparation time	nil	1'	1'	1'
Response time	determined by/negotiated with interlocutor			

Table 5.2
Key features of selected tasks, tape version, December 1992 trial

Task	Description	Narration	Discussion	Role play
Topic	work setting	car accident	work	party invitation
Type	unplanned open monologic	planned closed monologic	planned open monologic	unplanned open monologic
No. of questions	3	1	4	1
Language functions expected	describing, giving opinions	narrating, explaining	describing, narrating, explaining, giving opinions, speculating	apologising, explaining, making excuses
Preparation time	1'	1'	1'	1'
Response time	2'	2'	4'	45"

A detailed transcription of these tasks using the live and tape audio recordings of the 20 subjects selected was then carried out. This provided a total of 160 language samples for this discourse analytic study. In the excerpts reproduced for the analyses below the following transcription notation is used:

1 *Unfilled pauses and gaps:* periods of silence, timed in tenths of a second by counting 'beats' of elapsed time in accordance with the rhythm of the preceding speech. Micropauses, those of less than 0.2 seconds are symbolised (.) within parentheses; longer pauses appear as time within parentheses: e.g. (0.8) = 0.8 seconds. Where 'real' time is indicated (e.g. in between the end of task instructions and the beginning of the candidate's response, brackets ({ }) are used.

2 *Repair phenomena:* reformulations are indicated by a hyphen (-).

3 *Intonation:* a period (.) indicates a falling intonation, a question mark (?) marks a rising intonation and a comma (,) is used for continuing intonation.

4 *Overlapping talk:* brackets ([ ]) are used to indicate overlaps, i.e. where utterances start and/or end simultaneously.

5 *Transcription doubt or uncertainty:* these are marked by a question mark within parentheses (?).

6 *Quiet talk:* per cent signs (% %) are used to mark the boundaries of quiet talk.

7 *Latched utterances* i.e. where there is no interval between utterances: equals signs (=) are used at the end of the first utterance and at the beginning of the second utterance.

8 *Lengthened sounds or syllables:* a colon (:) is used; more colons prolong the stretch.

9 *Speakers:* the interlocutor on the live version is indicated by (I), the recorded instructor's voice on the tape version by (V) and the candidate on both versions by (C).

10 *Focus of analysis:* an asterisk (*) is used.

Discourse Study A: The qualitative analysis

Each of the discourse features used by Shohamy (1994), with the exception of lexical density (see Study B), was used to compare the audio recordings obtained from the live and tape versions of the *access:* oral interaction sub-test. For each feature the results are compared with those reported by Shohamy for the Hebrew OPI and SOPI.

Rhetorical functions and structure

In Shohamy's (1994) study rhetorical functions refer to the nature of the prompts used to elicit test taker speech while rhetorical structure (or scheme) refers to the underlying discourse organisation or macro-structure of the whole speech event. Shohamy found that the OPI mainly consisted of direct questions such as 'Where do you live?' and 'What is your profession?' while the SOPI mostly consisted of task prompts in the form of instructions such as 'Discuss the season you like best' and 'Give a speech'. The rhetorical structure of the OPI was therefore question – answer – question – answer while in the SOPI the rhetorical structure was task – performance – new task – new performance.

In this study, the rhetorical functions of the live and tape versions of the *access:* oral interaction sub-test were very similar. Both versions used task prompts in the form of instructions to elicit test taker speech. In the four matching tasks selected for this study task prompts included, for example, 'Describe the building in which you studied', 'Use the pictures to tell the story', 'Make excuses for not being able to go to lunch' and 'Describe a colleague you have admired' on the live version and 'Describe the building in which you work', 'Use the pictures to tell the story', 'Apologise and explain why you can't go your sister's party' and 'Describe some of the ways work is changing in your profession' on the tape version. The overall rhetorical structure of both the live and tape versions therefore was task – performance – new task – new performance. The following excerpts from candidate 27 performances on the description and role play tasks across the two versions illustrate the similarity in rhetorical functions and structure. Each interviewer prompt has been highlighted with an asterisk (*).

[Candidate 27: Live description]

*   I: I would like you to describe to me either the university you attended or the last school you attended. (0.5) Which one would you like to describe?

    C: Maybe the institution I mean the (?) polytechnical institute where I used to study (.) seven years ago (0.5).

*   I: OK I'll just get you to describe to me the external appearance and the location of the buildings.

    C: Mm uh it was a beautiful place (.) w-with a lot of trees er (0.4) m-maybe twenty or twenty-five large buildings or different departments, uh pretty location not far from the centre of town.

    I: Mm mm all right (0.8) secondly, describe the internal layout of the building or buildings, for example the number of floors, the number of classrooms, offices, etcetera.

    C: A big variety of different buildings from two storey buildings to (0.3) say twenty-four storey buildings so they were very different, some of them were built one hundred fifty years ago because it's a very old institution and some of them were almost new, one years old.

    I: Mm mm.

    C: Very different.

*   I: All right, finally, please describe one of the classrooms you were familiar with.

    C: The cl-classrooms are very different too because some of them were (1.0) designed for (0.5) two hundred two hundred fifty students and some of them just for a small group of ten twenty people.

    I: Mm mm all right.

[Candidate 27: Tape description]

*   V: ... Imagine that somebody is coming to visit you at work and they have never been there before. You must (0.5) one, describe to them the external appearance and the location of the building in which you work. Two, describe the internal layout of the building for example, the number of floors, the location of your office or work area. Three, describe the room in which you work. (0.8) You now have one minute to think about what you will say. You should respond to all three questions. Begin speaking after the beep. You will have two minutes to respond. {1 minute} beep

    C: {1.2} Well I'm working in the building of the English language centre of RMIT. It's located on 560 Elizabeth street. You should go along the Elizabeth street and you'll see the sign, blue sign saying er (0.5) English learning centre RMIT. Er this building is three storey and I'm working on the second floor. You (0.9) you going upstairs to the second floor and er going along the corridor and then turn (0.8) on the right and you'll see my room in the front of you with the number 206. Uh (0.9) the building (0.4) where I work (0.4) er doesn't have the ve – very interesting features, it's just look like other buildings in – on the street, er you can recognise it easier by the (side?) that I told you before, hmm, there are (0.3) three (0.5) – it is three storey building, there are three floors, and er (2.2) er (0.8) well (0.7) what could I (2.40 %location% (0.8) er (0.7) my office located in the middle of the floor, it's in the middle of the corridor, it's very suitable location, there are – there is air conditioner in my room so you always feel comfortable in my premises (cut off by recorded voice)

[Candidate 27: Live role play]

I: Now look at the second role play. I'll give you a couple of minutes
   to consider the information in your booklet. Ah, this time I'll
   begin. {1 minute 43 seconds} [Role play card ends with * instruction
   'Respond to your workmate by making up some excuses for not being
   able to go to lunch.']
I: Okay?
C: Okay.
I: Hi, it's Friday. Lunch?
C: Oh, yes, fantastic. It's lunch time but er I'm afraid I've got some
   problem to go to lunch today.
I: What? You always come on Friday.
C: Yeah, always but you know I'm married so I'm completely depend on my
   wife.
I: What?
C: (?) (?). You know, yes, (0.5) yeah.
I: You're joking.
C: Yeah, you know your feel like, like slave when your marriage. You can
   do nothing without permission of your wife (laughter).
I: Oh come on! Exert your [independence].
C: [Oh yeah] yeah I promised to buy one of
   these terrible expensive dresses today so she is waiting for me,
   exactly in this time. I was trying to explain to her it's important
   for me to go to the (?) - to this lunch to communicate with my
   friend
I: Oh.
C: (0.7) but you know I can do nothing about it.
I: You've got problems [there   ].
C: [Otherwise] I'll be in terrible trouble.
I: Couldn't you meet her after lunch or just ring her up and say look
   you'll be half an hour late?
C: Oh yeah, I'll try to contact her if I will be early bi (0.3)
   earlier. Really.
I: Cause I've got a friend who knows you and is dying to meet you and
   he's only got lunchtime today.
C: But wait, only lunch time? Have you got his phone number? Maybe I'll
   contact him to see him later.
I: I don't think he's contactable at the moment. He's in and out. He's
   not quite sure where he's staying. You sure you can't make it?
C: Oh, really, I'm so sorry about it but er I really can't go there.
I: Oh.
C: (0.8) So maybe we can arrange it another time.
I: Sorry about that. Okay.

[Candidate 27: Tape role play]

V1: Read the message your daughter has left for you at home. {30 seconds}
    When you ring your sister Ruth back, no-one is answering so you will
    have to leave a message on her answering machine.
*   (0.8) You should apologise and explain why you and the rest of the
        family can't go to the party. {5 seconds} Now listen to Ruth's
        recorded message. Begin speaking after the beep. You will have 45
        seconds to leave your message.
V2: Hello this is 562-4532. We can't answer the phone at the moment.
    Please leave a message and we'll get back to you as soon as possible.
C: Hello Ruth. How are you? G. calling. Told me that er you invite us
   for a birthday. (0.6) It could be so great to go there but
   unfortunately we can't go because of our circumstances. You know my
   wife's now is so sick and we should be with her in the hospital. Er,
   would you (0.4) we'll call you back as soon as we can. Thank you.
   Bye bye.
V: That is the end of this section.

Genre

In discourse analysis the term genre refers to a particular class of speech events which share distinctive characteristics such as prayers, sermons, conversations and speeches. In Shohamy's (1994) study the genre of the OPI was found to be a 'conversational interview' while the genre of the SOPI was a 'reporting monologue'.

The genre of the description, narration and discussion tasks in both versions of the *access:* oral interaction sub-test was essentially a *reporting or narrative 'monologue'*. Candidates responded to a series of scripted prompts with either minimal verbal feedback (the live version) or none at all (the tape version). The excerpts from candidate 27's performance on the live and tape description task (quoted above) illustrate the similarity between the two versions in this respect. While the tape role play was also a monologue, the live role play took the form of a *conversation*. Again, candidate 27's performances on these two tasks (quoted above) illustrate this difference.

Speech moves

Speech moves refer to units of spoken discourse which may be smaller than an utterance. In Shohamy's (1994) study the analysis of speech moves focused particularly on the presence or absence of expansions and elaborations in test taker responses beyond the immediate requirements of the test questions or tasks. She found a much higher incidence of expansion and elaboration beyond the specific questions (such as negotiations for meaning and creating new directions in the discourse) on the OPI than on the SOPI, where test takers mostly restricted their responses to reporting and describing what was directly relevant to the task at hand with little if any additional information.

In the 'monologic' tasks (i.e. the description, narration and discussion tasks) on both versions of the *access:* oral interaction sub-test, candidate responses rarely included expansions and elaborations beyond the requirements of the assigned tasks. In the case of the live version this may seem surprising given its interactive potential. However, it needs to be remembered that interlocutors were under instruction to limit their contribution to the script assigned to them and not to encourage further discussion in all tasks except the live role play. In addition, the rhetorical structure of this live test (i.e., task – performance – new task – new performance) may not have been as conducive to the kinds of expansions and elaborations reported by Shohamy (1994) on the Hebrew OPI where participants engage in a more fluid, interactive conversational interview. The following examples illustrate the parity between responses to the matched 'monologic' tasks on the live and tape versions. The beginning of the candidate's response in each instance is asterisked. Firstly, the more 'closed' narration task for candidate 2:

[Candidate 2: Live narration]

```
    I:  ...I'm now going to give you a minute to look at the pictures and
        think about your story. When you've had time I'll ask you to start.
        {30 seconds}
    C:  So I can use some of the pictures.
    I:  Mmm
    C:  and can start.
    I:  So A. what happened? Why are you so late arriving tonight?
*   C:  Umm. (0.7) When I was riding a car and my car umm was um get into
        the problem. Is there something wrong which I don't know. I didn't
        know what were happening so I get out of the car and tried to -
        tried to fix it up which I couldn't do it so (0.6)
    I:  Mmm
    C:  um behind me there's a house but it's um-  it's very dark inside but
        I tried to um um I approaching and tried to knock the door and
        hopefully is there so - is somebody there. (0.7) Umm when I knocked
        the doors there was no answer. Umm I was try my best but it's um
        nothing happen - it's nothing happen so I um - I come back to my car
        umm and try - I was trying to fix it again but it also doesn't work.
        (0.5) Um I was standing next to my car and er mm far away another
        car approaching to my car and because ah my cars is um doesn't have
        light show another car would hit by another car. Mm (1.4) mm (0.8) so
        um [I went - ]
    I:      [That's OK]
    C:  I was get into trouble so ah I was arrive very late -late.
    I:  Good good thanks A.
```

[Candidate 2: Tape narration]

```
    V:  ... You now have one minute to look at the pictures and think about
        the story. Begin after you hear the beep. You have two minutes to
        tell your story. (1 minute) beep
*   C:  I was walk - I was walking on the road. (0.7) I didn't see a car so
        the, the driver, um, (right?) (again?) and hit in the, er, in the
        back of me. I was falling down. I was sitting on the crow and the
        car hit me again. Mm the car was um absolutely um damage. Sure the
        lady come to ask me what was happened. (0.6) I told her I was hit by
        the car and see - she, she went to the telephone box nears that and
        she called the ambulant. (0.5) Minute later the ambulant arrive but
        the ambulant um, um, the staff who sitting inside er ambulant saw me
        and says um I'm worse than, - I was, - I didn't hurt sho and um
        another truck come and pick up the damaged car. (0.4) Um, I was still
        sitting on the road and the truck um pick up the car and (run?)
        away. I was sitting there and think um who was ... um, I don't - I
        was ... um the car, the damage car was repair. I still sitting on
        the road and didn't know (whas?) (wa?) happening.
```

Secondly, the more 'open' discussion task for candidate 13, again comparing the live and tape versions:

[Candidate 13: Live discussion]

I: ... Question one. What qualifications and/or experience are necessary to enter your profession?

* C: Uh, to enter my profession there - you need to have at least ah - you have to - you should finish ah post graduates level ah

I: Mm

C: means ah master degree and especially Bachelor of Commerce in my field of study [(?) (?)]

I: [Okay]

C: Yes.

I: Can you describe some wa (0.7) some of the ways work is changing in your profession?

* C: Mm. In the past ah most of the work wor - most of the task is emphasi - was empha - emphasi on er teaching

I: Mm hmm.

C: but ah about - from about last ten year on until, until now ah the concept of the work is change. Ah, now we, we not only emphasi on mm teaching but also in research

I: Mm hmm

C: so that there - there - three (1.0) there - so that we, we can get ah more knowledge and more experience and can ah transfer this other knowledge and experience to the student.

I: Okay. Very good.

C: Yes.

I: What experience do you have of working independently and as part of a team?

* C: Yes, I have mos er (0.7), I have both experience ah working independently and working as a group. I prefer working ah independently. Ha.

I: Mm.

C: Ha.

I: Quite.

C: because I think mm, we, we no need to depend on other person in our group sometime if we work in a group, in, they ah, they might (0.8) it's quite difficult to, to, to, separate the task - how much you, you are, you are learn, how much I have to do

I: Mm hmm.

C: and sometime I get (?) you have to do (it].

I: [yes]

C: have to?

I: Ha ha.

C: so I, I feel its, its, my - for me it's, I prefer to work er, independently.

I: Okay. The last question. We have all worked with people we admire. Please describe to me a colleague whom you have respected and admired.

* C: Yes. I have mm one of my er lecturer and now is my colleague. Ah, he, him er I respect and er ad - admire him. Ah, he is very kind and normally work is the high (pollity(?)) and he alway ah suggest

I: [cough cough]

C: he's in the suggest means very useful, ah useful (?) for things.

I: Mm hmm.

C: but I (?) (?) (?) (?) (?) (?). Yes.

I: Okay.

C: Yeah.

[Candidate 13: Tape discussion]

```
V:  ...You will have one minute to complete your answer for each
    question, and then you will hear the next question. (1.0) Question
    one. What qualifications and or experience are necessary to enter
    your profession. beep
*   C:  To enter my profession you should have er (0.5) the second degree. I
        mean you should have ah (0.6) you should finish mm post graduate
        study level ah especially in Agricultural Economics. And for the
        experience er is not necessary if you ah finish ah
        the - er you second degree.
    V:  Question two. Describe some of the ways work is changing in your
        profession. beep
*   C:  The changing of the work in my profession is er the - is mainly about
        the ah the emphasise on ah teaching. Now it (0.8) before - in the
        previous ah we emphasise on teaching but er now-a-day er it's change.
        We have to get more experience in the research work so that we can
        gain more knowledge and experience to teach the student and that's
        why now we are keep equally important or on teaching and research.
    V:  Question three. What experience do you have of working independently
        and as part of a team? beep
*   C:  Er, I have both - I have experience both in the case of mm working
        independently and working in a group. Mm, in a teaching some subject
        I, I (0.5) t - ah teach er (solely?) er nobody help. But sometime,
        some subject, I have to ah teach and share with the other teacher -
        other lecturer. In my experience I think er it's (0.9) there's some
        mm benefit and er disadvantage in working in group or working in
        independently. Ah, if you're working independently at some time we
        are f - we, we are more freely, we work ah more convenience by -
    V:  Question four. Describe a colleague you have admired. beep
*   C:  Ah, I have admired one of my colleagues. Ah, he is ah my former
        lecturer but now he's the senior staff in m, my university. He alway
        works ah in the (?) (?) ah (?) and his is very kind and he alway
        suggest - recommend to me about what I should do and what I should
        not do which is very er useful for me in the working.
    V:  That is the end of this section.
```

Thus, in both the more 'closed' narration task and the more 'open' discussion task it is apparent that there was little expansion and/or elaboration beyond the specified requirements. However, it is worth noting that the 'monologic' tape tasks generally elicited as much discourse as their live counterparts possibly due to the *access:* test developers', careful attempts to balance the demands of matching tasks across the two versions. This contrasts with Shohamy's (1994) study where responses on the SOPI seem to have been often much shorter than on the OPI.

In contrast to the 'monologic' tasks, the role play segment produced much greater expansion and hence more discourse than its counterpart in the tape version because of its dialogic nature and the fact that interlocutors were less constrained on this task. The transcripts of the live and tape role plays for Candidate 5 reproduced below clearly illustrate this difference. The excerpt from the live version here also demonstrates that much greater expansion and elaboration including negotiation of meaning were involved on the role play task than on any of the other live tasks. All of the candidate's contributions from the two excerpts are asterisked.

[Candidate 5: Live role play]

I: ... Okay, now look at the um second role play and I'll give you a couple of minutes to consider the information. {1 min 6 secs}

I: Okay?

C: Yeah.

I: All right, this, this time C. I will begin. Hi C., are you all right for lunch today?

* C: Er, mm yes but you know I have a, a problem today.

I: Mm.

* C: I mean I must go and carry out my children to the doctor. I have an appointment. It is very important to them so

I: Mm. But, I've, I've got someone coming from your home town specially just to see you. It's a surprise for you, and you've just got to come. Can't you make the, the appointment later?

* C: Mm. Hm. I don't know because er (0.8), because you know, we can't er, put off

I: Mm

* C: this appointment. We have to enter my a er my wife is, is sick just now.

I: She's sick?

* C: Yes [yes]

I: [oh]

* C: she's sick. She can't carry out my children so she ring me. Very upset.

I: Mm. You er, you can't find another way around it

C: (?)

I: because we really would love to have lunch [with you].

* C: [Yes I   ] appreciate (area?), yes I appreciate this, this time. I would be, I would, I would be very happy to lunch with you but (?), (0.6) health of my children is very important to us.

I: Oh, all right I understand that and we'll have to see you another time. I hope they are okay soon.

[Candidate 5: Tape role play]

V1: ...Now listen to Ruth's recorded message. (0.4) Begin speaking after the beep. (1.0) You will have 45 seconds to leave your message.

V2: Hello (0.2) this is 562-4532. (0.4) We can't answer the phone at the moment. (0.5) Please leave a message and we'll get back to you as soon as possible.

* C: Er, sorry we can't mm er, we are very sorry but we can't attend you mm you er birthday er (1.0) because my wife is very sick and we have to stay at home. I wish you very er, I wish you nice birthday (0.9) and all very - all the best to Paul. Thank you very much.

V: That is the end of this section.

Communicative properties

In Shohamy's (1994) study *communicative properties* refers to first, whether one-way or two-way communication is involved; secondly, whether the test is conducted in the test taker's first language (L1) or second language (L2); thirdly, the nature of the boundaries from one topic or section to another; and finally, whether parts of the question were repeated in the answer. Shohamy found that the OPI consisted entirely of a two-way channel of communication conducted in the test taker's L2 where the boundaries between topics were fluid and smooth. The SOPI, on the other hand, involved one-way communication and sharp, abrupt shifts from one task to the next. The tasks were presented in test takers' L1 and responded to in their L2.

Both versions of the ***access:*** oral interaction sub-test were conducted in English, i.e., the test taker's L2. In both formats the boundaries between tasks were rigid, i.e., there were clear shifts from one task to the next (see 'rhetorical functions and structure' above). The 'monologic' tasks on the live version did exhibit a slightly more two-way communicative character than their tape counterparts insofar as some form of verbal feedback (mostly minimal responses) was given to test takers during and at the end of their responses. This difference can be shown by contrasting the live and tape narration tasks for candidate 60. The interlocutor's feedback on the live version is asterisked.

[Candidate 60: Live narration]

```
        I:  ... All right, I am now going to give you a minute to look at the
            pictures and think about your story. {20 seconds} Okay so why are you
            so late tonight?
        C:  Oh I'm very sorry after I attended the conference, (0.6) I drove down
            with Auburn road,
   *    I:  Mm mm,
        C:  and (0.4) suddenly my car stuck before a big building, this part of
            the (0.3)- it was un (.) fa - I was unfamiliar with this part of the
            suburb, (0.4) - I went down to er (0. 7) the closest door to me,
   *    I:  Yes=
        C:  =rang the bell and (.) I knock at the door (0.7) but no-body answer
            my (0.4) knock er either my ringing of the bell. (0.5) I went back
            to my car, I parked it unfortunately in front of the gate of the
            owner of the house,
   *    I:  Mm mm,
        C:  and (0.5) at that moment I think that I forgot to (2.0)  my - my
            brake - handbrake and when I was walking down (0.3) to the - to my
            car the owner of the car (0.4) opened the door,
   *    I:  Mm mm,
        C:  and slammed it into my car. (0.5) So er I got a slight accident as
            well as a breakdown.
   *    I:  Ah!
        C:  That's the reason why (I'm?) late.
   *    I:  Mm right okay, thank you.
```

[Candidate 60: Tape narration]

V: ... You now have one minute to look at the pictures and think about
    the story. Begin after you hear the beep. You have two minutes to
    tell your story. (1 minute) beep
C: {2 seconds} I was er just turning to the left when I was er (0.5)
    going forwards (0.5) (the car?) was suddenly (0.3) came into my way
    (0.4) (?) (0.5) and I was so shocked but fortunately (0.5) I ran to
    the telephone and: (0.4) phoned the ambulance (0.6) to pick him up.
    The thing is that er I was so fortunate I didn't er (.) bumped him
    (0.5) dead. (0.8) And I phoned the ambulance and ambulance was er
    there in minutes and also the breakdown to pick my car up. (1.2) I
    was so (0.7) happy to see that he was (0.5) not unconscious, he was
    just (.) hit down. So er I think that er he will cover – recover
    when I take him to the hospital. (0.4) The ambulance came after the
    (0.8) – I phoned the ambulance but by the time the garage was there
    – the man from the garage, (0.5) the ambulance was not there. (0.3)
    So er (0.6) the problem is that er the ambulance was late to take
    him to the hospital. (0.6) I don't know exactly (1.2) what is the
    problem with the ambulance (0.3) that it er (0.5) didn't turn up. I
    was waiting for (0.2) him (0.7) er at the spot where uh had the
    accident. (1.8) So by the time when the (1.2) breakdown was there
    the ambulance didn't turn out so er I wait there (0.2) at the spot
    where the accident happened. {9 seconds}

Finally, as illustrated in the contrast between candidate 5's live and tape responses in terms of speech moves (see previous sub-section), the role play tasks differed in that the live task was essentially dialogic, allowing for 'authentic' interaction between candidate and interlocutor, while its tape equivalent remained entirely monologic.

Discourse strategies

In Shohamy's (1994) study *discourse strategies* refers to the procedures adopted by test takers to cope with the communicative demands of the testing situation. Shohamy reported that test takers used a greater range of discourse strategies on the OPI than on the SOPI. On the OPI these strategies included deliberation, avoiding direct answers, hesitation, self-correction, disagreeing, qualifying, switching to L1 for communicative purposes and demands for clarification. On the SOPI these strategies were restricted to paraphrasing, repetition of phrases in the eliciting questions, switching to L1, self-correction and silence when no answer was available.

In the *access:* oral interaction sub-test the discourse strategies employed by test takers appeared to be very similar in the two versions for both the 'monologic' and role play tasks. These strategies were mostly deliberation, hesitation and self-correction. In some instances, however, there were requests for clarification on the live version and longer periods of hesitation on the tape version. Both of these features can be illustrated by comparing matching excerpts from candidate 50's responses on the live and tape discussion tasks:

[Candidate 50: Live discussion (part)]

```
I:   And ah we have all worked with people we admire. Please describe to
     me a colleague whom you have respected and admired.
*   C:   Just a colleague?
    I:   Mm. Oh anyone that
*   C:   Ah!
    I:   [you've] ah
*   C:   [(?) of] my friends in (?) ah just one year older than me but he got
         much more experience than me. He is Chinese, English and Chinese; he
         is at the - his studies good. (0.6) He graduated from Calin -
         Californian University, yeah. And as the - not like many offices
         graduate ah he's ah work, he's ah well provide.
    I    Mm.
```

[Candidate 50: Tape discussion (part)]

```
    V:   Question four. Describe a colleague you have admired. beep
*   C:   I have a colleague from - graduated from University of California in
         the US (1.0) A and (1.5) he always encouraged me to do better and
         better and don't worry about my qualification. (1.8) Even though he
         graduated from California he persuade me to do better as well as h-
         him because in his opinion we are the same different only (0.9) the
         university we come from er don't worry about the (1.4) (?) because we
         are the same you are the same with me as well so don't worry about
         your (1.2) domestic cred - university. And (0.9) he is one year older
         than me but he has ah good skill in the finance and management as
         well. I admire him.
    V:   That is the end of this section.
```

Content and topics of discourse

In Shohamy's (1994) study the range of topics covered in the OPI depended on the test taker's level of proficiency. The topics covered with low proficiency test takers were mostly personal, even trivial, while those covered with high proficiency test takers included work, politics and educational subjects. On the SOPI the same topics covering a broad range of personal, social, work and educational issues were included for all test takers.

In the *access:* oral interaction sub-test (as in the SOPI) the content and topics of the tasks were the same within each of the two versions for all test takers irrespective of their proficiency level on all four matching tasks. The topics in the four tasks selected for this study included educational, social and occupational issues on both versions. Other parts of the two versions included topics on recreation, housing and the environment. The range of topics test takers were required to address was therefore both broad and uniform *within* each version. However, only in one of the four matching tasks – the discussion – was the topic identical *across* the two versions. For the other three tasks the topics were similar (see Tables 5.1 and 5.2 above).

Prosodic/paralinguistic features and contextualisation

Shohamy (1994) found that responses on the OPI included a greater range of *prosodic features,* such as changes in intonation and voice quality, as well as laughter and humming. These features tended to be absent on the SOPI.

In the 'monologic' tasks of the *access:* oral interaction sub-test there was a slightly greater variety of intonation and voice quality evident in test taker responses on the live version compared to the tape version, where answers tended to sound a little more flat and monotonous. This difference generally appeared to increase on the live versus tape role plays. While these lesser and greater differences in prosodic features (particularly voice quality) were not immediately apparent in examining the transcripts, they became clearer after re-listening to the audio recordings.

Shohamy also found signs of *contextualisation* (including paralinguistic features) on the part of test takers in the OPI (but not the SOPI) i.e., test takers used expressions of embarrassment and laughter, addressed the interviewer directly (such as 'Listen!'), shared personal information and referred to objects in the examination room to explain or demonstrate a point being made. However, there were few signs of such contextualisation on the part of the candidate in either version of the *access:* oral interaction sub-test. In the case of the live 'monologic' tasks this may have been due to the fact that the interlocutor's contribution was tightly scripted thereby eliciting a more formal, decontextualised response from the test taker than might have occurred if greater interaction had been allowed. Candidate 48's responses on the live and tape description tasks typify the lack of contextualisation on both versions:

[Candidate 48: Live description]
```
   I:  I would like you to describe to me either the university you attended
       or the last school you attended. Which one would you like to
       describe?
*  C:  Mmm. I, I didn't go to university but I, I did some tertiary course
       so I like to um describe that i - institute.
   I:  An institute. Okay, now I'm going to ask you a few questions about
       your institute. Firstly, please describe to me the external
       appearance and the location of the building.
*  C:  Ohm. (0.5) The building er that institution is in China, Shanghai.
       Hm, it's not in Australia. And it's er mm, I think it's er in the
       east part of Shanghai and er in just near the (Wampul?) River and
       the, mm, the building is er about it's not big about three buildings.
   I:  Mm hm. Second, describe the internal layout of the building (or one
       of the buildings) (e.g. the number of floors, the number of
       classrooms, offices, etc).
*  C:  Um. There three floors of that b - one of the building and every
       floor (0.6) floor they got about ten classrooms and the - one
       teachers' office and two toilets.
   I:  Finally, please describe one of the classrooms you were familiar
       with.
```

```
*    C:  Mm. The classroom is about er fifty, fifty square metres and er in
         front of the classroom there is blackboard and er about er forty
         seats and twenty desks and er two students sit together and share one
         desk and er there are six windows both side of the classroom.
     I:  Thank you.
```

[Candidate 48: Tape description]

```
     V:  ... Begin speaking after the beep. You will have two minutes to
         respond. {1 minute} beep
*    C:  This is the food processing industry. It's ah located on the Mainpole
         street oh at Bayswater. (0.9) Where you go into the company the f -
         on the right your side of the building is the men and the ladies
         changing room a - and (0.8) when you go into the main building in
         front of you this is a packing area and past packing area there is ?
         fitting room and I work in that area. There's only one floor (2.4)
         and and er sometimes they are ten people in the in - working on the
         line but er sometimes only three people. This depend on products.
         When you go into the working area you have to change your uniform and
         wear ca- hat and a boots because this is the food industry.
```

The tape role play displayed the same lack of contextualisation as the other tape tasks. In the case of the live role play there appeared to be only a slight increase in the level of contextualisation (e.g. laughter, embarrassment) perhaps because both participants were acting out prescribed roles and their level of personal involvement was therefore fairly low. The live and tape role play performances of candidates 5 and 27 quoted above are illustrative of the general lack of contextualisation on these tasks.

Types of speech functions

The term *speech function* refers to the purpose(s) for which an utterance is used. Functions are often described as categories of behaviour such as requesting, apologising, complaining and congratulating. Shohamy (1994) found that test takers used a much wider range of speech functions, including requesting clarification, agreeing and disagreeing, sharing personal information and negotiating on the OPI. The functions on the SOPI were mainly restricted to reporting, describing and narrating.

The speech functions identified in test taker responses on the live and tape 'monologic' tasks of the **access:** oral interaction sub-test were very similar and included describing, narrating, negotiating, explaining, making excuses, making suggestions, persuading, giving opinions and speculating. However, on the live version, there were also occasional requests for clarification (see, for example, the excerpt from candidate 50 under *Discourse strategies* above) as well as negotiation about the focus of the response, particularly in the description task where test takers were given a choice of topic. The following excerpt from the beginning of candidate 53's answer on this task illustrates the kind of negotiation which took place at this point:

[Candidate 53: Live description (part)]

```
    I:  I would like you to describe to me either the university you attended
        or the last school you attended.
    C:  Yes, right.
    I:  Which one would you like to describe?
*   C:  I can describe about er any university here? I had been to Monash on
        a couple of days.
*   I:  Okay, now I'm going to ask you a few questions about your university,
        about Monash.
*   C:  I'm not doing any course there.
*   I:  No, but you, you went there.
*   C:  Yes.
*   I:  Attended.
*   C:  Just, just like that with somebody else who is doing a course. I went
        with him two or three times.
*   I:  Okay. Er, well that's going to be difficult. What about in, in your
        country in India? Did you go to university there (?) (?) (?) (?).
*   C:  I did (1.4) I did training from India.
*   I:  Right.
*   C:  about thirteen years back.
*   I:  Right. Can you remember the, the institution you attended.
*   C:  Yeah, yeah I can remember.
```

In respect to the live and tape role plays the range of speech functions differed insofar as the live role play also included disagreeing, negotiating a solution and reaching a compromise. Again the performances of candidates 5 and 27 (quoted above) illustrate this difference.

Discourse markers

Discourse markers refer to words or phrases which help to provide coherence and cohesion in a text. On the OPI Shohamy (1994) found test takers used a variety of these markers which included, but were not limited to, 'and', 'but', 'although', 'however', and 'it depends'. On the SOPI the use of markers was mainly restricted to 'and', 'but', 'although' and 'however'.

In the ***access:*** 'monologic' tasks an equally broad range of discourse markers was used by test takers on the two versions, including connectors such as 'but', 'and', 'however', 'although', 'well', 'maybe', 'so', 'first', 'then', 'finally', 'now', 'then' and 'anyway'. However, there appears to have been a slight tendency on the tape version to use them less frequently (see previous examples). The live and tape role play tasks were also similar in this respect except that in the live role play other more conversational markers such as 'I mean', 'y'know' and 'anyway' were also used.

Register

The term *register* is used by Shohamy (1994) to refer to differences in speech formality. She found that there were no significant register shifts during the course of either the OPI or the SOPI, although there was a slight change to more formal speech in one part of the SOPI.

In the ***access:*** live and tape 'monologic' tasks there were very few register shifts. On the whole the register of test taker responses on these tasks seemed to be very similar, i.e. quite formal. The excerpts included under the previous categories illustrate this parity. However, on the live role play there was often a shift to a more informal register on the part of both the candidate and interlocutor which was appropriate, given the nature of the task. Test taker responses on the tape role play, however, remained quite formal even though the answering machine message was supposed to be left for a member of the immediate family. Candidate 40's performance on the live and tape role play tasks clearly illustrates this difference:

[Candidate 40: Live role play]

```
  I: Now look at the second role play. I will give you a couple of
     minutes to consider the information. {53 seconds} This time I will
     begin.
  I: Oh hello E. Er, coming to lunch today?
* C: Oh I'm really sorry. I'm unable to make it because I've got some
     urgent shopping to do. I've got to catch up with the weekly shopping.
  I: Oh, that's no good E. Um, you know we always get together on Fridays.
     You've got to come this week.
* C: Yeah, it is true I normally come (0.7) but this Friday I am really
     sorry I'm unable to make it because this evening I've got - I'm
     invited over to a friend's place for a birthday
  I: can't
* C: and he can't do the weekly shopping.
  I: Can't you do it tomorrow on Saturday morning?
* C: No, my (0.8) I've got only one car. My wife takes the car, she's
     working on Saturdays.
  I: I've er got a particular friend coming er to join us for the lunch
     today and um he's going to be very disappointed about it because he
     actually comes from your town.
* C: (?) I would like to meet him really but er unfortunately I am unable
     to make it today.
  I: Mm, you can't change the time?
  C: Mm.
  I: You know that can wait.
* C: It's, it's ju - it's really difficult to change it and almost
     impossible unless I wouldn't make a fuss over it. You know how I
     always join the parties every week.
  I: I, I know you do. That's why I relied on your being there today and
     invited the friend along.
* C: Yes, but it's, it's really something I wouldn't ah, manage this
     Friday. I hope to catch up with you next Friday.
  I: Well I hope that he's still around next Friday.
* C: Yes, let's hope so.
  I: Okay E.
* C: Yeah, thank you.
```

[Candidate 40: Tape role play]

```
V1: ... Now listen to Ruth's recorded message. (0.4) Begin speaking after
    the beep. (1.0) You will have 45 seconds to leave your message.
V2: Hello (0.2) this is 562-4532. (0.4) We can't answer the phone at the
    moment. (0.5) Please leave a message and we'll get back to you as
    soon as possible.
```

```
*  C:  Ruth, this is E. speaking. (0.7) Thank you very much for inviting us
       over to Paul's birthday party on Saturday the twentieth.
       Unfortunately (0.6) we are unable to come since we have already
       another engagement on the same day. A very close friend of mine has
       invited us over and (0.6) we have already accepted his invitation.
       (0.4) So thank you very much for calling us over but sorry we won't
       be able to attend.
   V:  That is the end of this section.
```

Summary of findings

Table 5.3 below summarises the findings of the study to this point and compares them with those obtained by Shohamy's (1994) study of the Hebrew OPI and SOPI. For the sake of clarity the results have been reduced to three categories: same, similar and different.

The comparison of discourse features analysed to this point appeared to indicate that there was much greater parity between test taker responses on the live and tape 'monologic' tasks in the *access:* oral interaction sub-test than in Shohamy's OPI/SOPI study. Thus, the careful efforts of *access:* test developers to match these tasks (particularly by controlling and limiting the interlocutor's contribution on the live version through the use of a script) seemed to have been rewarded in terms of the parity of language obtained from the two versions. However, the findings also suggest that the cost of this achievement was a certain 'unnaturalness' (i.e. stiffness and formality) in test taker output on the live version. The less controlled live role play, on the other hand, appears to have elicited language which more closely approximated to conversation than the other live tasks. Yet, the price to be paid for its greater 'authenticity' seems to have been a sharp lack of comparability with its tape counterpart. The final stage in the examination of the test taker language output was to conduct a more detailed, quantitative comparison of the two versions from the perspective of lexical density. This study is reported in the next section.

Table 5.3

**Summary of findings (Discourse Study A):
O'Loughlin (2001) and Shohamy (1994)**

Category	*access:* live and tape versions		Hebrew OPI/SOPI
	'monologic' tasks	role play tasks	
Rhetorical structure & functions	same	same	different
Genre	same	different	different
Speech moves	same	different	different
Communicative properties	similar	different	different
Discourse strategies	similar	similar	different
Content/ topics	similar (description & narration) same (discussion)	similar	similar
Prosodic features	similar	different	different
Contextualisation	same	similar	different
Speech functions	similar	different	different
Discourse markers	similar	similar	different
Register	similar	different	similar

Discourse Study B: Lexical density

Introduction

This study focuses on the remaining category used by Shohamy (1994) in comparing the language produced in the Hebrew OPI and SOPI. This category is *lexical density*, which provides a quantitative measure of the relationship between lexical and grammatical items in spoken or written discourse. It is usually expressed simply as the percentage of lexicon in a given text. Recall from Chapter 2 that Shohamy reported an average lexical density figure of 40% in the OPI compared to 60% on the SOPI. Shohamy suggests that this result indicated that the SOPI elicited a more 'literate' type of language output than the OPI, another important difference between the language samples obtained on the two tests. This study looks at whether the degree of lexical density differed across the two versions of the *access:* oral interaction sub-test.

The structure of this section is as follows: first, the history of lexical density is traced; secondly, the purpose and methodology used in the study are outlined; and thirdly, the results of the investigation are reported and discussed. In the conclusion to the chapter, the implications of the findings from both Study A and Study B for the equivalence of the direct and semi-direct versions of the *access:* oral interaction test are explored.

Background

The term *lexical density* was originally coined by Ure (1971) to provide a measure of the relationship between 'lexical' as opposed to 'grammatical' words as a percentage of the total number of words in a text. On the basis of her analysis of a wide range of written and spoken texts (N = 64) she found, in general, that the spoken texts had a lexical density of less than 40% (ranging from 24% to 43%) and the written texts a density of greater than 40% (ranging from 36% to 57%).

Of more direct relevance to the study reported in this chapter was Ure's focus on the presence or absence of verbal and non-verbal feedback to the main speaker in the spoken texts. Ure's (1971: 448) findings indicated that 'feedback was an even more powerful factor in determining lexical density than the spoken/written choice'. With only one exception, spoken texts without feedback (i.e. monologues) all had a lexical density of more than 37% and all of those with feedback (i.e. dialogues) under 36%. Finally, this research also indicated that plannedness may be another important determinant of lexical density, with prepared spoken texts all having a lexical density of 37% or higher.

Ure's findings are important for the current study as they suggest that degree of lexical density is highly responsive to the presence or absence of feedback in spoken discourse. However, her study is deficient in that it does not clearly articulate the distinction between 'lexical' and 'grammatical' words and therefore the results should be regarded with some caution. In addition, it should be noted that different subjects produced the spoken and written data in this study. As Zora and Johns-Lewis (1989) suggest, this is likely to be another source of variation influencing the degree of lexical density.

Halliday (1985) used lexical density to compare written and spoken texts in English. Like Ure, he demonstrates that written texts typically contain a higher degree of lexical words than spoken texts. He concludes that the complexity of written language is lexical and that of spoken language is grammatical. He does not, however, examine how the degree of lexical density in a text may also be influenced by other factors such as those identified by Ure.

Halliday provides a useful (albeit fairly limited) framework for distinguishing between lexical and grammatical items in a text. Grammatical items are *function* words and operate in *closed,* finite systems in the language. Conversely, lexical items are *content* words and enter into *open* sets which are infinitely extendable. Thus, in English, he suggests, determiners, pronouns, most prepositions, conjunctions and some classes of adverbs are grammatical items. Rather oddly, also included in his initial list are finite verbs but elsewhere, in the examples he uses, these are treated as lexical items. In these examples the verb forms which are consistently classified as grammatical items appear, appropriately enough, to be modals and auxiliaries as well as all forms of the verbs 'to be' and 'to have'. In addition, all pro-forms (not simply pronouns) and interrogative and negative adverbs are consistently labelled as grammatical. All other adverbs used in the example are treated as lexical items.

Halliday (1985: 63) is not prescriptive about this method of classification, acknowledging that there is, in fact, a continuum from lexis into grammar. He argues that it does not matter so much where the line is drawn provided it is done consistently. Still, it appears that a detailed taxonomy needs to be devised in order for this analysis to proceed in a principled fashion. One apparent weakness in Halliday's framework is that the division of items under the headings lexical and grammatical is made essentially at the sentence level only. Important discourse phenomena which occur naturally in speech such as discourse markers (words and expressions used to structure discourse including linking and sequencing devices), interjections, (e.g. *gosh, wow*), reactive tokens (*yes, no, OK,* etc.) as well as lexical and non-lexical filled pauses appear to be largely neglected within this system of classification.

Halliday (1985: 64–5) does, however, make an important modification to the calculation of lexical density by distinguishing between high and low frequency lexical items. High frequency lexical items are those which occur either commonly in the language in general (e.g. in English *people, thing, way, do, make, get, be, have* and *good*) or else more than once in an individual text since repetition reduces the effect of density. In calculating the final lexical density figure the high frequency items are given half the value of the low frequency ones. This would seem to provide a truer, more fine-grained estimate of the overall lexical density.

More recent research on lexical density (for example, Stubbs 1986; Hasan 1988; Zora and Johns-Lewis 1989) has focused on sources of variation in spoken discourse, particularly discourse form. In Stubbs' (1986) study, the lexical density figures were lowest for telephone conversations (e.g. 44% for business calls and 45% for calls between friends) and highest for radio commentaries (e.g. 54% for a commentary on cricket and 56% for one on a state funeral). Zora and Johns-Lewis (1989) report interviews to have a lexical density of 48.03% compared with 46.96% for informal conversations. In both studies the subjects were educated native speakers of English.

In a study focusing on discourse variability in native–non-native speaker spoken interaction in and out of the EFL classroom, Hasan (1988) found that the mean lexical density per T-unit of the non-native group was substantially lower when they participated as interviewees in formal interviews (33.67%) compared to formal and informal classroom interactions (38.96% and 40.64% respectively), informal classroom discussions (43.69%) and informal conversations with native speakers outside the classroom (41.60%). The figures for the native speaker group, on the other hand, were substantially higher in the formal interviews where they acted as interviewers (47.02%). The formal and informal classroom interactions as well as the informal classroom discussions in which the native speakers were EFL teachers yielded fairly similar results (38.25%, 41.15% and 37.97% respectively). Finally, the figure for informal conversations with non-teacher native speakers outside the classroom (42.48%) was almost identical to that obtained for the non-native speakers. In general, these findings suggest that the context or setting, the type of interaction and the role of the speakers all influence the degree of lexical density.

It is important to note that Stubbs and Zora and Johns-Lewis report considerably higher lexical density figures than does Ure for her spoken data. Zora and Johns-Lewis list eight possible sources of variation to account for the different percentages reported in the studies cited here: 1) the basis for calculating lexical density, i.e. differences in allocating items to lexical as opposed to grammatical classes; 2) expected interruption and length of speaking turn i.e. texts of a more monologic nature may predispose speakers to a higher degree of lexical density; 3) the function of component units of text; 4) self-consciousness/self-monitoring; 5) personal attributes; 6) group attributes; 7) planning time; and 8) topic.

As noted earlier, Shohamy's (1994) comparative study of the OPI and SOPI indicated that the SOPI elicited language which was of a significantly higher lexical density than the OPI. This would appear to reflect the fact that the OPI was a much more interactive language event in which verbal and non-verbal feedback played an important role. However, her analysis is perhaps somewhat limited insofar as it takes no account of other important variables apart from test format (i.e. direct or semi-direct) which may affect lexical density such as task type and plannedness. Furthermore, in relation to the variables of personal and group attributes suggested by Zora and Johns-Lewis (1989), it is unclear whether the samples analysed by Shohamy were produced by the same subjects. In addition, there is a lack of explicitness about her method of calculating lexical density, i.e. how precisely lexical and grammatical items were differentiated and whether high and low frequency lexical items were weighted differently for the analysis.

Research hypotheses

The present study focuses mainly on the effects of two key variables potentially having an input on candidate output in the *access:* oral interaction sub-test – first, test format (i.e. live or tape-mediated) and secondly, task type. It addresses this question by examining the degree of lexical density which characterised selected language samples from the two versions of this sub-test in the December 1992 trial. In order to explore these issues the following experimental hypotheses were formulated:

H_{A1}: There is an effect on lexical density for test format.

H_{A2}: There is an effect on lexical density for task type.

H_{A3}: There is an interaction effect on lexical density for test format and task type.

The closely matched format of the two versions permitted a perhaps more direct, tighter comparison of the language samples than in Shohamy's (1994) study of the Hebrew OPI and SOPI (described in detail in Chapter 2), at least at the micro-analytic level. In the case of the *access:* oral interaction sub-test there was a broad range of matching tasks which attempted to elicit a similar range of language functions in each case. The structure of both versions was essentially the same, i.e. task – performance – new task – new performance. While this is also the case in the SOPI test, the structure of the OPI is basically question – answer – question – answer.

Method

This study used the same data as in Discourse Study A, i.e. the transcripts obtained from a stratified sample of 20 candidates on the four matching tasks (description, narration, discussion and role play) under the two test conditions (live and tape).

In the studies cited previously in this chapter it is the word (used synonymously with the term *item*) that has been adopted as the basic unit of lexical density. However, while this may be a satisfactory method for an approximate comparison of the relative weight of lexis and grammar in a text, it is proposed that a more refined approach to this analysis would be to focus on the notion of a linguistic *item* as the more appropriate unit of measurement and to differentiate it from the concept of the *word*.

There is, in fact, no one-to-one correspondence between linguistic items and words in English. An item may consist of more than one word e.g. multi-word verbs such as *catch up on*, phrasal verbs such as *drop in* – and idioms such as *kick the bucket*. Conversely, a word may consist of more than one item e.g. contractions such as *they're* and *isn't*. In addition, different items may be realised by the same word, e.g. *lap*: *lap1* (noun or verb as in a race), *lap2* (verb as in 'the cat laps the milk') and *lap3* (noun as in 'sit on my lap'). On the other hand, different words may be realised by the one lexical item (e.g. *different* and *difference* are alternate word forms of *differ*). Finally, the term 'item' (unlike the term 'word') does not so readily exclude what are sometimes called 'particles' such as *oh* and *mm,* which can play important functions (apart from simply expressing hesitation) in spoken discourse. In this study, therefore, it is linguistic items which were counted to measure lexical density in the language samples collected.

A preliminary taxonomy of lexical and grammatical items was drawn up based on a framework devised by Halliday (1985). There were three categories: grammatical items, high frequency lexical items and low frequency lexical items. In order to distinguish high and low frequency lexical items the 700 most frequently used words in English (excluding those deemed to be grammatical items), as identified in the COBUILD Dictionary project (see Willis and Willis 1988), were classified as high frequency lexical items and all others as low frequency items.

The framework was then refined after attempting the analysis on a limited number of the language samples. In order to confirm the viability and robustness of the revised classification system, two independent counts of lexical and grammatical items for three of the candidates on both versions of the test were carried out by the author and a research assistant. The framework was further refined following this stage, and then the final version (see Table 5.4 below) was used to analyse the live and tape-based audio recordings of all 20 candidates. All stages of this process were carried out manually rather than automatically using a computer program. As Zora and Johns-Lewis (1989) suggest, the manual approach appears to be more accurate since each item is analysed by the researcher in its real context.

In carrying out the analysis all phrasal and multi-word verbs were counted as low frequency lexical items since the COBUILD list of high frequency items only included single words. In addition, only fully audible items were counted. In context, partially or completely inaudible items appear in most cases to have been mispronounced lexical items so that the final lexical density estimates for most of the samples may have been a little lower because of the exclusion of these items. Furthermore, since non-lexical filled pauses (e.g. *er, um*) were so frequently used by all candidates, they were excluded from the analysis; it was ultimately considered that their inclusion as grammatical items might have significantly obscured the relationship between lexical and grammatical items in the samples collected for this study. Finally, where candidates used self-repair only the final version of an item or utterance figured in the analysis.

The numbers of low and high frequency lexical items and grammatical items in the candidates' output for each of the tasks on both versions were then tallied as frequency counts. The lexical density calculations were subsequently undertaken in two ways following Halliday (1985: 64–5). First, no distinction was made between high and low frequency lexical items in calculating the overall lexical density figures – the number of all lexical items was simply expressed as a percentage of the total number of items in each case. Secondly, the high frequency lexical items were given half the weight of the low frequency lexical items and the weighted number of lexical items then expressed as a percentage of the total number of items in a given task. Halliday suggests that this second method represents a more refined approach to determining lexical density. Carrying out the calculations in both ways provided a test of whether it was really necessary to distinguish between high and low frequency lexical items using the weighting system outlined above for this kind of comparative analysis.

For both of these methods the resulting data sets consisted of the total percentage of lexical items (as opposed to grammatical items) in the candidate's output as a measure of the dependent variable lexical density for each of the eight tasks: live description, live narration, live discussion, live role play, tape description, tape narration, tape discussion and tape role play. Percentages are most safely treated as ordinal data, and the most appropriate measures of central tendency and variability therefore are the median and range respectively. These were calculated for each of the eight tasks.

Table 5.4

Lexical density: Classification of items

A Grammatical items	Verbs 'to be' and 'to have'. All modals and auxiliaries. All determiners including articles, demonstrative and possessive adjectives, quantifiers (e.g. *some, any*) and numerals (cardinal and ordinal). All pro-forms including pronouns (e.g. *she, they, it, someone, something*), pro-verbs (e.g. *A: Are you coming with us? B: Yes I am*), pro-clauses (e.g. *this, that* when used to replace whole clauses). Interrogative adverbs (e.g. *what, when, how*) and negative adverbs (e.g. *not, never*). All contractions. These were counted as two items (e.g. *they're = they are)* since not all NESB speakers regularly or consistently use contractions. All prepositions and conjunctions. All discourse markers including conjunctions (e.g. *and, but, so*), sequencers (e.g. *next, finally*), lexicalised clauses (e.g. *y'know, I mean*), meta-talk (e.g. *what I mean, the point is*), temporal deictics (e.g. *now, then*), spatial deictics (e.g. *here, there*) and quantifier phrases (e.g. *anyway, anyhow, whatever*). All lexical filled pauses (e.g. *well, I mean, so*). All interjections (e.g. *gosh, really, oh*). All reactive tokens (e.g. *yes, no, OK, right, mm*).
B High frequency lexical items	Very common lexical items as per the list of the 700 most frequently used words in English (accounting for 70% of English text) identified in the COBUILD Dictionary project (1987). This list is included in the *Collins* COBUILD *English Course*, Level 1 Student's book pp 111–12 (Willis and Willis 1988). It includes nouns (e.g. *thing, people*), adjectives (e.g. *good, right*), verbs (e.g. *do, make, get*), adverbs of time, manner and place (e.g. *soon, late, very, so, maybe, also, too, here, there*). No items consisting of more than one word are included in this category as the COBUILD list consists of words not items. Repetition of low frequency lexical items (see below) including alternate word forms of the same item (e.g. *student/study*).
C Low frequency lexical items	Lexical items not featuring in the list of 700 most frequently used English words cited above, including less commonly used nouns, adjectives, verbs including participle and infinitive forms (all multi-word and phrasal verbs count as one item), adverbs of time, place and manner and all idioms (also counted as one item).

In the study design there were two independent variables: first, test format (with two conditions) and task type (with four conditions); the samples were dependent and the data was on an ordinal scale. The experimental hypotheses focused on whether there were significant differences in the degree of lexical density for text format and task type. The most appropriate inferential statistic therefore was a 4 x 2 non-parametric factorial procedure with repeated measures using non-specific hypotheses. The procedure used here is taken from Meddis (1984: 325–9).

Results

Descriptive statistics

Appendices 5.1 and 5.2 tabulate the lexical density figures by task for all individual subjects using both methods of calculation. Tables 5.5 and 5.6 below show the median percentage scores, the range of scores, the sum of the ranks and the mean sum of the ranks for each of the eight tasks using both methods of calculating lexical density. In these tables, the tasks are abbreviated as follows: "Des" = description, "Nar" = narration, "Dis" = discussion and "RP" = role play.

Table 5.5

**Method A: Unweighted lexical items
(high frequency lexical items assigned the same weight
as low frequency lexical items)**

Test format	LIVE				TAPE			
Task	Des	Nar	Dis	RP	Des	Nar	Dis	RP
– median (%)	40.0	38.0	40.0	35.0	42.0	41.0	43.0	41.5
– range (%)	31–49	32–44	36–47	31–40	33–50	35–45	37–47	35–49
– sum of ranks	93.0	66.0	92.5	36.0	111.0	92.5	121.5	107.5
– mean sum of ranks (N=20)	4.7	3.3	4.6	1.8	5.6	4.6	6.1	5.4

Table 5.6

**Method B: Weighted lexical items
(high frequency lexical items assigned half the weight
of low frequency lexical items)**

Test format	LIVE				TAPE			
Task	Des	Nar	Dis	RP	Des	Nar	Dis	RP
– median (%)	33.5	31.0	32.5	29.0	36.0	34.5	34.5	36.5
– range (%)	26–43	26–36	28–39	23–32	29–44	27–40	30–45	27–44
– sum of ranks	87.5	65.5	80.5	31.0	121.0	96.0	119.0	119.5
– mean sum of ranks (N=20)	4.4	3.3	4.0	1.6	6.1	4.8	6.0	6.0

For the first method, where high and low frequency lexical items were not distinguished, the median scores *across* the tasks fall between 35.0 and 43.0 per cent. For the second method, where high frequency items were assigned half the weight of the low frequency ones, the median scores for the eight tasks, not surprisingly, are now lower falling between 29.0 and 36.5 per cent. Graphical representations of these results are useful here in providing an overview of the median scores for each of the two methods (see Figures 5.1 and 5.2).

Figure 5.1

**Median scores (%) for lexical density analysis
with underweighted lexical items (N = 20)**

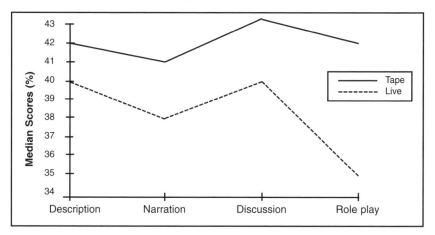

Figure 5.2

**Median scores (%) for lexical density analysis
with weighted lexical items (N = 20)**

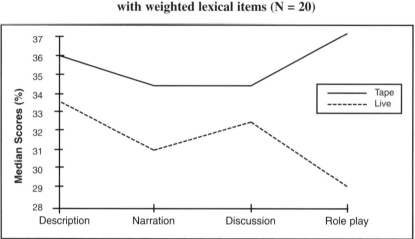

Looking at the range figures for the first method, the difference between the maximum and minimum scores for *each* of the eight tasks was fairly broad, from 10 to 18 percentage points. There is a fairly strong disparity between the sums of the ranks – from 36.0 to 121.5. This difference is also reflected in their means, which fall between 1.8 and 5.6. For the second method, the difference in the maximum and minimum scores for *each* of the eight tasks is between 10 and 17 percentage points. Finally, the sums of the ranks fall between 31.0 and 121.0 and their means between 1.6 and 6.1.

Inferential statistics

The results of the non-parametric factorial procedure which was used to examine the three experimental hypotheses were as follows:

Method A: Unweighted lexical items

H_{A1}: There is a significant effect on lexical density for test format
(H = 21.9, df = 1, p< 0.01).

H_{A2}: There is a significant effect on lexical density for task type
(H =14.7, df = 3, p< 0.01).

H_{A3}: There is no significant effect on lexical density for the
interaction between test format and task type
(H = 7.2, df = 3, n.s.).

Method B: Weighted lexical items

H_{A1}: There is a significant effect on lexical density for test format
(H = 38.0, df = 1, p< 0.01).

H_{A2}: There is a significant effect on lexical density for task type
(H = 10.0, df = 3, p< 0.05).

H_{A3}: There is a significant effect on lexical density for the interaction between test format and task type (H = 9.4, df = 3, p<0.05).

For the two methods of calculating lexical density the results are similar but not identical. In both cases the effect for test format is significant at the 0.01 level, while the effect for task type is significant at the 0.01 level and at the 0.05 level respectively. In statistical terms, the most important difference occurs in the results for the interaction effect between text format and task type. The result is not significant using the first method but significant at the 0.05 level when the second method was employed. The findings using the more finely tuned second method of determining lexical density (where high frequency lexical items were assigned half the weight of low frequency items) are probably the more accurate here. The discrepancy in the results based on the two methods suggests that this more refined analysis is probably warranted in formal investigations of lexical density, especially where inferential statistical procedures are to be employed.

In any event, all of the findings reported above require further interpretation as they provide no real indication about the nature or size of the particular effect, even where it is significant. In the absence of a suitable *post hoc* procedure, a visual representation of the mean sums of the ranks for the two methods of determining lexical density makes it possible to clarify the statistical results more fully (see Figures 5.3 and 5.4).

Figure 5.3

Sample rank means for lexical density analysis
with unweighted lexical items (N = 20)

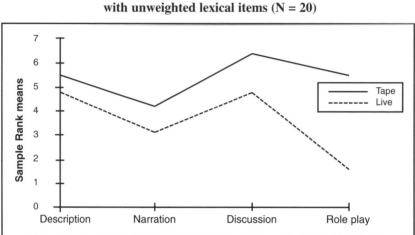

Figure 5.4

Sample rank means for lexical density analysis
with weighted lexical items (N = 20)

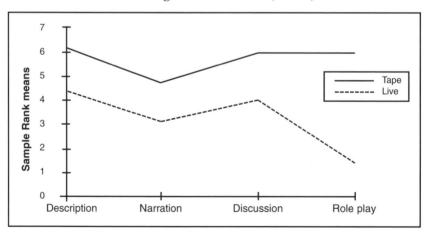

   Clearly, in both graphs the lexical density in candidate output on the tape-based version is higher for all four tasks than on the live version. This finding is consistent with those of Ure (1971) and Stubbs (1986), indicating that monologic texts are characterised by higher levels of lexical density. In addition, it appears that the degree of lexical density was lower for the narration task than for the description and discussion tasks for both versions. In the case of the role play, the degree of lexical density was similar to the description and discussion tasks in the tape version but clearly lower on the live version than all of the other three tasks.

In relation to the third hypothesis, the fact that in both graphs the two lines run almost perfectly parallel for the first three tasks and then diverge on the role play task suggests that any real interaction effect overall between test format and task type stems from the larger difference in lexical density on this last task compared to the other three tasks. The fact that the interaction effect was not statistically significant when the high and low frequency lexical items were unweighted in calculating the lexical density but significant when weighted appears to be simply a function of the size of the difference between the sums of the ranks for the live and tape role play tasks in each case. This difference was slightly greater using the weighted method and the result obtained for the interaction effect hence reaches the 0.05 significance level.

Discussion

The most important of the findings for the question of test equivalence reported above are those which relate first, to the effect of test format and secondly, to the interaction effect between test format and task type. In terms of the effect of test format, the results indicate that there was a significantly higher level of lexical density in candidate output on the tape tasks compared to the live tasks overall using both methods of analysis (i.e. weighted and unweighted lexical items). In relation to the interaction effect between test format and task type, it is evident from both the graphical representations of the median percentage scores (Figures 5.1 and 5.2) and the sample rank means (Figures 5.3 and 5.4) that the lowest level of lexical density occurred in candidates' responses on the live role play task. A possible explanation for these findings relates to the degree of *interactivity* for each of the eight tasks examined in this study.

As previously noted, the description, narration and discussion tasks on both the live and tape versions were designed to be 'monologic' language events. In the live format interlocutors were instructed not to intervene actively once candidates began their responses on these tasks. However, it appears that interaction could not be prevented on the live version, even in these tasks. This is evidenced by the fact, as noted in Study A, that interlocutors consistently used verbal feedback in the form of reactive tokens such as *mm*, *yes* and *right* while candidates responded on all three tasks. A distinguishing feature of the tape version, on the other hand, was the total absence of feedback to the candidate. The fact that the median percentage scores for the three tasks on the tape version were significantly higher than on the live version therefore supports Ure's (1971) finding that the use of verbal feedback results in a significantly lower level of lexical density.

The other important result in this study was the finding that the lowest level of lexical density occurred in candidates' responses on the live role play. This can be explained by the fact that the live role play was designed to incorporate a much higher degree of interaction than the other three live tasks examined here while the tape role play (like the other tape tasks) remained essentially non-interactive. In the live role play interlocutors were required to make a substantial contribution to the interaction, their input throughout the conversation playing a crucial role in shaping the content of the candidate's output. The fact that the *level* of lexical density is clearly lower in the live role play than in the other three live tasks and lower still than in all four tape tasks suggested that the level of interactivity in any given task strongly influences the degree of lexical density, i.e. the *higher* the level of interaction the *lower* the degree of lexical density in candidate output. This conclusion supports the suggestion by Zora and Johns-Lewis (1989) that as the expected degree of interruption diminishes and the length of speaking turn increases, the level of lexical density becomes higher.

The differences in lexical density between the direct and semi-direct versions found in this study, although statistically significant, were not as large as those reported in Shohamy (1994), i.e. an average of 40% on the OPI and 60% on the SOPI. It is difficult to determine why this may have been the case. The results from these two studies may point to a greater difference in interactivity between the OPI and SOPI than between the live and tape versions of the *access:* oral interaction sub-test overall. Another possible explanation is that the presence of feedback has a greater impact on lexical density in candidate output in Hebrew than in English.

On the basis of the results for the effect of task type, it appears that task structure may also have an impact on candidate output in tests of oral proficiency, i.e. 'open' tasks seem to elicit language with a higher degree of lexical density than 'closed' tasks (except for the live role play for reasons outlined above). In either case the candidate's response will only be as lexically dense as the task allows for. In each of the more 'closed' narration tasks the stories to be told (using the sequence of pictures) were fairly simple with little room for interpretation, potentially limiting the use of the candidate's lexical resources. Perhaps the more challenging requirement of these tasks is relating the pictures appropriately to each other using discourse markers, pro-forms and other cohesive devices – all grammatical items. This may account for the relatively lower levels of lexical density in both narration tasks. By contrast, in the more open tasks – notably, the description and interview – candidates are not constrained by any stimulus material and may therefore be able to display a greater range of their lexical resources. Hence the higher degree of lexical density in these cases. However, again, as the differences in the median scores between tasks are not great, such an interpretation is only offered tentatively.

Although not addressed in the experimental hypotheses, there are other factors which may influence the degree of lexical density in the samples collected. One of those suggested in Zora and Johns-Lewis (1989) is whether or not candidates planned their responses, i.e. planned answers are likely to be more lexically dense than unplanned ones. If this was the case, then there should be a greater difference between the two description tasks – the live one which did not include planning time and the tape-based one which did – than either of the other tasks which had provision for preparation on both versions of the test. But examination of the median scores and the sum of the ranks for both methods of calculating lexical density does not yield a clear answer to this question. This is a problematic variable to investigate, however, since, even where planning time is provided, there is no guarantee it will be effectively used by the candidate on either version.

Another relevant variable given in Zora and Johns-Lewis is topic. The only task with the same topic on the two versions used for this study was the discussion task. It is interesting to note, however, that the difference between the median scores on the live and tape versions for the discussion tasks (using both methods of calculating lexical density) is very similar to the description and narration tasks where the topics were very different on the two formats. This suggests that topic was not a significant source of variation in this study.

In sum, there are probably a number of factors, including task structure as well as preparation and response time, which influence candidate output in oral proficiency tests, not simply whether the candidate is talking to another person face-to-face or to a microphone *per se*. Nevertheless, format (i.e. live or tape-based) emerges as probably the single most important determinant of candidate output in this study.

Conclusion

The broad qualitative study of a range of discourse features (the same as those used in Shohamy's (1994) study of the Hebrew OPI and SOPI) in Discourse Study A suggested that the language produced in the direct and semi-direct versions of the *access:* oral interaction sub-test on the three 'monologic' tasks (i.e. description, narration and discussion) was strongly similar, but that the live and tape role plays produced a different kind of discoursal output. On the basis of these initial results it appeared that the careful efforts of the *access:* test designers to match all tasks except the live and tape role plays seemed to have been rewarded in terms of the parity of language elicited under the two test conditions. These findings contrasted with those of Shohamy, where differences between the OPI and SOPI were found on nearly all of the discourse features examined.

In Discourse Study B, however, the live version elicited language of a significantly lower lexical density than the tape version in all four matching tasks. It was argued that this result can be mainly attributed to the inextinguishable presence of interaction throughout the live version despite the careful attempt by the test designers to minimise it in all tasks except the role play. Furthermore, the results also indicated that the *higher* the degree of interaction the *lower* the level of lexical density in candidate output. This was clearly demonstrated in the figures from the live role play task where the communication between candidate and interlocutor was the least constrained of all the tasks on that version. The degree of lexical density was found to be correspondingly significantly lower on this task than any of the other live tasks. It seems that lexical density may have been the more sensitive measure of difference in language output in this study, at least from the perspective of interactivity.

A possible explanation for the differences found in candidate output on the live and tape versions, especially in terms of lexical density, then, is that the two versions were drawing on different language skills overall, i.e. interactive versus monologic speaking ability, despite the careful attempt to minimise interaction in nearly all the live tasks. This, in turn, may have accounted for the apparent lack of equivalence between the test scores on the two formats in the December 1992 trial reported in Chapter 4, since it is likely that at least some candidates would not perform equally well in tests which tap such different oral skills. This is not to say that the test scores obtained from the live and tape versions in this trial could be usefully correlated with the lexical density figures to confirm this conclusion since lexical density was not used as a scoring category. Nor would it have been valid to do so: while lexical density provides valuable clues about the speaking abilities being tapped in the two versions of the test, it does not actually measure any meaningful component of language proficiency.

At this point, therefore, the findings were still only tentative and partial. It was therefore decided to examine a later trial from a naturalistic perspective in order to pursue the equivalence question. Specifically, the next stage in the research involved examining first, the processes of test design, test taking and rating candidate performance and, secondly, the test scores from the June 1994 trial. The results of the study of test processes are reported in Chapter 6 and the analyses of test scores in Chapter 7.

6 Trial 2: The study of test processes

Introduction

The analyses of test scores and test taker language output in the December 1992 trial yielded important but nevertheless incomplete answers to the equivalence issue. It was therefore decided to adopt a very different perspective on a new trial held in Melbourne in June 1994. In theoretical terms, this involved comparing the direct and semi-direct versions of the *access:* oral interaction sub-test from a naturalistic perspective. Specifically, this stage of the research involved examining the processes of test design, test taking and rating in this trial using a range of data based on observation, interviews and questionnaires. This new perspective provided the basis for a very different comparison between the two versions than had been undertaken up to this point. After providing relevant information about the trial on which this study was based, the methods used to collect the various forms of data collected are described. The key findings are then reported and discussed.

The June 1994 trial

As outlined in Chapter 1, important revisions to the original test specifications for the oral interaction sub-test, including the tasks and the scoring criteria, had been completed by May 1994. Preparation for the trialling of new live and tape versions of the test then began. Table 6.1 summarises the main stages in the work done leading up to, during and after the trial conducted in Melbourne on 4 June 1994. This process was completed between May and July 1994. This trial was the focus of the study reported in this chapter.

Table 6.2 below lists the test tasks and scoring criteria (as per the revised test specifications) used in the June 1994 trial. The test now aimed to identify candidates reliably at both the Functional and Vocational levels. (Previously, only the Vocational level had been targeted by the test.)

The scoring criteria were now assessed on a seven-point scale with appropriately modified descriptors. The complete revised set of descriptors for each of the scoring criteria is given in Appendix 6.1. Further details about changes to the oral interaction sub-test at this time are provided in Chapter 1.

In this trial 120 volunteer NESB students, who were recruited from several local tertiary institutions, completed all four sub-tests of a new form of the test i.e. reading, writing, listening and speaking (both direct and semi-direct versions). Each test taker was paid AUD$70 upon completion of the trial test.

Table 6.1

**Stages in developing new live and tape versions (Form D)
of the oral interaction sub-test, May–July 1994**

Stage 1	Project team designed new tasks for both live and tape formats in accordance with test specifications. These were assembled in combination with previously used tasks as anchors to ensure comparability with earlier versions in relation to standard setting (= draft 1).
Stage 2	Item Editorial Committee vetted new tasks in draft 1.
Stage 3	Test developers revised draft 1 (= draft 2).
Stage 4	Item Editorial Committee members provided written feedback on draft 2.
Stage 5	Project team revised draft 2 to create trial versions which included interlocutor and candidate booklets for the live format and a candidate booklet, tapescript and ultimately a sound recording for the tape format. Questionnaires for candidates, interlocutors and raters were then prepared.
Stage 6	Training session for the trial interviewers was conducted.
Stage 7	Live and tape formats were administered to trial population. Audio recordings were made of candidate performances in both instances.
Stage 8	Each audiotape from both live and tape formats was independently assessed by two trained raters.
Stage 9	Multi-faceted Rasch analyses were carried out on trial test scores using the FACETS program.
Stage 10	Test revised in the light of the analyses of test scores as well as written feedback from candidates, interviewers and raters in preparation for an overseas administration in September 1994.

The trial cohort represented diverse cultural and linguistic backgrounds as well as a wide range of age groups. As in the December 1992 trial, candidates can be divided into two broad groups on the basis of how closely they resembled the target overseas test population using data obtained from questionnaires completed by them on the day of the trial administration. The more 'non-target-like' group (i.e. NESB students, generally under twenty-five and living in Australia on a temporary basis while completing their tertiary studies) comprised 58% of the test cohort. The remaining 42% belonged to the 'target-like' group which was composed of NESB professionals qualified in a wide range of fields including engineering, medicine, teaching, administration, computing, librarianship and architecture. However, insofar as they had mostly already obtained permanent residence, had been in Australia for more than 18 months and were undertaking the test here, even this group did not closely represent the target test taker population either.

Given these differences between the trial and operational test populations (as in the December 1992 trial), the findings reported here cannot be directly applied to the operational context. Nevertheless, they do have *potential* implications for any group of people undertaking the test and indeed for the interchangeability of other direct and semi-direct speaking tests.

Of the 120 trial candidates in the June 1994 trial, approximately half were administered the live version first, and half were administered the tape version first. As in the December 1992 trial, their performances on both versions were all audio taped so that they could be rated retrospectively. Sixteen tape-based recordings and ten live recordings were unsuccessful due to technical faults in the recording equipment, and these candidates were therefore excluded. Thus, the analysis was based on the scores from a total of 94 candidates on both the direct and semi-direct versions of the test.

Table 6.2

Test tasks and scoring criteria Form D (trial), June 1994

LIVE	TAPE

1. Warm up (unassessed)
2. A) Description
    – fluency
    – grammar
    – vocabulary
   B) Narration
    – grammar
    – vocabulary
    – coherence and cohesion
	1. Warm up (unassessed)
	2. A) Description (1)
	    – fluency
	    – grammar
	    – vocabulary
	   B) Narration
	    – grammar
	    – vocabulary
	    – coherence and cohesion
	   C) Summary
	    – fluency
	    – grammar
	    – vocabulary

3. Role play
    – fluency
    – grammar
    – intelligibility
4. A) Exposition (1)
    – fluency
    – vocabulary
    – coherence and cohesion
   B) Exposition (2)
    – fluency
    – vocabulary
    – coherence and cohesion
5. Discussion
    – fluency
    – grammar
    – intelligibility
	3. Role play
	    – fluency
	    – grammar
	    – intelligibility
	   A) Exposition
	    – fluency
	    – vocabulary
	    – coherence and cohesion
	   B) Instructions
	    – fluency
	    – vocabulary
	    – coherence and cohesion
	5. Discussion
	    – fluency
	    – grammar
	    – intelligibility
	6. Description (2)
	    – fluency
	    – grammar
	    – vocabulary

Global criteria
    – communicative effectiveness
    – comprehension
	Global criteria
	    – communicative effectiveness

Method

The investigation into the comparability of the direct and semi-direct versions of the oral interaction sub-test reported in this chapter was undertaken from a naturalistic (constructivist) viewpoint. From a naturalistic perspective, human behaviour, in this instance test performance, cannot be fully understood without incorporating into the research the perceptions and insights of those involved in the study, not simply the researcher. Typically (although not exclusively), it employs observation, interviews and other sources of qualitative data as methods of data collection.

There were three related phases in the investigation: first, the study of test design processes prior to the trial; secondly, the study of test taking processes during the trial; and, finally, the study of rating processes following the trial administration of the test. The procedures used to collect data in each of these phases will now be outlined.

The study of test design processes

In this first phase of the study the researcher obtained permission from the oral interaction sub-test development co-ordinator to attend the forthcoming Item Editorial Committee (IEC) meeting for the June 1994 trial as a non-participant observer. As outlined in Chapter 2, the role of the IEC was to evaluate new tasks in preparation for trialling in terms of their suitability, difficulty and the clarity of their requirements. Its membership included the chair of the *access:* Test Development Committee (TDC), four members of the oral interaction sub-test development team and several external language testing experts. Due to the last minute absence of the chair of the TDC, the researcher was asked to participate actively in the IEC meeting. Despite taking on this unexpected role, he was able to observe the meeting entirely as a newcomer since he had not attended one previously.

The day before the meeting an initial draft of the test tasks was distributed to members of the IEC in preparation for the meeting. This first draft was then edited on the basis of feedback in the meeting. The revised draft test was later sent to individual IEC members for further comment. The trial versions of the test were then finalised by the test development team.

In the IEC meeting the researcher made brief written notes. Since the opportunities for notetaking during the course of the meeting were highly restricted, he concentrated his efforts on recording any points directly related to the comparability of the live and tape versions. Following the IEC meeting the researcher interviewed all six members of the oral interaction sub-test development team. The three team members who designed the tasks for this trial were interviewed together first of all, followed by the two team members responsible for organising the rating of the trial and finally the co-ordinator.

The *informal conversational interview* was deemed by the researcher to be the most appropriate format for eliciting the views of all members of the test development team. In adopting this approach, the interviewer 'attempts to engage the interviewee in a natural conversation in which questions arise more-or-less spontaneously' (Lynch 1996: 126).

The informal conversational interview is often employed in contexts where the interviewer has already established some sort of relationship with the interviewee – hence its appropriateness in this instance for interviewing peers with whom the researcher had already developed a professional and, in some cases, a personal relationship. A more formal, structured type of interview would have been highly 'artificial' in the circumstances and therefore likely to have stifled the interaction.

Following completion of these interviews a *member check* session was conducted with the test development team as a whole. The aim of this session was to check that the researcher's interpretations of their comments in the interviews were correct and to draw the group's attention to the divergent views of individual members about key issues with the hope of stimulating further discussion.

The study of test taking processes

This part of the study involved close observation of two candidates' performances under both the live and tape-mediated formats. The criteria for selecting these candidates and relevant bio-data about each of them are given below. Subsequent interviews with each of them and with their respective interlocutors (in the live version) were also included as methods of data collection. This triangulation provided a series of 'snapshots' of the two candidates taken from different perspectives. Responses to questionnaires provided by 77 of the 94 test takers who participated in the trial formed additional data about test taker reactions to the two tests. These questionnaires were completed after candidates had undertaken both versions of the oral interaction sub-test.

In order to find two suitable people for the study, six test takers were approached by the researcher before they undertook both versions of the oral interaction test on the day of the trial administration. Given the impossibility of representativeness in studying only two test takers out of a large test cohort, the only criteria for selection were that one of these people would have done the live test first and the other the tape test and that one would be male and the other female. The six trial candidates were informed about the purpose of the study and the nature of their participation i.e. they would be observed while completing the two versions and then interviewed afterwards. They were also made aware that their test performances would be video taped and their interviews audio taped but that confidentiality with respect to their identities would be maintained at all stages of the project.

Two very different people, henceforth referred to by the pseudonyms 'Abdul' and 'Wing Li' ultimately agreed to take part in the project. Abdul was an Egyptian male, 52 years of age who had worked as a TV director in Egypt before arriving in Australia and taking up permanent residence in 1992. He was unemployed at the time of the trial and studying general English full-time. Wing Li was a Chinese female, 25 years of age, who arrived in Australia as a temporary resident in 1993. She was a student of tourism and hospitality at the time of the trial. Both candidates reported having studied English for ten years before coming to Australia. Abdul completed the live then tape version of the speaking sub-test in the morning before undertaking the rest of the test. By contrast, Wing Li did the tape then live version of the speaking sub-test in the early afternoon after undertaking the reading and writing modules but prior to completing the listening sub-test. Abdul's interlocutor in the live version was a male ESL teacher while Wing Li's interlocutor was a female primary, non-ESL trained teacher. The findings, using a wide variety of evidence, are outlined in the following section.

At the time the two test takers undertook each version the researcher made detailed observation notes of their performances. In undertaking this stage of the study the researcher used non-participant observation i.e. he did not have a role to play other than observer. In the live test, once the video camera was set up, he sat at the side of the room taking written notes without speaking. In the tape version he did much the same except that he also wore headphones in order to hear the candidate he was observing more clearly. A week later, another set of notes were taken from the video recordings without consulting the earlier ones in order to check the reliability and validity of the original set of observations. On both occasions the researcher made unstructured, descriptive field notes as described in Lynch (1996: 116). Field notes are typically used where there are no a priori decisions about what is to be focused upon in the observation. The two sets of observation notes are included in Appendix 6.2 as they constitute the basis of the judgements and interpretations about the performances of each of the test takers (under both the live and tape conditions) which are summarised in the next section of this chapter.

Even though the researcher attempted to make himself and the camera as unobtrusive as possible, it is important to consider the possibility that these observed and video recorded test performances may have been changed in the very act of studying them. This follows from Labov's (1972) 'observer's paradox' that data about how people behave naturally (i.e. when not being observed) can only be obtained through observation. In order to take this effect into account in interpreting the findings both candidates and interlocutors (in the live version) were questioned about what impact the presence of these two 'observers' had on them during their interviews with the researcher.

In carrying out the subsequent interviews with the candidates and their interlocutors on the live version the *interview guide approach* (as described by Lynch (1996: 128) was chosen. This procedure, which is neither completely structured nor unstructured in design, allows the interviewer to specify a range of questions to be covered in advance without needing to formulate either the wording of the questions or the order for posing them until the interview is in progress. It also allows for the inclusion of follow-up questions as deemed appropriate by the interviewer. This method aims to give the interviewee some degree of control over the shape and direction of the interview as well as to enhance its interactiveness and reduce the level of formality. A major advantage of this approach is that it allows the interviewer to be efficient, systematic and yet flexible across interviews. The interview guide approach was considered by the researcher to be most appropriate for both the candidates and their interlocutors particularly given the very limited time available for the interviews to be conducted on the day of the trial administration. The questions planned for the candidates and their interlocutors are included in Appendices 6.3 and 6.5.

A post-test questionnaire adminstered to all test takers was also used in the study. It was based on an earlier version which was used to examine test taker reactions to the two formats in the December 1992 trial (Hill 1997) and is included as Appendix 6.4. The questionnaire was designed to be completed as quickly and efficiently as possible at the conclusion of the trialling. Candidates were required to provide relevant bio-data before answering questions about the two versions considered separately and then together. Nearly all of the questions about the test could be completed by circling one of two or three alternative answers. The only exception was the final question asking for any additional comments about the test.

The study of rating processes

Twenty-two raters were engaged to mark the live and tape audio recordings from this trial. As in the December 1992 trial, the rating design was such that no rater assessed any particular candidate on either version more than once. This meant that each candidate was assessed by four different raters, i.e. two on the live version and two on the tape version. By this time the rating process had become more intensive than in the December 1992 trial where raters completed their scoring at home over a period of one week. From September 1993 raters were required to complete their assessments instead over a weekend in the language laboratory of a local English language centre for reasons of increased security and administrative efficiency. They assessed approximately ten live and ten tape versions over the two days. Prior to carrying out their work, raters attended a short two-hour calibration session during which they compared their scoring of sample audio recordings from both the live and tape versions.

The researcher conducted interviews with each of the raters who had marked a live or tape performance by either Adbul or Wing Li immediately after the assessment was completed. The raters were asked to explain their scoring of the candidate and to give their views on the equivalence of the two versions in general. Once again, the interview guide approach was used. The questions designed for the rater interviews are included in Appendix 6.7. At the conclusion of the rating process all 22 raters completed a written questionnaire designed to provide additional, broader feedback about the comparability of the two versions from their perspective. The questionnaire (see Appendix 6.8) consisted of four questions allowing for fairly detailed written responses.

The test scores of the two candidates focused upon in the study (see Appendix 6.6) were then examined in relation to the rest of the test cohort (see Chapter 7). Further data collection and analyses were later undertaken to check the reliability of the original ratings of the two candidates and to gain deeper insight into some of the factors affecting their test scores in each version. This process included further assessments of the two candidates under both test conditions and detailed comments made by an additional rater.

Peer debriefing session

After all of the data from each of these three stages had been gathered, coded and analysed for the first time, the researcher arranged a two hour debriefing session with a group of 'disinterested' colleagues (PhD students and academic staff) in the department of Applied Linguistics and Language Studies at Melbourne University. After introducing the two versions of the oral interaction sub-test using the test specifications, he presented the preliminary findings from this study (including the analysis of test scores reported in Chapter 7). This provided valuable feedback on the strengths and weaknesses of his initial interpretations of the data collected for this study.

Findings

The findings from this study are reported chronologically in order to evoke the test experience and/or views of participants at the particular stage of the test process they were investigated. Thus, this 'narrative' aims to contextualise their behaviour and ideas about the comparability of the live and tape versions of the oral interaction sub-test more fully than would be possible if, for example, the results were grouped thematically instead. In this way, it is hoped that the coherence and unity of their experiences are preserved in the analysis.

Test design processes

This section reports the findings from first, observation of the Item Editorial Committee (IEC) meeting and secondly, the interviews with the test development team held prior to the trial administration. Only the findings most directly relevant to the question of the comparability between the live and tape versions of the oral interaction sub-test in terms of their design are discussed.

Observation of the IEC meeting

The meeting consisted of detailed discussion of the test tasks. The first, most striking fact was that all the draft test tasks were presented to the IEC in the live format ready for inclusion in the interlocutor's booklet. It was therefore difficult, if not impossible, to envisage how the tasks proposed for the tape version would appear in the appropriate candidate's booklet.

The second notable feature of this meeting was that the proposed test tasks were evaluated without reference to the test specifications which set out the task types (including task structure and format), the expected language functions and the scoring criteria for each task. Thus, the guidelines for matching live and tape tasks in the test blueprint appeared to be ignored at this crucial point in the test process. Furthermore, even without the test specifications, no serious attempt was made in the discussion to compare individual matching tasks on the two versions in any respect. A clear example of this was the examination of the proposed live and tape exposition tasks where the two sets of questions appeared to elicit very different responses in terms of language functions.

The evaluation of the draft test therefore looked at each proposed task entirely in isolation, assessing each task in terms of what IEC members considered to be its potential interest, difficulty and clarity for candidates. There were, in fact, only a couple of moments where the comparability issue emerged at all. The first of these points was when the researcher asked how the decision to allocate supposedly matching tasks to either the live or tape version was reached. A test development team member indicated that 'the task which appeared easier to us would go on the tape version'. This comment suggests that the tape tasks needed to be easier than their live counterparts to compensate for the fact that the tape format was intrinsically more difficult. The second concerned the equivalence of the live and tape role plays. As one of the IEC members who was also a rater remarked, responses to the tape role play (the telephone answering machine) tended to be brief and often simplistic. As such it was no real match in terms of its communicative demands for its live counterpart where candidates were normally required to negotiate solutions to often fairly complex problems with the interlocutor. This comment supports the observation made in relation to the equivalence of these two tasks in Chapter 1.

In general, close scrutiny of the IEC meeting suggested that securing the equivalence of the two versions in terms of their design was not an important concern for either the test development team or the rest of the IEC members. This conclusion is further supported by an examination of the subsequent written exchanges between the test developers and the other IEC members about the next draft of these new versions of the oral interaction sub-test. Again, there was minimal attention given to the comparability issue. At a more general level, the lack of reference to the test specifications when evaluating the proposed test tasks in the IEC meeting was rather surprising. Both of these issues were pursued in the interviews which followed.

Interviews with the test development team

As outlined previously, three separate interviews were conducted with the test development team. The three team members who designed the tasks for this trial were interviewed together first of all, followed by the two team members responsible for organising the rating of the trial and finally the co-ordinator. Again, the primary focus of the reporting here is the comparability issue from the perspective of test design. However, given that much of the discussion in these interviews compared the design and 'execution' (i.e. test in action) stages of the two versions, the team members' comments on both these stages are included since they help to illuminate each other.

i The team members responsible for designing the tasks for the trial

The most important points raised in this interview centred on the comparability issues which emerged in the IEC meeting discussed above.

The researcher initially queried why all of the tasks in the draft distributed to the IEC members were presented as if for incorporation into the interlocutor's booklet of the live version. The team members indicated that this had become standard practice in designing new tasks as they found it easier to write for the live format. Translating a new task into the tape format was then a relatively straightforward process. They did agree, however, that this strategy was less than ideal and should be remedied in future by designing tasks in the format for which they were intended. Where it was unclear to which format a given task would ultimately be assigned it was agreed that the task should be written up in both live and tape formats for the IEC to examine.

Another important point raised in this interview related to the researcher's observation that reference to the test specifications was entirely absent in the IEC meeting. One of the team members suggested that this was not really necessary as they had consulted the specifications in designing the new tasks prior to the IEC meeting and, in this way, adherence to the guidelines for each task was assured. Another team member, however, argued that the test specifications should have been used in the meeting to ensure that the issue of maintaining the equivalence of the two versions was not forgotten while attempts were made by the committee to improve individual tasks. According to this team member ' ... the other committee members [those who are not part of the test development team] tend to judge each task on its clarity and level of difficulty instead of whether it follows the guidelines in the specs'. This observation is an important one given the important role of the IEC in the production of the final trial live and tape versions of the oral interaction sub-test. It is possible that a lack of explicit reference to the test blueprint in these meetings could have undermined the attempt in that document to secure the equivalence of the two versions.

The researcher also sought clarification of the explanation given in the IEC meeting with regard to the basis on which alternate tasks were allocated to either the live or tape version. According to these team members, allocation of the easier of two alternate tasks to the tape version meant that the tape task was less likely to be ambiguous or to require clarification from the interlocutor. This seemed to suggest that the tape tasks needed to be especially clear and straightforward with lower syntactic and lexical complexity in both the stimulus materials and instructions than their live counterparts.

These three team members agreed that securing the equivalence of the two versions in terms of test design was important, given that they were treated as being the same test in the analysis of test results. However, two of them considered that the two test 'events' were so different that absolute equivalence was an unrealistic goal, the live version being dialogic in nature and the tape version essentially monologic. Thus, as one team member suggested:

> *The direct version involves substantial negotiation of meaning ... the only sense of interaction in the other [semi-direct] version is whether the candidate appears to understand what is on the tape.*

The third team member felt that the live version was only slightly more interactive than the tape version, given its highly scripted nature and that the two versions were therefore fairly evenly matched.

One of the team members who felt that the two test conditions were not the same pointed out that in the live version candidates were able to use both verbal language and non-verbal language (e.g. gestures, eye contact and other facial expressions) to communicate meaning, whereas on the tape version they were restricted to verbal language. Since candidates were rated from audio recordings under both conditions their non-verbal language performance on the live version was ignored. This was unfair since non-verbal communication may have played an extremely important role in the production of meaning.

This team member also stressed that interlocutors were equally able to employ both verbal and non-verbal feedback in communicating with candidates on the live version. Even where interlocutors followed their instructions by adhering strictly to their script and 'behaved as much like a tape as possible' there was still substantial opportunity to use both kinds of feedback. Whether this feedback enhanced or inhibited candidates' performances would depend on how effectively it was communicated to them.

The other team member who considered the two formats to be different pointed out that the live and tape role plays, in particular, were not well matched and also that the summary task on the tape version had no counterpart on the live version. In any case, she felt that this task was primarily a test of listening comprehension and therefore inappropriate in a test of oral proficiency.

In general, therefore, the comments of two of these team members suggested that a high degree of interactivity was integral to the live version despite the attempt to minimise it at the design stage, particularly through the use of an interlocutor script. The tape version, on the other hand, was characterised by a complete absence of two-way interaction. The other interviewee played down this difference although she did concede that the quality of the candidate's performance could be partly determined by the skill of the interlocutor.

ii The team members responsible for organising the rating of the trial

The team members interviewed in this case considered that the scoring criteria, as set out in the test specifications, were applicable to both versions. However, one of them did suggest that different descriptors might be needed for some of the scoring categories across the two versions. For example, the various levels of *Fluency* or *Cohesion* might need to be defined differently in monologic compared to dialogic communication. This interviewee also queried why *Comprehension* was not included as a category on the tape version. One of them also suggested that *Communicative effectiveness* in the live version may have been used by raters to assess the candidate's ability to interact with the interlocutor, especially since there were no level descriptors accompanying this scoring category.

Both team members also remarked that trial candidates did not always perform equally well on the two versions. One of them suggested that how well individual candidates performed on either format might depend on their personalities and their test 'know-how'. Talking to an interlocutor in a face-to-face setting on the live version and responding within fixed times to a recorded voice in a language laboratory surrounded by other candidates called different test taking strategies into play. Some candidates, these interviewees claimed, clearly had a wider range of these strategies and were therefore not disadvantaged by either format. Others seemed to fall foul of one version or the other because they were unable to adjust to the communicative demands of the setting.

In addition, these interviewees argued that interlocutors rarely had a neutral impact on candidate performance. In some instances their behaviour positively influenced the candidate, particularly when they provided supportive verbal and non-verbal feedback without straying too far from their script. Where the interlocutor failed to provide such support and/or didn't follow the script very closely these members of the project team felt the candidate's performance was likely to be adversely affected.

Finally, these team members claimed raters were encouraged to mark the live and tape versions similarly, although some of them showed a tendency to be harsher on one version than the other. They also pointed out that raters often compensated candidates for being matched with a poor interlocutor in their assessments. One of them who had also rated the test in the past suggested that 'if I thought a candidate was getting a raw deal from the interlocutor I'd be more lenient in my marking'. This view is consistent with the findings of McNamara and Lumley (1993) in relation to the Occupational English Test (OET) described in Chapter 2.

iii   The test co-ordinator

The co-ordinator of the test development team initially emphasised the similarity of the two versions of the oral interaction sub-test in her interview. She argued that the live version closely resembled the tape version, first, because of its extremely low level of interactivity, i.e. it was a 'highly scripted test' with interlocutors being given 'strict instructions about the role they should play and what they should say in terms of the questions they asked in the test'. The sole exception was the live role play where the contribution of interlocutors was less restricted although their overall role was still highly circumscribed. The second reason why the two versions were highly similar was because, in both instances, the scoring criteria did not focus on the candidate's ability to interact, but rather on 'more concrete language criteria such as fluency, grammar, vocabulary and intelligibility'.

However, later in the interview when questioned about which of the two versions was fairer to test takers the test co-ordinator pointed to some important differences between them. In this instance she argued that 'every candidate gets the same quality of input' on the tape version, whereas on the live version this cannot be guaranteed because of variability in interlocutor performance. Examples of such variability included how closely interlocutors conformed to the script of the task prompts and whether they gave encouraging feedback during and at the end of candidate responses. She considered that 'the interlocutor variable is always going to have a large impact on candidates' scores and you can't ever get rid of it'.

These comments on the relative fairness of the two versions raise two issues central to the interchangeability question. First, the co-ordinator's suggestion that a candidate's result is, in fact, significantly affected (either positively or negatively) by the interlocutor's performance points to a higher level of interactivity on the live version in practice than was anticipated at the design stage. The implication is that the candidate's performance on the live version (but not the tape version) is jointly achieved or co-constructed despite the attempt to minimise interaction in this format at the design stage. If, in turn, interactive and monologic speaking skills constitute different language abilities, it is highly likely that at least some candidates will perform better on one version than the other. The fact that the scoring criteria do not focus explicitly on interaction may not prevent these candidates from achieving a higher overall result on one version, since they are likely to demonstrate stronger competence in some or all of the rating categories currently used in the test anyway. It is also conceivable that the candidate's interactive ability may be indirectly assessed on some or all of the task specific scoring criteria on the live version despite the fact that they do not explicitly focus on this skill. Even if that is not generally the case, it is highly probable that judgement of the candidate's interactive competence would be considered in scoring the general category *Communicative effectiveness* on the live version (as suggested earlier by one of the other team members), especially given that there are no level descriptors accompanying this criterion which might direct raters away from this ability. In addition, it is likely that any judgement of the candidate's skill in this respect would be linked to raters' perceptions of the overall success of the interaction, so that their assessment of the interlocutor's performance could also (albeit indirectly) inform their scoring.

Secondly, the fact that the quality of input remains the same for all candidates on the tape format may not make it automatically fairer to all candidates. Other factors peculiar to the tape format, such as the candidate's level of comfort with the language laboratory as a test environment, are likely to either have a positive or negative impact on the candidate's performance in the tape version.

Notwithstanding these counterarguments, the test co-ordinator's comments in this interview illustrate her sensitivity to the problems associated with attempting to minimise interactivity on the live version.

Test development team member check

All six members of the test development team later attended a group session where the researcher checked his interpretations of their individual comments in the interviews above. The session also provided them with the opportunity to compare their views on the equivalence of the two versions of the oral interaction sub-test.

After the group had had the opportunity to listen to and discuss the researcher's report of the earlier interviews, conflicting views about the equivalence of the two versions still persisted. On the one hand, two members of the group strongly defended their interchangeability based on the view, as one of them suggested, 'that the live version – apart from the role play – isn't interactive because it's so tightly scripted and the scoring criteria don't assess interaction anyway'. The other four team members, on the other hand, remained more sceptical about the equivalence of the two versions mainly on the grounds, as one of them suggested, that 'interaction can't be got rid of in the live version however hard we try to wipe it out in the tasks and in the marking'.

In conclusion, the relative interactivity of the live and tape versions of the oral interaction sub-test emerged from this first phase of the study of test processes as a central and highly contentious issue in determining their interchangeability. This provided a major focus for the next two phases of the study – the investigation of the processes of test taking and rating.

Test taking processes

The findings from the second phase of the study which focused on the performances of two trial candidates as well as feedback from candidates and raters on the comparability issue are reported below.

Observation of candidates

The conclusions drawn about the two trial candidates, 'Abdul' and 'Wing Li' in this sub-section are based on the observation notes made, first, at the time the live and tape versions of the oral interaction sub-test were administered to them and, secondly, a week later using video recordings of these performances. These two sets of observation notes are included in Appendix 6.2.

Abdul appeared to perform better in the live than the tape version at least partly because of the role played by his interlocutor in the interaction. This involved ample patience (allowing the candidate plenty of time to respond), reassurance and positive feedback of both a verbal and non-verbal nature. The interlocutor's verbal feedback consisted mainly of reactive tokens (such as *mm, yep* and *that's fine*) and was often used most effectively to encourage Abdul to keep talking when he was silent or hesitating. His non-verbal communication, on the other hand, mainly took the form of sustained eye contact, nodding and smiling, again, it appears, designed to reassure and encourage further response from the candidate. Like his interlocutor, Abdul made extensive use of non-verbal as well as verbal language throughout the interaction. His confidence appeared to grow as the test progressed, as evidenced by a gradual increase in his recourse to nodding, smiling, laughter, as well as a range of hand gestures and a matching decrease in the amount of hesitation in his responses.

On the other hand, Wing Li seemed to perform less well on the live version for two main reasons. Firstly, she was paired with an interlocutor who tended to rush her through the test. In particular, this interlocutor appeared to use verbal and non-verbal feedback – whether consciously or unconsciously – in such a way as to finish the test as quickly as possible. Both types of feedback, consisting mainly of reactive verbal tokens (such as *mm* or *yep*), nodding and half-smiles, tended to be given in a curt, almost abrupt manner often while the candidate was still speaking or else the moment after the end of an utterance. This behaviour seemed to have the effect of closing down Wing Li's responses even when she may have been able to extend them further. This interlocutor, therefore, displayed little of the patience, reassurance and encouragement that was so evident in the case of Abdul's interlocutor. Secondly, Wing Li's body language, which included a consistently stiff posture, sometimes with her arms tightly folded and at other times with her hands firmly clasped, seemed to indicate that she was ill at ease under the live condition. She only sporadically used non-verbal communication such as eye contact and hand gestures, mainly, it seemed, in response to the interlocutor's reluctance herself to interact more than was absolutely necessary to complete the test.

Despite the test developers' careful attempt to eliminate, or at least minimise, interaction in all tasks apart from the role play in order to match the conditions of the tape version, observation of Abdul and Wing Li undertaking the live version suggested that the effectiveness of the interaction between candidate and interlocutor played a major role in determining the quality of the candidate's overall performance in this format. In other words, it seems that, in practice, the test assessed the interactive competence of both participants.

In the tape version Wing Li appeared to be more proficient in 'remote', one-way communication than Abdul. She seemed to be better able to prepare and respond at length to each task without the support of a live interlocutor compared to Abdul. She also appeared to adapt much better to the more constrained conditions of the tape test than Abdul, who often appeared unable to process the requirements of the tasks and then produce a response in the time allowed for on nearly all of the tasks. Both were frequently cut off by the next question but Wing Li usually seemed closer to completing her answer. Abdul, on the other hand, often seemed to be still gathering his thoughts when the signal to begin talking was given and at the mid-point of his response when stopped short by the recorded voice.

Furthermore, Wing Li appeared more relaxed than Abdul throughout the tape test. This difference was underlined by their body language: Wing Li sat erect and alert without any obvious signs of tension throughout this version. Nor did she appear to be unduly distracted by the voices of those around her. (In fact, as a 'positive' test taking strategy, Wing Li noted in her post-test interview that it was actually possible to remain silent and listen to neighbouring candidates for ideas before starting to respond!) Abdul, on the other hand, seemed to grow progressively more tense in the course of the tape version. He gradually leant more and more over the desk holding his sides while answering a question. He also showed signs of being distracted by the voices of those around him when he was speaking, such as turning his head towards them and frowning during the response time. His brow also became increasingly furrowed and sweaty during the preparation times. In contrast to the live version, where he showed signs of amusement and even enjoyment, he looked increasingly anxious and frustrated as the tape test progressed. It should be noted in relation to these comments that Wing Li may have been slightly better prepared for the tape version of the oral interaction sub-test than Abdul by virtue of the fact that, unlike this other candidate, she had already completed the listening sub-test conducted in the language laboratory earlier in the day.

In conclusion, despite the best intentions of the test developers to match the two versions, observation of Abdul and Wing Li under the live and tape test conditions appeared to indicate that the live version was fundamentally interactive in practice while the tape version was essentially monologic. This conclusion lends support to the majority view of the team members interviewed prior to the trial administration that the speaking skills being tapped by the two formats are not the same whatever attempts are made to equate them. It also appears that candidates may not necessarily possess these different abilities in equal measure.

Candidate interviews

Interviews with both candidates were conducted by the researcher on the day of the trial administration after they had completed the two versions of the oral interaction sub-test. As outlined above, a set of questions were prepared in advance (see Appendix 6.3). However, some flexibility in the precise wording and order in which they were asked was employed in conducting the interviews.

Abdul reported feeling more nervous on the tape version and found it more difficult than the live version. He was critical of the lack of interaction in the tape format: he felt it was easier to talk to another person than to a microphone because 'you can ask questions when you don't understand what to do' (which he did on several occasions) and 'take your time to answer'. He was very satisfied with his interlocutor, who built his confidence by giving him 'plenty of time to think about and answer the questions'. On the tape version he reported needing more time to prepare for some questions, feeling frustrated at being unable to ask clarification questions and also pressured to finish his answers before being cut off by the instructions for the next task. In general, therefore, he felt the live version was a better test of his ability to speak English. He claimed not to be disconcerted by my presence as the observer or the video camera in either test.

Wing Li preferred the live version overall. She felt more confident on the tape version but liked the fact there is a interlocutor who responds in the live version. She also felt that the live version gave her more opportunity to talk. On the other hand, she found the live tasks slightly harder. She was highly positive about the fact that all of the instructions on the tape version were written as well as spoken. This provision meant that 'if you didn't understand the voice you could read the instructions as well'. Wing Li also reported feeling more nervous in the live version as she was anxious about whether she would understand the interlocutor and, more particularly, whether the interlocutor would comprehend her. In other words, she perceived the live version (unlike the tape version) to be essentially a test of her ability to interact with another person. In general, she felt the live version was a much better test of her proficiency because she was more aware of the need to communicate and therefore tailor her language appropriately. Surprisingly, she expressed no dissatisfaction with her interlocutor's performance in the live version, a view which was at odds with my own observation (see above). This discrepancy will be explored later in this chapter. Finally, like Abdul, she claimed not to be distracted by my presence or the video camera.

In retrospect, another important piece of information that should have been obtained from each of the candidates in these interviews related to their previous experience with language laboratories in general and tape-mediated tests in particular. This may have provided another important perspective on why their performances on the two versions appeared to differ so markedly. However, because of the very limited time frame in which these interviews could be conducted on the day of the trial administration, the focus was entirely restricted to the candidates' experiences of the live and tape events in this test.

Candidate questionnaires

Seventy-seven of the 94 candidates who undertook both versions completed the questionnaire about their reactions to the two test formats at the end of the trial administration (included as Appendix 6.4). As previously noted this questionnaire was a revised form of the one used earlier in the December 1992 trial. Table 6.3 provides a summary of test taker reactions to the main questions together with the matching figures, where applicable, from an earlier study undertaken by Hill (1997) of the December 1992 trial. The results indicate a clear preference for the live test in both trials. However, despite the fact that the overwhelming majority of candidates thought the live version a better test, it is worth noting that more than half of them (58%) in the 1994 trial still felt the tape version was a good test of their spoken English.

Table 6.3

Candidate reactions: June '94 and December '92 trials
of the oral interaction sub-test

Which test made you feel more nervous?

| June '94: | Tape 68% | Live 27% | Same 5% |
| (Dec '92: | Tape 60% | Live 40% | Same –) |

Which test was more difficult for you?

| June '94: | Tape 95% | Live 5% |
| (Dec '92: | Tape 85% | Live 15%) |

Which test gave you more opportunity to speak English?

| June '94: | Live 95% | Tape 5% |

Do you think the tape version was a good test of your spoken English?

| June '94: | Yes 58% | No 26% | Not sure 16% |

Do you think the live version was a good test of your spoken English?

| June '94: | Yes 94% | No – | Not sure 6% |

Which one was a better test of your spoken English?

| June '94 | Live 94% | Tape 5% | Same 1% |
| (Dec '92: | Live 90% | Tape 10% | Same –) |

Both Abdul and Wing Li completed the questionnaire and their responses provide an additional source of information about their reactions to the two versions of the test. Generally these responses were consistent with those given earlier on the same day in their interviews and my own observations.

Both candidates felt the live version gave them more opportunities to speak English and that it was a better test of their spoken English. Abdul felt more nervous on the tape test and also found it more difficult. Wing Li, on the other hand, felt more nervous in the live version and found it more difficult than the tape version.

In their responses to other more detailed questions dealing with the tape version separately, both candidates reported that the tape was always audible, the instructions were clear, that the test was pitched at the appropriate level of difficulty overall but that there was sometimes insufficient time given to complete their answers. Abdul did not always have enough time to both prepare and answer the questions and was not sure whether it was a good test of his spoken English. Wing Li, on the other hand, felt there was always adequate preparation time but sometimes insufficient time to respond on the tape. She also thought that the tape test was not a good test of her spoken English.

The responses of the two candidates to the parallel questions on the live version were identical. They both always felt they understood the instructions and had enough time to prepare and answer the questions. They thought the interlocutor was consistently helpful, the test pitched at the appropriate level of difficulty overall and this version to be a good test of their spoken English.

Interlocutor interviews

The interlocutor interviews were conducted immediately after the two candidates had completed the live version. The questions initially devised for these interviews are included in Appendix 6.5.

Interlocutor 1 thought that Abdul did well and improved as the test progressed. He also felt that he performed well as an interlocutor, that he had not been too intrusive and allowed the candidate sufficient time to complete his responses. In this instance his self-assessment was consistent with my own observations about his performance. Furthermore, he claimed not to be distracted by the presence of an observer and the video camera.

This interlocutor also believed that the live version would be superior to the tape version because 'we normally use language with other people'. Thus 'the interactive (sic) version was more natural' and provided 'the sort of props you normally get from other people in a communicative situation'. He felt the tape version would be much more 'artificial' and 'impersonal' for the candidates.

Interlocutor 2 thought that Wing Li performed fairly well but that she seemed more comfortable with the last two sections of the test, the exposition and discussion tasks. She also felt that her own performance as an interlocutor was creditable, that she had been encouraging and had allowed the candidate the opportunity to respond fully on each of the tasks. This self-assessment ran contrary to my own evaluation of her performance. In addition, although at the time of the interview she suggested that the video camera had not distracted her unduly, she later volunteered that it had made her uneasy and that this may have negatively affected her interaction with the candidate.

This interlocutor also considered that the live version offered a better context for assessing oral proficiency because of the participation of 'hopefully sympathetic interlocutors who could put the candidates at ease by encouraging and reassuring them'.

Rating processes

Before completing their assessments all raters (and the researcher as a non-participant observer) attended a calibration session conducted by a member of the test development team. This provided raters with the opportunity to compare their scoring of a small sample of live and tape performances from the trial. These sessions represented an important component of raters' on-going training whose major goal, as outlined in Chapter 3, is to achieve high levels of self-consistency (as opposed to absolute agreement) amongst raters. It was interesting to note in observing this particular calibration session that the comparability of the two versions was not specifically addressed. This suggested that the test equivalence issue was not an important concern in the assessment process for either those conducting the training sessions (members of the test development team) or the raters themselves.

The particular raters assigned to Abdul and Wing Li were as follows:

ABDUL: LIVE	RATERS 7 & 89
ABDUL: TAPE	RATERS 3 & 46
WING LI: LIVE	RATERS 3 & 72
WING LI: TAPE	RATERS 7 & 39

The raw scores assigned by these raters (and rater 12 – see below) to Abdul and Wing Li are tabulated in Appendix 6.6.

Rater interviews

Each of these six raters was subsequently interviewed about the performance of their assigned candidate. The questions prepared for these interviews are included in Appendix 6.7. Since raters 3 and 7 had carried out more than one of these assessments they were interviewed on two different occasions. While the whole group of 22 raters was informed beforehand that they might be interviewed over the course of the two-day rating period, these six raters were not aware that they would be questioned about either Abdul or Wing Li until they had completed their assessment of them.

The two raters who assessed Abdul's live performance felt he had performed fairly but had improved as the test progressed. Rater 7 remarked that he had shown himself to fullest advantage in the final discussion task where he was 'given most room to develop his answer'. Rater 89 suggested that the interaction between candidate and interlocutor had been successful both because the interlocutor had been 'very effective in supporting Abdul' and because Abdul himself had displayed 'strong interactive skills'.

Those raters who assessed Abdul's tape performance both indicated that he seemed ill at ease under this test condition ('a bit phased' in the words of rater 3) and would probably have performed better on a live test where, as rater 46 suggested, 'he could have been prompted to speak more'. Both raters remarked on how slow he often was to begin responding. This would normally result, as rater 3 pointed out, in him having insufficient time to complete his answers.

The raters who scored Wing Li's live test agreed that she had performed inconsistently across the various tasks. However, they had very different views on the performance of her interlocutor and of how interlocutors should behave in general. Rater 3 applauded the fact that the interlocutor had adhered very strictly to her designated script. This was consistent with her belief that 'interlocutors must be rigidly consistent, otherwise they're giving someone an advantage over someone else by helping them too much'. Rater 72, on the other hand, felt that the interlocutor 'stuck too much to the script' and that she should have been 'more flexible' in order to encourage the candidate to speak at greater length. This suggests that raters may have conflicting views about the behaviour of 'good interlocutors' in the live version of this test. This is confirmed by Morton and Wigglesworth (1994) in a study where raters were required to classify interlocutor behaviour on the live version of the *access:* test as poor, average or good. They found it was quite common for two raters to disagree on their classifications of an interlocutor's performance with any particular candidate. Using multifaceted Rasch analysis, McNamara and Lumley (1993) also report a lack of consensus in rater perceptions of interlocutor competence in the speaking sub-test of the Occupational English Test (OET) introduced in Chapter 2.

Raters 3 and 72 also disagreed about whether Wing Li had provided sufficient output in order to be reliably assessed on the live version. Unlike rater 3, rater 72 considered that Wing Li had often failed in this respect. She felt that this was a function of the candidate's 'poor interactive skills' as well as the interlocutor's inability or reluctance to 'draw her out more'. Thus, rater 72's judgements about the interactive competence of both the interlocutor and candidate appear to have been informing her ratings even though the scoring criteria did not specifically address this ability. This point will be pursued in Chapter 7.

Finally, the raters who assessed Wing Li's tape test both felt the candidate had performed very well overall. Rater 89 also remarked that Wing Li had 'given an extremely consistent performance'. Rater 39 commented that the candidate had seemed 'pretty relaxed and confident in tackling the test'. However, this rater also reported experiencing difficulty deciding between the upper levels for most of the relevant rating criteria, especially levels 5 and 6, in scoring this candidate. He felt the descriptors did not distinguish clearly enough between the different levels of performance 'for more able candidates'. This sentiment was not shared by rater 89 overall. However, she did comment that the descriptors used to distinguish higher levels of performance for the category *Fluency* could have been clearer.

The feedback obtained from these raters will be further examined in relation to their scoring of the two candidates in Chapter 7.

Rater questionnaires

All 22 raters who participated in this trial were given a written questionnaire consisting of four questions requiring them to express their opinions about the comparability of the two versions (see Appendix 6.8). The first three questions focused upon, first, whether the live and tape-based versions served equally well as tests of oral proficiency; secondly, whether the scoring criteria and accompanying level descriptors were appropriate for both versions; and, thirdly, whether one version was more difficult to rate than the other. In the final question, raters were invited to raise any other issue related to the comparability question.

Overall, raters were fairly even-handed in their responses to the first question. On the one hand, the live version was deemed to be a more 'natural' and 'authentic' communicative event but on the other hand, the performance of the candidate was felt to be strongly influenced by the interlocutor's performance. On the positive side, the tape version was generally considered to be more impartial because the quality of the input is the same for all candidates. On the negative side, it was felt to be a more 'artificial' context for oral communication ('like talking into a black hole' in the words of one rater) and also that candidates' familiarity with the language laboratory may have significantly affected their performance. In general, despite these format specific differences, raters felt that the two versions served equally well as tests of oral proficiency.

In their responses to the second question, the overwhelming majority of raters felt that the scoring criteria and accompanying level descriptors were appropriate for rating both versions. However, several questioned why *Comprehension* was not included as a category on the tape version.

Answers to the third question suggested that both versions were at times difficult to rate for quite different reasons. The tape version was considered problematic to rate where candidate responses were very brief or else totally irrelevant in relation to the task requirements (even though relevance was not targeted by any of the scoring criteria). At times it was felt that candidates had insufficient time to answer appropriately, especially those who used part of the response time to continue preparing or spoke slowly. In these cases raters felt there was often an inadequate sample of language to make a reliable assessment. Several raters complained of variable sound quality on the tape version, although this appears to have been a more widespread problem on the live version. Audibility is a serious concern in speaking tests where candidates are rated from audio recordings. In their study of the OET using multifaceted Rasch analysis, McNamara and Lumley (1993) found that imperfectly audible tapes were rated significantly more harshly than perfectly audible tapes.

Where raters found the live version difficult to assess it was usually because of what was perceived to be poor interlocutor behaviour, making it almost impossible for them to focus solely on the candidate's performance. The quality of the interlocutor's input and feedback was therefore seen to have a strong bearing on the candidate's performance. This was particularly the case on the role play where poor interviewers tended to dominate the exchange resulting in limited, sometimes insufficient candidate output. Some raters claimed to take the interlocutor variable into account in their assessments, i.e. they tended to compensate in their ratings where the interlocutor's performance was less than satisfactory. The study by McNamara and Lumley also lends strong support to this finding. Again using multifaceted Rasch analysis, they found a significant overall trend for raters to favour candidates paired with interlocutors they perceived to be less competent. As suggested above, audibility in the live version was another major problem consistently raised by raters, even though interlocutors were instructed to check the quality of the recording after the first part of the test (the warm up phase). Quite a few raters also claimed that the live version was less efficient to rate than the tape-based version, where the counter could be used to fast forward to the next response because of the standardisation of input, preparation and response times.

Overall, neither version clearly emerged as more difficult to assess from the rater questionnaires. The factor that appeared to most strongly influence raters' perceptions of comparative ease of marking was the performance of interlocutors on the live version. One rater probably summed up the feeling of the group as a whole by suggesting the following overall order of difficulty in assessing candidate performance on the two versions: a live test with a 'good' interviewer was the easiest to rate followed by the tape test and then the live test with a 'poor' interviewer.

Finally, no significantly new points about the comparability issue emerged in the more open-ended final question. In general, this question was used by raters to elaborate their responses to the earlier questions, particularly their views on the relative difficulty of assessing the two versions.

The additional rater

Since, as noted previously, the rating design for the trial was such that no rater assessed any individual test taker twice, i.e. under both live and tape conditions, it was decided that a more direct comparison of each candidate's performances under the two test conditions from the perspective of a single rater should also be obtained. One of the most experienced and reliable raters (rater 12), who had not originally been assigned to either Abdul or Wing Li in the scoring of this trial administration, was therefore engaged to assess both their live and tape performances several weeks after the other ratings had been completed. Rater 12 carried out these assessments using the video recordings of the performances of Abdul and Wing Li. (See Appendix 6.6 for a complete list of the raw scores rater 12 allocated to Abdul and Wing Li.)

In a follow-up interview with the researcher rater 12 was questioned about his own judgements of the test performances of the two candidates. He was also invited to comment on both the researcher's observations about how well Abdul and Wing Li performed under the two test conditions and on the post-test feedback given by each of them as well as by their respective interlocutors and raters. This provided a test of the reliability of the conclusions drawn by the researcher based on these various sources of evidence.

Rater 12's scoring of the two candidates is discussed in Chapter 7 where the comparability of test scores from the June 1994 trial is examined. The focus of attention at this stage is the follow-up interview where he provided valuable insight into the performances of Wing Li, in particular. He agreed that Wing Li performed less well on the live version and that this may be explained by *both* her discomfort in undertaking a test involving interaction and not being well supported by her interlocutor. Because Wing Li was nervous herself, he suggested, she may not have been aware of 'how much the interlocutor was feeding into her anxiety' by rushing through the test and providing minimal support in the interaction. In any case, the interlocutor's more formal, less supportive demeanour, rater 12 suggested, may have been in accordance with the candidate's expectations about the behaviour of examiners in oral language tests. These reasons might then explain why she expressed no dissatisfaction with her interlocutor afterwards. On the tape version, however, rater 12 felt that Wing Li seemed more confident and relaxed, and therefore more able to demonstrate her oral proficiency. She appeared to be 'quite familiar with the language laboratory environment' and 'to use both the preparation and response times very efficiently' under these conditions. This rater also observed that Wing Li was always ready to begin speaking when the cue to do so was given and considered that she had always provided sufficient language output for an accurate assessment to be made even though her response was sometimes cut off by the next question. Finally, while rater 12 considered that Wing Li's performance on the tape version was generally superior to the live version, he stressed that the difference was probably not great.

Rater 12 felt that Adbul performed better on the live version than the tape version. He agreed that Abdul's interlocutor was more successful than Wing Li's in drawing him out with 'encouragement, patience and positive verbal as well as non-verbal feedback'. Adbul seemed less comfortable ('a bit wooden') on the tape version: he appeared to have more difficulty planning effectively and then providing a coherent response in the time allowed. However, his overall level of performance did not appear to be significantly lower than on the live version.

Finally, rater 12 considered Wing Li had outperformed Abdul on both the live and tape versions of the test. In his view, Wing Li consistently demonstrated a higher level of oral proficiency (as defined by the scoring categories used to rate the test) under both test conditions.

Conclusion

The examination of the processes reported in this chapter appear to support the conclusion drawn from the analysis of candidate output in Chapter 5 that the two versions of the *access:* oral interaction sub-test tapped distinctly different components of the oral proficiency construct, i.e. interactive versus monologic speaking ability. Despite the test developers' careful attempt to minimise interaction in all tasks except the role play on the live version in order to equate the two versions, it appears that the live format, in practice, called into play the candidate's interactive competence in a sense that is absent from the tape version. This was clearly evidenced in the live performances of the two trial candidates studied in the June 1994 trial, where both the interlocutor and the candidate in each case relied on a broad range of 'unscripted' verbal *and* non-verbal feedback to communicate with each other throughout all stages of the test.

Thus, notwithstanding its highly scripted nature, the live version turned out to be a sustained, two-way face-to-face exchange between the interlocutor and candidate which involves substantial negotiation of meaning. The tape version, on the other hand, consisted entirely of a series of one-way 'remote' exchanges in which the candidate prepares and responds within rigid time limits to an audio recorded voice. Given that the two versions draw on such different oral skills, it is perhaps unsurprising that some test takers perform distinctly better in either one of these communicative settings. Both Abdul and Wing Li, the two candidates tracked in the June 1994 trial, fell into this category.

However, the study of these two individuals also suggested that any given candidate's final result on either version may be significantly affected by factors other than their oral language proficiency (under either the live or tape-based conditions). The most salient of these factors was the quality of the interaction between candidate and interlocutor on the live version. However, the adequacy of preparation and response times on the tape version and the candidate's level of comfort under the two conditions as test environments also appeared to influence the quality of the performance. Such factors pose threats to the reliability of measurement across the two versions.

It seems, therefore, that the two formats tap different speaking skills *and* may also fail to yield a satisfactory level of consistency in the measurement process. Both factors could well explain the apparent lack of test score equivalence found in the December 1992 trial (Chapter 4). The question of test score equivalence for both the entire test cohort and the two candidates tracked in the June 1994 trial will be examined in Chapter 7.

7 Trial 2: The analysis of test scores

Introduction

The previous chapter provided a naturalistic perspective on the equivalence issue focusing on the test design, test taking and rating processes. A range of qualitative and quantitative data was gathered using observation, interviews and questionnaires collected before, during and after the June 1994 trial of the *access:* oral interaction sub-test. This chapter reverts to a more positivistic orientation focusing on the analysis of scores from the same trial, although it also uses some of the qualitative data obtained from the rater interviews to interpret these scores. As in the December 1992 trial the scores were analysed using the multi-faceted Rasch measurement computer program, FACETS (Linacre 1989–95).

As outlined in Chapter 6, the audio recordings of a total of 94 candidates obtained from both versions of the test were independently scored by two raters. For this trial the analysis of candidate performance was based on two different methods of generating ability estimates from the FACETS program: first, the difficulty estimates from a number of previously trialled items were 'anchored', i.e. preset in the analysis and secondly, the analysis was carried out without this modification (as per the analysis of the December 1992 trial in Chapter 4). The chapter also reports on the use of an additional rater to clarify the scores originally assigned to the two candidates tracked in the trial (see Chapter 6). Finally, the findings from the application of bias analysis to investigate the interaction between individual raters and both candidates and format are discussed.

Analysis with anchored item difficulty estimates

Following the first trial in December 1992 it became standard practice, when trialling new forms of the live and tape versions of the oral interaction sub-test, to include several previously trialled tasks. The difficulty estimates of the items from these tasks were then 'anchored' in the control file prior to running the FACETS program, i.e. the difficulty estimates for these items were preset into the analysis in advance using the figures from the earlier trials. This process enabled results from one form of the test to be meaningfully compared with earlier forms of the test. It also allowed cut-off points for the different proficiency levels of the oral interaction sub-test (see Table 2.4 in Chapter 2) to be carried forward from one administration to the next. In this trial the 'anchors' were the description and exposition tasks on the live version and the summary task on the tape version. In addition, only three facets were now included in the analysis to ensure stability of estimate of facets: (1) candidate, (2) rater and (3) item.

Initially, in accordance with the established procedure for analysing test scores from both trial and overseas administrations, the live and tape data were treated as coming from the same test and combined to obtain ability estimates for each of the 94 candidates. The FACETS analysis in this case included the anchored difficulty estimates previously obtained for the items listed above. In addition, for the purpose of this study, separate analyses of the entire live and tape data sets, this time anchoring all of the item ability estimates obtained from the combined analysis, were then carried out. This was done so that the established cut-off scores would apply to the results from the two formats taken separately. The results for the three facets candidate, rater and item from the analyses using the combined, live and tape data sets are given in Appendix 7.1. Table 7.1 below provides summary statistics for these analyses.

Table 7.1

Summary statistics, oral interaction sub-test, FACETS analysis (1), June 1994 trial (N = 94)

	LIVE	TAPE	COMBINED
Number of items	20	25	45
Candidates:			
Mean logit score	-0.31	0.31	0.14
SD (logits)	2.19	2.22	1.75
Mean standard error (logits)	0.27	0.24	0.20
Person separation reliability (like K-R 20)	0.98	0.99	0.99

The candidate ability estimates obtained for the live and tape versions correlated only moderately well at $r = 0.80$. Figure 7.1 (below) illustrates graphically the performance of all candidates on the two versions.

Figure 7.1

**Scattergram of candidate ability estimates (logits) on the live and
tape version of the oral trial interaction sub-test, FACETS analysis (1),
June 1994 trial (N = 94)**

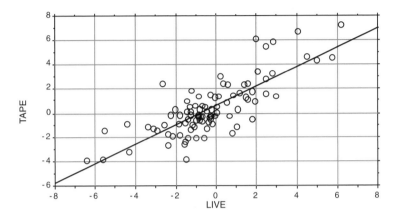

The cut-off scores (logits) established in September 1993 (see Chapter 1
for a description of this process) for the three key levels of proficiency
targeted by the test were as follows: Level 4: Functional = -0.8, Level 5:
Vocational = 0.8 and Level 6: Vocational+ = 1.8. All candidates were then
classified according to the level of proficiency they attained in both versions.
Table 7.2 below summarises this information.

Table 7.2

**Correspondence between candidate proficiency levels on the live
and tape versions of the oral interaction sub-test,
June 1994 trial (N = 94)**

		TAPE			
		-F	F	V	V+
	-F	24	14	3	2
LIVE	F	3	17	3	3
	V	2	2	4	2
	V+	-	-	4	11

-F = below Functional   *V = Vocational*
F = Functional   *V+ = Vocational+*

Overall these results indicated that 40% of all candidates were assigned a different level of proficiency on the two versions of the test. 28% did better on the tape test and 12% on the live test. In some cases (11% of all candidates) there was a discrepancy of more than one level. These findings suggest relatively poor consistency of measurement across the two formats of the oral interaction sub-test.

While these figures certainly indicate a significant difference in terms of overall performance on the two versions, they should still be interpreted with some degree of caution. The fact that a significant percentage of candidates were classified differently by the two versions of the oral interaction sub-test in both the December 1992 trial (12%) and even more so in this trial may have been partially a function of the way in which the cut-off scores were established. This is a highly problematic issue in criterion-referenced tests and is a major ongoing source of concern amongst measurement specialists (see, for example, Cizek 1993). It appears from the research in this area that different standard-setting methods lead to different classifications. It could be, for instance, that the degree of correspondence between results on the two versions of the test might have been higher using a different method of standard setting other than the ASLPR.

In the cases of two candidates tracked in the trial, candidates 39 (Abdul) and 88 (Wing Li), there was a sharp discrepancy between their live and tape ability estimates as shown in Table 7.3 below. In Abdul's case, however, this did not affect the overall proficiency level to which he was allocated in the final analysis, making him one of the 60% of candidates who achieved the same level on the two versions. Wing Li, on the other hand, achieved the highest possible proficiency level on the tape version and the lowest possible level on the live version. She thus formed part of the 40% of candidates who were allocated different proficiency levels on the two tests and, more particularly, of the 11% for whom there was a discrepancy of more than one proficiency level.

Table 7.3

Proficiency levels achieved by Abdul and Wing Li on the live and tape versions of the oral interaction sub-test, June 1994 trial (N = 94)

CANDIDATE	LOGIT	PROFICIENCY LEVEL
Wing Li: tape	1.84	Vocational +
Wing Li: live	-1.22	below Functional
Abdul: live	-1.56	below Functional
Abdul: tape	-2.64	below Functional

The discrepancy between Wing Li's logit scores on the two formats is clearly the more disconcerting set of results as the *access:* oral interaction sub-test aimed to identify candidates reliably at the Functional, Vocational and Vocational+ levels. It was not designed to distinguish accurately between candidates below Functional level. While the difference in Wing Li's results turned out to be highly significant, both of Abdul's results can simply be read as him not achieving Functional level on either version. A possible explanation for the strength of the discrepancy between Wing Li's final results will be pursued later in this chapter.

The data from the test taker questionnaires collected in this trial (see Chapter 6) also enabled analysis of these ability estimates from the two versions in relation to characteristics of test takers and of the test process. Of the 77 respondents, there were 39 males and 38 females. 57% of males and 45% of females gained higher scores on the live format, suggesting men were advantaged slightly more by the live version and women by the tape version. However, the reasons for these findings are unclear since gender differences in performance may stem from the rating process (i.e. the way in which raters responded to a particular gender) as much as features of the two test events such as the interaction between interlocutor and candidate on the live version or the degree of comfort with the laboratory as a test environment in the tape version. (See Sunderland (1995) for a discussion of these issues in speaking tests.)

A further issue in comparing test taker performance on the two versions in the trial situation relates to the possible extraneous influence of a 'practice effect' on test scores, given that candidates undertook both formats on the same day. It is worth remembering at this point that candidates in overseas administration only complete one version. 33 of the 77 candidates in this trial who completed the questionnaire undertook the live version first and 44 the tape version. 44% scored higher on the version they did first, a result which suggests that there was not a significant practice effect overall (in either a positive or negative sense) on candidate performance across the two versions.

The next section examines the output from the FACETS analysis of the June 1994 trial, where the difficulty estimates of previously trialled items were not 'anchored' in order to provide a more direct comparison with the results obtained from the analyses of the December 1992 trial, in which this was also the case. In both instances the lack of anchoring in the analysis can be understood to have yielded a more independent set of candidate ability estimates, i.e. they were uninfluenced by the results (specifically, the item difficulty estimates) obtained from earlier administrations of the test.

Analysis with unanchored item difficulty estimates

The set of procedures adopted in the second phase of the analysis was identical to those used to examine the comparability of the test scores from the December 1992 trial in Chapter 4. That is, the comparability of the direct and semi-direct versions of the oral interaction sub-test was examined from the perspectives of the psychometric unidimensionality and the relative difficulty of the two versions. Subsequent bias analyses were also carried out, in this case to investigate both the interaction between raters and candidates and the interaction between raters and the two test formats, i.e. live and tape-based.

Psychometric unidimensionality

Recall from Chapter 4 that the issue addressed here is whether it is possible to construct a single measurement dimension of speaking ability for the combined data from the two versions of the test. If so, this would provide compelling evidence in favour of the equivalence of test scores. In order to investigate this question three initial multi-faceted analyses using the FACETS program were undertaken: one for the combined data, one for the live data and one for the tape data. Only the following three facets were included in the analyses. Here these were: (1) candidate, (2) rater and (3) item. Appendix 7.2 shows the results for each of these facets in the analyses using the live, tape and combined data. Table 7.4 below provides summary statistics for candidates in each of the three analyses.

Table 7.4

Summary statistics, oral interaction sub-test, FACETS analysis (2), June 1994 trial (N = 94)

	LIVE	TAPE	COMBINED
Number of items	20	25	45
Candidates:			
Mean logit score	- 0.13	0.06	0.18
SD (logits)	2.27	2.23	1.75
Mean standard error (logits)	0.28	0.24	0.16
Person separation reliability (like K-R 20)	0.98	0.99	0.99

Table 7.5 below provides information on misfitting items and persons in the original FACETS analysis using the live, tape and combined data sets. As in the study of the December 1992 trial 'misfit' is defined operationally in terms of candidates, raters or items whose infit mean square value given in the FACETS output is more than 2 standard deviations above the average figure for the relevant set of candidates, raters and items. Using this baseline, there were no misfitting items in this initial set of analyses. However, the criterion *Intelligibility* almost fell into this category on the role play and discussion tasks for the live data taken separately, on the role play and discussion tasks for the tape data taken separately, and on all of these items in the output from the analysis of the combined data set. This suggests that *Intelligibility*, like *Appropriacy* as used in the December 1992 trial, may have been interpreted inconsistently by raters overall even though this criterion technically passes the 'fit' test. A possible way of offsetting this problem would have been for the level descriptors to be revised and for raters to have been more carefully trained and monitored in scoring this category. If *Intelligibility* still showed a consistent trend towards misfit following this process, then its relation to the other categories used in the test may have needed to be re-examined, i.e. it may have been assessing a different ability from the one measured by the other categories. Finally, *Comprehension* also fell just short of being misfitting here, thus confirming the conclusion from the earlier trial that its inclusion as an item in the live version only undermines the equivalence of the two tests.

Table 7.5

**Misfitting items and persons, FACETS analysis (2),
June 1994 trial (N = 94)**

	LIVE		TAPE		COMBINED	
	Mean	SD	Mean	SD	Mean	SD
Item infit	1.0	0.3	1.0	0.3	1.0	0.3
Person infit	1.0	0.3	1.0	0.3	1.0	0.4
Misfitting items and persons						
Items	–		–		–	
Persons	2		3		4	
	(#76,84)		(#58,60,98)		(#58,60,68,98)	

The five misfitting candidates from the live and tape versions taken separately were then removed from the data files. Given that their pattern of scoring was inconsistent with the general pattern of scoring for the test cohort overall it was decided, as in the analysis of the December 1992 trial score data, to exclude these candidates from the analysis in the interests of obtaining a clearer picture of the overall equivalence of test scores from the two versions. The edited data were then re-entered into the FACETS program using the same three facets, i.e. candidate, rater and item. Again there were three data files: one for the live data, one for the tape data and one for the combined data. Appendix 7.3 shows the results for each of the three facets using the live, tape and combined data sets. Table 7.6 below provides summary statistics for candidates in each of the three analyses.

Table 7.6

Summary statistics, oral interaction sub-test, FACETS analysis (3), June 1994 trial (N = 89)

	LIVE	TAPE	COMBINED
Number of items	20	25	45
Candidates:			
Mean logit score	- 0.10	0.06	0.17
SD (logits)	2.38	1.14	1.88
Mean standard error (logits)	0.28	0.24	0.17
Person separation reliability			
(like K-R 20)	0.99	0.99	0.99

Table 7.7 below provides information on misfitting items and persons obtained from the FACETS analyses using the edited live, tape and combined data sets. These results suggested (initially, at least) that when the edited live and tape test data were treated as a single test all items combined to define a single measurement dimension, and the overwhelming majority of candidates (with only one exception) had been measured meaningfully and reliably in terms of the dimension of ability so constructed. There was only one misfitting item across all three analyses – *Intelligibility* on the discussion tasks for the live data set. However, as in the initial analyses using the unedited data, the same criterion was almost misfitting on the role play task for the live data considered separately, on the role play and discussion tasks for the tape data taken separately, and on all of these items in the output from the analysis of the combined data set. Again, the item comprehension almost misfitted on the analysis using the combined data set.

Table 7.7

**Misfitting items and persons, FACETS analysis (3),
June 1994 trial (N = 89)**

	LIVE		TAPE		COMBINED	
	Mean	SD	Mean	SD	Mean	SD
Item infit	1.0	1.3	1.0	0.3	1.0	0.3
Person infit	1.0	0.3	1.0	0.2	1.0	0.2
Misfitting items and persons						
Items	1(#18)		–		–	
Persons	–		1(#12)		2(#68,100)	

Recall from Chapter 4 that if the two versions of the oral interaction sub-test taken together satisfy the psychometric unidimensionality assumption, then the person ability estimates derived from each version considered separately should be independent of the part of the test on which they were made. This would then suggest that the scores on the two versions were equivalent and that the two versions were therefore interchangeable, at least from this perspective. The same two statistical tests employed to examine the test scores from the December 1992 trial in Chapter 4 were used to address this issue.

The first test to be used was a Pearson correlation between the ability estimates obtained from the two versions of the test. The correlation between the two sets of ability estimates uncorrected for attenuation was $r = 0.80$ (the same result as in the previous section where anchored item difficulty estimates were used in the analyses). The result, when corrected for attenuation, was $r = 0.81$. This result suggested a weaker relationship between the ability estimates of candidates on the two versions than was the case in the December 1992 trial where $r = 0.94$. Figure 7.2 below graphically illustrates the relationship between scores on the live and tape versions in this trial.

Figure 7.2

Scattergram of candidate ability estimates (logits) on the live and tape version of the oral trial interaction sub-test, FACETS analysis (3), June 1994 trial (N = 89)

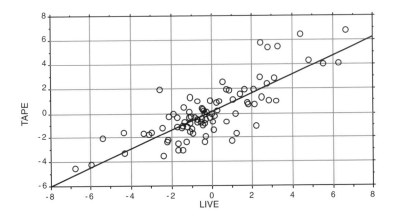

As suggested in relation to the analysis of the test score data from the December 1992 trial in Chapter 4, the correlation test only provides a measure of the linearity between two sets of scores. An additional, more rigorous test of the equality of ability estimates, a chi-squared (χ^2) procedure (as employed by McNamara (1991) and explained earlier in Chapter 4 in relation to the December 1992 trial results) was therefore used in order to determine the strength of relationship between the ability estimates obtained from the two versions of the oral interaction sub-test in the June 1994 trial. The resulting value of $\chi^2 = 1389.15$, df = 88, p< 0.001 suggests, as in the December 1992 trial, that the null hypothesis of equality between the two sets of ability estimates can be rejected. On the basis of results of this statistical procedure, therefore, it appears (as in the analysis of the test score data from the December 1992 trial in Chapter 4) that the assumption of psychometric unidimensionality has not been met. This finding therefore lends further support to the existence of a test method effect, the components of which are summarised later in this chapter.

Test difficulty

The next stage of the investigation concerned the question of comparative difficulty on the two versions of the test. The first step in this process was to map the 'item' difficulty estimates obtained from the FACETS analysis using the combined (live and tape) edited data. (See Table 6.2 in Chapter 6 for a complete list of items in this trial.) Figure 7.3 below suggests that the two versions matched each other fairly well in terms of overall difficulty (although perhaps not quite as closely as in the December 1992 trial – see Figure 4.3, Chapter 4) and that individual corresponding items tended to be of comparable difficulty in this trial. In this map items are again abbreviated according to task and criterion, in an identical manner to Figure 4.3. Thus, for example, 'DisV' stands for 'Discussion: *Vocabulary*' and 'NarF' for 'Narrative: *Fluency*'.

Figure 7.3

Item difficulty map, FACETS analysis (3) of the oral interaction sub-test using the combined live and tape data sets, June 1994 trial (N = 89)

Item difficulty (logits)	LIVE	TAPE
1.0		SumG; SumV
0.9		
0.8		RPG
0.7	NarG	NarG
0.6	DesV	
0.5	DesG; RPG	
0.4	NarV	Des1G; ExpV
0.3	NarC	Des1V;NarV;InsC;
	DisG; Des2G	
0.2		ExpC; InsV; ComEff
0.1		NarC; SumF; Des2V
0.0	Exp1V	RPF; ExpF
-0.1	DesF; DisG	Des 1F; DisF
-0.2	Exp2V; ComEff	Des2F
-0.3	Exp1F; Exp1C	InsF
-0.4	RPF; Exp2C	
-0.5		
-0.6		RPI
-0.7	Exp2F; DisI	
-0.8	RPI; DisF	
-0.9		DisI
-1.0		
-2.0		
-2.1		
-2.2		
-2.3	Comp	
-2.4		

As in the analysis of test difficulty for the December 1992 trial in Chapter 4, an additional FACETS analysis including the three facets, candidate, rater and format was later carried out using the combined data set to determine the overall relative difficulty of the two formats. Table 7.8 below shows that in this trial the tape version was 0.36 of a logit (or about 8%) more difficult than the live version overall. Although slightly larger than the difference in overall difficulty in the December 1992 trial (where the live version was 0.06 of a logit or 2% harder than the tape version), this discrepancy is still small enough to suggest that, in practical terms, the live and tape versions are of comparable difficulty.

As argued in Chapter 4 in relation to the December 1992 trial, the finding that the live and tape versions were highly comparable in difficulty does not, however, imply that the two versions of the oral interaction sub-test are psychometrically unidimensional. The more appropriate measure of test score equivalence was the chi-squared (χ^2) test (see above) which compared the candidate ability estimates obtained from the scores on the live and tape versions of the test taking into account the relative difficulty of the two formats. This procedure (as in the earlier trial) indicated that the two sets of ability estimates were not equivalent and thus confirmed the existence of a significant test method effect.

Table 7.8

Relative difficulty of the live and tape versions of the oral interaction sub-test, FACETS analysis (3), June 1994 trial (N = 89)

Obs score	Obs count	Obs avrge	Fair avrge	Measure (logits)	Model SE	Infit Mean sq	
16582	3533	4.7	4.6	- 0.18	0.02	1.0	Live
19878	4401	4.5	4.4	0.18	0.02	0.9	Tape

On the basis of the results illustrated in Figure 7.3 above it appears that *Grammar* was the most harshly scored criterion followed by *Vocabulary, Communicative effectiveness, Fluency, Intelligibility* and finally, *Comprehension* (live version only). This order of harshness is very similar to that obtained in the December 1992 trial except that the order for *Intelligibility* and *Fluency* was reversed in this trial and *Appropriacy* did not feature as a scoring criterion. Once again, *Comprehension* was the most leniently scored criterion, in this case by a considerable margin. The fact that the tape version was a little harder overall than the live version appears to be in large part the result of including comprehension on the live test only. It is worth underscoring the fact that, as in the December 1992 trial, its inclusion on one version but not the other may, in fact, have jeopardised test score equivalence with the tape version since the construct of oral proficiency across the two versions is not the same as a result.

Bias analysis

Introduction

We return now to the two candidates tracked in the trial, in particular Wing Li. Recall that while the difference between Abdul's logit scores from the FACETS analysis using the anchored item difficulty estimates did not affect the general proficiency level to which he was allocated on the two versions of the test, Wing Li was assigned to the lowest possible level (below Functional) distinguished by the test on the live version and the highest possible level (Vocational+) on the tape version. Some of the reasons for the difference between Wing Li's final results on the two versions were suggested in Chapter 6. (Particularly salient factors for her were a higher level of anxiety and a fairly unsupportive interlocutor in the live version, and an apparently good degree of familiarity with the language laboratory environment.) While Wing Li did appear to perform better on the tape version for these reasons, the magnitude of the difference between her final results was still somewhat perplexing. In order to explore this discrepancy, the scoring of the additional rater (introduced in Chapter 6) who assessed both candidates under the live and tape conditions was examined.

The additional rater (rater 12) ranked the four performances in the same order as the ability estimates derived from the FACETS analysis indicated (see Table 7.3 above). However, his total raw scores did not indicate as wide a discrepancy between the live and tape performances of Wing Li as suggested by her final proficiency level allocations on the two versions. This suggested the possibility that one or more of Wing Li's original raters may have been uncharacteristically harsh or lenient in their scoring. This hypothesis was investigated using bias analysis, previously introduced in Chapter 4.

Rater – candidate interaction

The initial focus of the bias analysis here was on the interaction between rater and candidate. The analysis was based on the edited combined data set (N = 89) to which was added rater 12's raw scores for Abdul (candidate 39) and Wing Li (candidate 88) on both the live and tape versions. The results for these two candidates are shown in Tables 7.9 and 7.10.

7 Trial 2: The analysis of test scores

Where the Z-score values fall between -2.0 and +2.0, the rater may be considered to be scoring that candidate without significant bias. Where the value falls below -2.0 the rater is marking the candidate significantly more leniently in relation to the way that rater does other candidates. On the other hand, where the value is greater than +2.0 the rater is scoring the candidate significantly more harshly compared to the way that rater treats other candidates. In this analysis the infit mean square value indicates how similar the rater's scoring is for the candidate over all of the items. Where the value is less than 0.7 the rater's scoring of the candidate lacks variation. Conversely, where it is greater than 1.3 the scores are too independent.

Table 7.9

Bias calibration report, June 1994 trial, rater–candidate interactions for Abdul (candidate 39)

Rater	Obs score	Exp score	Obs-Exp average	Bias (logit)	Error	Z-score	Infit mn sq
3	81	84.4	-0.13	0.27	0.28	1.0	0.5
7	86	80.8	0.26	-0.60	0.34	-1.8	0.5
12	198	196.3	0.04	-0.08	0.22	-0.4	0.5
46	94	91.3	0.11	-0.24	0.34	0.7	0.8
89	80	83.5	-0.18	0.41	0.34	1.2	0.6

Table 7.10

Bias calibration report, June 1994 trial, rater–candidate interactions for Wing Li (candidate 88)

Rater	Obs score	Exp score	Obs-Exp average	Bias (logit)	Error	Z-score	Infit mn sq
3	85	85.7	-0.04	0.08	0.34	0.3	0.3
7	119	115.0	0.16	-0.33	0.29	-1.2	0.5
12	228	231.9	-0.09	0.17	0.21	0.8	0.9
39	134	115.1	0.76	-1.53	0.28	-5.4	0.4
72	76	94.2	-0.91	2.03	0.33	6.0	1.1

The Z-scores in Table 7.10 indicate that two of Wing Li's sets of ratings were significantly biased and thus unreliable. Rater 39 assessed Wing Li's tape performance significantly more leniently compared to other candidates while rater 72 scored the same candidate's live performance significantly more harshly than other candidates. These findings would seem to explain, at least in part, the strength of the discrepancy between the live and tape logit scores for this candidate as the ability estimates calculated by the FACETS program do not take this kind of interaction into account. None of the raters who assessed Abdul appeared to be significantly biased in their ratings. Finally, Tables 7.9 and 7.10 indicate that seven of the ten sets of ratings showed a tendency for raters to score the test items for these two candidates too similarly. The other three sets of ratings were within the accepted range of fit.

Possible reasons for the erratic behaviour of two of Wing Li's raters were suggested in the rater interviews discussed in Chapter 6. Rater 39 reported difficulty in distinguishing between levels 5 and 6 for this candidate. Inspection of Wing Li's raw scores indicates that this rater gave her the benefit of the doubt on about 50% of the items, all of which were in the second half of the test. This may explain why his set of ratings for this candidate emerged as significantly more lenient than usual. In rater 72's case her unexpected harshness appears to relate to two factors: she seems to have penalised the candidate heavily for insufficient output linked to what she perceived to be her poor interactive competence, as well as the interlocutor's reluctance or inability to draw her out. This seems to confirm, as suggested in Chapter 6, that judgements about the interactive competence of both the interlocutor and candidate were informing rater 72's ratings even though the scoring criteria did not specifically address this ability. Rater 3, who also assessed Wing Li's live performance, expressed no such criticisms of either the candidate or interlocutor.

On the basis of the results of the bias analysis for Wing Li, it appears that there may be a significant interaction effect between some raters and candidates which is contributing to measurement error on both versions of the oral interaction sub-test and, therefore, to the discrepancy between individual candidates' final performance levels under the two conditions. This question was further investigated by examining the relevant figures from the bias analysis for the rest of the trial test cohort. In about 60% of cases there was evidence of rater bias, i.e. at least one of the four raters allocated to each trial candidate (two for the live version and two for the tape version) showed a tendency to mark the candidate either significantly more harshly or more leniently than s/he did other candidates. There was also a clearly discernible trend for the strength of this interaction effect to increase in the case of candidates who were subsequently assigned different proficiency levels on the two versions (i.e. 40% of candidates). This was particularly marked in the case of candidates where there was a difference of two or more proficiency levels (i.e. 11% of the test cohort). Given that the interaction effect between rater and candidate appears to be contributing strongly, in general, towards measurement error on the ability estimates obtained from both versions of the test, it would seem highly advisable to employ a third rater where one of the two original raters showed evidence of strong bias in relation to a particular candidate.

7 Trial 2: The analysis of test scores

Rater–format interaction.

Another potential source of measurement error in the ability estimates produced by the FACETS program is the interaction between raters and format (i.e. live or tape-based). This issue was investigated in relation to the December 1992 trial in Chapter 4.

In the analysis of test difficulty reported previously in this chapter the effect of test format over all raters, candidates and items was found not to be large, i.e. the tape version was 0.36 of a logit (or about 8%) more difficult than the live version overall. However, as in the December 1992 trial, it was still conceivable that individual raters judged performances on one format significantly more harshly or leniently than the other. Table 7.11 below shows the results from the bias analysis, again using the edited combined data set, for raters in this category (five from the total number of 22 raters used in this trial).

Table 7.11

Bias calibration report, June 1994 trial,
rater – format interactions (part)

Rater	Format	Obs score	Exp score	Obs-Exp average	Bias (logit)	Error	Z-score	Infit mn sq
39	live	935	880	-0.30	-0.65	0.11	-5.9	1.4
45	live	702	734	-0.18	0.37	0.11	3.5	0.5
46	live	398	413	-0.15	0.31	0.14	2.2	0.7
50	live	1062	1021	0.21	-0.48	0.11	-4.4	0.8
56	live	885	860	0.13	-0.26	0.10	-2.6	0.9
39	tape	1102	1156	-0.22	0.47	0.09	5.1	1.4
45	tape	1056	1024	0.13	-0.27	0.09	-2.9	0.6
46	tape	349	334	0.18	-0.40	0.16	-2.5	1.0
50	tape	816	857	-0.21	0.44	0.10	4.3	0.8
56	tape	926	951	-0.11	0.23	0.10	2.4	0.5

These figures indicate that raters 45 and 46 were significantly more severe on the live version while raters 39, 50 and 56 were significantly more harsh on the tape version. Rater 39 also showed a significant tendency to be inconsistent with an infit mean square value of 1.4 on both versions. In practical terms, however, the effects of rater bias in relation to the average difference it makes to the raw scores allocated by these raters are not substantial. In all five cases the raters were, on average, less than half a score point (on a seven-point scale) more or less severe on the live version than the tape version.

160

The results of the two bias analyses undertaken here, therefore, suggest that the more significant interaction in terms of its overall impact on candidates' final results was between rater and candidate rather than rater and format. Wigglesworth (1993; 1994) also used bias analysis to examine the interaction between rater and item on the oral interaction sub-test and then used the results as feedback to raters as part of their ongoing training. While her initial findings seemed to indicate that rater performance would improve as a result of this process, the results of the second study were less clear in their support of this claim. Given the lack of conclusive findings in relation to the effects of training on rater consistency, a more important concession to candidates (as noted above) may be to routinely carry out a bias analysis focusing on the rater – candidate interaction (as undertaken above) and to then use a third rater where either or both of the two original raters show evidence of significant bias in relation to a particular candidate.

Conclusion

This analysis of test scores and band levels obtained by candidates (N = 94) in the June 1994 trial confirmed the apparent lack of equivalence between test scores reported in the December 1992 trial. Again, contrary to the more standard measures of unidimensionality, the more rigorous measure of the relationship between candidate ability estimates (the chi-squared procedure) indicated that a single measurement dimension of speaking ability could not be constructed for the combined data obtained from the live and tape versions.

However, the lack of equivalence between test scores was most clearly revealed earlier in this chapter when band levels obtained by the trial candidates on the live and tape versions were compared. This analysis revealed that 40% of all candidates were assigned a different level of proficiency on the two versions with 28% doing better on the tape test and 12% on the live test. In the case of the two individual candidates tracked in the trial, Abdul's results were consistent insofar as he failed to achieve Functional level on both versions whereas Wing Li achieved the highest possible band level on the tape version and the lowest possible level on the live version. She thus formed part of the 11% of candidates for whom there was a discrepancy of more than one level.

In addition, further bias analyses of the June 1994 test score data indicated an additional important source of measurement error on both versions, i.e. rater bias with respect to individual candidates. These analyses indicated that in about 60% of cases there was evidence of rater bias, i.e. at least one of the four raters allocated to each trial candidate (two for the live version and two for the tape version) showed a tendency to mark the candidate either significantly more harshly or more leniently than s/he did other candidates.

There was also a clearly discernible trend for the strength of this interaction effect to increase in the case of candidates who were subsequently assigned different proficiency levels on the two versions (i.e. 40% of candidates). This was particularly marked in the case of candidates where there was a difference of two or more proficiency levels (i.e. 11% of the test cohort).

Finally, taking account of the findings in Chapters 5, 6 and 7, it appears that the scores obtained from the two versions may not be equivalent, first, because different language abilities are being tapped on the two versions, i.e. interactive and monologic speaking skills *and*, secondly, because the measurement process was not sufficiently constrained so as to yield a satisfactory level of reliability across the two formats in both trials. It appears that there are a variety of factors in the testing process currently contributing towards a lack of consistency in the measurement process on the two formats. These include the factors identified in Chapter 6 (i.e. the quality of the interaction between the candidate and interlocutor on the live version, the adequacy of the preparation and response times on the tape version, and the candidate's level of stress under each of the two conditions as test environments) as well as the existence of rater bias, particularly with respect to individual candidates on both versions, which has emerged in Chapter 7 as a significant source of measurement error. While there may be other potential threats to reliability, the insights gained from this investigation reveal some of the complexity of the factors other than the language ability in question which affect test scores and how they interact.

Chapter 8 summarises the findings reported in the last four chapters and explores their implications.

8 Summary and conclusions

Overview

This chapter begins by providing a summary of the findings from the various studies reported in the previous four chapters. The summary illustrates how each of the methods used in the study provided important but nevertheless partial insight into the equivalence of the two versions of the oral interaction sub-test. However, it also reveals that the use of multiple methods ultimately yielded a clearer, more comprehensive picture than would have been the case if only a single method had been adopted.

The chapter then explores the potential implications of these findings, first, for the *access:* oral interaction sub-test; secondly, for the equivalence of direct and semi-direct tests of oral proficiency more generally; thirdly, for comparability studies in language testing; fourthly, for combining positivistic and naturalistic approaches to research in language testing; and finally, for the interpretation of test scores in performance tests.

Summary of findings

A preliminary examination of the test specifications (see Chapter 2) indicated that the live version of the oral interaction sub-test had been designed to match the tape-mediated version as closely as possible partly in response to concerns expressed in the literature about the potential non-equivalence of the two formats. To this end a careful attempt was made by the test developers to minimise interaction between candidate and interlocutor on the live version (with the exception of the role play task) by carefully scripting the interlocutor's contribution. It was suggested that this attempt to equate the two versions at the design stage gave the study its unique character since previous research has investigated the comparability of direct and semi-direct tests (see Chapter 1) where this has not been the case.

The first major part of the study involved several different quantitative analyses of numerical score patterns in the December 1992 trial (N = 83) from the perspective of psychometric unidimensionality using the multi-faceted Rasch program, FACETS (Linacre, 1989–95) (see Chapter 4).

Standard analyses of the FACETS output (including a study of misfitting persons and items and also the strength of correlation between the candidate ability estimates) appeared to provide support for the assumption of psychometric unidimensionality in relation to the two versions of the test. However, a more rigorous measure of the relationship between the ability estimates, the chi-squared (χ^2) procedure, failed to confirm that a single measurement dimension of speaking ability could be constructed for the combined data obtained from the live and tape versions. In other words, contrary to the more standard measures of unidimensionality, this procedure indicated that the candidate ability estimates obtained from the two versions were not equivalent.

While the lack of equivalence between test scores obtained from the more rigorous test of unidimensionality was compelling, this finding appeared somewhat puzzling at this point, given the discrepancy between the different measures used to address this question. Furthermore, even if this conclusion was accurate, it was unclear from the statistical analyses alone about *why* this might be so.

Further analyses of a very different kind were then initiated. A selection of the audio taped performances of candidates who had completed both versions in the December 1992 trial (N = 20) were transcribed and their discourse features compared both qualitatively and quantitatively using a framework developed by Shohamy (1994) in her study of the Hebrew OPI and SOPI (see Chapter 5). Four alternate tasks were chosen as the focus of analysis – the description, narration, discussion and role play tasks. The first three tasks were 'monologic' in character on both versions, i.e. during the response only the test taker was required to speak in order to successfully fulfil the demands of the task. The live and tape role play tasks, however, differed in terms of their requirements for candidates. The live role play consisted of a two-way exchange based on an information gap while the tape role play remained monologic.

This analysis of language output was carried out in two separate stages. In the first stage (Discourse Study A), a range of discourse features, including rhetorical structure and functions, genre, speech moves, communicative properties, discourse strategies, content and topic of discourse, prosodic/paralinguistic features and contextualisation, type of speech functions, discourse markers and register, were examined. These features invited broad qualitative discourse analyses of the language samples obtained from the trial. In the second stage (Discourse Study B) a detailed quantitative examination of test taker language output was carried out focusing solely on lexical density. Using Shohamy's (1994) categories enabled a direct comparison to be drawn between her findings and the results of this study.

The broad qualitative study of a range of discourse features in Discourse Study A suggested that the language produced in the direct and semi-direct versions of the oral interaction sub-test on the three 'monologic' tasks (i.e. description, narration and discussion) was strongly similar but that the live and tape role plays produced a different kind of discoursal output. On the basis of these initial results it appeared that the careful efforts of the test designers to match the test tasks (except the live and tape role plays) had been rewarded in terms of the parity of test taker language elicited in the two versions. However, the findings also suggested that the cost of this achievement was a certain 'unnaturalness' (i.e. stiffness and formality) in candidate output on the live version, brought about by controlling and limiting the interlocutor's contribution through the use of a script. The less controlled live role play, on the other hand, appeared to have elicited language which more closely approximated to conversation than the other live tasks. Yet, the price to be paid for its greater 'authenticity' seems to have been a sharp lack of comparability with its tape counterpart.

The findings in Discourse Study A contrasted with those of Shohamy (1994) where consistent differences between the OPI and SOPI were found on nearly all of the discourse features examined (see Chapter 5, in particular Table 5.3).

In Discourse Study B, however, the live version elicited language of a significantly lower lexical density than the tape version in all four matching tasks. (See Chapter 5, Tables 5.5 and 5.6 as well as Figures 5.1, 5.2, 5.3 and 5.4.) It was argued that this result could be mainly attributed to the inextinguishable presence of interaction throughout the live version despite the attempt by the test designers to eliminate, or at least minimise, it in all tasks except the role play. Furthermore, the results also indicated that the *higher* the degree of interaction the *lower* the level of lexical density in candidate output. This was clearly demonstrated in the figures from the live role play task where the communication between candidate and interlocutor was the least constrained of all the tasks on that version. The degree of lexical density was found to be correspondingly significantly lower on this task than any of the other live tasks. Lexical density therefore proved to be the more sensitive measure of difference in language output in this study, at least from the perspective of interactivity (see Chapter 5).

On the basis of these findings, particularly those related to lexical density, it appeared possible that the two versions were drawing on different language skills overall, i.e. interactive versus monologic speaking ability, despite the efforts made by the test development team to minimise interaction on nearly all the live tasks in the interests of test equivalence. It was suggested that this, in turn, may have accounted for the apparent lack of equivalence between the test scores on the two formats in the December 1992 trial, since it is likely that at least some candidates would not perform equally well in tests which tap such different oral skills.

While the analyses of test scores and test taker language output provided some important initial answers to the equivalence question, they were still tentative and even partially contradictory. This led to the adoption of a third, very different perspective from which to address the research question in a subsequent trial. In the June 1994 trial the equivalence issue was addressed from a naturalistic perspective and the investigation focused on test *processes*, including the processes of test design, test taking and rating.

The findings from this part of the study confirmed that, despite the efforts of the test designers to equate the two versions, the live format, in practice, called into play the candidate's interactive competence in a sense that is absent from the tape version. This difference was most clearly and unambiguously revealed in the two individual case studies ('Abdul' and 'Wing Li') reported in Chapter 6. In the live version both trial candidates and their interlocutors relied on a broad range of 'unscripted' verbal and non-verbal feedback to communicate with each other throughout all stages of the test. The tape version was wholly lacking in two-way communication. Interactivity on the live version was also a recurrent theme in the interviews with test developers, candidates, interlocutors and raters, with most of these interviewees directly or indirectly agreeing that it was an integral feature of the live version.

Thus, notwithstanding its highly scripted nature, the live version turned out to be a sustained, two-way face-to-face exchange between the interlocutor and candidate which involved substantial negotiation of meaning through verbal and non-verbal communication. The tape version, on the other hand, consisted entirely of a series of one-way 'remote' exchanges in which the candidate prepares and responds within rigid time limits to an audio recorded voice.

The findings in Chapter 6 supported the conclusion drawn from Discourse Study B that the two versions of the *access:* oral interaction sub-test tapped distinctly different components of the oral proficiency construct, i.e. interactive versus monologic speaking ability, despite the best intentions of the test developers. Given that the two versions draw on such different oral skills it is perhaps unsurprising that some test takers perform distinctly better in either one of these communicative settings.

However, the findings in Chapter 6 also suggested that any given candidate's final result on either version may be significantly affected by factors other than their oral language proficiency (under either the live or tape-based conditions). The most salient of these factors was the quality of the interaction between candidate and interlocutor on the live version. However, the adequacy of preparation and response times on the tape version and the candidate's level of comfort under the two conditions as test environments also appeared to influence the quality of the performance. Such factors pose threats to the reliability of measurement across the two versions.

It seemed, therefore, that the two formats tapped different speaking skills *and* also failed to yield a satisfactory level of consistency in the measurement process. Both factors could well explain the apparent lack of test score equivalence found in the December 1992 trial (refer to Chapter 4). The issue of test score equivalence for both the entire test cohort and the two candidates tracked in the June 1994 trial was then examined in order to compare the results with those obtained from the December 1992 trial (see Chapter 7).

This analysis of test scores and band levels obtained by candidates (N = 94) in the June 1994 trial confirmed the apparent lack of equivalence between test scores reported in the December 1992 trial. Again, contrary to the more standard measures of unidimensionality, the more rigorous measure of the relationship between candidate ability estimates (the chi-squared (χ^2) procedure) indicated that a single measurement dimension of speaking ability could not be constructed for the combined data obtained from the live and tape versions. This lack of equivalence between test scores was most clearly revealed when band levels obtained by the trial candidates on the live and tape versions were compared. This analysis revealed that 40% of all candidates were assigned a different level of proficiency on the two versions with 28% doing better on the tape test and 12% on the live test. While Abdul's results were consistent insofar as he failed to achieve Functional level on both versions, Wing Li achieved the highest possible band level on the tape version and the lowest possible level on the live version. She thus formed part of the 11% of candidates for whom there was a discrepancy of more than one level.

Finally, further bias analyses of the June 1994 test score data indicated an additional important source of measurement error on both versions, i.e. rater bias with respect to individual candidates. These analyses indicated that in about 60% of cases there was evidence of rater bias, i.e. at least one of the four raters allocated to each trial candidate (two for the live version and two for the tape version) showed a tendency to mark the candidate either significantly more harshly or more leniently than s/he did other candidates. There was also a clearly discernible trend for the strength of this interaction effect to increase in the case of candidates who were subsequently assigned different proficiency levels on the two versions (i.e. 40% of candidates). This was particularly marked in the case of candidates where there was a difference of two or more proficiency levels (i.e. 11% of the test cohort).

On the basis of all the findings summarised in this section it is difficult to determine which was more responsible for the observed lack of equivalence between test scores on the two versions – the difference in what is being assessed in each format or the lack of consistency in the measurement process. It would seem, in any event, that both were playing a substantial role in this outcome.

The results of the various stages of the study in relation to the equivalence of the two versions of the oral interaction sub-test are shown in Table 8.1 below. This table shows that each stage provided important but sometimes conflicting insights into the equivalence of the two versions of the oral interaction sub-test. Thus, the use of multiple methods ultimately yielded a clearer, more comprehensive answer to the research question than would have been the case if only a single method had been adopted.

Table 8.1

Findings on the equivalence of the live and tape versions

Stage	Data	Method	Character	Finding
1	*test scores* 12/92	standard Rasch analyses	quantitative	equivalent
2	*test scores* 12/92	Rasch-based χ^2 test	quantitative	not equivalent
3	*language output* 12/92	analysis of various discourse features	qualitative	'monologic' tasks equivalent but role play tasks not equivalent
4	*language output* 12/92	analysis of lexical density	quantitative	both 'monologic' *and* role play tasks not equivalent
5	*test processes* 6/94	naturalistic data analysis	qualitative	not equivalent
6	*test scores* 6/94	standard Rasch analyses	quantitative	equivalent
7	*test scores* 6/94	Rasch-based χ^2 test	quantitative	not equivalent
8	*band levels* 6/94	frequency counts and percentages	quantitative	not equivalent

Implications of findings

This section explores the potential implications of the findings in this study, first, for the equivalence of direct and semi-direct tests of oral proficiency; secondly, for comparability studies in language testing; thirdly, for combining positivistic and naturalistic approaches to research in language testing; and finally, for the interpretation of test scores in performance tests.

The equivalence of direct and semi-direct tests of oral proficiency

The findings from this study appear to support Shohamy's (1994) conclusion that direct and semi-direct tests are not interchangeable as tests of oral proficiency. In particular, the analysis of candidate output from the perspective of lexical density in Chapter 5 and the studies of two trial candidates, Abdul and Wing Li, undertaking the two versions in Chapter 6, together with the lack of test score equivalence found in both the December 1992 and June 1994 trials, suggest that these two kinds of tests may tap fundamentally different language abilities whatever efforts are made to equate them.

In addition, as Lazaraton (1996) and McNamara (1997) both underscore, performance in any direct test of speaking is jointly achieved by the participants (typically, a single candidate and interlocutor) in the interaction, or *co-constructed*. In semi-direct tests the candidate's performance is also jointly achieved but in this instance with an 'unresponsive' interactional partner. This fundamental difference between the two formats was most clearly evident in the two individual case studies reported in Chapter 6. One of the most important challenges for direct testing, therefore, is to determine how to take account of interlocutor performance, which appears to be highly variable, in the assessment of an individual candidate's communicative ability.

If the ability to interact is to be seen as integral to the construct of oral proficiency and not simply an optional component, then direct testing appears, under normal circumstances, to remain the most valid method of assessing speaking notwithstanding the problems associated with variability in interlocutor performance. The semi-direct format, on the other hand, might be employed, as van Lier (1989) suggests, in more specialised testing contexts where the assessment of monologic speaking ability is required.

Comparability studies in language testing

To date, as previously argued, much previous comparability research in language testing has relied primarily on *concurrent validation,* which focuses on the equivalence between test scores. Many of the empirical studies reviewed in the first chapter of this study attempt to establish the equivalence of direct and semi-direct speaking tests in this way using statistical correlations. However, it has been argued in this book that investigating the relationship between test scores provides necessary but insufficient evidence as to whether the same language constructs are being tapped in different tests. This position provided the rationale for moving beyond concurrent validation in order to investigate the equivalence of the direct and semi-direct versions of the *access:* oral interaction sub-test. In so doing, the study has demonstrated the need to examine language tests from multiple perspectives in order to obtain deeper insights into what they appear to measure and thus provide richer, more comprehensive evidence for *construct validity*, of which concurrent validity is only one (albeit important) component. In turn, it is argued, this approach provides a more solid and therefore more valid basis from which to draw conclusions about test comparability.

Combining positivistic and naturalistic approaches to research in language testing

This study has also illustrated the potential of combining both positivistic and naturalistic inquiry in language testing research. Because of its bias towards outcomes and the expert knowledge of the researcher the positivistic model appears particularly appropriate to the analysis of test products such as test scores (see Chapters 4 and 7) and candidate language output (see Chapter 5). On the other hand, because of its emphasis on process and the importance of incorporating the views of all interested parties, not simply the researcher, in attempting to understand human behaviour, the naturalistic model seems particularly well suited to 'inside' examinations of how tests are designed and how test scores are produced, taking into account the experiences of such players as test developers, test takers and raters (see Chapter 6).

Furthermore, while the naturalistic approach to research in language testing tends to yield greater *depth* of coverage by shedding light on the experiences and perceptions of various individual 'actors' representing these different players in the testing process, the positivistic approach typically allows greater *breadth* of coverage by providing an overview of group performance. Given their very different orientations, the two perspectives might be usefully employed to balance each other. In this way, for example, the full significance of findings based on in-depth studies of individual test takers could become clearer by examining where their scores stand in relation to the rest of the test cohort. Conversely, group differences in test score equivalence revealed through quantitative analyses may be illuminated through investigations of individual case studies. In an important sense, the evidence provided by the two approaches can therefore be seen as complementary.

Most importantly, as demonstrated in this study, the adoption of such a mixed strategy has the potential to eventually yield more solidly grounded, valid conclusions than is the case where only one paradigm has been used, because of its dual emphasis on both product and process and its reliance on both quantitative and qualitative research methods.

To date language testing research has operated mostly within the positivistic paradigm (Hamp-Lyons and Lynch 1995). As suggested in Chapter 3, this is probably unsurprising given the centrality of measurement in this enterprise. However, more recently there have been calls for researchers in educational testing to consider more naturalistic perspectives from which to undertake test validation (see for example Messick 1989; Moss 1994, 1996; Shephard 1993). This does not necessarily mean that the positivistic paradigm should simply be jettisoned in favour of the naturalistic paradigm. Moss (1996: 22), for example, suggests that

> *the issue for me is not whether we should adopt [one approach or the other] to the social sciences in general, or to assessment in particular; the issue is how we can use the contrast to highlight the taken-for-granted practices and perspectives of each approach and how, taken together, they can provide a more textured and productive view of the social phenomena we seek to understand.*

Such a perspective appears to offer a fruitful direction for future research in language testing. In particular, the richness of performance testing needs to be matched by a similar richness in the methods used to explore important issues of validity and reliability.

The interpretation of test scores in performance tests

Finally, the results of this study overall suggest that test scores should be interpreted cautiously, particularly when important decisions about individuals are to be based on them, such as in the *access:* test. While language testing continues to strive for a kind of objective purity or psychometric 'pristineness', even in the communicative era, it appears that test scores on performance tests are produced from a series of highly complex interactions between the candidate, the test format, the interlocutor (where applicable), the type of tasks, the rater(s), and the rating scale. Such a measurement process can hardly claim to be foolproof in terms of its reliability. Even more importantly, the issue of what language ability is being tapped in performance tests is not always easily resolved but remains nevertheless crucial to the interpretation of test scores. As Bernard Spolsky (1995: 358) suggests;

> *If the aim [of a language test] is to make some serious decision*
> *affecting the future of the persons being tested, language testers must*
> *accept full responsibility for the inevitable uncertainty of a powerful*
> *but flawed technology, and make sure not just of reliability but also of*
> *focused and relevant validity, and intelligent and sceptical*
> *interpretation of the multiple methods of measurement and assessment*
> *used.*

All 'high stakes' language tests, such as the ***access:*** test, require such rigorous on-going scrutiny in relation to both their reliability and validity. It is to be hoped that this study demonstrates the importance and complexity of that enterprise.

References

Alderson, J. C. 1980. Native and non-native speaker performance on cloze tests. *Language Learning* 30, 1: 59–76.

Alderson, J. C., C. Clapham and D. Wall. 1995. *Language Test Construction and Evaluation.* Cambridge: Cambridge University Press.

Alderson, J. C., K. J. Krahnke and C. W. Stansfield (eds.). 1987. *Reviews of English Language Proficiency Tests.* Washington, DC: Teachers of English to Speakers of Other Languages.

Anivan, S. (ed.). 1991. *Current Developments in Language Testing.* Singapore: RELC.

ARELS Examinations Trust 1989. *The Oxford-ARELS Examinations in English as a Foreign Language: Rationales, Regulations and Syllabuses.* Oxford: ARELS Examination Trust.

Bachman, L. F. 1988. Problems in examining the validity of the ACTFL oral proficiency interview. *Studies in Second Language Acquisition* 10, 2: 149–64.

Bachman, L. F. 1990. *Fundamental Considerations in Language Testing.* Oxford: Oxford University Press.

Bachman, L. F. 1991. What does language testing have to offer? *TESOL Quarterly* 25: 4, 671–704.

Bachman, L. F. and S. J. Sauvignon. 1986. The evaluation of communicative language proficiency: A critique of the ACTFL oral interview. *The Modern Language Journal* 70: 4, 380–90.

Benson, M. J. 1989. The academic listening task: A case study. *TESOL Quarterly* 23: 3, 421–45.

Brindley, G. and G. Wigglesworth (eds.). 1997. *access: Issues in Language Test Design and Delivery.* Sydney: National Centre for English Language Teaching and Research.

Brown, A. 1993. The role of test-taker feedback in the development process: test takers' reactions to a tape-mediated test of proficiency in spoken Japanese. *Language Testing* 10: 3, 277–304.

Cherryholmes, C. H. 1992. Notes on pragmatism and scientific realism. *Educational Researcher* 21: 6, 13–17.

Cizek, G. J. 1993. Reconsidering standards and criteria. *Journal of Educational Measurement* 30: 2, 93–106.

Clark, J. L. D. 1979. Direct versus semi-direct tests of speaking proficiency. In Briere and Hinofotis (eds.).

Clark, J. L. D. 1986. *Handbook for the Development of Tape-mediated ACTFL/ILR Scale-based Tests of Speaking Proficiency in the Less Commonly Taught Languages.* Washington, DC: Center for Applied Linguistics (ERIC document 278 265).

Clark, J. L. D. 1988. Validation of a tape-mediated ACTFL/ILR scale-based test of Chinese speaking proficiency. *Language Testing* 5: 187–98.

Clark, J. L. D. and R. T. Clifford. 1988. The FSI/ILR/ACTFL proficiency scale and testing techniques. *Studies in Second Language Acquisition,* 10: 129–47.

Clark, J. L. D. and Y. Li. 1986. *Development, Validation and Dissemination of a Proficiency-Based Test of Speaking Ability in Chinese and an Associated Model for Other Less Commonly Taught Languages.* Washington, DC: Center for Applied Linguistics. (ERIC Document No. ED 278 264).

Clark, J. L. D. and S. Swinton. 1979. *An Exploration of Speaking Proficiency Measures in the TOEFL Context.* TOEFL Research Report 4. Princeton, NJ: Educational Testing Service.

Clark, J. L. D. and S. Swinton. 1980. *The Test of Spoken English as a Measure of Communicative Ability in English-medium Instructional Settings.* TOEFL Research Report 7. Princeton, NJ: Educational Testing Service.

Coulthard, M. (ed.). 1986. *Talking about Text.* Birmingham: University of Birmingham, English Language Research.

Davies, A. 1991. *The Native Speaker in Applied Linguistics.* Edinburgh: Edinburgh University Press.

Denzin, N. K. and Y. S. Lincoln (eds.). 1994. *Handbook of Qualitative Research.* London: Sage.

Filipi, A. 1995. Interaction in an Italian oral test: The role of some expansion sequences. *Australian Review of Applied Linguistics* Series S, No. 11: 119–36.

Frith, J. R. (ed.). 1980. *Measuring Spoken Language Proficiency.* Washington, DC: Georgetown University Press.

Gardner, R. 1992. *Task Classification, Methodology and Task Selection.* Unpublished manuscript, Department of Linguistics and Applied Linguistics, University of Melbourne.

Gass, S. and C. Madden (eds.). 1985. *Input in Second Language Acquisition.* Rowley, MA: Newbury House.

Guba, E. G. (ed.). 1990a. *The Paradigm Dialog.* Newbury House, CA: Sage.

Guba, E. G. 1990b. The alternative paradigm dialog. In Guba (ed.).

Guba, E. G. and Y. S. Lincoln. 1989. *Fourth Generation Evaluation.* Newbury House, CA: Sage.

Halliday, M. A. K. 1985. *Spoken and Written Language.* Melbourne: Deakin University Press.

Hamilton, J., M. Lopes, T. F. McNamara and E. Sheridan. 1993. Rating scales and native speaker performance on a communicatively oriented EAP test. *Melbourne Papers in Language Testing,* 2, 1: 1–24.

Hamp-Lyons, L. and B. K. Lynch. 1995. Perspectives on validity: An historical analysis of the LTRC. Paper presented at the 17th annual Language Testing Research Colloquium, Longbeach, California.

Hasan, A.S. 1988. *Variation in Spoken Discourse In and Beyond the EFL Classroom.* Unpublished PhD thesis, University of Aston.

Hawthorne, L. The political dimension of English language testing in Australia. *Language Testing* 14, 3: 248–60.

Henning, G. 1987. *A Guide to Language Testing: Development, Evaluation, Research.* Cambridge, MA: Newbury House.

Hill, K. 1997. The role of questionnaire feedback in the validation of the oral interaction module. In Brindley and Wigglesworth (eds.).

Hoejke, B. and K. Linnell. 1994. 'Authenticity' in language testing: Evaluating spoken language tests for international teaching assistants. *TESOL Quarterly* 28: 1, 103–25.

Howe, K. R. 1988. Against the quantitative-qualitative incompatability thesis: Or dogmas die hard. *Educational Researcher* 17, 1: 10–16.

Hughes, A. (ed.). 1988. *Testing English for University Study.* ELT documents 127. Oxford: Modern English Publications and the British Council.

Hughes, A. 1989. *Testing for Language Teachers.* Cambridge: Cambridge University Press.

Ingram, D. E. and E. Wylie. 1984. *Australian Second Language Proficiency Ratings.* Department of Immigration and Ethnic Affairs, AGPS, Canberra.

Jaeger, R. M. (ed.). 1988. *Complementary Methods for Research in Education.* Washington, DC: American Educational Research Association.

James, G. 1988. Development of an oral proficiency component in a test of English for academic purposes. In Hughes (ed.).

Johnson, D. 1992. *Approaches to Research in Second Language Learning.* New York: Longman.

Labov, W. 1972. *Sociolinguistic Patterns.* Philadelphia, PA: University of Pennsylvania Press.

Lado, R. 1961. *Language Testing: The Construction and Use of Foreign Language Tests.* London: Longman.

Lazaraton, A. L. 1991. *A Conversation Analysis of Structure and Interaction in the Language Interview.* Unpublished PhD thesis, University of California, Los Angeles.

Lazaraton, A. L. 1996. Interlocutor support in oral proficiency interviews: The case of the CASE. *Language Testing* 13: 2, 151–72.

Lazaraton, A. and N. Saville. 1994. Process and outcomes in oral assessment. Paper presented at the 16th annual Language Testing Research Colloquium, Washington, DC.

LeCompte, M. and J. Goetz. 1982. Problems of reliability and validity in ethnographic research. *Review of Educational Research* 52: 1, 31–60.

Linacre, J. M. 1989–95. *FACETS: A Computer Program for Multi Faceted Rasch Measurement.* Chicago, IL: Mesa Press.

Linn, R.L. (ed.). 1989. *Educational Measurement* (3rd edition). New York: American Council on Education/McMillan.

Lowe, P., Jr. 1987. Interagency Language Roundtable Oral Proficiency Interview. In Alderson, Krahnke and Stansfield (eds.).

Lowe, P., Jr. 1988. The unassimilated history. In Lowe, Jr. and Stansfield (eds.).

Lowe, P., Jr. and R. T. Clifford. 1980. Developing an indirect measure of overall oral proficiency. In Frith (ed.).

Lowe, P., Jr. and C. W. Stansfield (eds.). 1988. *Second Language Proficiency Assessment: Current Issues.* Englewood Cliffs, NJ: Prentice Hall.

Luoma, S. 1997. *Comparability of a Tape-mediated and a Face-to-face Test of Speaking: A Triangulation Study.* Unpublished Licentiate thesis. Centre for Applied Language Studies, University of Jyvaskyla, Jyvaskyla.

Lynch, B. K. 1996. *Language Program Evaluation: Theory and Practice.* Cambridge: Cambridge University Press.

McNamara, T. F. 1987. *Assessing the Language Proficiency of Health Professionals. Recommendations for the Reform of the Occupational English Test. A Report submitted to the Council of Overseas Professional Qualifications.* Department of Russian and Language Studies, University of Melbourne, Melbourne.

McNamara, T. F. 1988. *The Development of an English as a Second Language Speaking Test for Health Professionals. Part One of a Report to the Council of Overseas Professional Qualifications on a Consultancy to Develop the Occupational English Test.* Department of Russian and Language Studies, University of Melbourne, Melbourne.

McNamara, T. F. 1990a. Item Response Theory and the validation of an ESP test for health professionals. *Language Testing* 7: 52–75.

McNamara, T. F. 1990b. *Assessing the second language proficiency of health professionals.* Unpublished PhD thesis, University of Melbourne.

McNamara, T. F. 1991. Test dimensionality: IRT analysis of an ESP listening test. *Language Testing* 8: 2, 139–59.

McNamara, T. F. 1996a. *Measuring second language performance: A new era in language testing.* London and New York: Longman.

McNamara, T. F. 1997. 'Interaction' in second language performance assessment: Whose performance? *Applied Linguistics* 18, 4: 446–66.

McNamara, T. F. and T. Lumley. 1993. The effects of interlocutor and assessment mode variables in offshore assessment of speaking skills in occupational settings. Paper presented at the 15th annual Language Testing Research Colloquium, Cambridge, England, August (ERIC Document Reproduction Service ED 364 066).

Meddis, R. 1984. *Statistics Using Ranks*. New York, NY: Basil Blackwell Inc.

Merriam, S. B. 1988. *Case Study Research in Education: A Qualitative Approach*. San Francisco: Jossey-Bass.

Messick, S. 1989. Validity. In Linn (ed.).

Miller, D. (ed.). 1983. *A Pocket Popper*. London: Fontana.

Morton, J. and G. Wigglesworth. 1994. Evaluating interviewer input in oral interaction tests. Paper presented at the Second Language Research Forum, Montreal.

Morton, J., G. Wigglesworth and D. Williams. 1997. Approaches to the evaluation of interviewer behaviour in oral tests. In Wigglesworth and Brindley (eds.).

Moss, P. A. 1994. Can there be validity without reliability? *Educational Researcher* 23: 2, 4–12.

Moss, P. A. 1996. Enlarging the dialogue in educational measurement: Voices from interpretive research traditions. *Educational Researcher* 25: 1, 20–8.

Neeson, S. 1985. *An Exploratory Study of the Discourse Structure of the Australian Second Language Proficiency Ratings Test of Oral Proficiency*. Unpublished M.A. thesis, University of Birmingham.

Nunan, D. 1992. *Research Methods in Education*. Cambridge: Cambridge University Press.

Perren, G. E. and J. L. M. Trim (eds.). 1971. *Applications of Linguistics*. Cambridge: Cambridge University Press.

Perrett, G. 1987. The language testing interview: A reappraisal. Paper given at the 8th World Congress of Applied Linguistics (AILA), Sydney.

Phillips, D. C. 1990. Postpositivistic science: Myths and realities. In Guba (ed.).

Pollitt, A. and N. L. Murray. 1993. What raters really pay attention to. Paper presented at the 15th annual Language Testing Research Colloquium, Cambridge and Arnhem.

Raffaldani, T. 1988. The use of situation tests as measures of communicative ability. *Studies in Second Language Acquisition* 10: 197–216.

Ross, S. and Berwick, R. 1993. The discourse of accommodation in oral proficiency interviews. *Studies in Second Language Acquisition* 14: 159–76.

Sato, C. J. 1985. Task variation in interlanguage phonology. In Gass and Madden (eds.).

Shephard, L. A. 1993. Evaluating test validity. *Review of Research in Education* 19: 405–50.

Shohamy, E. 1982. Affective considerations in language testing. *The Modern Language Journal* 66: 13–17.

Shohamy, E. 1983. The stability of the oral proficiency trait on the oral interview speaking test. *Language Learning* 33: 527–40.

Shohamy, E. 1994. The validity of direct versus semi-direct oral tests. *Language Testing* 11: 2, 99–23.

Shohamy, E., S. Donitsa-Schmidt and R. Waizer. 1993. The effect of the elicitation mode on the language samples obtained in oral tests. Paper presented at the 15th Language Testing Research Colloquium, Cambridge, England.

Shohamy, E., C. Gordon, D. M. Kenyon and C. W. Stansfield. 1989. The development and validation of a semi-direct test for assessing oral proficiency in Hebrew. *Bulletin of Hebrew Higher Education* 4: 1, 4–9.

Southard, B. and R. Sheorey. 1992. Measures of oral proficiency in English: A comparison of the rated interview and the test of spoken English. *College ESL* 2: 2, 52–67.

Spolsky, B. 1985. The limits of authenticity in language testing. *Language Testing* 2: 1, 31–40.

Spolsky, B. 1995. *Measured Words: The Development of Objective Language Testing.* Oxford: Oxford University Press.

Stake, R. E. 1988. Case study methods in educational research: Seeking sweet water. In Jaeger (ed.).

Stake, R. E. 1994. Case studies. In Denzin and Lincoln (eds.).

Stansfield, C. W. (ed.). 1985. *Technology and Language Testing.* Princeton, NJ: Education Testing Service.

Stansfield, C. W. 1991. A comparative analysis of simulated and direct oral proficiency interviews. In Anivan (ed.).

Stansfield, C. and D. Kenyon. 1988. *Development of the Portuguese Speaking Test.* Washington, DC: Center for Applied Linguistics.

Stansfield, C. and D. Kenyon. 1989. *Development of the Hausa, Hebrew and Indonesian Speaking Tests.* Washington, DC: Center for Applied Linguistics.

Stansfield, C. and D. Kenyon. 1992a. The development and validation of a simulated oral proficiency interview. *The Modern Language Journal* 72: 2, 129–41.

Stansfield, C. and D. Kenyon. 1992b. Research on the comparability of the oral proficiency interview and the simulated oral proficiency interview. *System* 20: 3, 347–64.

Stansfield, C., D. Kenyon, R. Paiva, F. Doyle, I. Ulsh and M. Cowles. 1990. The development and validation of the Portuguese speaking test. *Hispania* 73: 641–51.

Stevenson, D. 1985. Authenticity, validity, and a tea party. *Language Testing* 2: 1, 41–47.

Stubbs, M. 1986. Lexical density: A computational technique and some findings. In Coulthard (ed.).

Sunderland, J. 1995. Gender and language testing. *Language Testing Update* 17: 24–35.

UCLES 1999. *The IELTS Handbook 2000.* Cambridge: UCLES.

Underhill, N. 1987. *Testing Spoken Language: A Handbook of Oral Testing Techniques.* Cambridge: Cambridge University Press.

Ure, J. 1971. Lexical density and register differentiation. In G. E. Perren and J. L. M. Trim (eds.).

van Lier, L. 1989. Reeling, writhing, drawling, stretching, and fainting in coils: Oral proficiency interviews as conversations. *TESOL Quarterly* 23: 489–508.

Wigglesworth, G. 1993. Exploring bias analysis as a tool for improving rater consistency in assessing oral interaction. *Language Testing* 10: 3, 303–35.

Wigglesworth, G. 1994. *The Investigation of Rater and Task Variability using Multi-faceted Measurement.* Report for the National Centre for English Language Teaching and Research, Macquarie University, Sydney.

Wigglesworth, G. and K. O'Loughlin. 1993. An investigation into the comparability of direct and semi-direct versions of an oral interaction test in English. *Melbourne Papers in Language Testing* 2: 1, 56–67.

Willis, J. and D. Willis. 1988. *Collins COBUILD English Course, Level 1, Student's Book.* London: Collins.

Yin, R. 1989. *Case Study Research.* (second edition) Beverly Hills, CA: Sage Publications.

Zora, S. and C. Johns-Lewis. 1989. Lexical density in interview and conversation. *York Papers in Linguistics* 14: 89–100.

Appendices

1.1   Test specifications, *access:* oral interaction sub-test, May 1994

4.1   Scoring criteria and descriptors, oral interaction sub-test, December 1992

4.2   FACETS analyses (1) oral interaction sub-test, December 1992 trial (N = 83)

4.3   FACETS analyses (2) oral interaction sub-test, December 1992 trial (N = 76)

5.1   Lexical density figures (%) with unweighted lexical items, December 1992 trial (N = 20)

5.2   Lexical density figures (%) with weighted lexical items, December 1992 trial (N = 20)

6.1   Scoring criteria and descriptors, oral interaction sub-test, June 1994

6.2   Observation notes: Abdul and Wing Li, June 1994 trial

6.3   Questions for candidate interviews, June 1994 trial

6.4   Candidate questionnaire, June 1994 trial

6.5   Questions for interlocutor interviews, June 1994 trial

6.6   Raw scores allocated to Abdul and Wing Li, June 1994 trial

6.7   Questions for rater interviews, June 1994 trial

6.8   Rater questionnaire, June 1994 trial

7.1   FACETS analyses (1) with anchored item difficulty estimates, oral interaction sub-test, June 1994 trial (N = 94)

7.2   FACETS analyses (2) with unanchored item difficulty estimates, oral interaction sub-test, June 1994 trial (N = 94)

7.3   FACETS analyses (3) with unanchored item difficulty estimates, oral interaction sub-test, June 1994 trial (N = 89)

Appendix 1.1
Test specifications, *access:* oral interaction sub-test, May 1994

access:
australian assessment of communicative english skills

ORAL INTERACTION TEST SPECIFICATIONS

1 NATURE OF THE TEST

The Australian Assessment of Communicative English Skills Test (*access:*) is designed to assess the English language proficiency of certain categories of intending immigrants to Australia. Results of the assessment will be used to assist immigration personnel in making decisions concerning eligibility for immigration points and to provide information to educational authorities on-shore for educational placement purposes.

The Oral Interaction Test

The Oral Interaction Test is designed to measure candidates' oral interactive skills. Candidates undertake one of two formats: a live (direct) format consisting of face-to-face interactions conducted by a trained interlocutor, or a taped-based (semi-direct) format administered in a language laboratory. In selecting tasks for the test, cultural appropriacy and non-discriminatory language are considered. The assessment of the oral module complements those of the listening, reading and writing modules.

2 CONTENT

The contents of the direct and semi-direct format of the oral test are related to a variety of 'authentic' contexts. The contexts reflect those encountered by adults in Australia in the course of their everyday life, work or study. These tasks involve both transactional and interactional uses of language.

Possible topics:
advertising
celebrations and festivals
clothes and fashion
consumer issues education (e.g. systems and practices, providers,
    methods of teaching, study techniques)
employment (e.g. workplace practices – personnel, pay, regulations,
    holidays, health and safety, promotion, on-the-job training)

the environment
famous people
food
health and welfare
housing and architecture
immigration and settlement
the law
the media
money
places in Australia
recreation
transportation
social interaction
travel and tourism

3 LEVELS

The Oral Interaction Test is designed to measure the oral interactive skills of candidates within a range of five levels of proficiency. These levels can be broadly defined as follows:

Level five

Can communicate effectively in spoken English in a range of social, educational and work situations. Communication is appropriate with a high degree of fluency. Language is grammatically accurate most of the time with a wide range of vocabulary which is used effectively in most situations.

Level four

Can communicate adequately in spoken English to handle everyday communication in social, educational and work situations. Can communicate with a fair degree of fluency despite some grammatical inaccuracies. Vocabulary is wide enough to express most ideas, particularly in familiar situations.

Level three

Can communicate general information in spoken English in most everyday social situations. Can use basic grammatical structures although inaccuracies are frequent. Although vocabulary is limited at this level most common concepts can be expressed.

Level two

Can communicate in spoken English well enough to hold a very simple conversation. Limited control of basic grammatical structures. Vocabulary is limited to common words and phrases.

Level one

No practical speaking ability in English.

4 TEST STRUCTURE

Test length

Direct format

This format commences with an unassessed warm-up phase of 2–3 minutes, followed by the actual test of approximately 20 minutes' duration.

Semi-direct format

This format is tape mediated and administered in a language laboratory. An unassessed warm-up phase of 2–3 minutes' is followed by the actual test of approximately 30 minutes' duration.

Internal organisation

Both formats of the test have five sections, the first of which is an introductory warm up as outlined above. The number of items within each section will vary across versions, but the total length (approximately 20 minutes for the live format and 30 minutes for the tape-based format) will remain constant.

Tasks in the direct and semi-direct formats of the test are developed in tandem in an attempt to ensure the comparability of the two formats. Before administration of a test, a trialling procedure is carried out in which candidates undertake direct and semi-direct formats of the test. Subsequent statistical analyses of the trial results allow for concurrent validation of the two types of test.

5 ITEM TYPE/DISCOURSE FORM

For the purposes of comparability both formats of the test consist mainly of one-way exchanges (monologic) where the candidate is required to communicate information in response to prompts from the 'interlocutor'. However, on the direct format of the test, the role play allows for a more 'authentic' information gap activity in which meaning is negotiated between candidate and interviewer (dialogic).

Direct Format	Semi-direct Format
description	description
narration	narration
role play	role play
	summarising
exposition	exposition
discussion	discussion

6 LANGUAGE FUNCTIONS

Tasks on both formats of the test require candidates to use a range of language functions and sub-skills.

Sub-skills/functions
describing
comparing
interpreting
narrating
explaining
apologising
analysing
speculating
giving opinions
summarising
discussing

7 TASK FORMAT

Task stimuli

A variety of stimuli are used and some examples follow:

Direct Format	Semi-direct Format
cartoon pictures	cartoon pictures
photos	photos
set questions	set questions
role play cards	telephone messages
	recorded dialogue
maps, tables, charts, graphs	maps, tables, charts, graphs
brochures	brochures
memos	memos
advertisements	advertisements
notices	notices
circulars	circulars

Task structure

A Unplanned vs planned

- planned and unplanned activities are included
- planned tasks allow planning time and are designed to elicit more complex language
- unplanned tasks are designed to elicit spontaneous language

B Open vs closed

- both open tasks (those which are open ended with a range of possible solutions) and closed tasks (those which have a restricted set of responses) are included

C Divergent vs convergent

- divergent tasks are those which have no specific goal, and which involve decision making, using opinion and argument
- convergent tasks are problem-solving tasks in which the aim is to arrive at a common goal (see live role play)

8 SCORING PROCEDURE

For both formats of the test each candidate's tape is marked by two trained assessors in Australia. Individual tasks are assessed using appropriate scoring criteria such as fluency, grammar, intelligibility, vocabulary and cohesion. Each of these criteria is accompanied by a set of seven descriptors. All scoring is carried out on a Likert scale of 1 to 7. In both formats an overall or global assessment of the candidate's performance is made using the criterion of overall communicative effectiveness. This criterion does not have descriptors. In the live format, comprehension is also included as a global category. This is a measure of the candidate's ability to understand the interviewer, and is accompanied by a set of descriptors. A scoresheet and descriptors for all criteria are attached.

9 SUMMARY GRIDS

Summary grids of the two formats are included below.

SUMMARY GRID: LIVE FORMAT

Test structure	Task type	Language functions	Scoring
Section 1 Warm up 2–3 minutes	Interview: Monologic • 4–5 set questions • open, unplanned	stating personal details	unassessed
Section 2 **Part A** (i) 2–3 minutes (including 1 minute planning time)	Description: Monologic • 1–2 set questions about an illustration • planned, closed, 1-way information exchange	(i) detailed description	(i), (ii) & (iii) fluency, grammar, vocabulary
(ii) 2–3 minutes (including 1 minute planning time)	Description: Monologic • 1–2 set questions about a related illustration showing change or contrast vis-à-vis picture in (i) • planned, closed, 1-way information exchange	(ii) detailed description, comparing, contrasting	
(iii) optional, 1–2 minutes	Description: Monologic • 1 set question relating pictures to personal experience • planned, open, 1-way information exchange	(iii) detailed description, comparing, contrasting, speculating	
Part B 2–3 minutes (including 1 minute planning time if planned)	Narration: Monologic • 1–2 set questions about a sequence of 6–8 illustrations • planned or unplanned, closed, 1-way information exchange	narrating, describing, explaining, speculating	grammar, vocabulary, coherence & cohesion
Section 3 3–4 minutes (including 1 minute planning time)	Role play: Dialogic • Role-play cards (Interviewer – max 150 words, Candidate – max 100 words) • candidates play themselves & must have strong justification to negotiate • planned, closed, convergent, 2-way information exchange	negotiating, explaining, making excuses, making suggestions, apologising, persuading, describing	fluency, grammar, intelligibility
Section 4 2–3 minutes (including 1 minute planning time)	Describing a process: Monologic • 1–2 set questions about a diagrammatic display (e.g. map, set of illustrated instructions, chart, table of statistics) • planned, closed, 1-way information exchange	interpreting diagrams, describing, explaining, giving instructions, comparing, suggesting	fluency, vocabulary, coherence & cohesion
Section 5 up to 5 minutes (including 1 minute planning time if planned)	Discussion: Monologic • 4–5 set questions on issues of general personal/vocational interest • planned or unplanned, open, 1-way information exchange, (divergent if 2-way information exchange)	describing, narrating, explaining, giving opinions, speculating	fluency, grammar, intelligibility

Appendices

SUMMARY GRID: TAPE-BASED FORMAT

Test structure	Task type	Language functions	Scoring
Section 1 Warm up 10–20 seconds per question	Interview Monologic • 4–5 set questions • open, unplanned	stating personal details	unassessed
Section 2 **Part A** (i) 2–3 minutes (including 1 minute planning time)	Description: Monologic • 1–2 set questions about an illustration • planned, closed, 1-way information exchange	(i) detailed description	(i) & (ii) & (iii) fluency, grammar, vocabulary
(ii) 2–3 minutes (including 1 minute planning time)	Description: Monologic • 1–2 questions about a related illustration showing change or contrast vis-à-vis picture in (i) • planned, closed, 1-way information exchange	(ii) detailed description, comparing, contrasting	
(iii) optional, 1–2 minutes	Description: Monologic • 1 set question relating pictures to personal experience • planned, open, 1-way information exchange	(iii) detailed description, comparing, contrasting, speculating	
Part B 2–3 minutes (including 1 minute planning time if planned)	Narration: Monologic • 1–2 set questions about a sequence of 6–8 illustrations • planned or unplanned, closed, 1-way information exchange	narrating, describing, explaining, speculating	grammar, vocabulary, coherence & cohesion
Part C 3–4 minutes (including 1 minute planning time)	Summary: Monologic • 1–2 set questions • recorded dialogue or monologue (approx 300 words) on a general topic • planned, closed, 1-way information exchange	listening for main ideas, summarising	fluency, grammar, vocabulary
Section 3 up to 2 minutes (including 1 minute planning time)	Role play : Monologic • 3–4 sentence written telephone message and standard telephone answering machine recording • planned, closed, 1-way information exchange	explaining, apologising, making suggestions	fluency, grammar, intelligibility
Section 4 2–3 minutes (including 1 minute planning time)	Describing a process: Monologic • 1–2 set questions about a diagrammatic display (e.g. map, set of illustrated instructions, chart, table of statistics) • planned, closed, 1-way information exchange	interpreting diagrams, describing, explaining, giving instructions, comparing, suggesting	fluency, vocabulary, coherence & cohesion
Section 5 up to 5 minutes (including 1 minute planning time if planned)	Discussion: Monologic • 4–5 set questions on issues of general personal/vocational interest • planned or unplanned, open, 1-way information exchange	explaining, giving opinions, describing, narrating, intelligibility speculating	fluency, grammar

Appendix 4.1
Scoring criteria and descriptors, oral interaction sub-test, December 1992

FLUENCY
6 Speech is as fluent as, and of a speed similar to, an educated native speaker.
5 Speaks fluently with only occasional hesitation. Speech may be slightly slower than that of a native speaker.
4 Speaks more slowly than native speakers, with some hesitations and groping for words though without impeding communication.
3 A marked degree of hesitation, due to groping for words or inability to phrase utterances easily, impedes communication.
2 Speech is fragmented due to unacceptably frequent and long hesitations, pauses or false starts.
1 Fluency only evident in the most common formulaic phrases.

RESOURCES OF GRAMMAR
6 Range and control of a native speaker.
5 Able to communicate effectively using a broad range of structures with only minor errors.
4 Generally demonstrates control of a variety of structures with only occasional minor errors.
3 Is able to use a range of basic structures. Errors may be frequent and may sometimes interfere with communication.
2 Is able to use only a narrow range of basic structures. Errors are likely to be frequent and intrusive but limited communication is possible.
1 Severe limitations of grammar prevent all but the most basic communication.

VOCABULARY
6 Uses a wide range of vocabulary precisely, appropriately and effectively.
5 Has a wide vocabulary. Is able to use circumlocution easily and effectively.
4 Vocabulary is broad enough to allow the candidate to express most ideas well.
3 Vocabulary is adequate to express most simple ideas but limitations prevent expression of more sophisticated ideas.

2 Limited vocabulary restricts expression to simple ideas only. Circumlocution is laborious and often ineffective.

1 Very limited vocabulary. Able to express only the most basic ideas.

COHERENCE AND COHESION

6 Discourse is coherent. Cohesive devices are so smoothly and effectively managed as to attract attention.

5 Discourse is coherent. Cohesive devices are only occasionally misused.

4 Discourse is generally coherent. Cohesive devices may be limited in range or sometimes used inappropriately or inaccurately.

3 Usually able to link sentences using more common cohesive devices. Longer utterances may be incoherent.

2 Some evidence of connected discourse but overall effect is disjointed. Cannot sustain coherent structures in longer utterances.

1 Able to use only isolated words and formulaic phrases.

APPROPRIACY

6 Uses language as appropriately and effectively as an educated native speaker.

5 Sensitive to register requirements. Generally responds appropriately to unpredictable turns in conversation.

4 Demonstrates good awareness of social conventions and has some ability to respond to unpredictable turns in conversation, though may sound unnatural.

3 Has some awareness of social conventions but often has difficulty responding appropriately to unpredictable turns in conversation.

2 Has limited awareness of social conventions. Essentially unable to cope with unpredictable turns in conversation.

1 Essentially unable to respond appropriately to register requirements.

INTELLIGIBILITY

6 Speech can be followed effortlessly by the interlocutor.

5 Speech causes the interlocutor only occasional strain and can generally be followed effortlessly.

4 Speech requires some concentration and may require occasional clarification by the interlocutor.

3 Speech requires concentration and/or clarification by/on the part of the interlocutor.

2 Speech can only be understood with constant effort. Repeated clarification may be needed.

1 Speech often unintelligible even with considerable effort on the part of the interlocutor.

COMPREHENSION (live version only)

6 Rarely misunderstands, except occasionally when speech is very rapid or ambiguous.

5 Appears to have only occasional problems in understanding.

4 Appears to be able to understand most speech but may require repetition of details.

3 Generally able to get gist of most speech but may require repetition. More comfortable with slower rates of speech.

2 Often has difficulty understanding utterances. May require frequent repetition or reformulation.

1 Demonstrates only intermittent comprehension even of simplified speech.

OVERALL COMMUNICATIVE EFFECTIVENESS

Scale of 1 to 6 (6 = near native flexibility and range; 1 = limited).

Appendix 4.2
FACETS analyses (1) oral interaction sub-test, December 1992 trial (N = 83)

A   Live data

(i) Candidates

Obsvd Score	Obsvd Count	Obsvd Average	Fair Avrge	Calib Logit	Model Error	Infit MnSq	Infit Std	Outfit MnSq	Outfit Std	Cand
715	138	5.2	5.4	3.94	0.13	1.2	2	1.2	1	1
466	138	3.4	3.4	-0.37	0.13	0.8	-1	0.8	-1	2
482	138	3.5	3.5	-0.09	0.13	0.7	-2	0.7	-2	3
587	138	4.3	4.4	1.82	0.13	0.8	-1	0.8	-1	4
496	138	3.6	3.7	0.24	0.13	1.0	0	1.0	0	5
578	138	4.2	4.3	1.67	0.13	1.4	3	1.5	3	6
593	138	4.3	4.4	1.84	0.13	0.8	-2	0.8	-1	7
495	138	3.6	3.7	0.22	0.13	0.7	-3	0.7	-3	8
672	138	4.9	5.1	3.24	0.13	1.1	0	1.2	1	9
436	138	3.2	3.2	-0.80	0.13	1.0	0	0.9	0	10
616	138	4.5	4.3	1.82	0.13	1.1	0	1.1	0	11
562	138	4.1	4.0	0.94	0.13	0.9	0	0.9	0	12
506	138	3.7	3.6	0.08	0.12	1.1	1	1.1	0	13
560	138	4.1	4.0	1.00	0.13	0.8	-1	0.8	-1	15
417	138	3.0	2.9	-1.30	0.12	0.8	-1	0.8	-1	16
582	138	4.2	4.1	1.35	0.13	1.8	5	1.8	5	17
255	135	1.9	1.7	-3.81	0.14	1.1	1	1.0	0	18
536	138	3.9	3.8	0.63	0.12	1.1	0	1.1	0	19
629	138	4.6	4.4	2.03	0.13	1.6	4	1.5	3	20
541	138	3.9	3.9	0.46	0.13	0.8	-1	0.8	-1	22
780	138	5.7	5.7	5.19	0.18	1.0	0	1.1	0	24
377	138	2.7	2.6	-2.30	0.13	1.1	1	1.1	0	25
484	138	3.5	3.4	-0.60	0.13	0.7	-2	0.7	-2	26
674	138	4.9	4.9	2.81	0.14	0.9	0	0.9	0	27
734	138	5.3	5.4	4.04	0.15	0.8	-1	0.8	-1	28
591	138	4.3	4.3	1.33	0.13	0.7	-2	0.8	-1	29
569	138	4.1	4.1	0.86	0.13	1.0	0	1.0	0	30
620	138	4.5	4.5	2.18	0.13	1.1	1	1.1	1	31
601	138	4.4	4.3	1.85	0.13	0.9	0	0.9	0	32
494	137	3.6	3.5	-0.02	0.13	1.1	0	1.1	1	33
523	138	3.8	3.7	0.44	0.13	1.1	0	1.1	1	34
283	136	2.1	2.0	-3.76	0.14	1.3	2	1.3	2	35
555	138	4.0	4.0	1.02	0.13	1.1	0	1.1	0	36
702	138	5.1	5.2	3.67	0.13	0.9	0	1.0	0	37
336	131	2.6	2.4	-2.54	0.13	1.5	3	1.4	3	38
560	138	4.1	4.0	1.20	0.13	0.7	-2	0.7	-2	39
758	138	5.5	5.5	4.64	0.15	1.2	1	1.2	1	40
292	135	2.2	2.0	-3.36	0.13	1.2	1	1.0	0	43
577	137	4.2	4.1	1.02	0.13	0.9	-1	0.9	-1	45
713	138	5.2	5.1	3.30	0.14	0.7	-2	0.7	-2	46
268	138	1.9	1.8	-3.90	0.14	0.9	0	1.0	0	47
569	134	4.2	4.1	0.99	0.13	1.1	0	1.1	0	48

Live data – candidates (continued)

Obsvd Score	Obsvd Count	Obsvd Average	Fair Avrge	Calib Logit	Model Error	Infit MnSq	Std	Outfit MnSq	Std	Cand
557	138	4.0	3.9	0.56	0.12	0.9	0	0.9	0	49
556	137	4.1	3.9	0.70	0.12	0.9	-1	0.9	0	50
389	138	2.8	2.6	-2.10	0.13	1.2	1	1.2	1	51
499	138	3.6	3.4	-0.31	0.13	1.0	0	0.9	0	52
727	138	5.3	5.2	3.65	0.14	0.7	-3	0.7	-3	53
507	138	3.7	3.6	-0.08	0.13	0.8	-1	0.8	-2	54
538	138	3.9	3.7	0.34	0.13	1.0	0	1.0	0	55
646	138	4.7	4.5	2.14	0.13	0.9	0	0.9	0	56
351	138	2.5	2.3	-2.64	0.13	0.9	0	1.0	0	57
480	136	3.5	3.4	-0.49	0.13	1.0	0	1.0	0	58
694	137	5.1	5.0	3.08	0.14	0.9	-1	0.9	-1	60
676	138	4.9	4.8	2.67	0.13	1.1	0	1.1	1	61
648	138	4.7	4.7	2.51	0.14	0.9	0	0.9	0	62
530	138	3.8	3.8	0.36	0.13	1.0	0	0.9	0	63
538	138	3.9	3.9	0.50	0.13	0.7	-2	0.7	-2	64
500	138	3.6	3.6	-0.27	0.13	0.7	-2	0.7	-2	66
549	138	4.0	4.0	0.70	0.13	1.0	0	1.0	0	67
617	135	4.6	4.5	2.09	0.14	0.9	0	0.9	0	68
529	138	3.8	3.8	0.25	0.13	0.6	-4	0.6	-4	69
559	136	4.1	4.1	0.95	0.14	0.8	-1	0.8	-1	70
510	136	3.8	3.7	0.06	0.13	1.0	0	1.0	0	71
502	138	3.6	3.6	-0.16	0.13	1.2	1	1.2	1	72
538	135	4.0	3.7	0.21	0.13	1.3	2	1.3	2	74
548	138	4.0	3.7	0.21	0.13	1.1	0	1.1	0	75
738	138	5.3	5.2	3.69	0.15	1.1	0	1.2	1	77
697	138	5.1	4.8	2.79	0.14	1.1	0	1.0	0	78
583	138	4.2	3.9	0.67	0.13	0.9	-1	0.8	-1	79
559	138	4.1	3.8	0.38	0.13	1.4	2	1.3	2	80
575	138	4.2	3.8	0.55	0.13	1.0	0	1.0	0	81
674	138	4.9	4.6	2.24	0.14	0.7	-3	0.6	-3	82
634	138	4.6	4.3	1.52	0.13	0.7	-2	0.7	-2	83
489	138	3.5	3.4	-0.49	0.13	1.6	4	1.6	4	84
565	138	4.1	3.9	0.75	0.14	0.9	0	0.9	-1	85
670	138	4.9	4.7	2.75	0.14	1.0	0	1.0	0	86
502	138	3.6	3.5	-0.36	0.13	1.9	5	1.9	5	87
329	138	2.4	2.2	-3.02	0.13	0.9	0	1.0	0	88
650	138	4.7	4.6	2.36	0.14	1.0	0	1.0	0	89
761	138	5.5	5.5	4.76	0.16	0.9	0	0.9	0	90
515	138	3.7	3.6	-0.05	0.13	0.9	-1	0.9	-1	92
682	138	4.9	4.9	3.08	0.14	1.1	0	1.1	0	93
773	138	5.6	5.6	5.09	0.17	0.8	-1	0.7	-1	94

Obsvd Score	Obsvd Count	Obsvd Average	Fair Avrge	Calib Logit	Model Error	Infit MnSq	Std	Outfit MnSq	Std	Cand
558.7	137.6	4.1	4.0	0.90	0.13	1.0	-0.1	1.0	-0.2	Mean
117.4	1.1	0.8	0.9	2.00	0.01	0.2	1.9	0.2	1.9	S.D.

RMSE 0.13 Adj S.D. 2.00 Separation 14.87 Reliability 1.00
Fixed (all same) chi-square: 17033.94 d.f.: 82 significance: .00
Random (normal) chi-square: 81.96 d.f.: 81 significance: .45

(ii) Raters

Obsvd Score	Obsvd Count	Obsvd Average	Fair Avrge	Measure Logit	Model Error	Infit MnSq	Std	Outfit MnSq	Std	Rater
1489	457	3.3	2.7	1.14	0.07	0.9	-1	1.0	0	1
1120	363	3.1	2.9	1.00	0.07	0.9	-1	0.9	-1	2
1738	414	4.2	3.6	0.41	0.08	0.7	-4	0.7	-3	3
1910	459	4.2	3.9	0.07	0.08	1.1	1	1.1	1	4
1806	368	4.9	4.6	-1.36	0.08	1.2	2	1.1	1	5
1922	460	4.2	3.8	-0.78	0.07	0.9	-1	0.9	-1	6
1729	457	3.8	3.4	1.28	0.07	0.9	-1	0.9	-1	7
1737	414	4.2	3.8	-0.92	0.07	1.2	2	1.2	2	8
1765	414	4.3	3.9	0.84	0.09	1.0	0	0.9	0	9
7423	1900	3.9	3.5	0.04	0.04	1.0	0	1.0	0	10
6666	1902	3.5	3.1	0.91	0.04	1.2	5	1.2	5	11
8870	1909	4.6	4.4	-1.38	0.04	1.1	2	1.0	1	12
8193	1902	4.3	4.0	-1.25	0.04	0.8	-5	0.8	-5	13
3566.8	878.4	4.0	3.6	0.00	0.06	1.0	-0.2	1.0	-0.3	Mean
2857.8	683.9	0.5	0.5	0.98	0.02	0.1	2.8	0.1	2.7	S.D.

RMSE 0.07 Adj S.D. 0.97 Separation 14.66 Reliability 1.00
Fixed (all same) chi-square: 4532.47 d.f.: 12 significance: .00
Random (normal) chi-square: 12.00 d.f.: 11 significance: .36

(iii) Items

Obsvd Score	Obsvd Count	Obsvd Average	Fair Avrge	Measure Logit	Model Error	Infit MnSq	Std	Outfit MnSq	Std	Nu Item
2181	498	4.4	3.9	-0.79	0.07	1.0	0	1.0	0	1 DesF
1961	498	3.9	3.5	0.29	0.07	0.8	-3	0.8	-3	2 DesG
2010	497	4.0	3.6	0.04	0.07	1.0	0	1.0	0	3 DesV
2147	497	4.3	3.9	-0.64	0.07	0.8	-3	0.8	-3	4 NarF
1878	498	3.8	3.3	0.69	0.07	0.7	-4	0.7	-4	5 NarG
1905	498	3.8	3.4	0.56	0.07	0.8	-3	0.8	-3	6 NarV
2075	498	4.2	3.7	-0.26	0.07	1.0	0	1.0	0	7 NarC
2036	498	4.1	3.6	-0.07	0.07	1.0	0	1.0	0	8 Exp1F
1797	498	3.6	3.1	1.08	0.07	0.9	-2	0.9	-2	9 Exp1G
2050	497	4.1	3.7	-0.14	0.07	1.0	0	1.1	0	10 RP1F
1872	497	3.8	3.3	0.72	0.07	1.0	0	1.0	0	11 RP1G
1991	497	4.0	3.5	0.14	0.07	2.0	9	2.0	9	12 RP1A
2109	494	4.3	3.8	-0.48	0.07	0.9	-1	0.9	-1	13 RP2F
1893	492	3.8	3.4	0.55	0.07	0.9	0	0.9	0	14 RP2G
2047	494	4.1	3.7	-0.17	0.07	1.5	6	1.5	6	15 RP2A
2135	498	4.3	3.8	-0.56	0.07	0.8	-3	0.8	-3	16 Exp2F
1913	498	3.8	3.4	0.53	0.07	0.8	-4	0.8	-3	17 Exp2G
2169	497	4.4	3.9	-0.75	0.07	0.9	-2	0.8	-2	18 DisF
1910	496	3.9	3.4	0.51	0.07	0.8	-2	0.8	-2	19 DisG
2022	494	4.1	3.6	-0.07	0.07	0.9	-1	0.9	-1	20 DisV
2076	497	4.2	3.7	-0.28	0.07	1.3	4	1.3	4	21 Int
1975	494	4.0	3.5	0.15	0.07	0.9	-1	0.9	-1	22 ComEf
2216	494	4.5	4.1	-1.06	0.07	1.4	5	1.3	4	23 Comp

Live data – items (continued)

Obsvd Score	Obsvd Count	Obsvd Average	Fair Avrge	Measure Logit	Model Error	Infit MnSq	Std	Outfit MnSq	Std	Nu Item
2016.0	496.5	4.1	3.6	0.00	0.07	1.0	-0.4	1.0	-0.5	Mean
110.9	1.8	0.2	0.2	0.55	0.00	0.3	3.5	0.3	3.4|	S.D.

RMSE 0.07 Adj S.D. 0.55 Separation 7.77 Reliability 0.98
Fixed (all same) chi-square: 1400.51 d.f.: 22 significance: .00
Random (normal) chi-square: 22.00 d.f.: 21 significance: .40

(iv) Order

Obsvd Score	Obsvd Count	Obsvd Average	Fair Avrge	Measure Logit	Model Error	Infit MnSq	Std	Outfit MnSq	Std	N Order
20887	5384	3.9	3.6	0.05	0.02	1.0	2	1.0	11	First
25481	6035	4.2	3.6	-0.05	0.02	1.0	-1	1.0	-22	Second
23184.0	5709.5	4.1	3.6	0.00	0.02	1.0	0.3	1.0	-0.1	Mean
2297.0	325.5	0.2	0.0	0.05	0.00	0.0	1.9	0.0	2.0|	S.D.

RMSE 0.02 Adj S.D. 0.04 Separation 2.03 Reliability 0.80
Fixed (all same) chi-square: 10.21 d.f.: 1 significance: .00
Random (normal) chi-square: 1.00 d.f.: 0 significance: 1.00

B   Tape data

(i) Candidates

Obsvd Score	Obsvd Count	Obsvd Average	Fair Avrge	Calib Logit	Model Error	Infit MnSq	Std	Outfit MnSq	Std	Cand
686	142	4.8	4.8	2.89	0.14	0.8	-2	0.8	-1	1
464	144	3.2	3.3	-0.86	0.13	0.9	-1	0.9	-1	2
515	144	3.6	3.6	0.01	0.13	0.9	-1	0.9	-1	3
660	144	4.6	4.5	2.23	0.14	0.7	-3	0.7	-3	4
563	144	3.9	3.8	0.48	0.13	0.8	-1	0.8	-1	5
663	144	4.6	4.5	2.29	0.14	0.8	-1	0.8	-1	6
647	144	4.5	4.6	2.34	0.14	0.8	-2	0.8	-2	7
519	144	3.6	3.5	-0.28	0.13	0.9	-1	0.9	-1	8
668	144	4.6	4.6	2.38	0.14	1.2	1	1.1	1	9
537	143	3.8	3.7	0.09	0.13	1.3	2	1.3	2	10
717	144	5.0	4.9	3.48	0.15	1.0	0	1.0	0	11
584	144	4.1	4.0	0.91	0.13	1.0	0	1.0	0	12
510	143	3.6	3.5	-0.38	0.13	0.6	-3	0.6	-3	13
549	144	3.8	3.6	-0.07	0.13	0.9	-1	0.9	0	15
488	144	3.4	3.3	-0.82	0.13	0.8	-1	0.8	-1	16
488	116	4.2	3.9	0.82	0.15	0.8	-1	0.8	-1	17
331	136	2.4	2.0	-3.58	0.13	1.4	2	1.4	2	18
633	144	4.4	4.2	1.46	0.14	0.9	0	0.9	0	19
700	144	4.9	4.8	3.12	0.14	1.6	4	1.5	3	20
605	144	4.2	4.1	1.22	0.14	1.2	1	1.2	1	22
783	144	5.4	5.5	5.17	0.16	1.0	0	1.0	0	24
443	144	3.1	2.9	-1.75	0.14	0.9	0	1.0	0	25
499	144	3.5	3.5	-0.36	0.14	1.0	0	1.0	0	26
673	144	4.7	4.6	2.50	0.14	0.8	-1	0.9	0	27
737	144	5.1	5.0	3.78	0.15	0.9	0	0.9	0	28
612	144	4.3	4.1	1.35	0.14	1.0	0	1.0	0	29
568	144	3.9	4.0	0.89	0.13	1.0	0	1.0	0	30
607	144	4.2	4.2	1.57	0.14	1.4	3	1.5	3	31
623	144	4.3	4.3	1.87	0.14	0.6	-3	0.7	-3	32
487	144	3.4	3.3	-0.59	0.13	1.0	0	1.0	0	33
563	144	3.9	3.9	0.77	0.13	1.0	0	1.0	0	34
401	144	2.8	2.7	-2.07	0.13	0.8	-1	0.8	-1	35
521	144	3.6	3.6	0.02	0.13	1.0	0	1.0	0	36
751	144	5.2	5.1	4.08	0.15	0.9	-1	0.9	-1	37
366	142	2.6	2.3	-2.92	0.13	1.3	2	1.3	2	38
626	144	4.3	4.2	1.58	0.14	0.6	-3	0.6	-3	39
796	144	5.5	5.5	5.57	0.17	1.6	4	1.7	4	40
377	144	2.6	2.4	-3.01	0.14	1.4	3	1.4	2	43
580	144	4.0	3.9	0.72	0.13	1.0	0	1.1	0	45
742	144	5.2	5.2	4.11	0.14	1.3	2	1.3	2	46
462	144	3.2	3.0	-1.44	0.14	1.1	0	1.1	0	47
543	144	3.8	3.8	0.41	0.13	1.1	0	1.1	0	48
473	135	3.5	3.5	-0.33	0.14	2.2	7	2.3	7	49
596	144	4.1	4.0	1.00	0.13	0.7	-2	0.7	-2	50
461	143	3.2	3.2	-0.63	0.14	1.0	0	1.0	0	51
509	144	3.5	3.6	0.18	0.13	1.0	0	1.0	0	52
716	144	5.0	5.1	3.88	0.14	1.0	0	1.1	0	53
378	120	3.2	3.0	-1.18	0.15	0.7	-2	0.7	-2	54
593	144	4.1	4.2	1.68	0.13	1.1	1	1.2	1	55
581	143	4.1	4.1	1.54	0.13	0.7	-3	0.7	-2	56
462	144	3.2	3.1	-1.03	0.14	0.7	-2	0.7	-2	57
443	144	3.1	3.1	-1.03	0.14	1.2	1	1.2	1	58
624	144	4.3	4.4	2.23	0.13	0.9	0	0.9	-1	60
636	140	4.5	4.6	2.77	0.13	0.9	0	0.9	-1	61
706	144	4.9	4.8	2.96	0.13	0.7	-2	0.8	-2	62
546	144	3.8	3.6	0.25	0.13	0.9	-1	0.9	-1	63

Tape data – candidates (continued)

Obsvd Score	Obsvd Count	Obsvd Average	Fair Avrge	Calib Logit	Model Error	Infit MnSq	Std	Outfit MnSq	Std	Cand
533	144	3.7	3.6	0.02	0.13	0.9	0	0.9	-1	64
487	141	3.5	3.4	-0.28	0.14	0.8	-1	0.8	-1	66
579	143	4.0	3.9	0.89	0.13	0.8	-2	0.8	-1	67
713	143	5.0	5.0	3.53	0.14	0.6	-3	0.6	-3	68
527	143	3.7	3.7	0.33	0.13	0.8	-1	0.8	-1	69
638	144	4.4	4.4	2.15	0.13	0.8	-2	0.8	-1	70
590	144	4.1	4.1	1.35	0.13	1.0	0	1.0	0	71
630	144	4.4	4.2	1.67	0.13	0.8	-1	0.8	-2	72
569	144	4.0	3.9	0.95	0.13	1.3	2	1.3	2	74
500	138	3.6	3.6	0.22	0.13	1.7	4	1.7	4	75
691	144	4.8	4.8	3.09	0.13	0.7	-2	0.7	-2	77
683	144	4.7	4.7	2.95	0.13	0.9	0	1.0	0	78
530	144	3.7	3.8	0.63	0.13	1.0	0	1.1	0	79
561	143	3.9	3.9	0.87	0.13	0.8	-1	0.8	-1	80
482	143	3.4	3.4	-0.14	0.13	0.8	-1	0.9	-1	81
635	144	4.4	4.5	2.45	0.13	1.0	0	0.9	0	82
583	144	4.0	4.2	1.54	0.13	0.8	-1	0.8	-1	83
477	134	3.6	3.3	-0.62	0.14	1.4	2	1.5	3	84
612	144	4.3	4.1	1.50	0.13	1.5	3	1.5	3	85
683	144	4.7	4.6	2.73	0.13	0.9	0	0.9	0	86
469	144	3.3	3.1	-1.14	0.14	1.3	2	1.4	2	87
379	143	2.7	2.2	-3.11	0.13	1.1	0	1.1	0	88
719	144	5.0	4.9	3.37	0.14	1.0	0	0.9	0	89
771	144	5.4	5.3	4.41	0.15	1.1	1	1.2	1	90
587	144	4.1	3.8	0.72	0.13	0.7	-2	0.7	-2	92
734	144	5.1	4.8	3.30	0.14	1.1	0	1.1	0	93
776	143	5.4	5.3	4.61	0.16	1.0	0	1.0	0	94

Obsvd Score	Obsvd Count	Obsvd Average	Fair Avrge	Calib Logit	Model Error	Infit MnSq	Std	Outfit MnSq	Std	Cand
580.1	142.7	4.1	4.0	1.09	0.14	1.0	-0.2	1.0	-0.2	Mean
107.4	4.3	0.7	0.8	1.92	0.01	0.3	2.1	0.3	2.1	S.D.

RMSE 0.14 Adj S.D. 1.92 Separation 14.05 Reliability 0.99
Fixed (all same) chi-square: 15752.04 d.f.: 82 significance: .00
Random (normal) chi-square: 81.97 d.f.: 81 significance: .45

(ii) Raters

Obsvd Score	Obsvd Count	Obsvd Average	Fair Avrge	Measure Logit	Model Error	Infit MnSq	Std	Outfit MnSq	Std	Rater
1616	405	4.0	3.6	0.79	0.08	1.0	0	1.0	0	1
1425	455	3.1	2.6	1.59	0.07	0.8	-2	0.8	-2	2
1938	480	4.0	3.3	-0.30	0.07	0.8	-2	0.9	-2	3
1842	456	4.0	3.5	0.23	0.07	1.0	0	1.0	0	4
2101	455	4.6	4.3	-1.56	0.08	1.2	3	1.2	3	5
1754	432	4.1	3.5	1.35	0.08	1.0	0	1.0	0	6
1688	452	3.7	3.5	0.49	0.08	1.1	0	1.1	1	7
1438	360	4.0	3.6	-0.25	0.09	1.5	5	1.5	5	8
1920	480	4.0	3.7	-0.42	0.08	0.9	0	1.0	0	9
7233	1976	3.7	3.1	0.63	0.03	1.0	0	1.0	0	10
7522	1943	3.9	3.5	-0.12	0.04	1.1	2	1.1	2	11
9114	1973	4.6	4.2	-1.50	0.04	0.9	-2	0.9	-2	12
8558	1978	4.3	4.0	-0.93	0.04	0.9	-2	0.9	-1	13
3703.8	911.2	4.0	3.6	-0.00	0.06	1.0	-0.0	1.0	0.2	Mean
2971.1	704.9	0.4	0.4	0.94	0.02	0.2	2.4	0.2	2.3	S.D.

RMSE 0.07 Adj S.D. 0.94 Separation 14.00 Reliability 0.99
Fixed (all same) chi-square: 3764.40 d.f.: 12 significance: .00
Random (normal) chi-square: 12.00 d.f.: 11 significance: .36

(iii) Items

Obsvd Score	Obsvd Count	Obsvd Average	Fair Avrge	Measure Logit	Model Error	Infit MnSq	Std	Outfit MnSq	Std	Nu Item
2141	494	4.3	3.9	-0.72	0.07	1.2	2	1.2	3	24 TDesF
1930	494	3.9	3.4	0.41	0.07	0.8	-2	0.9	-1	25 TDesG
1946	493	3.9	3.4	0.31	0.07	1.0	0	1.1	0	26 TDesV
2078	497	4.2	3.7	-0.31	0.07	0.9	-1	0.9	0	27 TNarF
1839	497	3.7	3.2	0.95	0.07	0.7	-5	0.7	-5	28 TNarG
1850	496	3.7	3.2	0.87	0.07	0.8	-3	0.8	-2	29 TNarV
2028	496	4.1	3.6	-0.07	0.07	1.0	0	1.0	0	30 TNarC
1978	488	4.1	3.5	0.07	0.07	1.1	1	1.1	1	31 TExp1F
1818	487	3.7	3.2	0.91	0.07	0.9	-2	0.8	-2	32 TExp2G
2183	497	4.4	3.9	-0.88	0.07	1.1	1	1.1	1	33 TRP1F
1973	497	4.0	3.5	0.25	0.07	0.8	-2	0.8	-2	34 TRP1G
2211	496	4.5	4.0	-1.05	0.07	1.3	3	1.3	3	35 TRP11A
2109	489	4.3	3.8	-0.65	0.07	1.1	1	1.1	1	36 TRP2F
1909	489	3.9	3.4	0.43	0.07	0.9	-1	0.9	-1	37 TRP2G
1991	489	4.1	3.6	-0.01	0.07	1.8	9	1.9	9	38 TRP2A
2114	494	4.3	3.8	-0.56	0.07	0.9	-1	0.9	-1	39 TExp2F
1880	493	3.8	3.3	0.66	0.07	0.8	-2	0.8	-2	40 TExp2G
2136	494	4.3	3.8	-0.68	0.07	0.9	0	1.0	0	41 TDisF
1923	494	3.9	3.4	0.46	0.07	0.8	-2	0.8	-2	42 TDisG
1956	488	4.0	3.5	0.16	0.07	0.9	-1	0.9	-1	43 TDisV
2097	496	4.2	3.7	-0.43	0.07	1.3	4	1.3	3	44 TInt
2011	494	4.1	3.6	-0.03	0.07	0.9	-1	0.9	-2	45 TComEf
2137	497	4.3	3.8	-0.63	0.07	0.9	-1	0.9	-1	46 TSumF
1911	496	3.9	3.3	0.55	0.07	0.8	-3	0.8	-3	47 TSumG

Tape data – items (continued)

Obsvd Score	Obsvd Count	Obsvd Average	Fair Avrge	Measure Logit	Model Error	Infit MnSq	Std	Outfit MnSq	Std	Nu Item
2006.2	493.5	4.1	3.6	-0.00	0.07	1.0	-0.5	1.0	-0.3	Mean
112.7	3.3	0.2	0.2	0.59	0.00	0.2	3.0	0.2	3.0	S.D.

RMSE 0.07 Adj S.D. 0.58 Separation 7.95 Reliability 0.98
Fixed (all same) chi-square: 1535.03 d.f.: 23 significance: .00
Random (normal) chi-square: 23.00 d.f.: 22 significance: .40

(iv) Order

Obsvd Score	Obsvd Count	Obsvd Average	Fair Avrge	Measure Logit	Model Error	Infit MnSq	Std	Outfit MnSq	Std	N Order
25946	6314	4.1	3.5	0.17	0.02	1.0	0	1.0	1	First
22203	5531	4.0	3.6	-0.17	0.02	1.0	-1	1.0	-1	Second
24074.5	5922.5	4.1	3.6	0.00	0.02	1.0	-0.7	1.0	-0.1	Mean
1871.5	391.5	0.0	0.1	0.17	0.00	0.0	1.3	0.0	1.6	S.D.

RMSE 0.02 Adj S.D. 0.17 Separation 8.06 Reliability 0.98
Fixed (all same) chi-square: 131.86 d.f.: 1 significance: .00
Random (normal) chi-square: 1.00 d.f.: 0 significance: 1.00

C   Combined data

(i) Candidates

Obsvd Score	Obsvd Count	Obsvd Average	Fair Avrge	Calib Logit	Model Error	Infit MnSq	Std	Outfit MnSq	Std	Cand
1401	280	5.0	5.1	3.40	0.09	1.1	1	1.1	1	1
930	282	3.3	3.3	-0.48	0.09	0.8	-2	0.8	-2	2
997	282	3.5	3.6	0.03	0.09	0.8	-3	0.8	-2	3
1247	282	4.4	4.5	2.01	0.09	0.7	-4	0.7	-3	4
1059	282	3.8	3.8	0.51	0.09	0.9	0	0.9	-1	5
1241	282	4.4	4.4	1.96	0.09	1.1	0	1.1	0	6
1240	282	4.4	4.4	1.95	0.09	0.8	-2	0.8	-2	7
1014	282	3.6	3.6	0.16	0.09	0.8	-2	0.8	-2	8
1340	282	4.8	4.8	2.79	0.09	1.3	3	1.3	3	9
973	281	3.5	3.5	-0.13	0.09	1.1	0	1.1	1	10
1333	282	4.7	4.8	2.64	0.09	1.2	2	1.2	1	11
1146	282	4.1	4.1	1.12	0.09	0.9	-1	0.9	-1	12
1016	281	3.6	3.6	0.14	0.09	0.9	-1	0.9	-1	13
1109	282	3.9	4.0	0.83	0.09	1.0	0	1.0	0	15
905	282	3.2	3.2	-0.71	0.09	0.8	-3	0.8	-2	16
1070	254	4.2	4.2	1.44	0.09	1.4	4	1.4	3	17
586	271	2.2	2.1	-2.86	0.09	1.2	2	1.1	1	18
1169	282	4.1	4.2	1.30	0.09	1.0	0	1.0	0	19
1329	282	4.7	4.8	2.60	0.09	1.5	4	1.4	4	20
1146	282	4.1	4.0	1.08	0.09	0.8	-2	0.8	-2	22
1563	282	5.5	5.6	4.82	0.11	0.9	0	0.9	0	24
820	282	2.9	2.8	-1.45	0.09	0.9	0	0.9	0	25
983	282	3.5	3.4	-0.19	0.09	0.8	-2	0.8	-2	26
1347	282	4.8	4.8	2.70	0.09	0.8	-2	0.8	-2	27
1471	282	5.2	5.2	3.81	0.10	0.9	-1	0.9	-1	28
1203	282	4.3	4.2	1.54	0.09	0.8	-2	0.8	-2	29
1137	282	4.0	4.0	1.01	0.09	0.9	0	0.9	0	30
1227	282	4.4	4.4	1.85	0.09	1.3	3	1.4	3	31
1224	282	4.3	4.4	1.82	0.09	0.9	-1	0.9	-1	32
981	281	3.5	3.5	-0.09	0.09	1.0	0	1.1	0	33
1086	282	3.9	3.9	0.71	0.09	1.0	0	1.0	0	34
684	280	2.4	2.4	-2.23	0.08	1.2	2	1.2	2	35
1076	282	3.8	3.9	0.63	0.09	1.2	1	1.2	1	36
1453	282	5.2	5.2	3.80	0.10	1.0	0	1.0	0	37
702	273	2.6	2.5	-2.02	0.08	1.2	1	1.2	1	38
1186	282	4.2	4.2	1.52	0.09	0.6	-5	0.6	-5	39
1554	282	5.5	5.6	4.86	0.11	1.3	3	1.3	3	40
669	279	2.4	2.4	-2.29	0.08	1.1	1	1.1	1	43
1157	281	4.1	4.2	1.27	0.09	0.9	-1	0.9	-1	45
1455	282	5.2	5.3	3.71	0.10	1.0	0	1.0	0	46
730	282	2.6	2.6	-1.92	0.08	1.5	5	1.6	5	47
1112	278	4.0	4.0	1.03	0.09	1.1	1	1.1	1	48
1030	273	3.8	3.8	0.51	0.09	1.7	7	1.7	7	49
1152	281	4.1	4.1	1.24	0.09	0.9	-1	0.9	-1	50
850	281	3.0	3.1	-0.96	0.09	1.1	1	1.1	1	51
1008	282	3.6	3.6	0.18	0.09	0.9	-1	0.9	-1	52
1443	282	5.1	5.2	3.71	0.10	0.8	-2	0.8	-2	53
885	258	3.4	3.5	-0.18	0.09	0.9	-1	0.9	-1	54
1131	282	4.0	4.1	1.13	0.09	1.1	0	1.1	1	55
1227	281	4.4	4.4	1.92	0.09	0.9	-1	0.9	-1	56

Combined data – candidates (continued)

Obsvd Score	Obsvd Count	Obsvd Average	Fair Avrge	Calib Logit	Model Error	Infit MnSq	Std	Outfit MnSq	Std	Cand
813	282	2.9	2.9	-1.28	0.09	1.0	0	1.0	0	57
923	280	3.3	3.3	-0.40	0.09	1.0	0	1.1	1	58
1318	281	4.7	4.8	2.66	0.09	1.0	0	0.9	0	60
1312	278	4.7	4.8	2.72	0.09	1.0	0	1.0	0	61
1354	282	4.8	4.8	2.84	0.09	0.8	-2	0.8	-2	62
1076	282	3.8	3.8	0.68	0.09	0.8	-2	0.8	-2	63
1071	282	3.8	3.8	0.64	0.09	0.7	-3	0.7	-3	64
987	279	3.5	3.6	0.08	0.09	0.7	-4	0.7	-4	66
1128	281	4.0	4.0	1.11	0.09	0.8	-3	0.8	-2	67
1330	278	4.8	4.8	2.82	0.09	0.8	-2	0.8	-2	68
1056	281	3.8	3.8	0.56	0.09	0.6	-4	0.6	-5	69
1197	280	4.3	4.3	1.70	0.09	0.9	-1	0.9	-1	70
1100	280	3.9	4.0	0.95	0.09	1.1	0	1.1	0	71
1132	282	4.0	4.0	1.09	0.09	1.3	2	1.3	3	72
1107	279	4.0	4.0	0.86	0.09	1.3	3	1.3	3	74
1048	276	3.8	3.8	0.53	0.09	1.4	3	1.5	4	75
1429	282	5.1	5.1	3.47	0.10	0.9	-1	0.9	0	77
1380	282	4.9	4.9	3.02	0.09	1.0	0	1.0	0	78
1113	282	3.9	3.9	0.83	0.09	1.0	0	1.0	0	79
1120	281	4.0	4.0	0.91	0.09	1.2	2	1.2	2	80
1057	281	3.8	3.8	0.42	0.09	1.0	0	1.0	0	81
1309	282	4.6	4.7	2.42	0.09	0.8	-2	0.8	-2	82
1217	282	4.3	4.3	1.65	0.09	0.8	-3	0.8	-3	83
966	272	3.6	3.5	-0.17	0.09	1.3	3	1.3	3	84
1177	282	4.2	4.1	1.20	0.09	1.0	0	1.0	-1	85
1353	282	4.8	4.7	2.62	0.09	1.0	0	0.9	-1	86
971	282	3.4	3.4	-0.40	0.09	1.5	4	1.5	4	87
708	281	2.5	2.4	-2.29	0.08	0.9	-1	0.9	-1	88
1369	282	4.9	4.8	2.76	0.09	1.0	0	1.0	0	89
1532	282	5.4	5.4	4.33	0.11	1.0	0	1.1	1	90
1102	282	3.9	3.8	0.60	0.09	0.8	-3	0.8	-2	92
1416	282	5.0	5.0	3.16	0.10	1.1	0	1.1	1	93
1549	281	5.5	5.5	4.60	0.11	0.9	0	1.1	0	94

Obsvd Score	Obsvd Count	Obsvd Average	Fair Avrge	Calib Logit	Model Error	Infit MnSq	Std	Outfit MnSq	Std	Cand
1138.8	280.3	4.1	4.1	1.19	0.09	1.0	-0.2	1.0	-0.2	Mean
217.8	4.5	0.8	0.8	1.70	0.01	0.2	2.5	0.2	2.5	S.D.

RMSE 0.09 Adj S.D. 1.70 Separation 18.79 Reliability 1.00
Fixed (all same) chi-square: 28284.18 d.f.: 82 significance: .00
Random (normal) chi-square: 81.98 d.f.: 81 significance: .45

(ii) Raters

Obsvd Score	Obsvd Count	Obsvd Average	Fair Avrge	Measure Logit	Model Error	Infit MnSq	Infit Std	Outfit MnSq	Outfit Std	Rater
3105	002	3.0	3.0	0.68	0.05	1.2	3	1.2	4	1
2545	818	3.1	2.6	1.69	0.05	0.9	-2	0.9	-2	2
3676	894	4.1	3.3	-0.35	0.05	0.7	-6	0.8	-5	3
3752	915	4.1	3.6	-0.28	0.05	1.2	3	1.2	3	4
3907	823	4.7	4.2	-1.43	0.05	1.1	2	1.2	3	5
3676	892	4.1	3.5	-0.23	0.05	1.0	-1	1.0	-1	6
3417	909	3.8	3.3	0.54	0.05	0.9	-2	0.9	-2	7
3175	774	4.1	3.6	-0.31	0.05	1.3	5	1.3	6	8
3685	894	4.1	3.7	-0.28	0.05	0.9	-1	0.9	-2	9
14656	3876	3.8	3.2	0.62	0.02	1.0	-0	1.0	0	10
14188	3845	3.7	3.2	0.85	0.02	1.1	6	1.1	6	11
17984	3882	4.6	4.2	-0.84	0.02	0.9	-2	0.9	-3	12
16751	3880	4.3	3.9	-0.67	0.03	0.9	-5	0.9	-5	13
7270.5	1789.5	4.0	3.5	0.00	0.04	1.0	-0.0	1.0	0.1	Mean
5822.7	1388.0	0.4	0.4	0.80	0.01	0.2	3.8	0.2	3.9	S.D.

RMSE 0.04 Adj S.D. 0.80 Separation 17.97 Reliability 1.00
Fixed (all same) chi-square: 6205.84 d.f.: 12 significance: .00
Random (normal) chi-square: 12.00 d.f.: 11 significance: .36

(iii) Items

Obsvd Score	Obsvd Count	Obsvd Average	Fair Avrge	Measure Logit	Model Error	Infit MnSq	Infit Std	Outfit MnSq	Outfit Std	Nu Item
2181	498	4.4	3.8	-0.55	0.07	1.0	0	1.0	0	1 DesF
1961	498	3.9	3.3	0.47	0.07	0.8	-2	0.8	-2	2 DesG
2010	497	4.0	3.4	0.23	0.07	1.1	1	1.1	1	3 DesV
2147	497	4.3	3.7	-0.40	0.07	0.8	-2	0.8	-2	4 NarF
1878	498	3.8	3.1	0.84	0.07	0.7	-4	0.7	-4	5 NarG
1905	498	3.8	3.2	0.72	0.07	0.8	-2	0.8	-2	6 NarV
2075	498	4.2	3.6	-0.05	0.07	1.1	1	1.1	1	7 NarC
2036	498	4.1	3.5	0.13	0.07	1.0	0	1.0	0	8 Exp1F
1797	498	3.6	3.0	1.20	0.07	0.9	-2	0.9	-2	9 Exp1G
2050	497	4.1	3.5	0.06	0.07	1.1	2	1.1	1	10 RP1F
1872	497	3.8	3.1	0.86	0.07	1.0	0	1.0	0	11 RP1G
1991	497	4.0	3.4	0.33	0.07	1.8	9	1.8	9	12 RP1A
2109	494	4.3	3.7	-0.26	0.07	1.0	0	1.0	0	13 RP2F
1893	492	3.8	3.2	0.71	0.07	0.9	-1	0.9	-1	14 RP2G
2047	494	4.1	3.5	0.03	0.07	1.3	4	1.3	4	15 RP2A
2135	498	4.3	3.7	-0.33	0.07	0.9	-1	0.9	-1	16 Exp2F
1913	498	3.8	3.2	0.68	0.07	0.8	-3	0.8	-3	17 Exp2G
2169	497	4.4	3.8	-0.51	0.07	0.9	-1	0.9	-1	18 DisF
1910	496	3.9	3.2	0.67	0.07	0.8	-2	0.8	-2	19 DisG
2022	494	4.1	3.5	0.12	0.07	1.0	0	1.0	0	20 DisV
2076	497	4.2	3.6	-0.07	0.07	1.4	5	1.4	5	21 Int
1975	494	4.0	3.4	0.33	0.07	1.1	1	1.1	1	22 ComEff
2216	494	4.5	3.9	-0.80	0.07	1.6	7	1.5	6	23 Comp
2141	494	4.3	3.9	-0.80	0.07	1.1	1	1.2	2	24 TDesF
1930	494	3.9	3.5	0.17	0.07	0.8	-2	0.9	-2	25 TDesG
1946	493	3.9	3.5	0.08	0.07	1.0	0	1.0	0	26 TDesV
2078	497	4.2	3.8	-0.45	0.07	0.9	-2	0.9	-1	27 TNarF
1839	497	3.7	3.2	0.63	0.07	0.7	-5	0.7	-4	28 TNarG

Combined data – items (continued)

Obsvd Score	Obsvd Count	Obsvd Average	Fair Avrge	Measure Logit	Model Error	Infit MnSq	Std	Outfit MnSq	Std	Nu Item
1850	496	3.7	3.3	0.56	0.07	0.8	-3	0.8	-3	29 TSNarV
2028	496	4.1	3.7	-0.24	0.07	1.0	0	1.0	0	30 TNarC
1978	488	4.1	3.6	-0.12	0.07	1.1	1	1.1	1	31 Texp1F
1818	487	3.7	3.3	0.60	0.07	0.9	-2	0.9	-2	32 TExp1G
2183	497	4.4	4.0	-0.94	0.07	1.0	0	1.1	0	33 TRP 1F
1973	497	4.0	3.5	0.03	0.07	0.9	-2	0.8	-2	34 TRP 1G
2211	496	4.5	4.0	-1.09	0.07	1.2	3	1.2	3	35 TRP1A
2109	489	4.3	3.9	-0.75	0.07	1.0	0	1.0	0	36 TRP2F
1909	489	3.9	3.5	0.18	0.07	0.9	-1	0.9	-1	37 TRP2G
1991	489	4.1	3.6	-0.19	0.07	1.8	9	1.8	9	38 TRP2A
2114	494	4.3	3.9	-0.67	0.07	0.8	-2	0.8	-2	39 Texp2F
1880	493	3.8	3.4	0.38	0.07	0.8	-3	0.8	-3	40 TExp2G
2136	494	4.3	3.9	-0.77	0.07	0.8	-2	0.9	-2	41 TDisF
1923	494	3.9	3.5	0.21	0.07	0.8	-2	0.8	-2	42 TDisG
1956	488	4.0	3.6	-0.04	0.07	0.8	-2	0.8	-2	43 TDisV
2097	496	4.2	3.8	-0.55	0.07	1.1	1	1.1	1	44 TInt
2011	494	4.1	3.6	-0.21	0.07	0.8	-2	0.8	-2	45 TComEf
2137	497	4.3	3.9	-0.72	0.07	0.9	-1	0.9	-1	46 TSumF
1911	496	3.9	3.4	0.29	0.07	0.8	-2	0.9	-2	47 TSumG

Obsvd Score	Obsvd Count	Obsvd Average	Fair Avrge	Measure Logit	Model Error	Infit MnSq	Std	Outfit MnSq	Std	Nu Item
2011.0	495.0	4.1	3.5	0.00	0.07	1.0	-0.3	1.0	-0.3	Mean
111.9	0.2	0.3	0.54	0.00	0.2	3.3	0.2	3.2	0.2	S.D.

RMSE 0.07 Adj S.D. 0.54 Separation 7.92 Reliability 0.98
Fixed (all same) chi-square: 2983.43 d.f.: 46 significance: .00
Random (normal) chi-square: 46.00 d.f.: 45 significance: .43

(iv) Order

Obsvd Score	Obsvd Count	Obsvd Average	Fair Avrge	Measure Logit	Model Error	Infit MnSq	Std	Outfit MnSq	Std	N Order
46833	11698	4.0	3.5	0.11	0.01	1.0	1	1.0	1	First
47684	11566	4.1	3.6	-0.11	0.01	1.0	-1	1.0	-1	Second

Obsvd Score	Obsvd Count	Obsvd Average	Fair Avrge	Measure Logit	Model Error	Infit MnSq	Std	Outfit MnSq	Std	N Order
47258.5	11632.0	4.1	3.6	-0.00	0.01	1.0	-0.1	1.0	0.1	Mean
425.5	66.0	0.1	0.0	0.11	0.00	0.0	1.3	0.0	1.3	S.D.

RMSE 0.01 Adj S.D. 0.11 Separation 8.11 Reliability 0.99
Fixed (all same) chi-square: 133.51 d.f.: 1 significance: .00
Random (normal) chi-square: 1.00 d.f.: 0 significance: 1.00

(v) Version

Obsvd Score	Obsvd Count	Obsvd Average	Fair Avrge	Measure Logit	Model Error	Infit MnSq	Std	Outfit MnSq	Std	Live/Tape
40308	11419	4.1	3.6	-0.18	0.01	1.1	3	1.0	2	1 Live
48149	11845	4.1	3.5	0.18	0.01	1.0	-3	1.0	-2	2 Tape
47258.5	11632.0	4.1	3.5	0.00	0.01	1.0	-0.1	1.0	0.1	Mean
890.5	213.0	0.0	0.1	0.18	0.00	0.0	3.8	0.0	2.7l	S.D.

RMSE 0.01 Adj S.D. 0.18 Separation 12.84 Reliability 0.99
Fixed (all same) chi-square: 331.54 d.f.: 1 significance: .00
Random (normal) chi-square: 1.00 d.f.: 0 significance: 1.00

Appendix 4.3
FACETS analyses (2) oral interaction sub-test, December 1992 trial (N = 76)
A Live data

(i) Candidates

Obsvd Score	Obsvd Count	Obsvd Average	Fair Avrge	Calib Logit	Model Error	Infit MnSq	Std	Outfit MnSq	Std	Cand
715	138	5.2	5.4	3.93	0.13	1.3	2	1.2	1	1
466	138	3.4	3.5	-0.42	0.13	0.8	-1	0.8	-1	2
482	138	3.5	3.6	-0.13	0.13	0.7	-2	0.7	-2	3
587	138	4.3	4.4	1.75	0.13	0.8	-1	0.8	-1	4
496	138	3.6	3.7	0.12	0.13	1.1	0	1.1	0	5
578	138	4.2	4.3	1.59	0.13	1.5	3	1.5	3	6
593	138	4.3	4.4	1.85	0.13	0.8	-1	0.8	-1	7
495	138	3.6	3.7	0.10	0.13	0.7	-2	0.7	-2	8
672	138	4.9	5.1	3.20	0.13	1.1	1	1.2	1	9
436	138	3.2	3.2	-0.97	0.14	1.0	0	1.0	0	10
616	138	4.5	4.4	1.83	0.13	1.1	1	1.1	1	11
562	138	4.1	4.0	0.91	0.13	0.9	0	0.9	0	12
506	138	3.7	3.6	0.00	0.13	1.2	1	1.2	1	13
560	138	4.1	4.0	0.88	0.13	0.9	0	0.9	0	15
417	138	3.0	2.9	-1.45	0.13	0.8	-1	0.8	-1	16
255	135	1.9	1.8	-4.23	0.14	1.2	1	1.1	1	18
536	138	3.9	3.8	0.49	0.13	1.2	1	1.2	1	19
541	138	3.9	3.9	0.36	0.13	0.8	-1	0.8	-1	22
780	138	5.7	5.7	5.30	0.18	1.0	0	1.1	0	24
377	138	2.7	2.7	-2.58	0.13	1.2	1	1.2	1	25
484	138	3.5	3.5	-0.67	0.13	0.8	-2	0.8	-2	26
674	138	4.9	4.9	2.77	0.14	1.0	0	0.9	0	27
734	138	5.3	5.4	4.04	0.15	0.9	-1	0.8	-1	28
591	138	4.3	4.3	1.25	0.13	0.8	-2	0.8	-1	29
569	138	4.1	4.1	0.86	0.13	1.0	0	1.0	0	30
620	138	4.5	4.5	2.21	0.13	1.2	1	1.2	1	31
601	138	4.4	4.4	1.87	0.14	0.9	0	0.9	0	32
494	137	3.6	3.6	-0.05	0.14	1.2	1	1.2	1	33
523	138	3.8	3.8	0.42	0.14	1.2	1	1.2	1	34
283	136	2.1	2.0	-4.05	0.14	1.4	3	1.4	3	35
555	138	4.0	4.0	1.02	0.14	1.1	0	1.1	0	36
702	138	5.1	5.2	3.65	0.13	0.9	0	1.0	0	37
560	138	4.1	4.1	1.11	0.14	0.7	-2	0.7	-2	39
758	138	5.5	5.6	4.74	0.15	1.2	1	1.2	1	40
292	135	2.2	2.0	-3.74	0.14	1.3	2	1.1	0	43
577	137	4.2	4.1	0.95	0.13	0.9	0	0.9	0	45
713	138	5.2	5.2	3.45	0.15	0.8	-1	0.7	-1	46
268	138	1.9	1.8	-4.31	0.14	1.0	0	1.1	0	47
569	134	4.2	4.2	1.00	0.13	1.1	0	1.1	0	48
556	137	4.1	4.0	0.61	0.13	0.9	0	0.9	0	50
389	138	2.8	2.6	-2.28	0.13	1.3	2	1.2	1	51
499	138	3.6	3.5	-0.36	0.13	1.0	0	1.0	0	52
727	138	5.3	5.2	3.72	0.15	0.7	-3	0.7	-2	53
507	138	3.7	3.6	-0.22	0.13	0.8	-1	0.8	-1	54
538	138	3.9	3.8	0.31	0.13	1.0	0	1.0	0	55
646	138	4.7	4.6	2.16	0.13	1.0	0	0.9	0	56
351	138	2.5	2.4	-2.94	0.13	1.0	0	1.1	0	57
480	136	3.5	3.4	-0.55	0.13	1.1	0	1.1	0	58
694	137	5.1	5.0	3.13	0.14	0.9	0	0.9	0	60

Live data – candidates (continued)

Obsvd Score	Obsvd Count	Obsvd Average	Fair Avrge	Calib Logit	Model Error	Infit MnSq	Std	Outfit MnSq	Std	Cand
676	138	4.9	4.8	2.71	0.14	1.2	1	1.2	1	61
648	138	4.7	4.7	2.45	0.14	0.9	0	0.9	0	62
530	138	3.8	3.9	0.24	0.14	1.0	0	1.0	0	63
538	138	3.9	3.9	0.39	0.14	0.8	-2	0.8	-2	64
500	138	3.6	3.7	-0.31	0.14	0.8	-2	0.8	-2	66
549	138	4.0	4.0	0.59	0.14	1.0	0	1.0	0	67
617	135	4.6	4.6	2.11	0.14	1.0	0	0.9	0	68
529	138	3.8	3.9	0.22	0.14	0.6	-4	0.6	-4	69
559	136	4.1	4.1	0.95	0.14	0.9	-1	0.8	-1	70
510	136	3.8	3.8	0.03	0.14	1.0	0	1.0	0	71
502	138	3.6	3.7	-0.28	0.14	1.2	1	1.3	1	72
538	135	4.0	3.7	0.07	0.13	1.3	2	1.3	2	74
738	138	5.3	5.2	3.63	0.16	1.1	0	1.2	1	77
697	138	5.1	4.8	2.71	0.14	1.1	0	1.0	0	78
583	138	4.2	4.0	0.64	0.13	0.9	-1	0.9	-1	79
559	138	4.1	3.8	0.25	0.13	1.4	3	1.4	3	80
575	138	4.2	3.9	0.51	0.13	1.1	0	1.1	0	81
674	138	4.9	4.6	2.25	0.14	0.7	-3	0.7	-3	82
634	138	4.6	4.3	1.51	0.13	0.7	-2	0.7	-3	83
565	138	4.1	4.0	0.74	0.14	0.9	0	0.9	0	85
670	138	4.9	4.8	2.81	0.14	1.0	0	1.0	0	86
329	138	2.4	2.3	3.35	0.13	1.0	0	1.0	0	88
650	138	4.7	4.6	2.40	0.14	1.0	0	1.0	0	89
761	138	5.5	5.5	4.86	0.16	0.9	0	0.9	0	90
515	138	3.7	3.7	-0.19	0.13	0.9	0	0.9	0	92
682	138	4.9	4.9	3.05	0.14	1.1	1	1.1	0	93
773	138	5.6	5.6	5.20	0.17	0.8	-1	0.8	-1	94

Obsvd Score	Obsvd Count	Obsvd Average	Fair Avrge	Calib Logit	Model Error	Infit MnSq	Std	Outfit MnSq	Std	Nu
559.2	137.5	4.1	4.0	0.86	0.14	1.0	-0.1	1.0	-0.1	Mean
121.2	1.2	0.9	0.9	2.16	0.01	0.2	1.7	0.2	1.6	S.D.

RMSE 0.14 Adj S.D. 2.16 Separation 15.70 Reliability 1.00
Fixed (all same) chi-square: 17592.96 d.f.: 76 significance: .00
Random (normal) chi-square: 75.96 d.f.: 75 significance: .45

(ii) Raters

Obsvd Score	Obsvd Count	Obsvd Average	Fair Avrge	Measure Logit	Model Error	Infit MnSq	Std	Outfit MnSq	Std	Rater
1489	457	3.3	2.7	1.07	0.07	0.9	0	1.0	0	1
858	294	2.9	2.9	1.09	0.09	0.9	-1	0.8	-1	2
1738	414	4.2	3.6	0.32	0.08	0.7	-3	0.8	-3	3
1910	459	4.2	3.9	-0.03	0.08	1.1	1	1.1	1	4
1576	322	4.9	4.6	-1.52	0.09	1.2	2	1.1	1	5
1758	414	4.2	3.8	-0.91	0.08	0.9	-1	0.9	-1	6
1729	457	3.8	3.4	1.23	0.07	0.9	-1	0.9	-1	7
1463	345	4.2	3.9	-1.25	0.08	1.1	0	1.1	0	8
1591	368	4.3	3.9	0.76	0.09	0.9	0	0.9	0	9
6898	1762	3.9	3.6	-0.08	0.04	1.0	0	1.0	0	10

Live data – raters (continued)

Obsvd Score	Obsvd Count	Obsvd Average	Fair Avrge	Measure Logit	Model Error	Infit MnSq	Std	Outfit MnSq	Std	Rater
6200	1764	3.5	3.2	0.81	0.04	1.2	4	1.2	4	11
8239	1771	4.7	4.4	-1.57	0.04	1.1	2	1.0	1	12
7612	1764	4.3	4.0	0.07	0.04	0.8	-5	0.8	-5	13

Obsvd Score	Obsvd Count	Obsvd Average	Fair Avrge	Measure Logit	Model Error	Infit MnSq	Std	Outfit MnSq	Std	Rater
3312.4	814.7	4.0	3.7	-0.00	0.07	1.0	-0.3	1.0	-0.3	Mean
2661.2	635.6	0.5	0.5	0.98	0.02	0.1	2.6	0.1	2.4	S.D.

RMSE 0.07 Adj S.D. 0.97 Separation 13.70 Reliability 0.99
Fixed (all same) chi-square: 3569.62 d.f.: 12 significance: .00
Random (normal) chi-square: 12.00 d.f.: 11 significance: .36

(iii) Items

Obsvd Score	Obsvd Count	Obsvd Average	Fair Avrge	Measure Logit	Model Error	Infit MnSq	Std	Outfit MnSq	Std	Nu Item
2026	462	4.4	4.0	-0.83	0.08	1.0	0	1.0	0	1 DesF
1818	462	3.9	3.6	0.33	0.07	0.8	-3	0.8	-2	2 DesG
1870	461	4.1	3.7	0.02	0.07	1.1	0	1.0	0	3 DesV
1996	461	4.3	4.0	-0.68	0.08	0.8	-2	0.8	-2	4 NarF
1739	462	3.8	3.4	0.76	0.07	0.7	-4	0.7	-4	5 NarG
1769	462	3.8	3.5	0.59	0.07	0.8	-2	0.8	-2	6 NarV
1930	462	4.2	3.8	-0.29	0.07	1.0	0	1.1	0	7 NarC
1888	462	4.1	3.7	-0.06	0.07	1.0	0	1.0	0	8 Exp1F
1659	462	3.6	3.2	1.20	0.07	0.9	-2	0.9	-2	9 Exp1G
1909	461	4.1	3.8	-0.18	0.07	0.9	0	1.0	0	10 RP1F
1733	461	3.8	3.4	0.78	0.07	0.9	-1	0.9	-1	11 RP1G
1857	461	4.0	3.7	0.11	0.07	1.9	9	1.9	9	12 RP1A
1965	458	4.3	3.9	-0.54	0.08	0.9	-1	0.9	-2	13 RP2F
1752	456	3.8	3.4	0.61	0.07	1.0	0	1.0	0	14 RP2G
1908	458	4.2	3.8	-0.22	0.07	1.5	6	1.5	6	15 RP2A
1983	462	4.3	3.9	-0.58	0.07	0.8	-3	0.8	-3	16 Exp2F
1773	462	3.8	3.5	0.57	0.07	0.8	-3	0.8	-3	17 Exp2G
2015	461	4.4	4.0	-0.79	0.08	0.9	-2	0.8	-2	18 DisF
1764	460	3.8	3.5	0.59	0.07	0.8	-2	0.8	-2	19 DisG
1879	458	4.1	3.7	-0.09	0.07	1.0	0	0.9	-1	20 DisV
1933	461	4.2	3.8	-0.32	0.07	1.3	3	1.3	3	21 Int
1841	458	4.0	3.7	0.12	0.07	0.9	0	0.9	-1	22 ComEf
2054	458	4.5	4.1	-1.09	0.08	1.4	5	1.3	3	23 Comp

Obsvd Score	Obsvd Count	Obsvd Average	Fair Avrge	Measure Logit	Model Error	Infit MnSq	Std	Outfit MnSq	Std	Nu Item
1872.2	460.5	4.1	3.7	0.00	0.07	1.0	-0.3	1.0	-0.5	Mean
105.6	1.8	0.2	0.2	0.59	0.00	0.3	3.4	0.3	3.2	S.D.

RMSE 0.07 Adj S.D. 0.59 Separation 7.86 Reliability 0.98
Fixed (all same) chi-square: 1432.84 d.f.: 22 significance: .00
Random (normal) chi-square: 22.00 d.f.: 21 significance: .40

B   Tape data

(i) Candidates

Obsvd Score	Obsvd Count	Obsvd Average	Fair Avrge	Calib Logit	Model Error	Infit MnSq	Std	Outfit MnSq	Std	Cand
686	142	4.8	4.8	3.05	0.14	0.8	-1	0.8	-1	1
464	144	3.2	3.2	-1.28	0.14	0.9	0	0.9	0	2
515	144	3.6	3.6	-0.34	0.14	0.9	0	0.9	0	3
660	144	4.6	4.6	2.37	0.14	0.7	-3	0.7	-2	4
563	144	3.9	3.9	0.54	0.14	0.9	-1	0.9	-1	5
663	144	4.6	4.6	2.43	0.14	0.9	-1	0.8	-1	6
647	144	4.5	4.5	2.12	0.14	0.8	-2	0.8	-2	7
519	144	3.6	3.6	-0.26	0.13	0.9	-1	0.9	-1	8
668	144	4.6	4.6	2.52	0.14	1.2	1	1.2	1	9
537	143	3.8	3.7	0.13	0.14	1.3	2	1.3	2	10
717	144	5.0	4.8	3.31	0.15	1.0	0	1.0	0	11
584	144	4.1	3.8	0.65	0.14	1.0	0	1.0	0	12
510	143	3.6	3.3	-0.72	0.14	0.7	-3	0.7	-2	13
549	144	3.8	3.6	-0.01	0.14	0.9	0	1.0	0	15
488	144	3.4	3.2	-1.21	0.14	0.9	0	0.9	-1	16
331	136	2.4	2.0	-3.87	0.13	1.4	2	1.4	3	18
633	144	4.4	4.2	1.58	0.14	1.0	0	1.0	0	19
605	144	4.2	4.2	1.34	0.14	1.2	1	1.2	1	22
783	144	5.4	5.4	5.05	0.16	1.1	0	1.1	0	24
443	144	3.1	3.0	-1.77	0.14	1.0	0	1.1	0	25
499	144	3.5	3.4	-0.66	0.14	1.1	0	1.1	0	26
673	144	4.7	4.7	2.66	0.14	0.9	-1	1.0	0	27
737	144	5.1	5.1	3.99	0.15	1.0	0	0.9	0	28
612	144	4.3	4.2	1.47	0.14	1.0	0	1.0	0	29
568	144	3.9	3.9	0.64	0.14	1.0	0	1.1	0	30
607	144	4.2	4.1	1.33	0.14	1.5	3	1.6	4	31
623	144	4.3	4.2	1.63	0.14	0.7	-3	0.7	-3	32
487	144	3.4	3.2	-0.91	0.14	1.0	0	1.1	0	33
563	144	3.9	3.7	0.50	0.14	1.0	0	1.0	0	34
401	144	2.8	2.6	-2.52	0.14	0.9	0	0.9	0	35
521	144	3.6	3.4	-0.28	0.14	1.1	0	1.1	0	36
751	144	5.2	5.1	4.30	0.15	0.9	0	0.9	0	37
626	144	4.3	4.2	1.69	0.14	0.6	-3	0.6	-3	39
796	144	5.5	5.4	5.49	0.17	1.7	4	1.8	4	40
377	144	2.6	2.5	-3.25	0.15	1.5	3	1.6	4	43
580	144	4.0	4.0	0.85	0.14	1.1	0	1.1	1	45
742	144	5.2	5.1	3.97	0.15	1.4	2	1.3	2	46
462	144	3.2	3.1	-1.42	0.14	1.2	1	1.2	1	47
543	144	3.8	3.7	0.17	0.14	1.1	0	1.1	1	48
596	144	4.1	4.1	1.15	0.14	0.7	-2	0.7	-2	50
461	143	3.2	3.1	-0.92	0.14	1.0	0	1.0	0	51
509	144	3.5	3.5	-0.09	0.14	1.0	0	1.0	0	52
716	144	5.0	4.9	3.73	0.14	1.1	0	1.1	1	53
378	120	3.2	3.0	-1.12	0.15	0.7	-2	0.7	-2	54
593	144	4.1	4.1	1.45	0.14	1.2	1	1.3	1	55
581	143	4.1	4.0	1.31	0.14	0.7	-2	0.7	-2	56
462	144	3.2	3.1	-0.98	0.14	0.7	-2	0.7	-2	57
443	144	3.1	3.0	-1.35	0.14	1.3	2	1.3	1	58
624	144	4.3	4.3	2.02	0.14	0.9	0	0.9	0	60
636	140	4.5	4.5	2.58	0.14	1.0	0	0.9	0	61
706	144	4.9	4.8	3.16	0.13	0.7	-2	0.8	-1	62
546	144	3.8	3.7	0.37	0.13	0.9	0	0.9	0	63
533	144	3.7	3.6	0.13	0.14	0.9	0	0.9	0	64
487	141	3.5	3.3	-0.55	0.14	0.8	-1	0.9	-1	66

Tape data – candidates (continued)

Obsvd Score	Obsvd Count	Obsvd Average	Fair Avrge	Calib Logit	Model Error	Infit MnSq	Std	Outfit MnSq	Std	Cand
579	143	4.0	3.9	1.03	0.13	0.8	-2	0.8	-1	67
713	143	5.0	4.9	3.38	0.14	0.6	-3	0.6	-3	68
527	143	3.7	3.6	0.09	0.14	0.9	-1	0.9	-1	69
638	144	4.4	4.3	1.97	0.13	0.8	-2	0.8	-2	70
590	144	4.1	4.0	1.15	0.13	1.0	0	1.0	0	71
630	144	4.4	4.2	1.83	0.13	0.8	-1	0.8	-1	72
569	144	4.0	4.0	1.04	0.13	1.4	2	1.4	3	74
691	144	4.8	4.9	3.26	0.14	0.7	-2	0.7	-2	77
683	144	4.7	4.8	3.12	0.14	0.9	0	1.0	0	78
530	144	3.7	3.7	0.34	0.13	1.1	0	1.1	1	79
561	143	3.9	4.0	0.96	0.13	0.9	-1	0.9	-1	80
482	143	3.4	3.4	-0.48	0.14	1.0	0	1.0	0	81
635	144	4.4	4.5	2.24	0.13	1.0	0	1.0	0	82
583	144	4.0	4.1	1.30	0.13	0.9	-1	0.9	-1	83
612	144	4.3	4.0	1.29	0.13	1.6	4	1.5	4	85
683	144	4.7	4.5	2.56	0.13	0.9	0	0.9	0	86
379	143	2.7	2.2	-3.33	0.14	1.2	1	1.2	1	88
719	144	5.0	4.7	3.22	0.14	1.0	0	0.9	0	89
771	144	5.4	5.1	4.28	0.15	1.2	1	1.2	1	90
587	144	4.1	3.8	0.83	0.14	0.8	-2	0.7	-2	92
734	144	5.1	4.8	3.50	0.14	1.2	1	1.1	0	93
776	143	5.4	5.2	4.53	0.16	1.0	0	0.9	0	94

Obsvd Score	Obsvd Count	Obsvd Average	Fair Avrge	Calib Logit	Model Error	Infit MnSq	Std	Outfit MnSq	Std	Cand
587.8	143.3	4.1	4.0	1.11	0.14	1.0	-0.2	1.0	-0.2	Mean
105.3	2.9	0.7	0.7	1.98	0.01	0.2	1.8	0.2	1.8	S.D.

RMSE 0.14 Adj S.D. 1.97 Separation 14.16 Reliability 1.00
Fixed (all same) chi-square: 14472.33 d.f.: 75 significance: .00
Random (normal) chi-square: 74.97 d.f.: 74 significance: .45

(ii) Raters

Obsvd Score	Obsvd Count	Obsvd Average	Fair Avrge	Measure Logit	Model Error	Infit MnSq	Std	Outfit MnSq	Std	Rater
1528	384	4.0	3.6	0.78	0.08	0.9	-1	0.9	-1	1
1353	431	3.1	2.6	1.56	0.07	0.8	-2	0.8	-2	2
1791	432	4.1	3.3	-0.44	0.07	0.8	-2	0.8	-3	3
1777	432	4.1	3.6	0.94	0.08	0.9	-1	0.9	-1	4
1677	359	4.7	4.3	-1.90	0.09	1.2	2	1.2	2	5
1754	432	4.1	3.6	1.26	0.08	1.0	0	1.0	0	6
1447	382	3.8	3.6	0.23	0.09	1.1	1	1.1	1	7
1358	336	4.0	3.6	0.62	0.10	1.5	5	1.5	5	8
1853	456	4.1	3.7	-0.49	0.08	0.9	-1	0.9	0	9
6740	1821	3.7	3.2	0.59	0.04	1.0	0	1.0	0	10
6999	1789	3.9	3.5	-0.25	0.04	1.1	2	1.1	2	11
8485	1821	4.7	4.3	-1.78	0.04	0.9	-2	0.9	-1	12
7914	1817	4.4	4.0	-1.10	0.04	0.9	-2	0.9	-1	13

Tape data – raters (continued)

Obsvd Score	Obsvd Count	Obsvd Average	Fair Avrge	Measure Logit	Model Error	Infit MnSq	Infit Std	Outfit MnSq	Outfit Std	Rater
3436.6	837.0	4.0	3.6	0.00	0.07	1.0	-0.2	1.0	-0.0	Mean
2763.7	650.3	0.4	0.4	1.07	0.02	0.2	2.5	0.2	2.5	S.D.

RMSE 0.07 Adj S.D. 1.06 Separation 14.77 Reliability 1.00
Fixed (all same) chi-square: 4255.02 d.f.: 12 significance: .00
Random (normal) chi-square: 12.00 d.f.: 11 significance: .36

(iii) Items

Obsvd Score	Obsvd Count	Obsvd Average	Fair Avrge	Measure Logit	Model Error	Infit MnSq	Infit Std	Outfit MnSq	Outfit Std	Nu Item
1990	455	4.4	3.9	-0.75	0.08	1.2	2	1.3	3	24 TDesF
1786	455	3.9	3.4	0.48	0.08	0.8	-2	0.9	-2	25 TDesG
1803	454	4.0	3.4	0.36	0.08	1.0	0	1.1	0	26 TDesV
1920	455	4.2	3.7	-0.33	0.08	0.9	-1	1.0	0	27 TNarF
1692	455	3.7	3.2	1.04	0.08	0.6	-6	0.6	-5	28 TNarG
1704	454	3.8	3.2	0.95	0.08	0.8	-3	0.8	-2	29 TNarV
1873	454	4.1	3.6	-0.07	0.08	1.0	0	1.0	0	30 TNarC
1853	451	4.1	3.6	0.03	0.08	1.1	0	1.1	1	31 TExp1F
1693	450	3.8	3.2	0.98	0.08	0.9	-1	0.9	-1	32 TExp1G
2016	455	4.4	3.9	-0.91	0.08	1.1	1	1.1	1	33 TRP1F
1815	455	4.0	3.5	0.31	0.08	0.9	-2	0.8	-2	34 TRP1G
2040	454	4.5	4.0	-1.09	0.08	1.3	4	1.3	4	35 TRPs1A
1985	455	4.4	3.9	-0.72	0.08	1.0	0	1.0	0	36 TRP2F
1795	455	3.9	3.4	0.43	0.08	0.9	-2	0.9	-1	37 TRP2G
1887	455	4.1	3.6	-0.13	0.08	1.7	9	1.7	9	38 TRP2A
1965	455	4.3	3.8	-0.60	0.08	0.9	-1	0.9	-1	39 TExp2F
1741	454	3.8	3.3	0.72	0.08	0.8	-2	0.8	-3	40 TExp2G
1987	454	4.4	3.9	-0.76	0.08	0.9	-1	0.9	-1	41 TDisF
1782	454	3.9	3.4	0.49	0.08	0.9	-2	0.9	-2	42 TDisG
1812	448	4.0	3.5	0.16	0.08	1.0	0	1.0	0	43 TDisV
1937	454	4.3	3.8	-0.46	0.08	1.3	3	1.3	3	44 TInt
1863	452	4.1	3.6	-0.07	0.08	0.9	-1	0.9	-1	45 TComEff
1978	455	4.3	3.8	-0.68	0.08	1.0	0	1.0	0	46 TSumF
1759	454	3.9	3.3	0.61	0.08	0.8	-2	0.8	-2	47 TSumG

Obsvd Score	Obsvd Count	Obsvd Average	Fair Avrge	Measure Logit	Model Error	Infit MnSq	Infit Std	Outfit MnSq	Outfit Std	Nu Item
1861.5	453.8	4.1	3.6	-0.00	0.08	1.0	-0.4	1.0	-0.3	Mean (Coun
105.9	1.8	0.2	0.2	0.63	0.00	0.2	3.0	0.2	3.0	S.D.

RMSE 0.08 Adj S.D. 0.63 Separation 8.05 Reliability 0.98
Fixed (all same) chi-square: 1571.11 d.f.: 23 significance: .00
Random (normal) chi-square: 23.00 d.f.: 22 significance: .40

C Combined data

(i) Candidates

Obsvd Score	Obsvd Count	Obsvd Average	Fair Avrge	Calib Logit	Model Error	Infit MnSq	Std	Outfit MnSq	Std	Cand
1401	280	5.0	5.1	3.43	0.10	1.1	0	1.1	0	1
930	282	3.3	3.3	-0.55	0.09	0.8	-1	0.8	-1	2
997	282	3.5	3.6	-0.02	0.09	0.8	-2	0.8	-2	3
1247	282	4.4	4.5	2.01	0.09	0.7	-3	0.7	-3	4
1059	282	3.8	3.8	0.47	0.09	1.0	0	1.0	0	5
1241	282	4.4	4.4	1.96	0.09	1.1	1	1.1	1	6
1240	282	4.4	4.4	1.96	0.09	0.8	-2	0.8	-2	7
1014	282	3.6	3.6	0.11	0.09	0.8	-2	0.8	-2	8
1340	282	4.8	4.8	2.81	0.09	1.3	3	1.3	3	9
973	281	3.5	3.5	-0.19	0.09	1.2	1	1.2	2	10
1333	282	4.7	4.7	2.67	0.09	1.2	1	1.2	1	11
1146	282	4.1	4.0	1.11	0.09	0.9	-1	0.9	0	12
1016	281	3.6	3.6	0.09	0.09	1.0	0	1.0	0	13
1109	282	3.9	3.9	0.81	0.09	1.0	0	1.0	0	15
905	282	3.2	3.2	-0.82	0.09	0.8	-2	0.8	-2	16
586	271	2.2	2.0	-3.10	0.09	1.3	3	1.3	2	18
1169	282	4.1	4.1	1.29	0.09	1.0	0	1.0	0	19
1146	282	4.1	4.0	1.06	0.09	0.9	-1	0.9	-1	22
1563	282	5.5	5.5	4.87	0.11	1.0	0	1.0	0	24
820	282	2.9	2.8	-1.55	0.09	1.0	0	1.0	0	25
983	282	3.5	3.4	-0.26	0.09	0.8	-1	0.8	-1	26
1347	282	4.8	4.7	2.72	0.09	0.8	-2	0.8	-2	27
1471	282	5.2	5.2	3.84	0.10	0.9	-1	0.9	-1	28
1203	282	4.3	4.2	1.52	0.09	0.8	-1	0.9	-1	29
1137	282	4.0	3.9	0.99	0.09	1.0	0	1.0	0	30
1227	282	4.4	4.4	1.86	0.09	1.4	3	1.4	4	31
1224	282	4.3	4.4	1.84	0.09	0.9	-1	0.9	-1	32
981	281	3.5	3.5	-0.14	0.09	1.1	1	1.1	1	33
1086	282	3.9	3.9	0.69	0.09	1.0	0	1.0	0	34
684	280	2.4	2.4	-2.44	0.09	1.2	2	1.2	1	35
1076	282	3.8	3.8	0.61	0.09	1.3	2	1.3	2	36
1453	282	5.2	5.2	3.86	0.10	1.0	0	1.0	0	37
1186	282	4.2	4.2	1.52	0.09	0.7	-4	0.6	-4	39
1554	282	5.5	5.6	4.93	0.11	1.3	3	1.3	3	40
669	279	2.4	2.3	-2.50	0.09	1.2	2	1.2	1	43
1157	281	4.1	4.1	1.27	0.09	0.9	0	0.9	0	45
1455	282	5.2	5.2	3.77	0.10	1.1	1	1.1	0	46
730	282	2.6	2.5	-2.09	0.09	1.7	7	1.8	7	47
1112	278	4.0	4.0	1.00	0.09	1.2	2	1.2	2	48
1152	281	4.1	4.1	1.24	0.09	1.0	0	1.0	0	50
850	281	3.0	3.0	-1.06	0.09	1.1	1	1.1	1	51
1008	282	3.6	3.6	0.15	0.09	0.9	-1	0.9	-1	52
1443	282	5.1	5.2	3.77	0.10	0.9	-1	0.8	-2	53
885	258	3.4	3.4	-0.22	0.09	0.8	-1	0.8	-1	54
1131	282	4.0	4.0	1.13	0.09	1.1	0	1.1	1	55
1227	281	4.4	4.4	1.94	0.09	1.0	0	0.9	0	56
813	282	2.9	2.9	-1.37	0.09	1.1	1	1.1	1	57
923	280	3.3	3.3	-0.46	0.09	1.1	1	1.2	1	58
1318	281	4.7	4.7	2.69	0.09	1.0	0	1.0	0	60
1312	278	4.7	4.7	2.76	0.09	1.0	0	1.0	0	61
1354	282	4.8	4.9	2.88	0.09	0.8	-2	0.8	-2	62
1076	282	3.8	3.8	0.65	0.09	0.8	-1	0.8	-1	63
1071	282	3.8	3.8	0.61	0.09	0.7	-3	0.7	-3	64

Combined data – candidates (continued)

Obsvd Score	Obsvd Count	Obsvd Average	Fair Avrge	Calib Logit	Model Error	Infit MnSq	Std	Outfit MnSq	Std	Cand
087	270	3.5	3.6	0.02	0.09	0.7	-3	0.7	-3	66
1128	281	4.0	4.0	1.10	0.09	0.8	-2	0.8	-2	67
1330	278	4.8	4.8	2.83	0.09	0.8	-2	0.8	-2	68
1056	281	3.8	3.8	0.52	0.09	0.7	-4	0.7	-4	69
1197	280	4.3	4.3	1.69	0.09	0.8	-2	0.8	-1	70
1100	280	3.9	3.9	0.92	0.09	1.0	0	1.0	0	71
1132	282	4.0	4.0	1.10	0.09	1.4	4	1.4	4	72
1107	279	4.0	4.0	0.84	0.09	1.4	3	1.4	4	74
1429	282	5.1	5.1	3.53	0.10	0.9	-1	0.9	-1	77
1380	282	4.9	4.9	3.07	0.10	1.0	0	1.0	0	78
1113	282	3.9	3.9	0.80	0.09	1.0	0	1.0	0	79
1120	281	4.0	4.0	0.88	0.09	1.3	3	1.3	3	80
1057	281	3.8	3.8	0.37	0.09	1.1	0	1.1	1	81
1309	282	4.6	4.7	2.43	0.09	0.9	-1	0.9	-1	82
1217	282	4.3	4.3	1.65	0.09	0.8	-2	0.8	-2	83
1177	282	4.2	4.0	1.18	0.09	1.0	0	1.0	0	85
1353	282	4.8	4.7	2.63	0.09	1.0	0	1.0	0	86
708	281	2.5	2.3	-2.45	0.09	0.9	0	1.0	0	88
1369	282	4.9	4.7	2.77	0.09	1.0	0	1.0	0	89
1532	282	5.4	5.4	4.40	0.11	1.1	0	1.2	2	90
1102	282	3.9	3.8	0.58	0.09	0.8	-2	0.8	-2	92
1416	282	5.0	4.9	3.20	0.10	1.1	1	1.1	1	93
1549	281	5.5	5.5	4.67	0.11	1.0	0	1.1	0	94

Obsvd Score	Obsvd Count	Obsvd Average	Fair Avrge	Calib Logit	Model Error	Infit MnSq	Std	Outfit MnSq	Std	Cand
1150.0	280.9	4.1	4.1	1.25	0.09	1.0	-0.2	1.0	-0.1	Mean
218.2	3.1	0.8	0.8	1.77	0.01	0.2	2.2	0.2	2.3	S.D

RMSE 0.09 Adj S.D. 1.77 Separation 19.21 Reliability 1.00
Fixed (all same) chi-square: 26940.28 d.f.: 75 significance: .00
Random (normal) chi-square: 74.99 d.f.: 74 significance: .45

(ii) Raters

Obsvd Score	Obsvd Count	Obsvd Average	Fair Avrge	Measure Logit	Model Error	Infit MnSq	Std	Outfit MnSq	Std	Rater
2974	821	3.6	3.0	0.65	0.05	1.2	3	1.2	4	1
2211	725	3.0	2.6	1.83	0.05	0.9	-2	0.9	-2	2
3529	846	4.2	3.3	-0.42	0.05	0.8	-5	0.8	-4	3
3616	868	4.2	3.7	0.92	0.06	1.1	2	1.1	2	4
3253	681	4.8	4.3	-1.59	0.06	1.1	2	1.2	3	5
3512	846	4.2	3.5	-0.28	0.05	0.9	-1	0.9	-1	6
3176	839	3.8	3.3	0.35	0.05	0.9	-1	0.9	-1	7
2821	681	4.1	3.7	-0.62	0.06	1.3	5	1.3	5	8
3444	824	4.2	3.6	-0.39	0.06	0.9	-2	0.9	-2	9
13595	3563	3.8	3.2	0.61	0.02	1.0	0	1.0	0	10
13152	3531	3.7	3.2	0.81	0.03	1.2	6	1.2	6	11
16663	3569	4.7	4.2	-0.96	0.03	0.9	-2	0.9	-3	12
15455	3558	4.3	3.9	-0.93	0.03	0.9	-5	0.9	-4	13

Combined data – raters (continued)

Obsvd Score	Obsvd Count	Obsvd Average	Fair Avrge	Measure Logit	Model Error	Infit MnSq	Std	Outfit MnSq	Std	Rater
6723.2	1642.5	4.0	3.5	-0.00	0.05	1.0	-0.1	1.0	0.1	Mean
5397.9	1276.6	0.4	0.5	0.91	0.01	0.1	3.5	0.2	3.7	S.D

RMSE 0.05 Adj S.D. 0.91 Separation 19.13 Reliability 1.00
Fixed (all same) chi-square: 6706.57 d.f.: 12 significance: .00
Random (normal) chi-square: 12.00 d.f.: 11 significance: .36

(iii) Items

Obsvd Score	Obsvd Count	Obsvd Average	Fair Avrge	Measure Logit	Model Error	Infit MnSq	Std	Outfit MnSq	Std	Nu Item
2008	456	4.4	3.9	-0.74	0.07	1.1	1	1.1	1	1 DesF
1804	456	4.0	3.4	0.32	0.07	0.8	-2	0.9	-2	2 DesG
1855	455	4.1	3.5	0.04	0.07	1.2	2	1.1	2	3 DesV
1979	455	4.3	3.8	-0.60	0.07	0.9	-1	0.9	-1	4 NarF
1724	456	3.8	3.2	0.73	0.07	0.7	-4	0.7	-4	5 NarG
1755	456	3.8	3.3	0.57	0.07	0.9	-1	0.9	-1	6 NarV
1914	456	4.2	3.7	-0.24	0.07	1.1	1	1.1	1	7 NarC
1871	456	4.1	3.6	-0.02	0.07	1.0	0	1.0	0	8 Exp1F
1645	456	3.6	3.0	1.13	0.07	0.8	-2	0.8	-2	9 Exp1G
1890	455	4.2	3.6	-0.13	0.07	1.1	0	1.1	0	10 RP1F
1715	455	3.8	3.2	0.77	0.07	0.9	-1	0.9	-1	11 RP1G
1834	455	4.0	3.5	0.16	0.07	1.7	8	1.7	8	12 RP1A
1954	454	4.3	3.8	-0.49	0.07	1.0	0	0.9	0	13 RP2F
1744	453	3.8	3.3	0.59	0.07	0.9	-1	0.9	-1	14 RP2G
1898	454	4.2	3.6	-0.19	0.07	1.4	4	1.4	4	15 RP2A
1965	456	4.3	3.8	-0.51	0.07	0.9	-1	0.9	-1	16 Exp2F
1760	456	3.9	3.3	0.55	0.07	0.8	-3	0.8	-3	17 Exp2G
2003	455	4.4	3.9	-0.74	0.07	0.9	-1	0.9	-1	18 DisF
1754	454	3.9	3.3	0.55	0.07	0.8	-3	0.8	-3	19 DisG
1869	452	4.1	3.6	-0.09	0.07	1.0	0	1.0	0	20 DisV
1915	455	4.2	3.7	-0.27	0.07	1.4	4	1.3	4	21 Int
1828	452	4.0	3.5	0.12	0.07	1.1	2	1.1	1	22 CommEff
2041	452	4.5	4.0	-1.02	0.07	1.6	7	1.5	6	23 Comp
1990	455	4.4	3.8	-0.67	0.07	1.1	1	1.2	3	24 TDesF
1786	455	3.9	3.4	0.39	0.07	0.9	-2	0.9	-1	25 TDesG
1803	454	4.0	3.4	0.29	0.07	1.0	0	1.0	0	26 TDesV
1920	455	4.2	3.7	-0.30	0.07	0.9	-2	0.9	-1	27 TNarF
1692	455	3.7	3.1	0.87	0.07	0.7	-4	0.7	-4	28 TNarG
1704	454	3.8	3.2	0.78	0.07	0.8	-3	0.8	-3	29 TNarV
1873	454	4.1	3.6	-0.08	0.07	1.0	0	1.0	0	30 TNarC
1853	451	4.1	3.5	0.01	0.07	1.1	0	1.1	1	31 TExp1F
1693	450	3.8	3.2	0.81	0.07	0.9	-1	0.9	-1	32 TExp2G
2016	455	4.4	3.9	-0.81	0.07	1.1	0	1.1	1	33 TRP1F
1815	455	4.0	3.4	0.24	0.07	0.9	-1	0.9	-1	34 TRP1G
2040	454	4.5	4.0	-0.96	0.07	1.3	3	1.3	3	35 TRP1A
1985	455	4.4	3.8	-0.64	0.07	0.9	-1	0.9	0	36 TRP2F
1795	455	3.9	3.4	0.35	0.07	0.9	-1	0.9	-1	37 TRP2G
1887	455	4.1	3.6	-0.13	0.07	1.6	8	1.7	9	38 TRP2A
1965	455	4.3	3.8	-0.53	0.07	0.8	-2	0.8	-2	39 TExp2F
1741	454	3.8	3.3	0.60	0.07	0.8	-3	0.8	-3	40 TExp2G
1987	454	4.4	3.8	-0.67	0.07	0.8	-3	0.8	-2	41 TDisF
1782	454	3.9	3.4	0.40	0.07	0.8	-2	0.9	-2	42 TDisG

Combined data – items (continued)

Obsvd Score	Obsvd Count	Obsvd Average	Fair Avrge	Measure Logit	Model Error	Infit MnSq	Std	Outfit MnSq	Std	Nu Item
1812	448	4.0	3.5	0.12	0.07	0.9	-2	0.9	-2	43 TDisV
1937	454	4.3	3.7	-0.41	0.07	1.1	1	1.1	1	44 TInt
1863	452	4.1	3.6	-0.08	0.07	0.9	-1	0.9	-2	45 TCommEff
1978	455	4.3	3.8	-0.60	0.07	0.9	-1	1.0	0	46 TSumF
1759	454	3.9	3.3	0.50	0.07	0.9	-1	0.9	-1	47 TSumG

Obsvd Score	Obsvd Count	Obsvd Average	Fair Avrge	Measure Logit	Model Error	Infit MnSq	Std	Outfit MnSq	Std	Nu Item
1859.6	454.3	4.1	3.5	-0.00	0.07	1.0	-0.2	1.0	-0.2	Mean
105.5	1.6	0.2	0.2	0.55	0.00	0.2	3.1	0.2	3.0	S.D.

RMSE 0.07 Adj S.D. 0.54 Separation 7.51 Reliability 0.98
Fixed (all same) chi-square: 2683.28 d.f.: 46 significance: .00
Random (normal) chi-square: 46.00 d.f.: 45 significance: .43

Appendix 5.1
Lexical density figures (%) with unweighted lexical items, December 1992 trial (N = 20)

ID	Description Live	Tape	Narration Live	Tape	Interview Live	Tape	Role play Live	Tape
2	38	41	36	45	37	37	37	41
5	49	47	32	41	46	45	33	46
9	34	36	37	35	38	44	34	40
10	43	42	39	44	41	43	39	40
13	31	44	38	35	42	39	32	43
16	38	41	32	37	38	40	32	47
22	41	41	38	39	40	43	37	42
27	43	38	32	43	44	41	37	41
29	49	49	41	41	47	52	34	48
31	38	33	37	41	39	38	31	44
40	42	50	44	43	40	46	40	49
43	36	42	38	41	41	46	39	41
45	39	41	41	38	43	44	35	35
46	41	42	33	37	40	45	35	46
48	36	42	39	36	42	47	32	37
50	43	42	40	45	37	40	33	39
51	44	35	41	42	39	40	39	42
53	42	36	39	44	36	39	33	35
60	38	43	41	36	37	41	38	35
78	35	42	38	38	44	44	35	48

Appendix 5.2
Lexical density figures (%) with weighted lexical items,
December 1992 trial (N = 20)

ID	Description Live	Tape	Narration Live	Tape	Interview Live	Tape	Role play Live	Tape
2	32	35	28	36	27	30	30	36
5	41	42	27	37	37	38	28	40
9	27	33	30	30	31	36	23	33
10	34	36	32	35	32	34	31	35
13	26	37	32	28	34	33	25	38
16	34	33	26	31	31	34	25	40
22	32	32	31	30	32	35	27	38
27	35	31	27	37	38	35	30	34
29	43	43	34	36	39	45	29	44
31	30	31	31	35	33	31	25	38
40	35	44	36	40	34	41	32	41
43	29	38	30	34	31	36	30	36
45	33	36	35	34	35	37	30	29
46	34	37	30	31	32	39	26	37
48	31	36	32	32	34	39	25	27
50	35	37	32	38	29	33	24	34
51	40	29	32	39	31	34	30	38
53	35	32	34	37	31	32	27	33
60	30	36	31	27	28	33	29	29
78	27	36	31	32	34	34	27	39

Appendix 6.1
Scoring criteria and descriptors, oral interaction sub-test, June 1994

FLUENCY
7 Speech is marked by a very high degree of fluency.
6 Speech is marked by a high degree of fluency with occasional hesitation.
5 Speech is fluent but with some hesitation or deliberation.
4 Noticeable hesitation and some groping for words is present, but does not impede communication.
3 A marked degree of hesitation, grasping for words or inability to phrase utterances easily impedes communication.
2 Speech is fragmented because of hesitations, pauses or false starts.
1 Fluency is evident only in the most formulaic phrases.

GRAMMAR
7 Range and control of grammatical structures are precise and sophisticated.
6 Candidate uses a broad range of structures with only occasional minor errors.
5 Communication is generally grammatically accurate with a range of structures; minor errors may be noticeable.
4 Satisfactory communication is achieved despite a limited range of structures and/or obvious grammatical inaccuracies.
3 Communication is less than satisfactory because of a limited range of structures and/or the presence of frequent errors.
2 Limited communication is possible but errors are likely to be frequent and intrusive.
1 Severe limitations of grammar prevent all but the most basic communication.

VOCABULARY

7 Candidate uses a wide range of vocabulary precisely, appropriately and effectively.

6 Candidate uses a wide range of vocabulary effectively though occasionally may be imprecise.

5 Vocabulary is broad enough to allow the candidate to express ideas well. Circumlocution is smooth and effective, if required.

4 Vocabulary is broad enough to allow the candidate to express most ideas. Can usually circumlocute to cover gaps in vocabulary, if required.

3 Vocabulary is broad enough to allow the candidate to express simple ideas. Circumlocution is sometimes ineffective.

2 Limited vocabulary restricts expression to common words and phrases. Circumlocution is laborious and often ineffective.

1 Vocabulary is very limited.

INTELLIGIBILITY

7 Speech is clear and can be followed effortlessly.

6 Speech is generally clear and can be followed with little effort.

5 Speech can be followed though at times requires some concentration by the listener.

4 Speech can generally be followed though sometimes causes strain.

3 Speech can generally be followed though frequently causes strain.

2 Speech requires constant concentration to be understood.

1 Speech can only be followed intermittently and then only with considerable effort.

COHESION

7 Cohesive devices are smoothly and effectively managed.

6 A good range of cohesive devices is used but occasionally these may be inappropriate.

5 A range of cohesive devices is used but these may be inappropriate.

4 Cohesive devices are limited in range and may be used inappropriately or inaccurately.

3 Very simple cohesive devices are used to link sentences but errors are frequent.

2 There is some evidence of connected discourse but the overall effect is disjointed.

1 Candidate is able to use only isolated words and formulaic phrases.

COMPREHENSION (live version only)

7 Candidate rarely misunderstands, except occasionally when speech is very rapid or ambiguous.

6 Candidate appears to have only occasional problems in understanding.

5 Candidate appears to be able to understand most speech but may require repetition of some details.

4 Candidate is generally able to get the gist of most speech although s/he may require repetition, and is more comfortable with slower rates of speech.

3 Candidate often has difficulty understanding utterances, and may require frequent repetition or reformulation.

2 Candidate is only able to understand simplified speech.

1 Candidate demonstrates only intermittent comprehension.

OVERALL COMMUNICATIVE EFFECTIVENESS

Scale of 1 to 7 without descriptors (7 = near native flexibility and range; 1 = limited).

Appendix 6.2
Observation notes: Abdul and Wing Li, June 1994 trial

1 Notes recorded at the time the test was conducted

A Abdul

(i) Live version
A = Abdul
I = Interlocutor
Setting
Small classroom. Quiet with natural lighting.

Section 1 (warm up)
I asks questions in a relaxed, informal manner, smiling with sustained eye contact. A a little tentative: clasping hands, feet crossed. Responses are OK: speaks with careful phrasing and emphasis. At the end I checks cassette recorder is working. He smiles and they both laugh.

Section 2a
Q1: During preparation time A studies picture carefully. When responding looks at I for confirmation. I keeps smiling and nodding. He also provides some verbal feedback e.g. 'Mm' or 'Yep'. Q2: A again studies pictures carefully. Asks what 'accommodation' means. I reads question very naturally, clearly. A answers still looking closely at pictures, not looking much at I. A speaks quite fluently but softly. Again, I provides occasional verbal feedback ('mm', 'yea'). Q3: A speaks with more animation (wider voice range), uses hand gestures and establishes better eye contact with I. A still looking at pictures (for ideas?), silent at such times. I allows silences for thinking time and doesn't comment. At the end of A's answer I says 'Yep, that's fine'.

Section 2b
A studies pictures very carefully in preparation time. A talks while still looking closely at pictures, occasionally glancing at I. I nods, smiles and provides occasional verbal feedback ('mm', 'yea'). A seems unsure about last two pictures: hesitates before continuing the story at these two points. I says 'OK, that's fine' at the end.

Section 3
I reads instructions for role play and smiles reassuringly. During preparation time A appears a little anxious: body slightly tense, shifting feet back and forward. I starts role play off. A is rather tentative at first. I speaks quite a lot, especially at the outset. A appears to gradually relax and

enter into his role more enthusiastically. Problem posed by the situation in the role play is satisfactorily resolved at the end. I says 'good' and both laugh.

Section 4a

A asks what the terms 'attitudes' and 'patterns' mean. I explains first word but says 'I'm not sure how much I can tell you' in response to query about second word. Q1: A looks at graph while talking and I says very little. Q2: A uses more eye contact and hand gestures, speaks more confidently. Sometimes not intelligible when speaking softly. Q3: A is quite relaxed, even joking and smiling at times. Eye contact is maintained throughout. I smiles slightly, raises eyebrows and nods at times and occasionally says 'Yep'.

Section 4b

A appears to prepare carefully, studying graph and questions in detail. A answers all four questions quite confidently. I is more strict with the amount of time he allows A to answer in.

Section 5

A responds fluently and confidently although he pauses for a while some-times. I does not fill these pauses and allows A the time to think. A is more expansive in this section and speaks more loudly, using a lot of hand gestures as well.

(ii) Tape version

A = Abdul

Setting

Language lab with 20 candidates. Room is hot and stuffy with no natural light. Supervisor adopts a formal manner (e.g. 'Don't open your test booklets until I tell you to.')

Section 1 (warm up)

A appears relaxed and answers questions calmly and confidently.

Section 2a

Q1: A looks very closely at first picture during prep time. Still looking at picture while speaking. He uses very careful phrasing. Appears to be having trouble monitoring himself with noise of other people speaking around him. Even listening to him with headphones is difficult because of the other people talking. A is cut off by next segment. Q2: A is again cut off by next question. Q3: A is speaking more slowly than in live test but is not cut off in this case.

Section 2b

A appears more tense: furrowed brow, body seems a bit rigid. Uses pictures to create a descriptive commentary rather than a story ('In picture 1, in picture 2'). Response completed with plenty of time to spare here.

Section 2c

A takes notes as suggested while dialogue is playing. Continues writing during preparation time. When prompted to speak A seems to be struggling to find what he wants to say in his notes and doesn't end up saying very much. He's looking very tense at this point with pursed lips and a very furrowed brow.

Section 3

A still looks anxious as he reads and prepares his response. He mouths the words on the page as he reads them. He seems to struggle again to find the right words when he speaks. His response becomes a little more fluent towards the end but it is still marred by a lot of pauses and hesitations.

Section 4a

Q1: A still speaking very slowly and deliberately but a bit more confidently now. Still looking tense and pressured – perhaps concerned about being cut off? Q2: A repeats question in answer, seems to complete response in time on this occasion. Q3: Response seems clear enough although there is a long pause in the middle.

Section 4b

A provides a full, fairly fluent response but cut off at the end by next section.

Section 5

Q1: A talking a bit more quickly and confidently here, finishes on time. Q2: A hesitates a fair bit but the answer is quite coherent. Cut off once again. Q3: A gives fairly full answer, in fact seems to be adding further detail just to fill up the time at the end. Q4: A speaks more slowly again but not so hesitatingly.

Section 6

Q1: A studies pictures very carefully before and while speaking. Q2: A very engaged by this task. Doesn't hesitate or pause much and gives what appears to be a complete answer. Q3: Some pausing and hesitation here as well as slower speech.

B Wing Li

(i) Tape version

W = Wing Li

Setting

Language lab: 13 other candidates, rather stuffy with no natural light. Supervisor seems more relaxed than in the morning sessions.

Section 1 (warm up)

W sitting in a fairly relaxed manner. Answers questions in a relaxed, fairly confident manner: appears quite at home with language lab environment.

Section 2a

Q1: W answers quite fluently even though she is still studying the pictures throughout her response. When almost finished she is cut off by the next question. Q2 and Q3: Very clear answers and in both instances she finishes on time.

Section 2b

W delivers a very clear narrative. She speaks very fluently apart from a few pauses and hesitations.

Section 2c

W has hand on forehead while recorded dialogue is playing. She doesn't take many notes. She starts talking immediately after the beep and provides a very clear answer which is cut off at the end.

Section 3

W again concentrates very hard in question time. Begins talking immediately after she is prompted to do so. However, in this case her speech is a little more disjointed than in the previous sections. She is cut off at the end but again she appears to have almost completed her answer.

Section 4a

Q1: W responds quite fully with some hesitation. She is cut off at the end. Q2: Again she doesn't finish her response but it is very clear. Q3: Speaks very confidently and fluently. She seems to be merely filling up the remaining silence at the end however, without having much left to say.

Section 4b

Handles this task very competently. Her response is fluent and clear.

Section 5

Q1: W hesitates somewhat. She seems to be responding to Q2 in part. Q2: Unusually, she pauses before beginning speaking. She also repeats some of her answer to Q1. She is cut off at the end although her answer appeared to be complete. Q3 and Q4: Fluent, clear answers. She is cut off in both questions but appears to be merely filling in time towards the end, especially in Q4.

Section 6

Q1: Very full and interesting response. Q2: Cut off, this time without appearing to finish the main thrust of her answer. Q3: W shows some hesitation here. Her answer includes some self-repair and pausing. She is also cut off again, but, as is usually the case, she appears to have presented the major part of her answer.

(ii) Live version

W = Wing Li

I = Interlocutor

Setting

Large classroom. Quiet but without natural lighting.

Section 1 (warm up)

The I seems to be rushing through these questions. She asks each one quickly and begins the next one as soon as W has provided even the most minimal answer. W appears a little ill at ease: her body seems stiff and she is clasping her hands. I also seems uncomfortable: she doesn't smile much and her gaze seems expectant but not very friendly.

Section 2a

I reads instructions rapidly. In preparation time W looks rather anxious while studying pictures. Her answer to Q1 is a bit tentative. She looks to I for reassurance but I gives little aural/visual feedback. W is still rather hesitant in her answers to Q2 and Q3. I still seems rather ill at ease. She doesn't use much verbal feedback although she does nod occasionally and establish eye contact sporadically.

Section 2b

In preparation time W seems to want clarification. She asks whether the person in the story has a sore back. I evades the question by telling her to think about the story for a minute and then she can talk. W is a bit more confident in her response on this task. W still glances occasionally at the I for confirmation, without much success on the whole. W still clasping her hands while talking. Her response is quite comprehensive and clear. She laughs at the end although the reason for this is unclear – is she embarrassed or beginning to relax? I gives a quick smile and nods several times towards the end of W's answer. She seems eager for W to finish.

Section 3

In role play I speaks a lot and uses gestures in acting out her role. W seems rather inhibited, even a little embarrassed. She doesn't contribute much although the I doesn't really give her much room to talk anyway.

Section 4a

W speaks quite freely and more confidently in this task. I gives very little feedback, either verbal or non-verbal. I seems more tense than W at this point.

Section 4b

W is definitely more relaxed now, sometimes smiling at I while listening and talking. I has slowed a bit in the speed of her delivery of the instructions and questions but she still gives the impression of wanting the test to be over as quickly as possible. W's responses are generally clear although she hesitates in places.

Section 5

In preparation time W talks to herself quietly as if rehearsing her answer. I appears to relax a little in this final section. At the end of Q1 she says 'Sounds good' and provides more consistent verbal feedback throughout all four questions. However, I still appears keen to bring the test to an end: she moves quickly on to each successive question. W is reasonably relaxed, even laughs on occasions (although again this could be the result of nervousness). Her answers are fairly clear although she appears to be speaking quite deliberately, monitoring herself carefully.

2 Notes based on video recordings

A Abdul

(i) Live version
A = Abdul
I = Interlocutor
Setting: large, bright room. Some extraneous traffic noise.

Section 1 (Warm up)

I reads questions, smiles. He folds his hands on the table, leaning forward slightly in his chair. A sits upright, hands together underneath the table. A speaks fairly intelligibly though rather softly and carefully initially. I smiles encouragingly and A begins to speak more freely and loudly. I checks cassette recorder is working. A smiles as he listens to himself on tape.

Section 2a

A changes glasses to look at page 2. A studies pictures carefully in prep time, looks up once at I. I allows full amount of prep time for Q1. A studies picture while talking. He uses an occasional hand gesture but doesn't look at I very much. I sits with hands folded, not saying much. He looks alternately at A and at the pictures. A looks up at I after finishing his answer to Q1 and smiles. I says 'That's good', then moves on to next question. Full preparation time for Q2 allowed. A begins talking immediately when prompted to do so. He still looks at the pictures while talking although he occasionally looks up at the I. Again I looks alternately at the booklet and at A. In Q3 A still looks at the picture even though the question doesn't really require him to do so. He uses hand gestures frequently now, both it seems to highlight meaning and to compensate for problems in English. I eventually terminates A's response when it appears he has nothing important left to say.

Section 2b

I reads instructions. A studies pictures. Full prep time allowed. I folds arms and asks questions which cue A's response. A discusses content of each picture in present rather than past time. A looks up occasionally at I for confirmation. I nods in response. A appears a little unsure of what is happening in several of the pictures. He hesitates at one point and says he can't really understand what's happening. The I smiles sympathetically but doesn't actively assist him. A perseveres and eventually finishes the task. I says 'That's fine'.

Section 3

I reads instructions for the role play. A studies the role play card in the prep time. Full prep time allowed. Both I and A appear to be comfortable with their respective roles. I talks a fair bit, probably more than A. Neither of them look at the booklets much at all in this task. Both laugh together at the end.

Section 4a

A studies graph and questions in prep time. He asks what 'attitudes' means. I appears rather uncomfortable at this point and says, 'I'm not sure how much I can tell you.' They laugh together. I then explains the meaning. Full prep time allowed. A answers Q1 immediately when prompted to begin. He talks while studying the graph and looks up occasionally. I alternately looks at A and at his own booklet. In Q2 and Q3 A is still looking at the graph while talking though not as much as in Q1. He uses hand gestures sometimes. He smiles fairly often and holds his hands together on the table most of the time. I is attentive, smiles and nods often. At the end of this section he says to A, 'All right, that's good.'

Section 4b

Full prep time allowed. Once again A studies graph while talking most of the time. He answers Q1 briefly but confidently, Q2 and Q3 a bit hesitantly but in some detail and Q4 quite briefly and then laughs at the end.

Section 5

Full prep time allowed. A answers questions in detail and less hesitantly than most other questions. He also maintains eye contact with I more continuously. He only occasionally glances at relevant page in booklet to check questions.

(ii) Tape version

A = Abdul

Section 1 (warm up)

In Q1 A starts to speak before instead of after the bell. He does the same in Q2 but this time starts again after the bell. He begins talking after the bell in Q3 and Q4 but is cut off by the next questions. He begins appropriately in Q5 and finishes within the time allowed.

Section 2a

A studies pictures intently in prep time. His neighbour looks to see what he's doing. A is leaning forward with his elbows on the desk. He appears to be concentrating very intensely while he responds to Q1. At one point he says 'Sorry' and starts again. He is speaking fairly slowly and deliberately, giving the impression he is closely monitoring his speech. He is cut off at the end. In Q2 he speaks a little more quickly but is still cut off. He completes Q3 in time.

Section 2b

A studies pictures closely in prep time. When prompted to begin talking he describes the actions in each of the eight pictures in the present tense. He rushes a little in this section, as if worried he'll be cut off again.

Section 2c

Again, A studies his booklet very carefully. He takes notes while he listens, as advised for this task. He shifts around in his chair a little. He is still taking notes when the announcement finishes (his neighbour tries to read them). He begins talking immediately when given the cue but soon begins to pause for long periods and ends up actually saying very little. His last phrase is cut off.

Section 3

A studies booklet both during and after the prep time. He speaks more fluently in this task with only a couple of hesitations. He is cut off at the end.

Section 4a

A studies booklet very carefully in prep time. He begins speaking immediately after the bell. His answer to Q1 is fairly fluent with only minor hesitations. He speaks with even greater ease in Q2. He is more hesitant in Q3 and there are several long pauses. Not cut off in any of these questions.

Section 4b

Again, A studies questions very closely in prep time. He is breathing heavily now and looks tired and a little stressed. Nevertheless, he speaks quite fluently and confidently. He is cut off at the end.

Section 5

A prepares carefully. In Q1 he speaks quite confidently and easily. He finishes well within the time. In Q2, Q3 and Q4 he is a little more hesitant but still quite fluent. He is cut off in Q4.

Section 6

A prepares carefully as usual. In Q1 he hesitates a little. He looks intently at pictures while speaking. In Q2 he speaks quite quickly at first, then slows down and pauses a little as his response continues. He is cut of by the next question. In Q3 he hesitates a little but his answer is reasonably clear.

B Wing Li

(i) Tape version
W = Wing Li

Section 1 (warm up)

Not recorded

Section 2a

Q1: W studies picture, blinking with hand under chin. She speaks fairly softly but confidently without hesitations. Q2 and Q3: W speaks quite fluently, again with little hesitation or pausing. She is cut off in Q2 but in both questions she provides a comprehensive answer.

Section 2b

W folds arms on top of desk to prepare. She studies the pictures closely. She seems a bit more hesitant in her response on this task. Her version of the story is quite coherent staying close to the pictures. There are some re-phrasings. She is cut off just before finishing.

Section 2c

W yawns while instructions are read, listens intently while interview is played, hand over head then under her chin. She takes some notes during and at the end of the interview. She speaks quite animatedly and fluently, providing a comprehensive summary. She is cut off just prior to completion.

Section 3

W appears to be listening and reading her instructions very carefully with her hands under her chin. She is rather hesitant in her response but quite coherent, leaning forward over the desk. She is cut off again.

Section 4a

W prepares carefully, studying the questions and graph closely. Q1: She begins talking immediately. She gives a fluent answer but is cut off at the end. Q2: As for Q1. Her answer here includes a good range of vocabulary. Q3: Clear, coherent comparison between China and Australia.

Section 4b

As usual, W appears to be concentrating intently on the task at hand in the prep time. She answers comprehensively but is cut off prior to completing her answer.

Section 5

Initially, W appears to be answering all four questions simultaneously here. She realises her mistake after Q2 is read aloud. She handles this confusion well and her next three responses are more specifically geared to the individual questions. She is cut off in Q1 and Q3.

Section 6

W appears to be studying the pictures and questions carefully in the prep time with her arms folded on the desk. Q1: She begins talking in a confident manner and provides a clear answer with few hesitations. Q2: This answer is a bit hesitant but still coherent. She is cut off by the next question. Q3: A fluent response but again cut off before finishing. However, W appears to have completed the major part of her answer and is simply filling in time by elaborating further. At the end of this section she takes the headphones off and smiles.

(ii) Live version

W = Wing Li

I = Interlocutor

Setting: Small classroom, a bit stuffy without natural light.

I reads general instructions about the test quickly, pushing her hair back. W nods.

Section 1 (warm up)

I asks each warm up question in fairly quick succession. W appears a bit awkward and embarrassed, laughing nervously especially in Q5 where she re-starts several times. I checks tape recorder is working. She also checks with W: 'That's OK isn't it?' without smiling. W nods in agreement.

Section 2a

I reads instructions fairly briskly and W studies the first picture. There is very little eye contact between them. I allows the full prep time for Q1 then asks question. W talks fairly hesitantly occasionally looking up at I. I nods or occasionally smiles with her head down. In Q2 and Q3 I appears a little tense and restless. She folds and then unfolds her arms on the table. W still speaking fairly hesitantly looking up at I at times as if for encouragement. I nods in a rather perfunctory manner, and, even more rarely, gives her a half smile at these moments.

Section 2b

I reads instructions fairly quickly. W asks for clarification about what happens to the woman in the story. I replies, 'You just think about it for a minute and then I'll ask that question.' She therefore appears to miss the point of W's question, whether deliberately or not. W is clearly confused about what is happening in the sequence of pictures and needs assistance. I has a sip of water and waits one minute before cuing W's response. W tells the story rather tentatively. I moves the tape recorder close to W while she's talking. W looks up at several points and I nods curtly when she does this. W has her hands folded fairly tightly on the desk and sometimes switches them to below the desk. I has her hands behind her head, then over her forehead, then behind her head again and finally folded in front of her while W speaks. W smiles at the end of her answer. I gives a quick, rather tight smile in response. Both of them seem quite anxious at this point.

Section 3

I reads instructions a bit more slowly here. W asks for clarification about their respective roles. W reads her role play card, hands clasped on table. I sits with arms folded tightly leaning on the table. I looks up after one minute and begins the role play. I pretends to be looking for photos in a drawer. Both smile, looking at each other. W puts up some resistance in her role as directed in the instructions for this task and refuses to accept the replacement film. I quickly agrees to W's demands as if she wants to end the role play as soon as possible. Throughout the role play W and I often smiled reassuringly at each other, as if to acknowledge that the conflict they were involved in was fake.

Section 4a

I reads instructions quite rapidly again and W looks at the graph and questions. At the end of the prep time I says 'OK?' W nods but there is still no eye contact between them. W gives quite a lengthy answer to Q1 still without looking at I. I nods occasionally while W talks. In Q2 W responds more confidently, occasionally looking up at I who nods. I goes straight into Q3 when W pauses although it is unclear whether W has actually finished her answer. In Q3 W answers quite fluently. She looks up once at I during her answer. I nods but doesn't smile. W looks up at the end apparently to signal to I she has finished her answer.

Section 4b

I reads instructions quickly and W studies the questions and graphical information carefully in prep time. W gives a short answer for Q1 and longer answer for both Q2 and Q3. In both instances she looks up at I at times. I nods in reply. W looks up again when she has finished her answers. W is smiling more in this section. In Q4 W laughs in a fairly relaxed way when discussing the kind of technology she uses at home and I even manages a full smile in response.

Section 5

I reads instructions a little less hurriedly than in section 4. In this case I looks at W while she answers the questions. W is also looking more at I here. This behaviour might indicate they are more relaxed with each other now although the open nature of this task probably promotes more interaction. W answers all of the questions quite confidently. At the end both give each other a relaxed smile.

Appendix 6.3
Questions for candidate interviews, June 1994 trial

1. Is it OK if I record this interview?

2. TAPE TEST

    a. Were the voices on the tape clear?

    b. Were the instructions in the booklet and the tape clear?

    c. Which tasks were difficult/easy?

    d. Was there sufficient preparation time?

    e. Was there sufficient response time?

    f. Was it distracting having the other candidates talking at the same time?

    g. Was this a good test of your spoken English?

    h. Did you feel relaxed during this test?

    i. How did you feel about having me and the video camera in the room?

3. LIVE TEST

    a. Did you feel relaxed during this test?

    b. Did you find the interviewer easy to understand? Why/why not?

    c. Was the interviewer helpful?

    d. Which tasks were difficult/easy?

    e. Were the instructions clear/unclear?

    f. Was there sufficient preparation time?

    g. Was there sufficient response time?

    h. Was this a good test of your spoken English?

    i. How did you feel about having another person and a video camera in the room?

4. LIVE TEST versus TAPE TEST

    a. Did you feel more nervous on one test than the other? Why?

    b. Was it easier talking to a microphone or another person?

    c. Was one of the tests more difficult for you? Why?

    d. Which one was a better test of your spoken English?

Appendix 6.4
Candidate questionnaire, June 1994 trial

QUESTIONNAIRE

You did two speaking tests today. One was in the language laboratory (TAPE) and the other with an interviewer (INTERVIEW). To help us improve the speaking tests, we would like you to answer these questions.

NAME
1 Which speaking test did you do first (please circle)?   TAPE LIVE
2 Indicate your gender (please circle).   FEMALE MALE
3 How old are you?   years
4 How long have you been in Australia?
5 What is your occupation?
6 What is your native language?

Please circle ONLY ONE answer for each question.

The TAPE speaking test

1 Could you hear the tape clearly?

Always   /   Sometimes   /   Never

2 Did you understand the instructions?

Always   /   Sometimes   /   Never

3 Did you have enough time to think about the questions *before* you spoke?

Always   /   Sometimes   /   Never

4 Did you have enough time to answer the questions?

Always   /   Sometimes   /   Never

5 Did you feel the test was

Too difficult /   OK   /   Too easy

6 Do you think the tape test was a good test of your spoken English?

Yes   /   Not sure   /   No

Please circle ONLY ONE answer for each question.

The INTERVIEW speaking test

1 Did you understand the instructions?

       Always   /   Sometimes   /   Never

2 Did you have enough time to think about the questions *before* you spoke?

       Always   /   Sometimes   /   Never

3 Did you have enough time to answer the questions?

       Always   /   Sometimes   /   Never

4 Was the interviewer helpful?

       Always   /   Sometimes   /   Never

5 Did you feel the test was

       Too difficult /   OK   /   Too easy

6 Do you think the interview was a good test of your spoken English?

       Yes   /   Not sure   /   No

BOTH TESTS

1 Which test made you more nervous?

       Tape   Interview

2 Which test was more difficult for you?

       Interview   Tape

3 Which test gave you more opportunity to speak English?

       Tape   Interview

4 Which one was a better test of your spoken English?

       Interview   Tape

Any other comments?

Thank you for answering these questions. Please take the questionnaire to Registration and you will receive your payment.

Appendix 6.5
Questions for interlocutor interviews, June 1994 trial

1. What is your occupation?
2. Have you done interviewing in language tests before? Which ones?
3. Did you feel relaxed during the test?
4. Did you find the instructions clear?
5. How closely do you think you followed them? Did you normally allow the prescribed amount of preparation time?
6. Did you find you needed to add more instructions or clarifying statements?
7. Did you think the candidate was nervous?
8. Did you think the test was pitched at the right level for the candidate?
9. Did you think you helped the candidate to perform at his/her best? How did you do this?
10. Do you think you contributed the right amount in the role play?
11. How well did you think the candidate performed in each of the tasks/overall?
12. Were you distracted by my presence or the video camera?
13. Do you think this was a good test of the candidate's spoken English?
14. What did you think of your own performance overall?
15. Do you think this test is better than other tests of speaking in which you have been an interviewer?
16. How do you think a live test such as this one compares with a tape-based one done in a language laboratory?

Appendix 6.6
Raw scores allocated to Abdul and Wing Li, June 1994 trial

A LIVE

	ABDUL			WING	LI	
RATERS	7	89	12	3	72	12
Description						
– fluency	5	4	4	4	3	5
– grammar	4	4	4	4	3	5
– vocabulary	5	4	5	4	3	5
Narration						
– grammar	4	4	4	4	4	4
– vocabulary	4	4	4	4	4	5
– cohesion	3	3	4	4	5	4
Role play						
– fluency	4	4	5	4	4	5
– grammar	4	4	4	4	4	4
– intelligibility	5	4	5	4	4	5
Exposition (1)						
– fluency	4	5	5	4	3	5
– vocabulary	4	4	5	4	3	5
– cohesion	5	4	4	4	3	5
Exposition (2)						
– fluency	4	4	5	4	4	5
– vocabulary	4	4	5	4	4	5
– cohesion	4	5	4	4	4	4
Discussion						
– fluency	5	4	5	5	5	5
– grammar	4	4	4	4	4	4
– intelligibility	5	3	4	5	3	4
Global criteria						
– comm effectiveness	4	3	4	5	3	5
– comprehension	5	5	7	6	6	7

B TAPE

	ABDUL			WING	LI	
RATERS	3	46	12	7	39	12
Description (1)						
– fluency	3	4	5	5	5	6
– grammar	3	4	4	5	5	5
– vocabulary	3	4	5	5	5	6
Narration						
– grammar	4	4	4	4	5	4
– vocabulary	3	4	4	5	5	6
– cohesion	3	4	4	5	5	5
Summary						
– fluency	3	3	4	5	5	6
– grammar	3	3	4	5	5	5
– vocabulary	3	3	4	5	5	6
Role play						
– fluency	4	4	5	5	6	6
– grammar	4	4	4	5	5	4
– intelligibility	3	4	5	5	6	6
Exposition						
– fluency	3	4	4	4	5	5
– vocabulary	3	4	4	5	5	5
– cohesion		2	3	4	5	6
Instructions						
– fluency	4	4	5	4	5	5
– vocabulary	3	4	4	5	5	5
– cohesion	3	4	4	5	6	5
Discussion						
– fluency	3	4	5	5	5	5
– grammar	3	4	4	4	5	5
– intelligibility	4	4	4	5	6	6
Description (2)						
– fluency	4	4	5	4	6	5
– grammar	4	4	4	4	6	4
– vocabulary	3	3	4	5	6	6
Global criteria						
– comm effectiveness	3	3	4	5	6	6

Appendix 6.7
Questions for rater interviews, June 1994 trial

1. What is your experience as a rater of the ***access:*** oral interaction test?
2. How long is it since you marked last time?
3. Did the calibration session prove useful?
4. How many tapes have you rated so far? Live? Tape?

   The rest of the questions relate to the specific performance assessed by the rater immediately prior to the interview.

5. Is this a live or tape test performance?
6. Do you think the format
   a. was pitched at the right level for the candidate?
   b. provided clear instructions?
   c. provided adequate preparation and response time?
7. Were the scoring criteria appropriate overall for this version?
8. Were the descriptors for the criteria clear?
9. Was it difficult to rate the candidate?
10. Did the candidate seem nervous? confident?
11. How well did the candidate perform overall?
12. Did s/he perform consistently?
13. Do you think this was a good test of their speaking proficiency?
14. (live version only) How well did the interlocutor perform?
15. (live version only) Do you think it would have been easier to rate the live version with a videotaped recording?
16. In general, do you think either version provides a better test of proficiency in spoken English?

Appendix 6.8
Rater questionnaire, June 1994 trial

access: **oral interaction test**

RATER QUESTIONNAIRE

Name .... Rater no. ....

Please answer the following questions which focus on the comparability of the live and tape-based versions of the test in general. If there is insufficient space you can write on the back of the sheet.

1. Do you think the live and tape-based versions of the test serve equally well as tests of proficiency in spoken English? Please explain your answer.

2. Do you think the scoring criteria (fluency, grammar etc.) and their accompanying level descriptors are appropriate for rating both versions?

3. Is one version more difficult to rate than the other? Again, please explain your answer.

4. Is there anything else about the comparability of the two versions you'd like to add?

Appendix 7.1

FACETS analyses (1) with anchored item difficulty estimates, oral interaction sub-test, June 1994 trial (N = 94)

A Live data

(i) Candidates

Obsvd Score	Obsvd Count	Obsvd Average	Fair Avrge	Measure	Model S.E.	Infit MnSq	Infit Std	Outfit MnSq	Outfit Std	Num
172	40	4.3	4.0	-0.79	0.29	0.6	-1	0.6	-1	1
221	40	5.5	4.8	1.56	0.26	0.8	0	0.8	0	2
241	40	6.0	5.9	2.46	0.26	1.2	0	1.1	0	3
146	40	3.7	3.9	-2.02	0.25	0.9	0	0.8	0	4
160	37	4.3	4.1	-0.25	0.31	1.3	1	1.4	1	5
178	40	4.5	4.8	0.05	0.31	1.2	0	1.2	0	7
203	40	5.1	5.0	1.48	0.27	1.5	2	1.7	2	9
207	40	5.2	5.4	0.04	0.26	1.6	2	1.7	2	10
153	40	3.8	3.9	-2.93	0.32	1.2	0	1.2	0	12
199	40	5.0	4.9	0.60	0.23	0.8	0	0.8	0	13
167	40	4.2	4.2	-1.83	0.26	1.1	0	1.1	0	14
150	40	3.8	3.5	-3.38	0.28	1.0	0	1.0	0	15
252	40	6.3	6.4	2.49	0.26	0.7	-1	0.8	0	16
177	40	4.4	4.4	-0.29	0.28	0.6	1	0.6	2	17
180	40	4.5	4.3	-1.10	0.25	0.9	0	0.9	0	18
200	40	5.0	4.6	-0.68	0.21	1.1	0	1.1	0	20
257	40	6.4	6.3	2.83	0.30	0.9	0	0.8	0	21
184	40	4.6	3.8	-1.26	0.23	0.8	-1	0.8	-1	22
199	40	5.0	4.4	-0.37	0.21	0.5	-2	0.5	2	23
207	40	5.2	4.8	0.24	0.24	0.7	-1	0.7	-1	24
168	40	4.2	3.9	-1.03	0.24	0.4	3	0.5	2	25
258	40	6.5	6.5	5.01	0.34	1.2	0	1.3	0	26
168	40	4.2	4.3	-0.77	0.27	0.5	-3	0.5	-2	27
175	40	4.4	3.8	-1.00	0.30	0.6	-2	0.6	-2	28
229	40	5.7	5.3	2.95	0.28	0.6	-1	0.6	-1	29
172	40	4.3	4.4	0.06	0.32	1.2	0	1.1	0	30
178	40	4.5	4.5	-0.43	0.29	0.9	0	1.0	0	32
172	40	4.3	4.4	-1.41	0.27	0.6	-2	0.6	-2	33
198	40	5.0	5.5	1.07	0.27	0.6	-2	0.6	-2	35
169	40	4.2	4.5	-0.45	0.28	0.7	-1	0.9	0	36
225	40	5.6	5.7	1.58	0.26	0.8	-1	1.0	0	37
198	40	5.0	4.7	-0.53	0.29	1.1	0	1.2	0	38
166	40	4.2	4.1	-1.56	0.26	0.7	-1	0.7	-1	39
175	40	4.4	4.4	-1.29	0.26	1.2	0	1.1	0	40
214	40	5.3.	5.3.	2.45	0.31	0.9	0	0.9	0	41
189	40	4.7	4.6	-0.87	0.25	1.0	0	1.0	0	42
179	40	4.5	4.4	-0.67	0.27	1.6	2	1.6	2	43
183	40	4.6	4.1	-1.28	0.23	1.0	0	1.0	0	44
204	40	5.1	4.6	-0.06	0.20	1.3	1	1.4	1	45
250	40	6.3	5.7	1.99	0.21	1.2	0	1.2	0	47
109	40	2.7	2.3	-5.51	0.31	0.9	0	0.9	0	48
242	40	6.1	5.7	1.80	0.25	1.1	0	1.2	0	50
257	40	6.4	6.7	6.19	0.34	1.0	0	1.2	0	51
158	40	4.0	3.7	-0.85	0.30	1.3	1	1.3	1	53
171	34	5.0	4.7	0.69	0.29	1.0	0	1.0	0	55
233	40	5.8	5.8	2.80	0.26	0.8	-1	0.8	-1	56
230	40	5.8	5.8	4.03	0.27	0.5	-3	0.5	-3	57

Live data – candidates (continued)

Obsvd Score	Obsvd Count	Obsvd Average	Fair Avrge	Measure	Model S.E.	Infit MnSq	Infit Std	Outfit MnSq	Outfit Std	Num
172	40	4.3	4.5	-1.50	0.31	0.6	-2	0.6	-2	58
210	40	5.3	5.9	1.94	0.27	0.5	-3	0.5	-2	59
170	40	4.3	4.5	-0.37	0.27	1.2	0	1.3	1	60
230	40	5.8	5.7	2.07	0.29	1.3	1	1.5	1	61
174	40	4.3	4.2	-1.55	0.28	1.2	0	1.2	1	65
204	40	5.1	5.2	1.39	0.24	0.7	-1	0.7	-1	66
170	40	4.3	4.2	-0.84	0.27	0.6	-1	0.6	-1	67
161	40	4.0	3.9	-2.63	0.28	1.4	1	1.4	1	68
202	40	5.1	4.8	0.37	0.22	0.8	-1	0.7	-1	71
195	40	4.9	4.4	-0.57	0.26	0.3	-4	0.3	-4	72
195	40	4.9	4.0	-0.81	0.20	1.4	1	1.3	1	73
187	40	4.7	4.5	-0.67	0.22	0.9	0	0.9	0	74
150	40	3.8	3.5	-2.36	0.28	0.9	0	0.9	0	75
192	40	4.8	4.1	-0.21	0.24	1.7	2	1.7	2	76
199	40	5.0	4.9	-0.21	0.25	0.9	0	0.9	0	77
179	40	4.5	4.6	0.84	0.34	0.7	0	0.6	-1	78
147	40	3.7	3.8	-2.17	0.32	1.1	0	1.1	0	79
170	40	4.3	4.1	-1.44	0.28	0.8	-1	0.8	-1	80
240	40	6.0	6.5	4.50	0.29	0.9	0	0.9	0	81
171	40	4.3	4.3	-1.82	0.27	1.7	2	1.7	2	84
196	40	4.9	4.9	-0.32	0.29	0.9	0	1.0	0	85
192	40	4.8	5.2	1.03	0.26	1.5	1	1.5	1	86
161	40	4.0	4.0	-1.22	0.27	1.3	0	1.2	0	88
204	40	5.1	5.0	0.15	0.26	0.8	0	0.8	0	89
185	40	4.6	4.4	-1.53	0.27	1.0	0	1.1	0	90
193	40	4.8	4.8	-0.28	0.25	1.2	0	1.1	0	91
140	40	3.5	3.2	-3.10	0.26	0.8	0	0.9	0	92
161	40	4.0	3.9	-1.78	0.24	0.8	0	0.8	-1	94
189	40	4.7	4.3	-1.27	0.25	0.9	0	1.0	0	95
184	40	4.6	4.0	-1.01	0.23	0.7	-1	0.8	0	98
184	40	4.6	4.5	-1.17	0.25	0.7	-1	0.7	-1	99
203	40	5.1	5.1	1.78	0.31	0.8	0	0.8	0	100
160	40	4.0	3.6	-1.55	0.25	1.1	0	1.0	0	102
141	40	3.5	3.2	-4.42	0.29	1.4	1	1.4	1	103
274	40	6.8	6.8	5.76	0.45	0.6	-1	0.3	-1	104
156	40	3.9	3.9	-2.54	0.28	1.4	1	1.4	1	105
152	40	3.8	4.1	-2.39	0.34	1.0	0	1.1	0	107
117	40	2.9	3.2	-5.64	0.44	1.0	0	1.3	0	108
107	40	2.7	2.5	-6.41	0.40	0.9	0	1.2	0	109
101	22	4.6	4.5	-1.46	0.34	1.4	1	1.5	1	110
128	40	3.2	2.9	-4.31	0.27	1.3	1	1.2	0	112
200	40	5.0	5.1	1.17	0.26	1.1	0	1.2	0	114
176	40	4.4	4.6	-0.89	0.28	0.9	0	0.9	0	115
189	40	4.7	5.0	0.83	0.28	0.7	-1	0.6	-1	117
214	40	5.3	5.2	0.55	0.21	1.8	3	1.8	3	118
186	40	4.7	4.5	-1.41	0.25	0.4	-3	0.4	-3	119
167	40	4.2	3.7	-2.26	0.25	0.6	-1	0.7	-1	120

Live data – candidates (continued)

Obsvd Score	Obsvd Count	Obsvd Average	Fair Avrge	Measure	Model S.E.	Infit MnSq	Std	Outfit MnSq	Std	Num
186.6	39.7	4.7	4.6	-0.31	0.27	1.0	-0.4	1.0	-0.3	Mean
33.5	1.9	0.8	0.9	2.19	0.04	0.3	1.5	0.3	1.5	S.D.

RMSE 0.28 Adj S.D. 2.17 Separation 7.85 Reliability 0.98
Fixed (all same) chi-square: 4983.6 d.f.: 95 significance: .00
Random (normal) chi-square: 94.4 d.f.: 94 significance: .47

(ii) Raters

Obsvd Score	Obsvd Count	Obsvd Average	Fair Avrge	Measure	Model S.E.	Infit MnSq	Std	Outfit MnSq	Std	Rater
728	180	4.0	4.2	0.52	0.14	0.9	0	0.9	0	3
795	180	4.4	4.7	-0.26	0.12	0.7	-3	0.7	-3	7
932	180	5.2	5.4	0.16	0.11	1.2	1	1.1	1	12
366	80	4.6	4.7	-0.48	0.20	0.9	0	0.9	0	28
786	160	4.9	5.0	-0.27	0.13	0.9	0	0.9	0	32
855	180	4.8	5.2	-1.04	0.10	0.9	0	0.9	0	36
816	160	5.1	4.8	-0.06	0.11	1.0	0	1.0	0	37
818	180	4.5	5.0	-1.76	0.12	0.8	-2	0.8	-2	38
935	180	5.2	5.3	-1.15	0.11	0.8	-2	0.7	-1	39
940	180	5.2	5.0	0.04	0.12	1.0	0	1.1	0	43
702	180	3.9	3.8	1.85	0.16	0.8	-1	0.8	-1	45
398	100	4.0	3.9	0.73	0.20	1.1	0	1.1	0	46
810	191	4.2	4.3	-1.95	0.13	1.0	0	1.0	0	48
1062	191	5.6	5.0	-0.08	0.13	0.9	0	1.0	0	50
880	180	4.9	4.7	0.15	0.12	0.9	0	0.9	0	52
885	200	4.4	4.3	0.57	0.15	1.3	2	1.3	2	56
987	200	4.9	5.0	1.21	0.12	0.7	-3	0.7	-3	67
838	200	4.2	4.1	2.89	0.15	1.0	0	1.1	0	70
803	180	4.5	4.5	-0.24	0.11	0.9	0	0.9	0	72
877	171	5.1	5.2	0.05	0.13	1.4	2	1.5	3	82
798	180	4.4	4.9	-1.39	0.15	1.2	1	1.2	1	83
906	180	5.0	4.7	0.51	0.11	1.0	0	0.9	0	89

Obsvd Score	Obsvd Count	Obsvd Average	Fair Avrge	Measure	Model S.E.	Infit MnSq	Std	Outfit MnSq	Std	Num
814.4	173.3	4.7	4.7	-0.00	0.13	1.0	-0.4	1.0	-0.3	Mean
158.9	28.4	0.5	0.4	1.09	0.03	0.2	1.6	0.2	1.6	S.D.

RMSE 0.14 Adj S.D. 1.09 Separation 8.04 Reliability 0.98
Fixed (all same) chi-square: 1433.2 d.f.: 21 significance: .00
Random (normal) chi-square: 21.0 d.f.: 20 significance: .40

(iii) Items

Obsvd Score	Obsvd Count	Obsvd Average	Fair Avrge		Measure	Model S.E.	Infit MnSq	Std	Outfit MnSq	Std	Nu Item
890	191	4.7	4.7	A	0.07	0.12	1.0	0	1.0	0	1 DesF
841	191	4.4	4.5	A	0.47	0.12	0.7	-3	0.7	-3	2 DesG
837	191	4.4	4.4	A	0.71	0.12	1.0	0	1.0	0	3 DesV
835	192	4.3	4.4	A	0.65	0.12	0.6	-3	0.7	-3	4 NarG
853	192	4.4	4.5	A	0.43	0.12	0.9	0	0.9	-1	5 NarV
869	192	4.5	4.6	A	0.24	0.12	1.3	2	1.4	3	6 NarC
898	189	4.8	4.8		-0.35	0.12	1.0	0	1.0	0	7 RPF
833	189	4.4	4.4		0.61	0.12	0.7	-3	0.6	-3	8 RPG
933	189	4.9	5.0		-0.86	0.12	1.5	3	1.6	3	9 RPI
900	190	4.7	4.8	A	-0.21	0.12	0.8	-1	0.9	-1	10 Exp1F
874	190	4.6	4.7	A	0.07	0.12	0.9	-1	0.9	0	11 Exp1V
896	190	4.7	5.1	A	-0.93	0.12	1.2	1	1.3	2	12 Exp1C
920	189	4.9	5.0		-0.68	0.12	0.7	-2	0.8	-1	13 Exp2F
886	189	4.7	4.8		-0.18	0.12	0.7	-2	0.7	-2	14 Exp2V
901	189	4.8	4.8		-0.40	0.12	1.0	0	1.0	0	15 Exp2C
952	192	5.0	5.0	A	-0.78	0.12	0.8	-1	0.8	-1	16 DisF
893	192	4.7	4.7	A	-0.06	0.12	0.7	-3	0.7	-3	17 DisG
940	192	4.9	4.9	A	-0.63	0.12	1.6	4	1.5	3	18 DisI
897	192	4.7	4.7	A	-0.11	0.12	0.5	-5	0.6	-4	19 CommEf
1069	192	5.6	5.6	A	-2.27	0.12	1.4	3	1.3	1	20 Comp
Obsvd Score	Obsvd Count	Obsvd Average	Fair Avrge		Measure	Model S.E.	Infit MnSq	Std	Outfit MnSq	Std	Nu Item
895.9	190.6	4.7	4.8		-0.21	0.12	1.0	-0.7	1.0	-0.6	Mean
52.2	1.3	0.3	0.3		0.69	0.00	0.3	2.7	0.3	2.5	S.D.

RMSE 0.12 Adj S.D. 0.68 Separation 5.60 Reliability 0.97
Fixed (all same) chi-square: 634.5 d.f.: 19 significance: .00
Random (normal) chi-square: 19.0 d.f.: 18 significance: .39

B   Tape data

(i) Candidates

Obsvd Score	Obsvd Count	Obsvd Average	Fair Avrge	Measure	Model S.E.	Infit MnSq	Std	Outfit MnSq	Std	Cand
206	50	4.1	4.3	-0.63	0.23	0.8	0	1.2	0	1
273	50	5.5	5.5	2.40	0.29	0.9	0	1.0	0	2
261	50	5.2	5.4	1.58	0.20	1.4	1	1.6	2	3
222	50	4.4	4.7	0.28	0.22	1.4	1	1.4	1	4
205	50	4.1	4.2	-0.58	0.25	1.4	1	1.3	1	5
218	50	4.4	4.6	-0.06	0.19	0.4	-3	0.5	-3	7
258	50	5.2	5.5	1.26	0.22	0.8	0	0.9	0	9
186	50	3.7	4.3	-0.28	0.20	0.7	-1	0.7	-1	10
200	49	4.1	3.8	-1.46	0.26	1.5	1	1.5	1	12
261	50	5.2	5.9	2.32	0.22	0.7	-1	0.7	-1	13
208	50	4.2	4.0	-0.93	0.24	1.5	1	1.6	1	14
185	50	3.7	3.8	-1.17	0.26	1.0	0	1.1	0	15
301	50	6.0	6.4	5.70	0.24	1.5	2	1.3	1	16
245	50	4.9	5.0	1.53	0.23	0.8	-1	0.7	-1	17
197	50	3.9	3.9	-1.18	0.23	1.3	1	1.4	1	18
241	50	4.8	4.6	0.60	0.24	0.8	-1	0.8	-1	20
323	50	6.5	6.5	5.82	0.31	0.9	0	1.0	0	21
227	50	4.5	4.5	-0.16	0.18	0.5	-2	0.5	-2	22
227	50	4.5	3.9	-0.77	0.17	1.3	1	1.2	1	23
293	50	5.9	6.4	3.05	0.22	0.8	0	0.8	0	24
238	50	4.8	4.5	0.61	0.22	0.6	-2	0.6	-2	25
267	50	5.3	5.8	4.35	0.24	1.2	0	1.2	0	26
205	50	4.1	4.1	-0.32	0.26	0.6	-2	0.6	-2	27
210	50	4.2	4.3	-0.66	0.23	1.0	0	1.0	0	28
239	50	4.8	5.4	1.36	0.21	1.2	0	1.2	1	29
221	50	4.4	4.3	0.53	0.25	0.9	0	0.9	0	30
230	50	4.6	4.7	0.14	0.21	0.8	-1	0.7	-1	32
208	50	4.2	4.2	-0.56	0.22	1.3	1	1.4	1	33
244	50	4.9	5.1	0.26	0.18	0.7	-1	0.7	-1	35
181	50	3.6	3.1	-1.35	0.18	0.9	0	0.9	0	36
254	50	5.1	5.3	1.14	0.23	0.8	-1	0.8	-1	37
220	50	4.4	4.6	0.51	0.23	1.3	1	1.3	1	38
175	50	3.5	3.6	-2.64	0.27	0.8	-1	0.8	-1	39
217	50	4.3	4.3	0.51	0.27	1.0	0	1.0	0	40
286	50	5.7	5.8	2.82	0.23	1.0	0	1.1	0	41
250	50	5.0	4.9	1.34	0.22	0.8	0	0.9	0	42
200	50	4.0	4.2	-0.34	0.21	0.9	0	1.0	0	43
205	50	4.1	4.1	-1.40	0.24	0.9	0	0.9	0	44
248	50	5.0	5.2	1.24	0.23	1.4	1	1.5	1	45
334	50	6.7	6.8	6.11	0.31	0.8	-1	0.8	-1	47
203	50	4.1	2.9	-1.46	0.19	1.2	0	1.2	0	48
249	50	5.0	5.7	1.75	0.22	0.8	-1	0.8	-1	50
314	50	6.3	6.3	7.21	0.35	1.1	0	1.1	0	51
194	50	3.9	4.2	-0.38	0.26	0.9	0	0.8	-1	53
210	50	4.2	4.3	-0.23	0.22	1.3	1	1.4	1	55
271	50	5.4	5.5	3.24	0.24	0.4	-4	0.4	-3	56
321	50	6.4	6.7	6.71	0.28	1.1	0	1.1	0	57
103	37	2.8	3.0	-3.84	0.19	1.7	3	2.2	3	58
253	50	5.1	5.1	0.86	0.18	0.8	-1	0.8	-1	59
218	50	4.4	3.5	-0.95	0.18	1.9	3	2.0	3	60

Tape data – candidates (continued)

Obsvd Score	Obsvd Count	Obsvd Average	Fair Avrge	Model Measure	S.E.	Infit MnSq	Std	Outfit MnSq	Std	Cand
304	50	6.1	6.5	3.43	0.26	1.2	0	1.4	1	61
200	50	4.0	3.9	-0.87	0.26	1.0	0	0.9	0	65
247	50	4.9	5.2	2.36	0.24	0.9	0	0.9	0	66
231	50	4.6	4.4	-0.18	0.26	1.0	0	1.0	0	68
260	50	5.2	5.4	2.38	0.26	0.4	-3	0.4	-3	71
168	50	3.4	3.7	-2.07	0.25	0.8	0	0.8	0	72
218	50	4.4	4.2	0.24	0.25	0.9	0	0.9	0	73
195	50	3.9	4.1	-0.76	0.22	1.5	2	1.3	1	74
185	50	3.7	2.9	-1.76	0.19	0.8	0	0.8	0	75
14	3	4.7	5.3	-0.28	1.01	0.9	0	0.8	0	76
223	50	4.5	4.5	0.25	0.21	0.9	0	0.9	0	77
212	50	4.2	4.5	1.44	0.27	0.7	-1	0.8	-1	78
195	50	3.9	3.8	-1.92	0.24	0.6	-1	0.5	-1	79
224	50	4.5	4.4	0.05	0.26	0.8	0	0.9	0	80
308	50	6.2	6.5	4.67	0.27	0.8	0	0.8	0	81
234	50	4.7	5.1	0.10	0.20	1.4	1	1.2	1	84
222	50	4.4	4.4	-0.40	0.21	1.2	0	1.2	0	85
198	50	4.0	4.4	-1.18	0.21	0.8	-1	1.0	0	86
253	50	5.1	5.3	1.84	0.22	0.5	-2	0.7	-1	88
260	50	5.2	4.9	1.34	0.23	0.8	0	0.8	0	89
201	50	4.0	4.1	-0.84	0.26	0.7	-1	0.7	-1	90
102	23	4.4	4.4	-0.28	0.28	0.7	0	0.8	0	91
191	50	3.8	3.9	-1.31	0.22	0.9	0	0.9	0	92
154	44	3.5	4.0	-1.90	0.22	1.1	0	1.1	0	94
204	50	4.1	4.7	0.07	0.18	0.4	-3	0.4	-4	95
163	50	3.3	3.1	-2.08	0.21	1.7	2	1.6	2	98
197	50	3.9	4.2	-1.03	0.27	1.0	0	0.9	0	99
190	50	3.8	4.0	-0.60	0.28	1.4	1	1.4	1	100
144	44	3.3	3.4	-2.44	0.24	1.4	1	1.4	1	102
206	50	4.1	3.4	-0.97	0.19	1.2	1	1.2	1	103
298	50	6.0	6.2	4.53	0.25	1.4	1	1.4	1	104
211	50	4.2	4.2	-1.04	0.27	0.7	-1	0.7	-1	105
163	50	3.3	3.5	-2.70	0.22	0.5	-2	0.5	-2	107
135	50	2.7	2.6	-3.83	0.21	0.9	0	1.0	0	108
143	50	2.9	2.2	-3.94	0.20	1.0	0	1.0	0	109
241	50	4.8	5.7	0.95	0.23	0.7	-1	0.7	-1	110
143	41	3.5	3.2	-3.26	0.23	1.2	0	1.3	0	112
243	50	4.9	5.1	1.64	0.23	1.1	0	1.1	0	114
222	50	4.4	4.4	-0.30	0.21	0.6	-2	0.6	-2	115
201	50	4.0	4.2	-1.75	0.20	1.2	1	1.4	1	117
236	50	4.7	4.9	0.80	0.19	0.4	-3	0.5	-3	118
172	50	3.4	3.1	-2.09	0.19	0.6	-2	0.6	-2	119
213	50	4.3	4.5	-0.16	0.20	0.7	-1	0.6	-2	120
Obsvd Score	Obsvd Count	Obsvd Average	Fair Avrge	Model Measure	S.E.	Infit MnSq	Std	Outfit MnSq	Std	Num
219.5	48.9	4.5	4.6	0.31	0.24	1.0	-0.3	1.0	-0.3	Mean
49.4	5.7	0.8	1.0	2.22	0.09	0.3	1.6	0.3	1.6	S.D.

RMSE 0.25 Adj S.D. 2.21 Separation 8.72 Reliability 0.99
Fixed (all same) chi-square: 7823.0 d.f.: 96 significance: .00
Random (normal) chi-square: 95.9 d.f.: 95 significance: .45

(ii) Raters

Obsvd Score	Obsvd Count	Obsvd Average	Fair Avrge	Measure	Model S.E.	Infit MnSq	Std	Outfit MnSq	Std	Rater
1033	250	4.1	4.0	1.12	0.12	1.2	2	1.2	1	3
1094	250	4.4	4.5	-0.77	0.11	0.8	-1	0.9	-1	7
1219	250	4.9	5.0	-0.82	0.10	1.3	3	1.3	3	12
646	125	5.2	4.2	2.14	0.15	1.2	1	1.2	1	28
1091	231	4.7	4.8	-1.79	0.12	1.0	0	1.1	0	32
994	213	4.7	4.6	-0.00	0.09	0.9	0	1.0	0	36
1104	250	4.4	4.9	-0.18	0.08	0.9	-1	0.9	0	37
1237	247	5.0	5.1	0.74	0.10	0.8	-2	0.9	-1	38
1102	250	4.4	4.1	0.96	0.08	0.6	-5	0.6	-5	39
1083	250	4.3	4.6	-1.27	0.10	1.2	1	1.2	1	43
1056	250	4.2	4.0	1.24	0.11	0.8	-2	0.8	-2	45
349	85	4.1	4.6	-0.60	0.18	1.2	1	1.2	1	46
824	200	4.1	4.0	0.10	0.13	1.0	0	1.0	0	48
816	194	4.2	4.1	0.60	0.12	1.0	0	1.0	0	50
895	200	4.5	4.3	0.39	0.10	0.8	-2	0.8	-2	52
926	225	4.1	3.9	0.37	0.11	0.7	-3	0.7	-3	56
1019	224	4.5	4.7	0.06	0.14	0.9	0	0.9	0	67
891	225	4.0	4.1	0.14	0.11	1.2	1	1.1	1	70
933	197	4.7	4.7	-0.31	0.11	1.1	0	1.1	0	72
832	200	4.2	5.3	-2.93	0.09	1.2	1	1.2	1	82
1135	203	5.6	4.9	1.56	0.11	0.9	-1	0.9	0	83
1016	222	4.6	4.6	-0.74	0.11	1.0	0	1.0	0	89

Obsvd Score	Obsvd Count	Obsvd Average	Fair Avrge	Measure	Model S.E.	Infit MnSq	Std	Outfit MnSq	Std	Num
968.0	215.5	4.5	4.5	0.00	0.11	1.0	-0.4	1.0	-0.3	Mean
193.6	40.9	0.4	0.4	1.12	0.02	0.2	2.1	0.2	1.9	S.D.

RMSE 0.11 Adj S.D. 1.12 Separation 9.73 Reliability 0.99
Fixed (all same) chi-square: 2556.4 d.f.: 21 significance: .00
Random (normal) chi-square: 21.0 d.f.: 20 significance: .40

(iii) Items

Obsvd Score	Obsvd Count	Obsvd Average	Fair Avrge		Measure	Model S.E.	Infit MnSq	Std	Outfit MnSq	Std	Nu Item
876	191	4.6	4.5	A	0.03	0.11	1.0	0	1.1	0	21 TDes1F
840	191	4.4	4.3	A	0.47	0.11	0.8	-1	0.8	-1	22 TDes1G
851	191	4.5	4.3	A	0.34	0.11	1.2	1	1.2	1	23 TDes1V
807	190	4.2	4.1	A	0.79	0.11	0.8	-2	0.8	-1	24 TNarG
836	190	4.4	4.3	A	0.44	0.11	0.8	-1	0.9	-1	25 TNarV
855	190	4.5	4.4	A	0.22	0.11	1.2	1	1.2	1	26 TNarC
849	188	4.5	4.3	A	0.41	0.11	1.0	0	1.0	0	27 TSumF
781	188	4.2	4.1	A	0.96	0.12	0.7	-3	0.7	-3	28 TSumG
780	188	4.1	4.0	A	1.24	0.12	0.9	0	0.9	-1	29 TSumV
854	187	4.6	4.4	A	0.09	0.12	1.3	2	1.3	2	30 TRPF
795	187	4.3	4.1	A	0.81	0.12	0.8	-2	0.8	-1	31 TRPG
909	187	4.9	4.7	A	-0.58	0.12	1.5	3	1.6	4	32 TRPI
858	188	4.6	4.4	A	0.08	0.11	0.9	0	1.0	0	33 TExpF
831	188	4.4	4.3	A	0.40	0.11	0.9	0	0.9	-1	34 TExpV
845	188	4.5	4.4	A	0.24	0.11	1.4	3	1.4	3	35 TExp
900	191	4.7	4.6		-0.29	0.11	1.1	0	1.1	0	36 TInsF
854	191	4.5	4.3		0.30	0.11	1.0	0	1.0	0	37 TInsV
854	191	4.5	4.3		0.30	0.11	1.2	1	1.3	2	38 TInsC
881	191	4.6	4.5	A	-0.06	0.11	0.9	0	0.9	0	39 TDisF
846	191	4.4	4.3	A	0.35	0.11	0.5	-5	0.6	-4	40 TDisG
941	191	4.9	4.8	A	-0.78	0.11	1.3	2	1.3	2	41 TDisI
888	191	4.6	4.5		-0.13	0.11	0.8	-2	0.8	-1	42 TDes2F
841	190	4.4	4.3		0.42	0.11	0.6	-4	0.6	-4	43 TDes2G
863	191	4.5	4.4		0.19	0.11	0.9	-1	0.9	0	44 TDes2V
860	191	4.5	4.4		0.23	0.11	0.5	-5	0.6	-4	45 TComm

Obsvd Score	Obsvd Count	Obsvd Average	Fair Avrge	Measure	Model S.E.	Infit MnSq	Std	Outfit MnSq	Std	Nu Iteml
851.8	189.6	4.5	4.4	0.26	0.11	1.0	-0.6	1.0	-0.4	Mean
36.3	1.5	0.2	0.2	0.43	0.00	0.3	2.5	0.3	2.4	S.D.

RMSE 0.11 Adj S.D. 0.42 Separation 3.64 Reliability 0.93
Fixed (all same) chi-square: 352.3 d.f.: 24 significance: .00
Random (normal) chi-square: 24.0 d.f.: 23 significance: .41

C   Combined data

(i) Candidates

Obsvd Score	Obsvd Count	Obsvd Average	Fair Avrge	Measure	Model S.E.	Infit MnSq	Std	Outfit MnSq	Std	Cand
271	64	4.2	4.3	-0.38	0.19	0.7	-1	0.8	-1	1
352	64	5.5	5.5	2.07	0.20	0.6	-2	0.6	-2	2
356	64	5.6	5.4	1.60	0.17	1.1	0	1.2	0	3
262	64	4.1	4.3	-0.73	0.19	1.6	2	1.5	2	4
266	64	4.2	4.2	-0.37	0.21	1.1	0	1.1	0	5
286	64	4.5	4.8	0.11	0.18	0.7	-2	0.7	-1	7
328	64	5.1	5.2	1.52	0.19	0.8	-1	0.9	0	9
273	64	4.3	4.1	-0.48	0.16	1.0	0	1.0	0	10
256	64	4.0	4.0	-1.72	0.21	1.2	0	1.3	1	12
322	64	5.0	5.1	1.39	0.18	1.0	0	1.1	0	13
264	64	4.1	3.9	-0.81	0.20	1.1	0	1.1	0	14
237	64	3.7	3.8	-2.05	0.21	1.2	1	1.2	1	15
388	64	6.1	6.0	3.81	0.20	1.2	1	1.1	0	16
295	64	4.6	4.9	0.70	0.20	0.5	-3	0.5	-3	17
264	64	4.1	4.1	-1.13	0.20	1.1	0	1.2	1	18
307	64	4.8	4.6	0.01	0.18	0.7	-1	0.7	-1	20
410	64	6.4	6.7	5.03	0.27	1.2	0	1.4	1	21
291	64	4.5	4.6	-0.05	0.17	0.7	-1	0.7	-1	22
298	64	4.7	4.5	-0.18	0.16	1.5	2	1.7	3	23
356	64	5.6	5.5	1.55	0.17	1.2	0	1.4	1	24
288	64	4.5	4.5	0.03	0.18	0.6	-2	0.7	-1	25
370	64	5.8	6.0	3.65	0.20	1.0	0	1.0	0	26
267	64	4.2	4.2	-0.50	0.20	0.5	-3	0.5	-3	27
269	64	4.2	4.0	-0.90	0.19	0.7	-2	0.7	-2	28
331	64	5.2	5.3	1.78	0.19	1.6	2	1.6	2	29
277	64	4.3	4.5	-0.05	0.20	0.8	-1	0.8	-1	30
289	64	4.5	4.5	0.06	0.18	0.7	-1	0.7	-1	32
275	64	4.3	4.5	-0.41	0.20	1.0	0	1.0	0	33
314	64	4.9	5.0	0.91	0.18	0.6	-2	0.6	-2	35
251	64	3.9	3.9	-0.96	0.17	0.9	0	0.9	0	36
335	64	5.2	4.9	0.99	0.19	0.7	-1	0.8	0	37
292	64	4.6	4.4	-0.01	0.20	1.3	1	1.4	1	38
241	64	3.8	3.8	-1.46	0.21	0.9	0	1.0	0	39
279	64	4.4	4.3	-0.08	0.21	1.1	0	1.0	0	40
360	64	5.6	5.5	2.64	0.20	0.8	-1	0.7	-1	41
316	64	4.9	5.0	0.72	0.19	0.9	0	1.0	0	42
272	64	4.3	4.4	-0.24	0.19	1.0	0	1.2	1	43
275	64	4.3	4.3	-0.94	0.19	1.1	0	1.0	0	44
320	64	5.0	5.3	0.93	0.18	1.6	2	1.7	3	45
410	64	6.4	6.5	3.54	0.21	1.3	1	1.3	1	47
222	64	3.5	3.1	-2.14	0.16	1.5	2	1.4	1	48
345	64	5.4	5.5	1.79	0.18	1.0	0	1.0	0	50
406	64	6.3	6.3	5.44	0.28	1.0	0	1.0	0	51
251	64	3.9	3.9	-0.72	0.20	1.0	0	0.9	0	53
280	61	4.6	4.7	0.32	0.19	1.2	1	1.4	1	55
356	64	5.6	5.5	2.55	0.20	0.5	-3	0.5	-3	56
388	64	6.1	6.2	4.07	0.21	0.7	-1	0.7	-1	57
210	52	4.0	4.2	-1.26	0.24	0.8	0	0.8	-1	58
322	64	5.0	5.2	1.19	0.17	0.9	0	0.9	0	59
263	64	4.1	4.1	-1.02	0.19	1.7	3	1.7	3	60
378	64	5.9	5.8	2.50	0.20	1.0	0	1.0	0	61
264	64	4.1	4.0	-1.07	0.20	0.9	0	0.9	0	65
310	64	4.8	5.0	1.65	0.20	0.6	-2	0.6	-2	66
283	64	4.4	4.4	0.10	0.20	0.9	0	0.9	0	67

Combined data – candidates (continued)

Obsvd Score	Obsvd Count	Obsvd Average	Fair Avrge	Model Measure	Model S.E.	Infit MnSq	Infit Std	Outfit MnSq	Outfit Std	Cand
298	64	4.7	4.5	0.12	0.20	2.3	5	2.3	5	68
330	64	5.2	5.3	1.51	0.19	1.0	0	0.9	0	71
258	64	4.0	4.0	-1.13	0.17	0.9	0	0.9	0	72
293	64	4.6	4.8	0.12	0.17	0.9	0	0.9	0	73
268	64	4.2	4.3	-0.45	0.19	1.4	1	1.4	1	74
237	64	3.7	3.4	-1.79	0.19	0.9	0	0.9	0	75
135	28	4.8	4.6	0.54	0.25	1.6	1	1.7	2	76
301	64	4.7	4.6	0.27	0.18	0.8	-1	0.8	0	77
278	64	4.3	4.6	0.70	0.21	0.7	-1	0.7	-1	78
246	64	3.8	3.9	-1.51	0.20	0.6	-2	0.6	-2	79
278	64	4.3	4.3	-0.41	0.21	0.8	-1	0.8	-1	80
390	64	6.1	6.5	3.93	0.21	0.8	-1	0.8	-1	81
294	64	4.6	4.5	-0.09	0.18	1.3	1	1.2	1	84
305	64	4.8	4.7	0.11	0.19	0.9	0	0.8	0	85
278	64	4.3	4.5	-0.01	0.20	1.3	1	1.3	1	86
294	64	4.6	4.8	0.51	0.17	1.1	0	1.0	0	88
328	64	5.1	4.8	0.80	0.19	0.7	-2	0.7	-2	89
273	64	4.3	4.3	-0.90	0.21	1.0	0	1.0	0	90
172	37	4.6	4.5	-0.26	0.24	1.2	0	1.2	1	91
235	64	3.7	3.7	-1.64	0.19	0.8	-1	0.8	0	92
222	58	3.8	3.9	-1.42	0.18	1.0	0	0.9	0	94
276	64	4.3	4.4	-0.40	0.15	0.5	-3	0.6	-2	95
242	64	3.8	4.0	-1.10	0.17	2.2	5	2.3	5	98
266	64	4.2	4.2	-1.09	0.21	0.8	-1	0.8	-1	99
273	64	4.3	4.5	0.23	0.20	1.5	2	1.4	1	100
209	58	3.6	3.6	-1.89	0.20	1.4	1	1.4	1	102
249	64	3.9	3.7	-1.37	0.16	1.2	1	1.2	1	103
407	64	6.4	6.4	4.68	0.26	1.3	1	1.4	1	104
265	64	4.1	4.0	-1.16	0.20	1.1	0	1.0	0	105
225	64	3.5	3.8	-2.30	0.25	0.9	0	0.9	0	107
185	64	2.9	3.1	-3.59	0.22	1.0	0	1.0	0	108
181	64	2.8	2.4	-4.37	0.20	0.9	0	0.8	-1	109
274	58	4.7	4.8	0.12	0.20	1.1	0	1.5	2	110
180	55	3.3	3.1	-3.46	0.20	1.3	1	1.2	0	112
308	64	4.8	4.8	1.21	0.20	0.9	0	0.9	0	114
280	64	4.4	4.5	-0.29	0.20	0.8	-1	0.8	-1	115
275	64	4.3	4.4	-0.59	0.19	1.6	2	1.5	2	117
318	64	5.0	5.0	0.62	0.16	1.0	0	1.1	0	118
250	64	3.9	3.7	-1.64	0.17	0.7	-2	0.7	-2	119
266	64	4.2	4.3	-0.72	0.19	0.7	-1	0.7	-1	120

Obsvd Score	Obsvd Count	Obsvd Average	Fair Avrge	Model Measure	Model S.E.	Infit MnSq	Infit Std	Outfit MnSq	Outfit Std	Num
280.4	61.4	4.6	4.6	0.14	0.20	1.0	-0.2	1.0	-0.1	Mean
61.1	8.2	0.7	0.8	1.75	0.02	0.3	1.8	0.4	1.8	S.D.

RMSE 0.20 Adj S.D. 1.74 Separation 8.73 Reliability 0.99
Fixed (all same) chi-square: 6797.7 d.f.: 98 significance: .00
Random (normal) chi-square: 97.7 d.f.: 97 significance: .46

(ii) Raters

Obsvd Score	Obsvd Count	Obsvd Average	Fair Avrge	Model Measure	S.E.	Infit MnSq	Std	Outfit MnSq	Std	Rater
1243	306	4.1	4.0	0.65	0.10	1.0	0	1.0	0	3
1347	306	4.4	4.6	0.31	0.09	1.0	0	1.0	0	7
1521	306	5.0	4.9	-1.30	0.09	1.1	1	1.1	1	12
720	146	4.9	4.4	1.27	0.13	1.4	2	1.4	2	28
1325	280	4.7	4.9	0.25	0.10	1.0	0	1.0	0	32
1280	276	4.6	4.7	-0.03	0.08	1.0	0	1.0	0	36
1363	292	4.7	4.7	0.35	0.09	1.2	2	1.2	1	37
1469	303	4.8	4.8	-0.36	0.08	0.9	0	0.9	0	38
1439	306	4.7	4.6	0.12	0.07	0.7	-4	0.7	-4	39
1429	306	4.7	4.8	-0.49	0.08	1.1	1	1.2	1	43
1244	306	4.1	3.9	1.00	0.10	0.9	-1	0.9	0	45
513	127	4.0	4.2	0.10	0.14	1.1	0	1.1	0	46
1173	281	4.2	4.3	-1.10	0.11	1.1	1	1.1	0	48
1339	275	4.9	4.5	0.04	0.09	0.7	-3	0.7	-3	50
1258	270	4.7	4.5	0.43	0.09	0.7	-3	0.7	-3	52
1290	302	4.3	4.1	0.14	0.10	0.9	-1	0.9	-1	56
1430	302	4.7	4.8	-0.83	0.10	0.8	-2	0.8	-2	67
1225	296	4.1	4.1	2.35	0.11	1.0	0	1.0	0	70
1218	267	4.6	4.3	-0.06	0.09	1.2	2	1.2	2	72
1222	267	4.6	5.1	-1.61	0.09	1.6	5	1.7	6	82
1362	270	5.0	4.9	-0.18	0.10	1.1	0	1.2	1	83
1351	285	4.7	4.6	-1.03	0.09	1.1	0	1.1	0	89

Obsvd Score	Obsvd Count	Obsvd Average	Fair Avrge	Model Measure	S.E.	Infit MnSq	Std	Outfit MnSq	Std	Rater
1261.9	276.1	4.6	4.5	-0.00	0.10	1.0	0.1	1.0	0.2	Mean
224.8	46.5	0.3	0.3	0.87	0.02	0.2	2.3	0.2	2.3	S.D.

RMSE 0.10 Adj S.D. 0.87 Separation 8.99 Reliability 0.99
Fixed (all same) chi-square: 1683.1 d.f.: 21 significance: .00
Random (normal) chi-square: 21.0 d.f.: 20 significance: .40

(iii) Items

Obsvd Score	Obsvd Count	Obsvd Average	Fair Avrge		Measure	Model S.E.	Infit MnSq	Std	Outfit MnSq	Std	Nu Item
890	191	4.7	4.5	A	0.07	0.11	1.1	0	1.1	0	1 DesF
841	191	4.4	4.3	A	0.47	0.11	0.7	-2	0.7	-2	2 DesG
837	191	4.4	4.2	A	0.71	0.11	1.0	0	1.0	0	3 DesV
835	192	4.3	4.2		0.65	0.11	0.6	-3	0.7	-3	4 NarG
853	192	4.4	4.3		0.43	0.11	0.9	0	0.9	0	5 NarV
869	192	4.5	4.4		0.24	0.11	1.2	2	1.3	2	6 NarC
898	189	4.8	4.6		-0.27	0.11	1.0	0	1.1	0	7 RPF
833	189	4.4	4.3		0.50	0.11	0.7	-2	0.7	-2	8 RPG
933	189	4.9	4.8		-0.71	0.11	1.5	3	1.5	3	9 RPI
900	190	4.7	4.6	A	-0.21	0.11	1.0	0	1.0	0	10 Exp1F
874	190	4.6	4.5	A	0.07	0.11	0.9	0	1.0	0	11 Exp1V
896	190	4.7	4.9	A	-0.93	0.11	1.3	2	1.4	2	12 Exp1C
952	192	5.0	4.9		-0.78	0.11	1.0	0	1.0	0	16 DisF
893	192	4.7	4.5		0.06	0.11	0.7	-3	0.7	-3	17 DisG
940	192	4.9	4.8		-0.63	0.11	1.6	4	1.6	4	18 DisI
897	192	4.7	4.6		-0.11	0.11	0.6	-4	0.7	-3	19 CommEff
1069	192	5.6	5.6		-2.27	0.12	1.5	4	1.5	3	20 Comp
872	190	4.6	4.5		0.03	0.11	1.1	0	1.1	0	21 TDes1F
835	190	4.4	4.3		0.47	0.11	0.8	-2	0.8	-2	22 TDes1G
846	190	4.5	4.4		0.34	0.11	1.1	0	1.1	1	23 TDes1V
807	190	4.2	4.2		0.79	0.11	0.8	-1	0.8	-1	25 TNarV
855	190	4.5	4.4		0.22	0.11	1.1	0	1.1	1	26 TNarC
849	188	4.5	4.3	A	0.41	0.11	1.1	0	1.1	0	27 TSumF
781	188	4.2	4.1	A	0.96	0.11	0.7	-2	0.7	-3	28 TSumG
780	188	4.1	4.0	A	1.24	0.11	1.0	0	1.0	0	29 TSumV
854	187	4.6	4.5		0.09	0.11	1.3	2	1.3	2	30 TRPF
795	187	4.3	4.2		0.81	0.11	0.8	-2	0.8	-1	31 TRPG
909	187	4.9	4.8		-0.58	0.11	1.4	3	1.4	3	32 TRPI
857	187	4.6	4.5		0.08	0.11	0.9	0	1.0	0	33 TExpF
830	187	4.4	4.3		0.40	0.11	0.9	0	0.9	0	34 TExpV
844	187	4.5	4.4		0.24	0.11	1.4	3	1.4	3	35 TExpC
880	190	4.6	4.6		-0.06	0.11	1.0	0	1.1	1	39 TDisF
845	190	4.4	4.4		0.35	0.11	0.6	-4	0.6	-3	40 TDisG
940	190	4.9	4.9		-0.78	0.11	1.3	2	1.3	2	41 TDisI
860	191	4.5	4.4		0.18	0.11	0.6	-4	0.6	-3	45 TComm
Obsvd Score	Obsvd Count	Obsvd Average	Fair Avrge		Measure	Model S.E.	Infit MnSq	Std	Outfit MnSq	Std	Nu Item
867.5	189.8	4.6	4.5		0.10	0.11	1.0	-0.1	1.0	0.0	Mean
55.0	1.8	0.3	0.3		0.66	0.00	0.3	2.4	0.3	2.3	S.D.

RMSE 0.11 Adj S.D. 0.65 Separation 5.91 Reliability 0.97
Fixed (all same) chi-square: 1100.2 d.f.: 31 significance: .00
Random (normal) chi-square: 31.0 d.f.: 30 significance: .42

Appendix 7.2
FACETS analyses (2) with unanchored item difficulty estimates, oral interaction sub-test, June 1994 trial (N = 94)

A   Live data

(i) Candidates

Obsvd Score	Obsvd Count	Obsvd Average	Fair Avrge	Measure	Model S.E.	Infit MnSq	Infit Std	Outfit MnSq	Outfit Std	Cand
172	40	4.3	4.1	-0.65	0.30	0.7	-1	0.7	-1	1
221	40	5.5	4.9	1.83	0.26	0.8	0	0.8	0	2
241	40	6.0	6.0	2.76	0.27	1.2	0	1.2	0	3
146	40	3.7	3.9	-1.89	0.26	0.8	0	0.7	-1	4
160	37	4.3	4.1	-0.06	0.31	1.3	1	1.3	1	5
178	40	4.5	4.9	0.23	0.32	1.2	0	1.2	0	7
203	40	5.1	5.1	1.73	0.27	1.5	2	1.7	2	9
207	40	5.2	5.4	0.15	0.26	1.6	2	1.7	2	10
153	40	3.8	4.0	-2.81	0.33	1.2	1	1.3	1	12
199	40	5.0	5.0	0.82	0.23	0.8	0	0.9	0	13
167	40	4.2	4.3	-1.70	0.27	1.1	0	1.1	0	14
150	40	3.8	3.5	-3.29	0.29	1.0	0	1.0	0	15
252	40	6.3	6.5	2.80	0.26	0.8	-1	0.9	0	16
177	40	4.4	4.4	-0.10	0.29	0.6	-1	0.6	-1	17
180	40	4.5	4.4	-0.94	0.26	0.9	0	0.9	0	18
200	40	5.0	4.7	-0.51	0.22	1.0	0	1.0	0	20
257	40	6.4	6.4	3.17	0.30	0.9	0	0.8	0	21
184	40	4.6	4.0	-1.11	0.23	0.8	0	0.8	0	22
199	40	5.0	4.6	-0.17	0.21	0.5	-2	0.5	-2	23
207	40	5.2	4.9	0.46	0.25	0.8	0	0.8	0	24
168	40	4.2	4.0	-0.86	0.24	0.4	-3	0.5	-2	25
258	40	6.5	6.6	5.39	0.34	1.2	0	1.4	0	26
168	40	4.2	4.4	-0.60	0.28	0.5	-3	0.5	-2	27
175	40	4.4	3.9	-0.84	0.30	0.6	-2	0.6	-2	28
229	40	5.7	5.4	3.26	0.29	0.7	1	0.7	-1	29
172	40	4.3	4.5	0.22	0.32	1.1	0	1.1	0	30
178	40	4.5	4.5	-0.26	0.30	1.0	0	0.1	1	32
172	40	4.3	4.5	-1.26	0.27	0.6	0.2	0.5	-2	33
198	40	5.0	5.6	1.31	0.28	0.6	-2	0.6	-2	35
169	40	4.2	4.5	-0.27	0.28	0.8	0	1.0	0	36
225	40	5.6	5.8	1.83	0.27	0.9	0	1.2	0	37
198	40	5.0	4.8	-0.35	0.29	1.2	0	1.2	0	38
166	40	4.2	4.2	-1.42	0.26	0.8	-1	0.8	-1	39
175	40	4.4	4.5	-1.14	0.27	1.1	0	1.0	0	40
214	40	5.3	5.4	2.73	0.32	0.9	0	0.9	0	41
189	40	4.7	4.7	-0.70	0.25	1.0	0	1.0	0	42
179	40	4.5	4.5	-0.50	0.28	1.6	2	1.6	2	43
183	40	4.6	4.2	-1.13	0.23	1.1	0	1.0	0	44
204	40	5.1	4.8	0.15	0.21	1.4	1	1.4	1	45
250	40	6.3	5.8	2.32	0.21	1.3	1	1.4	1	47
109	40	2.7	2.4	-5.52	0.31	0.9	0	0.9	0	48
242	40	6.1	5.8	2.08	0.25	1.1	0	1.1	0	50
257	40	6.4	6.7	6.57	0.34	1.0	0	1.3	0	51
158	40	4.0	3.7	-0.70	0.30	1.3	1	1.3	1	53
171	34	5.0	4.7	0.91	0.29	1.1	0	1.1	0	55
233	40	5.8	5.8	3.10	0.27	0.8	0	0.8	0	56
230	40	5.8	5.9	4.37	0.27	0.5	-3	0.5	-3	57
172	40	4.3	4.6	-1.36	0.31	0.5	-2	0.5	-2	58
210	40	5.3	5.9	2.20	0.27	0.5	-2	0.5	-2	59

Live data – candidates (continued)

Obsvd Score	Obsvd Count	Obsvd Average	Fair Avrge	Measure	Model S.E.	Infit MnSq	Std	Outfit MnSq	Std	Cand
170	40	4.3	4.6	-0.19	0.28	1.3	0	1.4	1	60
230	40	5.8	5.7	2.34	0.29	1.3	1	1.5	1	61
174	40	4.3	4.3	-1.41	0.29	1.3	1	1.3	1	65
204	40	5.1	5.3	1.65	0.25	0.7	-1	0.7	-1	66
170	40	4.3	4.3	-0.68	0.27	0.6	-1	0.6	-1	67
161	40	4.0	4.0	-2.53	0.28	1.3	1	1.3	1	68
202	40	5.1	5.0	0.61	0.23	0.9	0	0.7	-1	71
195	40	4.9	4.5	-0.40	0.27	0.4	-3	0.3	-3	72
195	40	4.9	4.2	-0.64	0.21	1.3	1	1.3	1	73
180	40	4.7	4.7	-0.50	0.23	0.8	0	0.8	0	74
150	40	3.8	3.6	-2.24	0.28	0.9	0	0.9	0	75
192	40	4.8	4.2	-0.01	0.24	1.8	2	1.8	2	76
199	40	5.0	5.0	-0.02	0.25	0.9	0	1.0	0	77
179	40	4.5	4.6	1.02	0.35	0.7	-1	0.6	-1	78
147	40	3.7	3.8	-2.04	0.33	1.1	0	1.2	0	79
170	40	4.3	4.2	-1.30	0.29	0.8	-1	0.7	-1	80
240	40	6.0	6.6	4.87	0.29	0.9	0	0.9	0	81
171	40	4.3	4.3	-1.68	0.28	1.7	2	1.7	2	84
196	40	4.9	5.0	-0.14	0.30	0.9	0	0.9	0	85
192	40	4.8	5.3	1.26	0.27	1.6	2	1.6	2	86
161	40	4.0	4.0	-1.07	0.28	1.2	0	1.1	0	88
204	40	5.1	5.1	0.36	0.26	0.8	0	0.8	0	89
185	40	4.6	4.5	-1.39	0.28	1.0	0	1.0	0	90
193	40	4.8	4.9	-0.09	0.25	1.2	0	1.2	0	91
140	40	3.5	3.3	-3.00	0.26	0.8	-1	0.9	0	92
161	40	4.0	3.9	-1.65	0.24	0.9	0	0.8	0	94
189	40	4.7	4.4	-1.13	0.25	0.9	0	1.1	0	95
184	40	4.6	4.1	-0.84	0.23	0.6	-2	0.7	-1	98
184	40	4.6	4.6	-1.01	0.25	0.7	-1	0.7	-1	99
203	40	5.1	5.2	2.03	0.32	0.8	0	0.8	0	100
160	40	4.0	3.7	-1.42	0.25	1.1	0	1.0	0	102
141	40	3.5	3.3	-4.38	0.29	1.5	2	1.4	1	103
274	40	6.8	6.9	6.13	0.45	0.6	-1	0.3	0	104
156	40	3.9	4.0	-2.42	0.29	1.5	2	1.4	1	105
152	40	3.8	4.2	-2.27	0.34	1.1	0	1.2	0	107
117	40	2.9	3.2	-5.61	0.44	1.1	0	1.7	1	108
107	40	2.7	2.5	-6.39	0.40	0.9	0	1.2	0	109
101	22	4.6	4.6	-1.35	0.35	1.5	1	1.8	2	110
128	40	3.2	3.0	-4.25	0.28	1.3	1	1.1	0	112
200	40	5.0	5.2	1.41	0.27	1.2	0	1.2	0	114
176	40	4.4	4.7	-0.74	0.29	0.9	0	0.9	0	115
189	40	4.7	5.1	1.06	0.28	0.7	-1	0.7	-1	117
214	40	5.3	5.4	0.78	0.22	1.8	3	1.8	3	118
186	40	4.7	4.6	-1.27	0.26	0.4	-3	0.4	-3	119
167	40	4.2	3.7	-2.14	0.25	0.7	-1	0.7	-1	120

Obsvd Score	Obsvd Count	Obsvd Average	Fair Avrge	Measure	Model S.E.	Infit MnSq	Std	Outfit MnSq	Std	Num
186.6	39.7	4.7	4.7	-0.13	0.28	1.0	-0.3	1.0	-0.2	Mean
33.5	1.9	0.8	0.9	2.27	0.04	0.3	1.5	0.4	1.5	S.D.

RMSE 0.28 Adj S.D. 2.25 Separation 7.99 Reliability 0.98
Fixed (all same) chi-square: 5190.1 d.f.: 95 significance: .00
Random (normal) chi-square: 94.5 d.f.: 94 significance: .47

Appendices

(ii) Raters

Obsvd Score	Obsvd Count	Obsvd Average	Fair Avrge	Measure	Model S.E.	Infit MnSq	Std	Outfit MnSq	Std	Rater
728	180	4.0	4.2	0.54	0.14	0.9	0	0.9	0	3
795	180	4.4	4.7	-0.27	0.12	0.7	-3	0.7	-3	7
932	180	5.2	5.4	0.16	0.11	1.1	1	1.1	0	12
366	80	4.6	4.7	-0.48	0.20	0.9	0	0.9	0	28
786	160	4.9	5.0	-0.27	0.13	0.9	0	0.9	0	32
855	180	4.8	5.2	-1.08	0.10	1.0	0	1.0	0	36
816	160	5.1	4.8	-0.05	0.11	1.1	0	1.0	0	37
818	180	4.5	5.0	-1.80	0.12	0.8	-1	0.8	-1	38
935	180	5.2	5.3	-1.19	0.11	0.8	-1	0.7	-1	39
940	180	5.2	5.0	0.04	0.12	1.0	0	1.1	0	43
702	180	3.9	3.8	1.91	0.16	0.8	-1	0.8	-1	45
398	100	4.0	3.9	0.76	0.20	1.1	0	1.1	0	46
810	191	4.2	4.3	-2.00	0.14	1.0	0	1.0	0	48
1062	191	5.6	5.0	-0.09	0.13	1.0	0	1.0	0	50
880	180	4.9	4.7	0.13	0.13	0.9	0	0.9	-1	52
885	200	4.4	4.3	0.57	0.15	1.3	2	1.3	2	56
987	200	4.9	5.0	1.25	0.12	0.7	-4	0.7	-3	67
838	200	4.2	4.1	3.00	0.15	1.1	1	1.3	1	70
803	180	4.5	4.5	-0.25	0.12	1.0	0	0.9	0	72
877	171	5.1	5.2	0.04	0.13	1.4	3	1.6	4	82
798	180	4.4	4.9	-1.43	0.15	1.2	1	1.2	1	83
906	180	5.0	4.7	0.52	0.12	1.0	0	1.0	0	89

Obsvd Score	Obsvd Count	Obsvd Average	Fair Avrge	Measure	Model S.E.	Infit MnSq	Std	Outfit MnSq	Std	Num
814.4	173.3	4.7	4.7	-0.00	0.13	1.0	-0.3	1.0	-0.1	Mean
158.9	28.4	0.5	0.4	1.13	0.03	0.2	1.7	0.2	1.7	S.D.

RMSE 0.14 Adj S.D. 1.12 Separation 8.16 Reliability 0.99
Fixed (all same) chi-square: 1472.3 d.f.: 21 significance: .00
Random (normal) chi-square: 21.0 d.f.: 20 significance: .40

(iii) Items

Obsvd Score	Obsvd Count	Obsvd Average	Fair Avrge	Measure	Model S.E.	Infit MnSq	Std	Outfit MnSq	Std	Nu Item
890	191	4.7	4.7	0.11	0.12	1.1	0	1.1	0	1 DesF
841	191	4.4	4.4	0.85	0.12	0.7	-3	0.7	-2	2 DesG
837	191	4.4	4.3	0.92	0.12	1.1	0	1.0	0	3 DesV
835	192	4.3	4.3	1.01	0.12	0.7	-3	0.7	-2	4 NarG
853	192	4.4	4.4	0.74	0.12	0.9	0	0.9	0	5 NarV
869	192	4.5	4.5	0.50	0.12	1.3	2	1.5	3	6 NarC
898	189	4.8	4.7	-0.14	0.12	1.0	0	1.0	0	7 RPF
833	189	4.4	4.4	0.85	0.12	0.7	-3	0.7	-3	8 RPG
933	189	4.9	5.0	-0.68	0.12	1.5	4	1.6	4	9 RPI
900	190	4.7	4.7	-0.11	0.12	0.9	-1	0.9	0	1 Exp1
874	190	4.6	4.6	0.29	0.12	0.9	0	0.9	0	Exp1V
896	190	4.7	4.7	-0.05	0.12	1.1	0	1.2	1	12 Exp1
920	189	4.9	4.9	-0.48	0.12	0.7	-2	0.8	-1	13 Exp2F
886	189	4.7	4.7	0.04	0.12	0.8	-2	0.8	-2	14 Exp2V
901	189	4.8	4.8	-0.19	0.12	1.0	0	1.0	0	15 Exp2
952	192	5.0	5.0	-0.75	0.12	0.9	-1	0.9	-1	16 DisF
893	192	4.7	4.6	0.14	0.12	0.7	-2	0.7	-2	17 DisG
940	192	4.9	4.9	-0.57	0.12	1.6	4	1.6	4	18 DisI
897	192	4.7	4.7	0.08	0.12	0.5	-5	0.6	-4	19 CommEf
1069	192	5.6	5.7	-2.57	0.13	1.4	3	1.3	1	20 Comp

Obsvd Score	Obsvd Count	Obsvd Average	Fair Avrge	Measure	Model S.E.	Infit MnSq	Std	Outfit MnSq	Std	Nu Item
895.9	190.6	4.7	4.7	-0.00	0.12	1.0	-0.5	1.0	-0.3	Mean
52.2	1.3	0.3	0.3	0.79	0.00	0.3	2.7	0.3	2.5	S.D.

RMSE 0.12 Adj S.D. 0.78 Separation 6.32 Reliability 0.98
Fixed (all same) chi-square: 784.0 d.f.: 19 significance: .00
Random (normal) chi-square: 19.0 d.f.: 18 significance: .39

B   Tape data

(i) Candidates

Obsvd Score	Obsvd Count	Obsvd Average	Fair Avrge	Measure	Model S.E.	Infit MnSq	Std	Outfit MnSq	Std	Cand
206	50	4.1	4.2	-0.88	0.23	0.8	0	1.1	0	1
273	50	5.5	5.4	2.16	0.29	0.9	0	1.0	0	2
261	50	5.2	5.3	1.34	0.20	1.4	1	1.6	2	3
222	50	4.4	4.6	0.02	0.22	1.4	1	1.4	1	4
205	50	4.1	4.1	-0.84	0.25	1.4	1	1.3	1	5
218	50	4.4	4.4	-0.31	0.19	0.4	-3	0.5	-2	7
258	50	5.2	5.4	1.01	0.22	0.8	0	0.9	0	9
186	50	3.7	4.1	-0.54	0.20	0.7	-1	0.7	-1	10
200	49	4.1	3.7	-1.73	0.26	1.5	1	1.5	1	12
261	50	5.2	5.8	2.07	0.22	0.7	-2	0.7	-2	13
208	50	4.2	3.9	-1.18	0.24	1.5	1	1.6	1	14
185	50	3.7	3.7	-1.43	0.26	1.0	0	1.1	0	15
301	50	6.0	6.3	5.45	0.24	1.5	2	1.3	1	16
245	50	4.9	4.9	1.28	0.23	0.8	-1	0.7	-1	17
197	50	3.9	3.9	-1.43	0.23	1.3	1	1.3	1	18
241	50	4.8	4.5	0.35	0.24	0.8	-1	0.8	-1	20
323	50	6.5	6.5	5.60	0.31	0.9	0	1.0	0	21
227	50	4.5	4.4	-0.42	0.18	0.5	-2	0.5	-2	22
227	50	4.5	3.8	-1.03	0.17	1.3	1	1.3	1	23
293	50	5.9	6.3	2.81	0.22	0.8	-1	0.8	0	24
238	50	4.8	4.4	0.36	0.22	0.6	-2	0.6	-2	25
267	50	5.3	5.7	4.10	0.24	1.2	0	1.2	0	26
205	50	4.1	4.0	-0.58	0.26	0.6	-2	0.6	-2	27
210	50	4.2	4.2	-0.92	0.23	1.0	0	1.0	0	28
239	50	4.8	5.3	1.10	0.21	1.1	0	1.2	0	29
221	50	4.4	4.2	0.27	0.25	0.9	0	0.9	0	30
230	50	4.6	4.6	-0.11	0.21	0.8	-1	0.7	-1	32
208	50	4.2	4.1	-0.82	0.22	1.3	1	1.4	1	33
244	50	4.9	4.9	0.01	0.18	0.7	-1	0.7	-1	35
181	50	3.6	3.0	-1.61	0.18	0.9	0	0.9	0	36
254	50	5.1	5.1	0.89	0.23	0.8	-1	0.8	-1	37
220	50	4.4	4.5	0.26	0.23	1.3	1	1.3	1	38
175	50	3.5	3.6	-2.90	0.27	0.8	-1	0.8	-1	39
217	50	4.3	4.2	0.26	0.27	1.0	0	1.0	0	40
286	50	5.7	5.7	2.58	0.23	1.0	0	1.1	0	41
250	50	5.0	4.8	1.09	0.22	0.8	0	0.9	0	42
200	50	4.0	4.1	-0.60	0.21	0.9	0	1.0	0	43
205	50	4.1	4.1	-1.66	0.24	0.9	0	0.9	0	44
248	50	5.0	5.1	0.99	0.23	1.4	1	1.5	1	45
334	50	6.7	6.8	5.85	0.31	0.8	-1	0.8	-1	47
203	50	4.1	2.7	-1.72	0.19	1.2	0	1.2	0	48
314	50	6.3	6.2	6.93	0.35	1.1	0	1.2	0	51
194	50	3.9	4.1	-0.64	0.26	1.0	0	0.8	0	53
210	50	4.2	4.2	-0.49	0.22	1.3	1	1.4	1	55
271	50	5.4	5.4	3.00	0.25	0.4	-4	0.4	-4	56
321	50	6.4	6.6	6.42	0.28	1.1	0	1.1	0	57
103	37	2.8	2.8	-4.10	0.20	1.7	3	2.2	3	58
253	50	5.1	4.9	0.61	0.18	0.8	-1	0.8	-1	59
218	50	4.4	3.3	-1.21	0.18	1.9	3	2.0	3	60
304	50	6.1	6.4	3.19	0.26	1.2	0	1.4	1	61

Tape data – candidates (continued)

Obsvd Score	Obsvd Count	Obsvd Average	Fair Avrge	Measure	Model S.E.	Infit MnSq	Infit Std	Outfit MnSq	Outfit Std	Cand
200	50	4.0	3.8	-1.13	0.26	1.0	0	0.9	0	65
247	50	4.9	5.1	2.11	0.24	0.9	0	0.9	0	66
231	50	4.6	4.4	-0.43	0.23	1.0	0	1.0	0	67
254	50	5.1	4.8	2.16	0.26	1.0	0	1.0	0	68
260	50	5.2	5.3	2.13	0.27	0.4	-3	0.4	-3	71
168	50	3.4	3.6	-2.34	0.25	0.8	0	0.8	0	72
218	50	4.4	4.1	-0.02	0.25	1.0	0	0.9	0	73
195	50	3.9	4.0	-0.99	0.23	1.5	2	1.4	1	74
185	50	3.7	2.8	-2.03	0.19	0.8	0	0.8	0	75
14	3	4.7	5.2	-0.54	1.01	0.9	0	0.9	0	76
223	50	4.5	4.4	-0.01	0.21	0.9	0	0.9	0	77
212	50	4.2	4.4	1.19	0.27	0.7	-1	0.8	-1	78
195	50	3.9	3.7	-2.19	0.24	0.6	-1	0.5	-1	79
224	50	4.5	4.4	-0.20	0.26	0.8	0	0.9	0	80
230	50	4.6	3.4	-0.87	0.21	0.7	-1	0.7	-1	82
234	50	4.7	5.0	-0.16	0.20	1.4	1	1.3	1	84
222	50	4.4	4.3	-0.66	0.21	1.2	0	1.2	0	85
198	50	4.0	4.3	-1.44	0.21	0.8	-1	1.0	0	86
253	50	5.1	5.2	1.60	0.22	0.5	-2	0.7	-1	88
260	50	5.2	4.8	1.09	0.23	0.8	-1	0.8	0	89
201	50	4.0	4.1	-1.10	0.26	0.8	-1	0.8	-1	90
102	23	4.4	4.2	-0.53	0.28	0.7	0	0.8	0	91
191	50	3.8	3.8	-1.57	0.22	0.9	0	0.9	0	92
154	44	3.5	3.9	-2.16	0.22	1.1	0	1.1	0	94
204	50	4.1	4.5	-0.20	0.18	0.4	-3	0.4	-4	95
163	50	3.3	2.9	-2.34	0.21	1.7	2	1.7	2	98
197	50	3.9	4.1	-1.29	0.27	1.0	0	0.9	0	99
190	50	3.8	3.9	-0.85	0.28	1.4	1	1.4	1	100
144	44	3.3	3.3	-2.70	0.24	1.4	1	1.4	1	102
206	50	4.1	3.2	-1.23	0.19	1.2	1	1.2	1	103
298	50	6.0	6.2	4.29	0.25	1.4	1	1.4	2	104
211	50	4.2	4.1	-1.30	0.27	0.7	-1	0.7	-1	105
163	50	3.3	3.5	-2.96	0.22	0.5	-2	0.6	-2	107
135	50	2.7	2.5	-4.11	0.21	0.9	0	1.0	0	108
143	50	2.9	2.1	-4.21	0.20	1.0	0	1.0	0	109
241	50	4.8	5.5	0.70	0.23	0.8	-1	0.8	-1	110
143	41	3.5	3.0	-3.53	0.23	1.2	0	1.3	0	112
243	50	4.9	5.0	1.39	0.23	1.1	0	1.1	0	114
222	50	4.4	4.3	-0.55	0.21	0.6	-2	0.5	-2	115
201	50	4.0	4.1	-2.01	0.20	1.3	1	1.4	1	117
236	50	4.7	4.7	0.55	0.19	0.4	-3	0.5	-3	118
172	50	3.4	2.9	-2.36	0.19	0.6	-2	0.6	-2	119
213	50	4.3	4.4	-0.41	0.21	0.7	-1	0.6	-2	120

Obsvd Score	Obsvd Count	Obsvd Average	Fair Avrge	Measure	Model S.E.	Infit MnSq	Infit Std	Outfit MnSq	Outfit Std	Cand
219.5	48.9	4.5	4.4	0.06	0.24	1.0	-0.3	1.0	-0.3	Mean
49.4	5.7	0.8	1.0	2.23	0.09	0.3	1.6	0.3	1.6	S.D.

RMSE 0.25 Adj S.D. 2.21 Separation 8.72 Reliability 0.99
Fixed (all same) chi-square: 7821.0 d.f.: 96 significance: .00
Random (normal) chi-square: 95.9 d.f.: 95 significance: .45

Appendices

(ii) Raters

Obsvd Score	Obsvd Count	Obsvd Average	Fair Avrge	Measure	Model S.E.	Infit MnSq	Std	Outfit MnSq	Std	Rater
1033	250	4.1	4.0	1.13	0.13	1.2	2	1.2	1	3
1094	250	4.4	4.5	-0.77	0.11	0.8	-1	0.9	-1	7
1219	250	4.9	5.0	-0.81	0.10	1.3	3	1.3	3	12
646	125	5.2	4.2	2.11	0.15	1.1	1	1.2	1	28
1091	231	4.7	4.8	-1.79	0.12	1.0	0	1.1	0	32
994	213	4.7	4.7	-0.00	0.09	1.0	0	1.0	0	36
1104	250	4.4	4.9	-0.17	0.08	0.9	-1	0.9	0	37
1237	247	5.0	5.1	0.75	0.10	0.8	-2	0.9	-1	38
1102	250	4.4	4.1	0.95	0.08	0.6	-5	0.6	-5	39
1083	250	4.3	4.6	-1.27	0.10	1.2	1	1.2	1	43
1056	250	4.2	4.0	1.25	0.11	0.8	-2	0.8	-2	45
349	85	4.1	4.6	-0.58	0.18	1.2	1	1.2	1	46
824	200	4.1	4.0	0.11	0.13	1.0	0	1.1	0	48
816	194	4.2	4.1	0.61	0.12	1.0	0	1.0	0	50
895	200	4.5	4.3	0.39	0.10	0.8	-2	0.8	-2	52
926	225	4.1	3.9	0.38	0.11	0.7	-3	0.7	-3	56
1019	224	4.5	4.7	0.02	0.14	0.9	-1	0.9	-1	67
891	225	4.0	4.1	0.15	0.11	1.2	1	1.1	1	70
933	197	4.7	4.7	-0.35	0.11	1.1	0	1.1	0	72
832	200	4.2	5.3	-2.94	0.09	1.2	1	1.2	1	82
1135	203	5.6	4.9	1.56	0.11	0.9	-1	0.9	0	83
1016	222	4.6	4.6	-0.73	0.11	1.0	0	1.1	0	89

Obsvd Score	Obsvd Count	Obsvd Average	Fair Avrge	Measure	Model S.E.	Infit MnSq	Std	Outfit MnSq	Std	Num
968.0	215.5	4.5	4.5	-0.00	0.11	1.0	-0.4	1.0	-0.2	Mean
193.6	40.9	0.4	0.4	1.12	0.02	0.2	2.1	0.2	1.9	S.D.

RMSE 0.11 Adj S.D. 1.11 Separation 9.70 Reliability 0.99
Fixed (all same) chi-square: 2544.7 d.f.: 21 significance: .00
Random (normal) chi-square: 21.0 d.f.: 20 significance: .40

(iii) Items

Obsvd Score	Obsvd Count	Obsvd Average	Fair Avrge	Measure	Model S.E.	Infit MnSq	Std	Outfit MnSq	Std	Nu Item
876	191	4.6	4.6	-0.24	0.11	1.0	0	1.1	0	21 TDes1F
840	191	4.4	4.4	0.23	0.11	0.8	-1	0.8	-1	22 TDes1G
851	191	4.5	4.4	0.08	0.11	1.2	1	1.2	2	23 TDes1V
807	190	4.2	4.2	0.59	0.11	0.8	-2	0.8	-1	24 TNarG
836	190	4.4	4.4	0.21	0.11	0.8	-1	0.9	-1	25 TNarV
855	190	4.5	4.5	-0.04	0.11	1.2	1	1.2	1	26 TNarC
849	188	4.5	4.5	-0.05	0.12	1.0	0	1.0	0	27 TSumF
781	188	4.2	4.1	0.85	0.12	0.7	-3	0.7	-3	28 TSumG
780	188	4.1	4.1	0.87	0.12	0.9	0	0.8	-1	29 TSumV
854	187	4.6	4.5	-0.18	0.12	1.3	2	1.3	2	30 TRPF
795	187	4.3	4.2	0.61	0.12	0.8	-2	0.8	-1	31 TRPG
909	187	4.9	4.9	-0.91	0.12	1.5	3	1.6	4	32 TRP
858	188	4.6	4.5	-0.16	0.11	0.9	0	1.0	0	33 TExpF
831	188	4.4	4.4	0.20	0.11	0.9	0	0.9	-1	34 TExpV
845	188	4.5	4.5	0.01	0.11	1.4	3	1.4	3	35 TExp
900	191	4.7	4.7	-0.55	0.11	1.1	0	1.1	0	36 TInsF
854	191	4.5	4.5	0.04	0.11	1.0	0	1.0	0	37 TInsV
854	191	4.5	4.5	0.04	0.11	1.2	1	1.3	2	38 TInsC
881	191	4.6	4.6	-0.30	0.11	0.9	0	0.9	0	39 TDisF
846	191	4.4	4.4	0.15	0.11	0.5	-5	0.6	-4	40 TDisG
941	191	4.9	4.9	-1.09	0.12	1.4	2	1.4	2	41 TDisI
888	191	4.6	4.6	-0.39	0.11	0.8	-2	0.8	-1	42 TDes2F
841	190	4.4	4.4	0.16	0.11	0.6	-4	0.6	-4	43 TDes2G
863	191	4.5	4.5	-0.07	0.11	0.9	-1	0.9	0	44 TDes2V
860	191	4.5	4.5	-0.03	0.11	0.5	-5	0.6	-4	45 TComm

Obsvd Score	Obsvd Count	Obsvd Average	Fair Avrge	Measure	Model S.E.	Infit MnSq	Std	Outfit MnSq	Std	Nu Item
851.8	189.6	4.5	4.5	-0.00	0.11	1.0	-0.5	1.0	-0.3	Mean
36.3	1.5	0.2	0.2	0.45	0.00	0.3	2.5	0.3	2.5	S.D.

RMSE 0.11 Adj S.D. 0.44 Separation 3.81 Reliability 0.94
Fixed (all same) chi-square: 381.8 d.f.: 24 significance: .00
Random (normal) chi-square: 24.0 d.f.: 23 significance: .40

C   Combined data

(i) Candidates

Obsvd Score	Obsvd Count	Obsvd Average	Fair Avrge	Measure	Model S.E.	Infit MnSq	Std	Outfit MnSq	Std	Cand
378	90	4.2	4.3	-0.41	0.16	0.8	-1	0.8	-1	1
494	90	5.5	5.4	2.03	0.17	0.6	-2	0.6	-2	2
502	90	5.6	5.4	1.54	0.14	1.0	0	1.1	0	3
368	90	4.1	4.3	-0.72	0.17	1.3	1	1.3	1	4
365	87	4.2	4.2	-0.29	0.18	1.0	0	1.0	0	5
396	90	4.4	4.6	0.01	0.15	0.8	-1	0.8	-1	7
461	90	5.1	5.2	1.52	0.16	0.9	0	1.0	0	9
393	90	4.4	4.3	-0.31	0.14	0.9	0	1.0	0	10
353	89	4.0	3.9	-1.83	0.18	1.1	0	1.2	0	12
460	90	5.1	5.2	1.55	0.15	1.0	0	1.0	0	13
375	90	4.2	4.0	-0.70	0.17	1.2	1	1.2	1	14
335	90	3.7	3.7	-1.82	0.16	1.0	0	1.0	0	15
553	90	6.1	6.1	3.89	0.17	1.3	1	1.2	1	16
422	90	4.7	5.0	0.96	0.17	0.7	-2	0.7	-2	17
377	90	4.2	4.2	-1.01	0.17	1.3	1	1.3	1	18
441	90	4.9	4.7	0.13	0.15	0.8	-1	0.9	-1	20
580	90	6.4	6.5	5.01	0.22	1.1	0	1.3	1	21
411	90	4.6	4.6	-0.03	0.14	0.7	-2	0.7	-2	22
426	90	4.7	4.6	-0.02	0.13	1.2	1	1.4	2	23
500	90	5.6	5.5	1.55	0.15	1.0	0	1.1	0	24
406	90	4.5	4.5	0.06	0.15	0.5	-3	0.7	-2	25
525	90	5.8	6.1	3.85	0.17	1.1	0	1.1	0	26
373	90	4.1	4.1	-0.50	0.17	0.4	-4	0.5	-4	27
385	90	4.3	4.1	-0.65	0.16	0.7	-2	0.7	-2	28
468	90	5.2	5.3	1.83	0.16	1.1	0	1.1	0	29
393	90	4.4	4.5	0.01	0.17	0.7	-1	0.7	-1	30
408	90	4.5	4.5	0.08	0.15	0.7	-2	0.7	-2	32
380	90	4.2	4.3	-0.60	0.17	1.0	0	1.0	0	33
442	90	4.9	4.9	0.92	0.15	0.7	-2	0.6	-2	35
350	90	3.9	3.8	-0.98	0.14	0.9	0	0.9	0	36
479	90	5.3	5.0	1.22	0.16	0.8	-1	0.9	0	37
418	90	4.6	4.5	0.22	0.17	1.2	1	1.3	1	38
341	90	3.8	3.9	-1.37	0.17	0.8	-1	0.8	-1	39
392	90	4.4	4.2	-0.08	0.17	1.0	0	0.9	0	40
500	90	5.6	5.5	2.34	0.17	0.8	-1	0.8	-1	41
439	90	4.9	5.0	0.51	0.16	0.9	0	0.9	0	42
379	90	4.2	4.3	-0.42	0.16	1.2	0	1.3	1	43
388	90	4.3	4.3	-0.97	0.16	1.1	0	1.0	0	44
452	90	5.0	5.1	0.97	0.15	1.6	3	1.6	3	45
584	90	6.5	6.6	3.78	0.19	1.5	2	1.6	2	47
312	90	3.5	3.1	-2.07	0.14	1.2	1	1.1	0	48
491	90	5.5	5.6	1.92	0.15	0.9	0	0.9	0	50
571	90	6.3	6.3	5.42	0.25	1.1	0	1.2	0	51
352	90	3.9	3.9	-0.67	0.17	0.8	-1	0.8	-1	53
381	84	4.5	4.6	0.24	0.16	1.1	0	1.2	1	55
504	90	5.6	5.5	2.54	0.17	0.5	-3	0.5	-3	56
551	90	6.1	6.2	4.28	0.17	0.7	-2	0.7	-2	57
275	77	3.6	3.6	-2.36	0.17	2.5	5	2.2	3	58
463	90	5.1	5.1	1.36	0.15	0.9	0	0.8	-1	59
388	90	4.3	4.2	-0.54	0.16	2.0	4	1.9	4	60
534	90	5.9	5.9	2.62	0.17	1.0	0	1.1	0	61

Combined data – candidates (continued)

Obsvd Score	Obsvd Count	Obsvd Average	Fair Avrge	Model Measure	Model S.E.	Infit MnSq	Infit Std	Outfit MnSq	Outfit Std	Cand
374	90	4.2	4.1	-1.01	0.18	0.9	0	0.8	-1	65
451	90	5.0	5.2	2.05	0.16	0.7	-2	0.7	-2	66
401	90	4.5	4.5	0.19	0.17	0.8	-1	0.8	-1	67
415	90	4.6	4.4	-0.06	0.17	2.0	5	2.0	5	68
462	90	5.1	5.3	1.51	0.16	1.0	0	0.9	-1	71
363	90	4.0	4.0	-1.09	0.14	0.9	0	0.9	0	72
413	90	4.6	4.6	0.11	0.14	0.9	0	0.9	0	73
382	90	4.2	4.4	-0.30	0.16	1.3	1	1.3	1	74
335	90	3.7	3.4	-1.64	0.16	0.9	0	0.9	0	75
206	43	4.8	4.5	0.45	0.20	1.7	2	1.7	2	76
422	90	4.7	4.6	0.25	0.15	0.8	-1	0.8	-1	77
391	90	4.3	4.6	0.73	0.18	0.6	-2	0.6	-2	78
342	90	3.8	3.9	-1.58	0.17	0.6	-2	0.6	-2	79
394	90	4.4	4.1	-0.33	0.17	0.7	-1	0.8	-1	80
548	90	6.1	6.3	3.77	0.17	0.6	-3	0.7	-2	81
405	90	4.5	4.3	-0.30	0.15	1.4	2	1.4	2	84
418	90	4.6	4.5	-0.18	0.16	1.0	0	1.0	0	85
390	90	4.3	4.3	-0.01	0.16	1.3	1	1.3	1	86
414	90	4.6	4.8	0.51	0.14	1.0	0	0.9	0	88
464	90	5.2	4.9	0.86	0.16	0.7	-2	0.7	-2	89
386	90	4.3	4.3	-0.86	0.18	0.8	-1	0.8	-1	90
295	63	4.7	4.6	-0.06	0.18	1.1	0	1.2	1	91
331	90	3.7	3.6	-1.65	0.16	0.8	-1	0.8	-1	92
315	84	3.8	3.9	-1.45	0.15	0.9	0	0.9	0	94
393	90	4.4	4.4	-0.31	0.13	0.5	-4	0.6	-3	95
347	90	3.9	4.0	-1.02	0.15	2.0	4	2.1	5	98
381	90	4.2	4.2	-0.89	0.18	0.7	-2	0.7	-1	99
393	90	4.4	4.3	0.34	0.16	1.8	4	1.8	4	100
304	84	3.6	3.6	-1.72	0.17	1.2	1	1.1	0	102
347	90	3.9	3.7	-1.36	0.14	1.2	1	1.2	1	103
572	90	6.4	6.4	4.69	0.22	1.3	1	1.3	1	104
367	90	4.1	3.9	-1.37	0.18	1.1	0	1.0	0	105
315	90	3.5	3.7	-2.12	0.18	0.6	-2	0.8	-1	107
252	90	2.8	3.0	-3.14	0.14	0.8	-1	0.8	-1	108
250	90	2.8	2.2	-4.06	0.15	0.7	-1	0.8	-1	109
342	72	4.8	4.8	0.28	0.18	1.1	0	1.5	2	110
271	81	3.3	3.2	-3.44	0.17	1.2	1	1.1	0	112
443	90	4.9	4.9	1.45	0.16	0.9	0	0.9	0	114
398	90	4.4	4.6	-0.15	0.16	0.7	-2	0.7	-1	115
390	90	4.3	4.3	-0.46	0.15	1.5	3	1.4	2	117
450	90	5.0	5.0	0.58	0.14	0.9	0	1.0	0	118
358	90	4.0	3.7	-1.61	0.15	0.6	-2	0.6	-2	119
380	90	4.2	4.4	-0.59	0.16	0.9	0	0.9	0	120
Obsvd Score	Obsvd Count	Obsvd Average	Fair Avrge	Model Measure	Model S.E.	Infit MnSq	Infit Std	Outfit MnSq	Outfit Std	Num
396.1	86.4	4.6	4.6	0.18	0.16	1.0	-0.4	1.0	-0.3	Mean
85.7	11.1	0.8	0.8	1.75	0.02	0.4	2.1	0.4	2.0	S.D.

RMSE 0.17 Adj S.D. 1.74 Separation 10.52 Reliability 0.99
Fixed (all same) chi-square: 10071.8 d.f.: 98 significance: .00
Random (normal) chi-square: 97.8 d.f.: 97 significance: .46

(ii) Raters

Obsvd Score	Obsvd Count	Obsvd Average	Fair Avrge	Measure	Model S.E.	Infit MnSq	Infit Std	Outfit MnSq	Outfit Std	Rater
1761	430	4.1	4.0	0.81	0.09	1.0	0	1.0	0	3
1889	430	4.4	4.5	0.58	0.07	0.9	-1	0.9	0	7
2151	430	5.0	4.9	-1.00	0.07	1.1	1	1.1	1	12
1012	205	4.9	4.4	1.29	0.11	1.1	0	1.1	1	28
1877	391	4.8	5.0	0.18	0.08	0.9	-1	1.0	0	32
1849	393	4.7	4.6	-0.05	0.06	1.0	0	1.0	0	36
1920	410	4.7	4.7	0.50	0.07	1.3	3	1.3	3	37
2055	427	4.8	4.7	-0.15	0.07	0.9	-1	0.9	-1	38
2037	430	4.7	4.5	0.25	0.05	0.6	-6	0.6	-6	39
2023	430	4.7	4.7	-0.44	0.07	1.1	0	1.1	1	43
1758	430	4.1	3.9	1.18	0.08	0.8	-2	0.9	-2	45
747	185	4.0	4.2	0.48	0.12	1.0	0	1.0	0	46
1634	391	4.2	4.2	-1.54	0.09	1.2	2	1.2	2	48
1878	385	4.9	4.4	0.03	0.07	0.7	-4	0.7	-3	50
1775	380	4.7	4.4	0.49	0.08	0.7	-3	0.7	-3	52
1811	425	4.3	4.1	0.08	0.08	1.1	0	1.0	0	56
2006	424	4.7	4.8	-0.76	0.08	0.8	-3	0.8	-2	67
1729	425	4.1	4.1	0.40	0.07	1.1	1	1.1	1	70
1736	377	4.6	4.3	0.11	0.07	1.1	1	1.1	0	72
1709	371	4.6	5.0	-1.38	0.07	1.5	5	1.6	6	82
1933	383	5.0	4.8	-0.07	0.08	1.0	0	1.1	0	83
1922	402	4.8	4.6	-1.00	0.08	1.1	0	1.1	0	89

Obsvd Score	Obsvd Count	Obsvd Average	Fair Avrge	Measure	Model S.E.	Infit MnSq	Infit Std	Outfit MnSq	Outfit Std	Num
1782.4	388.8	4.6	4.5	0.00	0.08	1.0	-0.3	1.0	-0.1	Mean
314.6	64.7	0.3	0.3	0.74	0.01	0.2	2.7	0.2	2.6	S.D.

RMSE 0.08 Adj S.D. 0.74 Separation 9.21 Reliability 0.99
Fixed (all same) chi-square: 1799.3 d.f.: 21 significance: .00
Random (normal) chi-square: 21.0 d.f.: 20 significance: .40

(iii) Items

Obsvd Score	Obsvd Count	Obsvd Average	Fair Avrge	Measure	Model S.E.	Infit MnSq	Std	Outfit MnSq	Std	Nu Item
890	191	4.7	4.5	-0.14	0.11	1.1	0	1.1	0	1 DesF
841	191	4.4	4.3	0.44	0.11	0.7	-2	0.8	-2	2 DesG
837	191	4.4	4.2	0.48	0.11	1.0	0	1.0	0	3 DesV
835	192	4.3	4.2	0.55	0.11	0.7	-3	0.7	-3	4 NarG
853	192	4.4	4.3	0.34	0.11	0.9	0	0.9	0	5 NarV
869	192	4.5	4.4	0.16	0.11	1.2	1	1.2	2	6 NarC
898	189	4.8	4.6	-0.36	0.11	1.0	0	1.1	0	7 RPF
833	189	4.4	4.3	0.42	0.11	0.7	-2	0.7	-2	8 RPG
933	189	4.9	4.8	-0.79	0.11	1.5	3	1.5	3	9 RPI
900	190	4.7	4.6	-0.33	0.11	1.0	0	1.0	0	10 Exp1F
874	190	4.6	4.5	-0.02	0.11	0.9	0	1.0	0	11 Exp1V
896	190	4.7	4.6	-0.28	0.11	1.1	0	1.1	0	12 Exp1C
920	189	4.9	4.8	-0.63	0.11	0.8	-2	0.9	-1	13 Exp2F
886	189	4.7	4.6	-0.21	0.11	0.7	-3	0.8	-2	14 Exp2V
901	189	4.8	4.7	-0.40	0.11	1.0	0	1.0	0	15 Exp2C
952	192	5.0	4.9	-0.83	0.11	0.9	0	0.9	0	16 DisF
893	192	4.7	4.5	-0.13	0.11	0.7	-3	0.7	-3	17 DisG
940	192	4.9	4.8	-0.69	0.11	1.5	4	1.5	4	18 DisI
897	192	4.7	4.5	-0.17	0.11	0.6	-4	0.6	-3	19 CommEf
1069	192	5.6	5.5	-2.32	0.12	1.6	4	1.6	3	20 Comp
876	191	4.6	4.5	-0.02	0.11	1.1	0	1.1	0	21 TDes1F
840	191	4.4	4.3	0.40	0.11	0.8	-2	0.8	-2	22 TDes1G
851	191	4.5	4.4	0.27	0.11	1.1	0	1.1	1	23 TDes1V
807	190	4.2	4.2	0.71	0.11	0.8	-2	0.8	-1	24 TNarG
836	190	4.4	4.3	0.38	0.11	0.8	-1	0.9	-1	25 TNarV
855	190	4.5	4.4	0.16	0.11	1.1	1	1.2	1	26 TNarC
849	188	4.5	4.4	0.15	0.11	1.1	0	1.1	0	27 TSumF
781	188	4.2	4.1	0.94	0.11	0.7	-2	0.7	-2	28 TSumG
780	188	4.1	4.0	0.96	0.11	1.0	0	1.0	0	29 TSumV
854	187	4.6	4.5	0.05	0.11	1.3	2	1.4	3	30 TRPF
795	187	4.3	4.1	0.75	0.11	0.9	-1	0.9	0	31 TRPG
909	187	4.9	4.8	-0.61	0.11	1.5	3	1.5	3	32 TRPI
858	188	4.6	4.5	0.06	0.11	1.0	0	1.0	0	33 TExpF
831	188	4.4	4.3	0.37	0.11	1.0	0	0.9	0	34 TExpV
845	188	4.5	4.4	0.21	0.11	1.4	3	1.4	3	35 TExp
900	191	4.7	4.6	-0.30	0.11	1.1	1	1.1	1	36 TInsF
854	191	4.5	4.4	0.23	0.11	1.0	0	1.0	0	37 TInsV
854	191	4.5	4.4	0.23	0.11	1.2	1	1.3	2	38 TInsC
881	191	4.6	4.5	-0.08	0.11	1.0	0	1.1	0	39 TDisF
846	191	4.4	4.3	0.33	0.11	0.6	-3	0.6	-3	40 TDisG
941	191	4.9	4.9	-0.78	0.11	1.4	3	1.4	3	41 TDisI
888	191	4.6	4.6	-0.16	0.11	0.8	-2	0.8	-1	42 TDes2F
841	190	4.4	4.3	0.34	0.11	0.6	-4	0.6	-4	43 TDes2G
863	191	4.5	4.4	0.13	0.11	0.9	-1	0.9	-1	44 TDes2V
860	191	4.5	4.4	0.16	0.11	0.6	-4	0.6	-3	45 TComm

Obsvd Score	Obsvd Count	Obsvd Average	Fair Avrge	Measure	Model S.E.	Infit MnSq	Std	Outfit MnSq	Std	Nu Item
871.4	190.1	4.6	4.5	-0.00	0.11	1.0	-0.4	1.0	-0.2	Mean
49.2	1.5	0.2	0.3	0.56	0.00	0.3	2.4	0.3	2.3	S.D.

RMSE 0.11 Adj S.D. 0.55 Separation 5.06 Reliability 0.96
Fixed (all same) chi-square: 1136.9 d.f.: 44 significance: .00
Random (normal) chi-square: 43.9 d.f.: 43 significance: .43

Appendix 7.3
FACETS analyses (3) with unanchored item difficulty estimates, oral interaction sub-test, June 1994 trial (N = 89)

A   Live data

(i) Candidates

Obsvd Score	Obsvd Count	Obsvd Average	Fair Avrge	Measure	Model S.E.	Infit MnSq	Infit Std	Outfit MnSq	Outfit Std	Cand
172	40	4.3	4.1	-0.70	0.30	0.7	-1	0.8	0	1
221	40	5.5	5.0	2.06	0.27	0.6	-2	0.7	-1	2
241	40	6.0	6.0	2.82	0.27	1.3	1	1.3	1	3
146	40	3.7	3.9	-1.88	0.26	0.8	0	0.7	-1	4
160	37	4.3	4.1	-0.35	0.32	1.2	0	1.2	0	5
178	40	4.5	4.8	0.14	0.32	1.3	1	1.3	1	7
203	40	5.1	5.1	1.76	0.27	1.5	2	1.7	2	9
207	40	5.2	5.4	0.06	0.27	1.6	2	1.7	2	10
153	40	3.8	3.9	-3.10	0.33	1.2	1	1.3	1	12
199	40	5.0	5.0	0.84	0.23	0.8	0	0.9	0	13
167	40	4.2	4.3	-1.72	0.27	1.1	0	1.1	0	14
150	40	3.8	3.5	-3.37	0.29	1.0	0	1.0	0	15
252	40	6.3	6.5	2.78	0.26	0.8	-1	0.9	0	16
177	40	4.4	4.5	-0.11	0.30	0.7	-1	0.7	-1	17
180	40	4.5	4.4	-0.95	0.26	0.9	0	0.9	0	18
200	40	5.0	4.8	-0.46	0.21	1.0	0	0.9	0	20
257	40	6.4	6.4	3.27	0.30	0.9	0	0.9	0	21
184	40	4.6	4.0	-1.03	0.24	0.8	0	0.8	0	22
199	40	5.0	4.8	0.09	0.21	0.5	-2	0.5	-2	23
207	40	5.2	4.9	0.54	0.26	0.8	0	0.8	0	24
168	40	4.2	4.1	-0.50	0.24	0.5	-2	0.6	-2	25
258	40	6.5	6.6	5.53	0.34	1.2	0	1.4	0	26
168	40	4.2	4.4	-0.53	0.28	0.5	-3	0.5	-2	27
175	40	4.4	3.8	-1.22	0.30	0.6	-1	0.6	-2	28
229	40	5.7	5.4	3.20	0.29	0.8	-1	0.7	-1	29
172	40	4.3	4.5	0.25	0.33	1.1	0	1.1	0	30
178	40	4.5	4.6	-0.27	0.30	1.0	0	1.1	0	32
172	40	4.3	4.4	-1.35	0.28	0.6	-1	0.6	-2	33
198	40	5.0	5.5	1.17	0.28	0.6	-2	0.6	-2	35
169	40	4.2	4.5	-0.31	0.29	0.8	0	1.0	0	36
225	40	5.6	5.8	1.82	0.27	0.9	0	1.2	0	37
198	40	5.0	4.8	-0.41	0.29	1.2	0	1.2	0	38
166	40	4.2	4.2	-1.45	0.26	0.8	-1	0.8	-1	39
175	40	4.4	4.5	-1.14	0.26	1.1	0	1.0	0	40
214	40	5.3	5.4	2.72	0.32	0.9	0	0.9	0	41
189	40	4.7	4.7	-0.72	0.25	0.9	0	1.0	0	42
179	40	4.5	4.5	-0.49	0.28	1.6	2	1.6	2	43
183	40	4.6	4.3	-1.06	0.24	1.1	0	1.1	0	44
204	40	5.1	4.8	0.24	0.21	1.4	1	1.4	1	45
250	40	6.3	5.8	2.43	0.21	1.3	1	1.4	1	47
109	40	2.7	2.4	-5.39	0.32	0.9	0	0.9	0	48
242	40	6.1	5.9	2.46	0.25	1.2	0	1.3	1	50
257	40	6.4	6.7	6.63	0.34	1.0	0	1.3	0	51
158	40	4.0	3.7	-1.10	0.30	1.4	1	1.4	1	53
171	34	5.0	4.7	0.70	0.30	1.0	0	1.0	0	55
233	40	5.8	5.8	3.10	0.27	0.8	0	0.8	0	56
230	40	5.8	5.9	4.42	0.28	0.5	-3	0.5	-2	57
210	40	5.3	5.9	2.09	0.27	0.5	-2	0.6	-2	59

Live data – candidates (continued)

Obsvd Score	Obsvd Count	Obsvd Average	Fair Avrge	Measure	Model S.E.	Infit MnSq	Std	Outfit MnSq	Std	Cand
230	40	5.8	5.7	2.36	0.29	1.3	1	1.5	1	61
174	40	4.3	4.2	-1.48	0.29	1.3	1	1.3	1	65
204	40	5.1	5.3	1.64	0.25	0.7	-1	0.7	-1	66
170	40	4.3	4.3	-0.70	0.27	0.6	-2	0.6	-1	67
161	40	4.0	4.0	-2.54	0.28	1.3	1	1.4	1	68
202	40	5.1	5.0	0.72	0.23	0.9	0	0.8	-1	71
195	40	4.9	4.5	-0.37	0.27	0.4	-3	0.3	-3	72
195	40	4.9	4.4	-0.34	0.21	1.2	0	1.1	0	73
187	40	4.7	4.7	-0.44	0.23	0.9	0	0.9	0	74
150	40	3.8	3.6	-2.19	0.29	0.9	0	0.9	0	75
199	40	5.0	5.0	-0.00	0.25	1.0	0	1.0	0	77
179	40	4.5	4.6	1.05	0.35	0.7	-1	0.6	-1	78
147	40	3.7	3.8	-2.15	0.33	1.1	0	1.2	0	79
170	40	4.3	4.1	-1.71	0.30	0.8	-1	0.8	-1	80
240	40	6.0	6.5	4.83	0.29	0.9	0	0.9	0	81
196	40	4.9	4.9	-0.30	0.30	0.9	0	0.9	0	85
192	40	4.8	5.3	1.20	0.27	1.6	2	1.6	2	86
161	40	4.0	4.0	-1.06	0.28	1.2	0	1.2	0	88
204	40	5.1	5.1	0.34	0.26	0.9	0	0.8	0	89
185	40	4.6	4.4	-1.43	0.27	1.0	0	1.0	0	90
193	40	4.8	4.9	-0.09	0.25	1.2	0	1.2	0	91
140	40	3.5	3.3	-2.97	0.26	0.8	-1	0.9	0	92
161	40	4.0	4.0	-1.67	0.25	0.9	0	0.8	0	94
189	40	4.7	4.4	-1.11	0.25	0.9	0	1.1	0	95
184	40	4.6	4.6	-0.97	0.25	0.7	-1	0.7	-1	99
203	40	5.1	5.3	2.19	0.32	0.9	0	0.8	0	100
160	40	4.0	3.6	-1.65	0.26	1.4	1	1.3	1	102
141	40	3.5	3.3	-4.35	0.29	1.5	1	1.4	1	103
274	40	6.8	6.9	6.30	0.45	0.6	-1	0.4	-1	104
156	40	3.9	4.0	-2.41	0.29	1.6	2	1.5	1	105
152	40	3.8	4.2	-2.36	0.34	1.1	0	1.2	0	107
117	40	2.9	3.2	-5.98	0.44	1.1	0	1.7	1	108
107	40	2.7	2.5	-6.77	0.40	0.9	0	1.1	0	109
101	22	4.6	4.6	-1.38	0.35	1.5	1	1.9	2	110
128	40	3.2	3.0	-4.33	0.28	1.3	1	1.2	0	112
200	40	5.0	5.2	1.40	0.27	1.2	0	1.2	0	114
176	40	4.4	4.7	-0.86	0.29	0.9	0	0.9	0	115
189	40	4.7	5.1	0.99	0.28	0.7	-1	0.7	-1	117
214	40	5.3	5.3	0.78	0.22	1.9	3	1.9	3	118
186	40	4.7	4.6	-1.27	0.26	0.4	-3	0.4	-3	119
167	40	4.2	3.7	-2.12	0.26	0.7	-1	0.7	-1	120

Obsvd Score	Obsvd Count	Obsvd Average	Fair Avrge	Measure	Model S.E.	Infit MnSq	Std	Outfit MnSq	Std	Num
186.9	39.7	4.7	4.7	-0.10	0.28	1.0	-0.3	1.0	-0.2	Mean
34.4	2.0	0.8	0.9	2.38	0.04	0.3	1.5	0.3	1.4	S.D.

RMSE 0.28 Adj S.D. 2.36 Separation 8.31 Reliability 0.99
Fixed (all same) chi-square: 5248.24 d.f.: 89 significance: .00
Random (normal) chi-square: 88.53 d.f.: 88 significance: .46

(ii) Raters

Obsvd Score	Obsvd Count	Obsvd Average	Fair Avrge	Measure	Model S.E.	Infit MnSq	Std	Outfit MnSq	Std	Rater
728	180	4.0	4.2	0.54	0.14	0.9	0	0.9	0	3
795	180	4.4	4.7	-0.30	0.12	0.7	-3	0.7	-3	7
826	160	5.2	5.4	0.14	0.12	1.2	1	1.2	1	12
278	160	4.6	4.7	-0.29	0.25	0.9	0	0.9	0	28
786	160	4.9	5.0	-0.23	0.13	0.9	0	0.9	0	32
752	160	4.7	5.2	-0.96	0.11	1.0	0	1.0	0	36
816	160	5.1	4.8	0.00	0.11	1.1	0	1.1	0	37
818	180	4.5	5.0	-1.73	0.12	0.8	-1	0.8	-1	38
722	140	5.2	5.1	-0.73	0.13	0.7	-2	0.6	-2	39
940	180	5.2	5.0	0.12	0.12	1.0	0	1.1	0	43
702	180	3.9	3.8	1.96	0.16	0.8	-1	0.8	-1	45
398	100	4.0	4.0	0.67	0.20	1.1	0	1.1	0	46
735	171	4.3	4.5	-2.40	0.15	0.9	-1	0.9	0	48
1062	191	5.6	5.0	-0.12	0.13	1.0	0	1.1	0	50
880	180	4.9	4.7	0.12	0.13	0.9	0	0.9	0	52
723	160	4.5	4.4	0.58	0.16	1.3	2	1.3	2	56
898	180	5.0	5.1	1.09	0.13	0.7	-3	0.7	-2	67
760	180	4.2	4.1	2.84	0.16	1.1	0	1.3	1	70
711	160	4.4	4.5	-0.31	0.13	1.0	0	1.0	0	72
785	151	5.2	5.3	0.04	0.14	1.4	2	1.6	3	82
798	180	4.4	4.9	-1.55	0.15	1.2	1	1.2	1	83
906	180	5.0	4.7	0.50	0.12	1.0	0	1.0	0	89

Obsvd Score	Obsvd Count	Obsvd Average	Fair Avrge	Measure	Model S.E.	Infit MnSq	Std	Outfit MnSq	Std	Num
764.5	162.4	4.7	4.7	-0.00	0.14	1.0	-0.2	1.0	-0.1	Mean
160.5	29.4	0.4	0.4	1.12	0.03	0.2	1.7	0.2	1.6	S.D.

RMSE 0.15 Adj S.D. 1.11 Separation 7.60 Reliability 0.98
Fixed (all same) chi-square: 1276.67 d.f.: 21 significance: .00
Random (normal) chi-square: 20.98 d.f.: 20 significance: .40

(iii) Items

Obsvd Score	Obsvd Count	Obsvd Average	Fair Avrge	Measure	Model S.E.	Infit MnSq	Std	Outfit MnSq	Std	Nu Item
834	179	4.7	4.6	0.14	0.13	1.1	0	1.1	0	1 DesF
790	179	4.4	4.4	0.87	0.13	0.7	-2	0.7	-2	2 DesG
786	179	4.4	4.3	0.93	0.13	1.1	0	1.1	0	3 DesV
782	180	4.3	4.3	1.07	0.13	0.7	-3	0.7	-2	4 NarG
800	180	4.4	4.4	0.77	0.13	0.9	-1	0.9	-1	5 NarV
813	180	4.5	4.5	0.56	0.13	1.3	2	1.5	3	6 NarC
846	177	4.8	4.8	-0.20	0.13	1.0	0	1.0	0	7 RPF
782	177	4.4	4.4	0.86	0.13	0.7	-3	0.7	-3	8 RPG
876	177	4.9	5.0	-0.70	0.13	1.5	3	1.6	4	9 RPI
843	178	4.7	4.7	-0.08	0.13	0.9	0	0.9	0	10 Exp1F
820	178	4.6	4.6	0.30	0.13	0.9	0	0.9	0	11 Exp1V
841	178	4.7	4.7	-0.05	0.13	1.1	1	1.2	1	12 Exp1C
865	177	4.9	4.9	-0.52	0.13	0.7	-2	0.8	-1	13 Exp2F
834	177	4.7	4.7	-0.01	0.13	0.7	-2	0.7	-2	14 Exp2V
847	177	4.8	4.8	-0.22	0.13	1.0	0	1.0	0	15 Exp2C
894	180	5.0	5.0	-0.76	0.13	0.8	-1	0.8	-1	16 DisF
837	180	4.7	4.6	0.17	0.13	0.7	-2	0.7	-2	17 DisG
884	180	4.9	4.9	-0.60	0.13	1.7	5	1.6	4	18 DisI
843	180	4.7	4.7	0.07	0.13	0.5	-5	0.6	-4	19 CommEf
1002	180	5.6	5.7	-2.60	0.13	1.4	3	1.3	1	20 Comp

Obsvd Score	Obsvd Count	Obsvd Average	Fair Avrge	Measure	Model S.E.	Infit MnSq	Std	Outfit MnSq	Std	Nu Item
841.0	178.6	4.7	4.7	0.00	0.13	1.0	-0.5	1.0	-0.3	Mean (Cou
49.0	1.3	0.3	0.3	0.81	0.00	0.3	2.7	0.3	2.5	S.D.

RMSE 0.13 Adj S.D. 0.80 Separation 6.21 Reliability 0.97
Fixed (all same) chi-square: 757.68 d.f.: 19 significance: .00
Random (normal) chi-square: 18.98 d.f.: 18 significance: .39

B   Tape data

(i) Candidates

Obsvd Score	Obsvd Count	Obsvd Average	Fair Avrge	Measure	Model S.E.	Infit MnSq	Infit Std	Outfit MnSq	Outfit Std	Cand
206	50	4.1	4.2	-0.82	0.25	0.9	0	1.3	1	1
273	50	5.5	5.4	1.94	0.29	0.9	0	1.0	0	2
261	50	5.2	5.3	1.06	0.21	1.3	1	1.5	2	3
222	50	4.4	4.7	-0.08	0.22	1.4	1	1.4	1	4
205	50	4.1	4.1	-0.88	0.25	1.3	1	1.3	1	5
218	50	4.4	4.4	-0.29	0.20	0.6	-2	0.6	-2	7
258	50	5.2	5.3	0.82	0.22	0.9	0	0.9	0	9
186	50	3.7	4.3	-0.75	0.19	0.7	-1	0.8	-1	10
200	49	4.1	4.0	-1.82	0.28	1.8	2	1.8	2	12
261	50	5.2	5.7	1.89	0.22	0.7	-2	0.7	-2	13
208	50	4.2	3.9	-1.16	0.24	1.5	1	1.6	2	14
185	50	3.7	3.7	-1.68	0.27	1.1	0	1.1	0	15
301	50	6.0	6.3	5.40	0.24	1.5	2	1.4	1	16
245	50	4.9	4.8	1.07	0.24	0.8	-1	0.7	-1	17
197	50	3.9	4.0	-1.74	0.25	1.6	2	1.5	2	18
241	50	4.8	4.6	0.31	0.24	0.7	-1	0.7	-1	20
323	50	6.5	6.5	5.50	0.31	0.9	0	1.0	0	21
227	50	4.5	4.4	-0.32	0.19	0.6	-2	0.6	-2	22
227	50	4.5	3.6	-1.40	0.18	1.4	1	1.4	1	23
293	50	5.9	6.2	2.57	0.23	0.8	0	0.9	0	24
238	50	4.8	4.5	0.34	0.22	0.5	-2	0.5	-3	25
267	50	5.3	5.7	4.03	0.24	1.2	0	1.2	0	26
205	50	4.1	3.9	-0.79	0.26	0.5	-2	0.6	-2	27
210	50	4.2	4.0	-1.18	0.24	1.1	0	1.1	0	28
239	50	4.8	5.2	0.93	0.22	1.1	0	1.2	1	29
221	50	4.4	4.4	0.18	0.25	0.8	0	0.8	0	30
230	50	4.6	4.7	0.08	0.21	0.8	-1	0.7	-1	32
208	50	4.2	4.2	-0.79	0.23	1.4	1	1.5	1	33
244	50	4.9	4.9	-0.08	0.19	0.8	-1	0.7	-1	35
181	50	3.6	2.8	-1.92	0.18	0.8	0	0.8	0	36
254	50	5.1	5.2	0.73	0.23	0.8	-1	0.7	-1	37
220	50	4.4	4.5	0.23	0.23	1.2	0	1.2	0	38
175	50	3.5	3.5	-3.09	0.27	0.9	0	0.9	0	39
217	50	4.3	4.2	0.02	0.27	1.0	0	1.0	0	40
286	50	5.7	5.6	2.44	0.24	1.0	0	1.1	0	41
250	50	5.0	4.8	0.93	0.22	0.8	0	0.8	0	42
200	50	4.0	4.3	-0.48	0.21	1.1	0	1.2	0	43
205	50	4.1	4.1	-1.60	0.25	0.9	0	0.9	0	44
248	50	5.0	5.1	0.81	0.24	1.5	1	1.5	2	45
334	50	6.7	6.7	5.76	0.31	0.8	-1	0.8	-1	47
203	50	4.1	2.9	-2.08	0.20	1.3	1	1.4	1	48
249	50	5.0	5.5	1.30	0.22	0.9	0	0.9	0	50
314	50	6.3	6.2	6.76	0.35	1.1	0	1.2	0	51
194	50	3.9	4.0	-0.88	0.28	1.0	0	0.8	0	53
210	50	4.2	4.1	-0.72	0.22	1.3	1	1.3	1	55
271	50	5.4	5.6	2.86	0.25	0.4	-4	0.4	-3	56
321	50	6.4	6.6	6.44	0.28	1.1	0	1.1	0	57
253	50	5.1	5.0	0.77	0.18	0.8	-1	0.8	-1	59
304	50	6.1	6.4	2.98	0.26	1.2	0	1.4	1	61
200	50	4.0	4.0	-1.24	0.28	1.1	0	1.0	0	65

Tape data – candidates (continued)

Obsvd Score	Obsvd Count	Obsvd Average	Fair Avrge	Model Measure	Model S.E.	Infit MnSq	Infit Std	Outfit MnSq	Outfit Std	Cand
247	50	4.9	5.1	1.95	0.24	0.9	0	0.9	0	66
231	50	4.6	4.3	-0.55	0.23	1.1	0	1.0	0	67
254	50	5.1	4.8	1.98	0.26	1.0	0	1.0	0	68
260	50	5.2	5.5	1.99	0.27	0.4	-3	0.4	-3	71
168	50	3.4	3.5	-2.43	0.25	0.8	0	0.9	0	72
218	50	4.4	4.3	-0.11	0.25	1.0	0	0.9	0	73
195	50	3.9	4.0	-1.03	0.23	1.6	2	1.4	1	74
185	50	3.7	2.7	-2.40	0.19	0.8	0	0.8	0	75
223	50	4.5	4.4	-0.12	0.21	0.9	0	0.9	0	77
212	50	4.2	4.6	1.11	0.28	0.7	-1	0.8	0	78
195	50	3.9	3.6	-2.26	0.24	0.6	-1	0.5	-1	79
224	50	4.5	4.3	-0.41	0.26	0.8	0	0.9	0	80
308	50	6.2	6.4	4.34	0.27	0.8	0	0.8	0	81
222	50	4.4	4.3	-0.54	0.21	1.2	0	1.2	0	85
198	50	4.0	4.2	-1.72	0.22	0.8	-1	1.0	0	86
253	50	5.1	5.1	1.29	0.22	0.6	-2	0.7	-1	88
260	50	5.2	4.9	0.98	0.23	0.8	-1	0.8	-1	89
201	50	4.0	4.0	-1.14	0.26	0.7	-1	0.7	-1	90
102	23	4.4	4.3	-0.38	0.29	0.7	-1	0.7	-1	91
191	50	3.8	3.8	-1.61	0.23	0.9	0	0.9	0	92
154	44	3.5	3.7	-2.56	0.24	1.3	1	1.3	1	94
204	50	4.1	4.4	-0.45	0.18	0.4	-3	0.4	-3	95
197	50	3.9	4.1	-1.30	0.27	1.0	0	1.0	0	99
190	50	3.8	3.9	-1.09	0.28	1.5	1	1.5	1	100
144	44	3.3	3.2	-3.11	0.26	1.5	1	1.5	1	102
206	50	4.1	3.0	-1.61	0.19	1.2	0	1.2	0	103
298	50	6.0	6.3	4.13	0.25	1.4	2	1.5	2	104
211	50	4.2	4.1	-1.24	0.26	0.7	-1	0.7	-1	105
163	50	3.3	3.4	-3.57	0.29	0.7	-1	0.7	-1	107
135	50	2.7	2.4	-4.27	0.22	0.9	0	1.0	0	108
143	50	2.9	2.0	-4.53	0.20	0.9	0	1.0	0	109
241	50	4.8	5.4	0.46	0.23	0.8	-1	0.8	-1	110
143	41	3.5	3.1	-3.30	0.22	1.2	0	1.1	0	112
243	50	4.9	5.0	1.56	0.23	1.0	0	1.0	0	114
222	50	4.4	4.3	-0.38	0.21	0.6	-2	0.5	-2	115
201	50	4.0	3.9	-2.31	0.20	1.3	1	1.4	1	117
236	50	4.7	4.7	0.30	0.19	0.3	-4	0.4	-4	118
172	50	3.4	3.4	-2.39	0.21	0.6	-2	0.6	-2	119
213	50	4.3	4.5	-0.31	0.21	0.7	-1	0.7	-1	120

Obsvd Score	Obsvd Count	Obsvd Average	Fair Avrge	Model Measure	Model S.E.	Infit MnSq	Infit Std	Outfit MnSq	Outfit Std	Num
224.2	49.4	4.5	4.5	0.06	0.24	1.0	-0.3	1.0	-0.3	Mean
44.4	3.1	0.8	1.0	2.28	0.03	0.3	1.6	0.3	1.6	S.D.

RMSE 0.24 Adj S.D. 2.27 Separation 9.48 Reliability 0.99
Fixed (all same) chi-square: 7155.40 d.f.: 87 significance: .00
Random (normal) chi-square: 86.78 d.f.: 86 significance: .46

(ii) Raters

Obsvd Score	Obsvd Count	Obsvd Average	Fair Avrge	Measure	Model S.E.	Infit MnSq	Infit Std	Outfit MnSq	Outfit Std	Rater
1033	250	4.1	4.0	0.97	0.13	1.3	2	1.2	2	3
987	225	4.4	4.6	-0.94	0.12	0.9	-1	0.9	-1	7
1219	250	4.9	5.0	-1.05	0.11	1.3	3	1.3	3	12
646	125	5.2	4.3	2.00	0.15	1.2	1	1.2	1	28
930	194	4.8	4.8	-1.53	0.13	0.9	0	0.9	0	32
780	163	4.8	4.5	0.17	0.11	0.9	-1	0.9	0	36
874	200	4.4	4.8	0.06	0.10	0.8	-1	0.8	-1	37
1237	247	5.0	5.2	0.50	0.10	0.8	-1	0.9	0	38
1009	225	4.5	4.3	0.74	0.09	0.6	-5	0.6	-4	39
995	225	4.4	4.6	-0.51	0.11	1.1	1	1.1	1	43
1056	250	4.2	4.0	1.16	0.11	0.8	-2	0.8	-2	45
349	85	4.1	4.6	-0.63	0.18	1.2	1	1.2	1	46
824	200	4.1	4.1	-0.12	0.14	1.0	0	1.1	0	48
736	169	4.4	4.2	0.17	0.13	1.0	0	1.0	0	50
895	200	4.5	4.4	0.18	0.10	0.8	-2	0.8	-2	52
851	200	4.3	3.9	1.61	0.13	0.7	-3	0.7	-3	56
1019	224	4.5	4.6	0.02	0.14	0.9	-1	0.9	-1	67
839	200	4.2	4.1	0.38	0.14	1.1	1	1.1	0	70
933	197	4.7	4.7	-0.43	0.11	1.1	0	1.1	0	72
609	150	4.1	5.5	-3.34	0.10	1.2	1	1.2	1	82
1005	175	5.7	5.0	1.27	0.12	0.9	0	1.0	0	83
903	197	4.6	4.6	-0.67	0.11	1.0	0	1.0	0	89

Obsvd Score	Obsvd Count	Obsvd Average	Fair Avrge	Measure	Model S.E.	Infit MnSq	Infit Std	Outfit MnSq	Outfit Std	Num
896.8	197.8	4.5	4.5	-0.00	0.12	1.0	-0.4	1.0	-0.2	Mean
193.0	40.7	0.4	0.4	1.14	0.02	0.2	2.0	0.2	1.9	S.D.

RMSE 0.12 Adj S.D. 1.13 Separation 9.28 Reliability 0.99
Fixed (all same) chi-square: 2253.25 d.f.: 21 significance: .00
Random (normal) chi-square: 21.02 d.f.: 20 significance: .40

(iii) Items

Obsvd Score	Obsvd Count	Obsvd Average	Fair Avrge	Measure	Model S.E.	Infit MnSq	Infit Std	Outfit MnSq	Outfit Std	Nu Item
804	174	4.6	4.6	-0.24	0.12	1.0	0	1.0	0	21 TDes1F
772	174	4.4	4.4	0.25	0.12	0.8	-1	0.8	-1	22 TDes1G
781	174	4.5	4.5	0.11	0.12	1.2	1	1.3	2	23 TDes1V
748	174	4.3	4.3	0.61	0.12	0.8	-2	0.8	-1	24 TNarG
779	174	4.5	4.5	0.14	0.12	0.8	-1	0.9	0	25 TNarV
794	174	4.6	4.6	-0.09	0.12	1.1	1	1.2	1	26 TNarC
787	172	4.6	4.6	-0.08	0.12	1.0	0	0.9	0	27 TSumF
722	172	4.2	4.2	0.92	0.13	0.7	-3	0.7	-3	28 TSumG
722	172	4.2	4.2	0.92	0.13	0.9	0	0.8	-1	29 TSumV
789	171	4.6	4.6	-0.20	0.12	1.2	1	1.3	2	30 TRPF
733	171	4.3	4.2	0.67	0.12	0.7	-2	0.8	-1	31 TRPG
835	171	4.9	4.9	-0.90	0.12	1.5	3	1.6	4	32 TRPI
800	173	4.6	4.6	-0.22	0.12	0.9	0	1.0	0	33 TExpF
773	173	4.5	4.4	0.19	0.12	0.9	0	0.9	0	34 TExpV
784	173	4.5	4.5	0.02	0.12	1.4	2	1.4	2	35 TExp
833	176	4.7	4.7	-0.53	0.12	1.0	0	1.1	0	36 TInsF
794	176	4.5	4.5	0.04	0.12	1.0	0	1.0	0	37 TInsV
791	176	4.5	4.5	0.09	0.12	1.2	1	1.3	2	38 TInsC
819	176	4.7	4.7	-0.33	0.12	1.0	0	1.0	0	39 TDisF
787	176	4.5	4.5	0.15	0.12	0.5	-4	0.6	-4	40 TDisG
877	176	5.0	5.0	-1.19	0.12	1.4	2	1.3	2	41 TDisI
824	176	4.7	4.7	-0.40	0.12	0.8	-2	0.8	-1	42 TDes2F
782	175	4.5	4.4	0.16	0.12	0.6	-4	0.6	-4	43 TDes2G
801	176	4.6	4.5	-0.06	0.12	0.9	-1	0.9	0	44 TDes2V
798	176	4.5	4.5	-0.02	0.12	0.6	-4	0.6	-4	45 TComm
Obsvd Score	Obsvd Count	Obsvd Average	Fair Avrge	Measure	Model S.E.	Infit MnSq	Infit Std	Outfit MnSq	Outfit Std	Nu Item
789.2	174.0	4.5	4.5	-0.00	0.12	1.0	-0.6	1.0	-0.3	Mean
34.1	1.8	0.2	0.2	0.47	0.00	0.3	2.3	0.3	2.3	S.D.

RMSE 0.12 Adj S.D. 0.46 Separation 3.73 Reliability 0.93
Fixed (all same) chi-square: 367.96 d.f.: 24 significance: .00
Random (normal) chi-square: 23.98 d.f.: 23 significance: .40

C   Combined data

(i) Candidates

Obsvd Score	Obsvd Count	Obsvd Average	Fair Avrge	Measure	Model S.E.	Infit MnSq	Std	Outfit MnSq	Std	Cand
378	90	4.2	4.3	-0.49	0.16	0.8	-1	0.9	0	1
494	90	5.5	5.4	2.02	0.17	0.6	-3	0.6	-2	2
502	90	5.6	5.5	1.53	0.14	1.1	0	1.2	1	3
368	90	4.1	4.4	-0.77	0.17	1.3	2	1.3	1	4
365	87	4.2	4.3	-0.43	0.18	1.0	0	1.0	0	5
396	90	4.4	4.5	-0.06	0.15	0.9	0	0.9	0	7
461	90	5.1	5.2	1.52	0.16	0.9	0	1.0	0	9
393	90	4.4	4.4	-0.30	0.14	0.9	0	1.0	0	10
353	89	4.0	4.0	-2.14	0.20	1.4	2	1.4	1	12
460	90	5.1	5.1	1.52	0.15	0.9	0	0.9	0	13
375	90	4.2	3.9	-0.85	0.17	1.3	1	1.3	1	14
335	90	3.7	3.6	-2.18	0.18	1.1	0	1.1	0	15
553	90	6.1	6.0	3.84	0.17	1.3	1	1.2	1	16
422	90	4.7	4.9	0.92	0.17	0.7	-2	0.7	-2	17
377	90	4.2	4.2	-1.16	0.17	1.4	2	1.4	2	18
441	90	4.9	4.7	0.09	0.15	0.8	-1	0.8	-1	20
580	90	6.4	6.5	5.07	0.22	1.1	0	1.3	1	21
411	90	4.6	4.6	-0.02	0.14	0.7	-2	0.7	-2	22
426	90	4.7	4.6	-0.04	0.13	1.4	2	1.6	3	23
500	90	5.6	5.6	1.56	0.15	1.0	0	1.1	0	24
406	90	4.5	4.6	0.07	0.15	0.5	-3	0.7	-2	25
525	90	5.8	6.1	3.82	0.17	1.1	0	1.1	0	26
373	90	4.1	4.1	-0.67	0.17	0.5	-4	0.5	-4	27
385	90	4.3	4.0	-0.81	0.16	0.7	-1	0.7	-1	28
468	90	5.2	5.2	1.77	0.16	1.1	0	1.1	0	29
393	90	4.4	4.6	-0.06	0.17	0.8	-1	0.7	-1	30
408	90	4.5	4.6	0.06	0.15	0.7	-2	0.7	-2	32
380	90	4.2	4.2	-0.69	0.17	1.0	0	1.1	0	33
442	90	4.9	4.8	0.89	0.15	0.7	-2	0.6	-2	35
350	90	3.9	3.8	-1.03	0.14	0.9	0	0.9	0	36
479	90	5.3	5.1	1.14	0.16	0.8	-1	0.9	0	37
418	90	4.6	4.5	0.12	0.17	1.3	1	1.3	1	38
341	90	3.8	3.8	-1.54	0.18	0.8	-1	0.9	-1	39
392	90	4.4	4.2	-0.25	0.17	1.0	0	1.0	0	40
500	90	5.6	5.5	2.26	0.17	0.8	-1	0.8	-1	41
439	90	4.9	4.9	0.46	0.16	0.8	-1	0.9	-1	42
379	90	4.2	4.4	-0.46	0.16	1.2	1	1.4	2	43
388	90	4.3	4.3	-1.00	0.16	1.2	1	1.1	0	44
452	90	5.0	5.1	0.99	0.15	1.6	3	1.7	3	45
584	90	6.5	6.6	3.89	0.19	1.4	2	1.5	2	47
312	90	3.5	3.2	-2.28	0.15	1.3	1	1.2	1	48
491	90	5.5	5.7	1.92	0.15	1.0	0	1.0	0	50
571	90	6.3	6.2	5.38	0.25	1.1	0	1.2	0	51
352	90	3.9	3.8	-0.85	0.17	0.9	0	0.8	-1	53
381	84	4.5	4.5	0.13	0.16	1.1	0	1.2	1	55
504	90	5.6	5.6	2.48	0.17	0.5	-3	0.5	-3	56
551	90	6.1	6.3	4.33	0.18	0.8	-2	0.7	-2	57
463	90	5.1	5.1	1.35	0.15	0.9	-1	0.8	-1	59
534	90	5.9	5.8	2.62	0.17	1.0	0	1.2	0	61

Combined data – candidates data (continued)

Obsvd Score	Obsvd Count	Obsvd Average	Fair Avrge	Measure	Model S.E.	Infit MnSq	Infit Std	Outfit MnSq	Outfit Std	Cand
374	90	4.2	4.1	-1.14	0.18	0.9	0	0.9	0	65
451	90	5.0	5.2	2.00	0.16	0.7	-2	0.7	-2	66
401	90	4.5	4.4	0.08	0.17	0.8	-1	0.8	-1	67
415	90	4.6	4.4	-0.22	0.17	1.9	5	1.9	5	68
462	90	5.1	5.4	1.57	0.16	0.9	0	0.8	-1	71
363	90	4.0	4.1	-1.07	0.14	0.8	-1	0.8	-1	72
413	90	4.6	4.7	0.13	0.14	0.8	-1	0.9	-1	73
382	90	4.2	4.4	-0.34	0.17	1.4	2	1.4	2	74
335	90	3.7	3.3	-1.86	0.16	0.9	0	0.9	0	75
422	90	4.7	4.6	0.19	0.15	0.8	-1	0.8	-1	77
391	90	4.3	4.6	0.68	0.18	0.6	-2	0.6	-2	78
342	90	3.8	3.9	-1.80	0.18	0.7	-2	0.7	-2	79
394	90	4.4	4.1	-0.50	0.18	0.8	-1	0.8	-1	80
548	90	6.1	6.3	3.80	0.17	0.6	-3	0.7	-2	81
418	90	4.6	4.5	-0.24	0.16	1.0	0	1.0	0	85
390	90	4.3	4.3	-0.10	0.17	1.3	1	1.4	2	86
414	90	4.6	4.8	0.53	0.14	1.0	0	0.9	0	88
464	90	5.2	4.9	0.76	0.16	0.7	-2	0.7	-1	89
386	90	4.3	4.3	-0.97	0.18	0.9	-1	0.9	-1	90
295	63	4.7	4.5	-0.10	0.18	1.1	0	1.2	0	91
331	90	3.7	3.6	-1.75	0.17	0.8	-1	0.8	-1	92
315	84	3.8	3.8	-1.63	0.16	1.0	0	1.0	0	94
393	90	4.4	4.4	-0.30	0.13	0.5	-4	0.5	-3	95
381	90	4.2	4.3	-0.98	0.18	0.7	-1	0.8	-1	99
393	90	4.4	4.3	0.24	0.17	2.0	5	2.0	4	100
304	84	3.6	3.5	-1.96	0.18	1.3	2	1.3	1	102
347	90	3.9	3.6	-1.54	0.14	1.2	1	1.2	1	103
572	90	6.4	6.5	4.73	0.22	1.3	1	1.4	1	104
367	90	4.1	4.0	-1.48	0.19	1.2	0	1.0	0	105
315	90	3.5	3.6	-2.56	0.22	1.0	0	1.0	0	107
252	90	2.8	2.9	-3.97	0.18	1.0	0	1.0	0	108
250	90	2.8	2.1	-4.38	0.15	0.8	-1	0.8	-1	109
342	72	4.8	4.8	0.22	0.18	1.1	0	1.6	2	110
271	81	3.3	3.1	-3.54	0.17	1.3	1	1.2	0	112
443	90	4.9	5.0	1.42	0.16	0.9	0	0.9	0	114
398	90	4.4	4.5	-0.23	0.17	0.7	-2	0.8	-1	115
390	90	4.3	4.2	-0.58	0.16	1.6	3	1.5	2	117
450	90	5.0	5.0	0.60	0.14	0.9	0	1.1	0	118
358	90	4.0	3.8	-1.76	0.15	0.6	-2	0.6	-3	119
380	90	4.2	4.4	-0.62	0.16	0.9	0	0.9	0	120
Obsvd Score	Obsvd Count	Obsvd Average	Fair Avrge	Measure	Model S.E.	Infit MnSq	Infit Std	Outfit MnSq	Outfit Std	Num
410.8	89.1	4.6	4.6	0.17	0.17	1.0	-0.3	1.0	-0.2	Mea
72.8	3.7	0.8	0.8	1.88	0.02	0.3	1.9	0.3	1.9	S.D.

RMSE 0.17 Adj S.D. 1.87 Separation 11.20 Reliability 0.99
Fixed (all same) chi-square: 9880.85 d.f.: 88 significance: .00
Random (normal) chi-square: 87.83 d.f.: 87 significance: .45

(ii) Raters

Obsvd Score	Obsvd Count	Obsvd Average	Fair Avrge	Measure	Model S.E.	Infit MnSq	Std	Outfit MnSq	Std	Rater
1761	430	4.1	4.0	0.71	0.09	1.0	0	1.0	0	3
1889	430	4.4	4.6	0.37	0.08	1.0	0	1.0	0	7
2045	410	5.0	4.9	-1.15	0.07	1.1	1	1.1	1	12
924	185	5.0	4.4	1.39	0.12	1.1	0	1.1	0	28
1716	354	4.8	5.0	0.17	0.09	0.9	0	1.0	0	32
1532	323	4.7	4.6	-0.01	0.07	1.0	0	1.0	0	36
1805	385	4.7	4.7	0.54	0.08	1.3	3	1.3	3	37
2055	427	4.8	4.7	-0.22	0.07	0.9	0	0.9	0	38
1731	365	4.7	4.4	0.39	0.06	0.5	-7	0.5	-7	39
1935	405	4.8	4.8	0.24	0.08	1.0	0	1.1	0	43
1758	430	4.1	3.9	1.08	0.08	0.8	-2	0.9	-1	45
747	185	4.0	4.2	0.25	0.12	1.1	0	1.1	0	46
1559	371	4.2	4.3	-1.84	0.09	1.1	1	1.1	1	48
1693	340	5.0	4.5	-0.30	0.08	0.7	-3	0.8	-3	50
1775	380	4.7	4.4	0.43	0.08	0.8	-3	0.8	-3	52
1574	360	4.4	4.1	1.30	0.10	0.9	0	0.9	0	56
1815	384	4.7	4.8	-0.83	0.09	0.7	-3	0.8	-2	67
1599	380	4.2	4.2	0.33	0.10	1.0	0	1.1	0	70
1644	357	4.6	4.3	0.00	0.08	1.1	1	1.1	1	72
1394	301	4.6	5.1	-1.61	0.08	1.5	5	1.7	6	82
1803	355	5.1	4.9	-0.15	0.09	1.0	0	1.1	1	83
1809	377	4.8	4.6	-1.07	0.08	1.1	0	1.1	0	89

Obsvd Score	Obsvd Count	Obsvd Average	Fair Avrge	Measure	Model S.E.	Infit MnSq	Std	Outfit MnSq	Std	Num
1662.0	360.6	4.6	4.5	-0.00	0.08	1.0	-0.3	1.0	-0.0	Mean
305.0	64.9	0.3	0.3	0.84	0.01	0.2	2.7	0.2	2.7	S.D.

RMSE 0.09 Adj S.D. 0.84 Separation 9.82 Reliability 0.99
Fixed (all same) chi-square: 2047.81 d.f.: 21 significance: .00
Random (normal) chi-square: 20.98 d.f.: 20 significance: .40

(iii) Items

Obsvd Score	Obsvd Count	Obsvd Average	Fair Avrge	Measure	Model S.E.	Infit MnSq	Infit Std	Outfit MnSq	Outfit Std	Nu Item
824	177	4.7	4.5	-0.09	0.12	1.1	0	1.1	0	1 DesF
780	177	4.4	4.3	0.50	0.12	0.8	-2	0.8	-1	2 DesG
777	177	4.4	4.3	0.55	0.12	1.1	0	1.1	0	3 DesV
773	178	4.3	4.2	0.66	0.12	0.7	-3	0.7	-2	4 NarG
790	178	4.4	4.3	0.43	0.12	0.9	0	0.9	0	5 NarV
802	178	4.5	4.4	0.26	0.12	1.2	1	1.3	2	6 NarC
836	175	4.8	4.7	-0.39	0.12	1.0	0	1.0	0	7 RPF
772	175	4.4	4.3	0.49	0.12	0.7	-2	0.7	-2	8 RPG
864	175	4.9	4.9	-0.78	0.12	1.4	3	1.5	3	9 RPI
833	176	4.7	4.6	-0.29	0.12	0.9	0	1.0	0	10 Exp1F
810	176	4.6	4.5	0.03	0.12	1.0	0	1.0	0	11 Exp1V
830	176	4.7	4.6	-0.25	0.12	1.1	1	1.2	1	12 Exp1C
855	175	4.9	4.8	-0.65	0.12	0.8	-2	0.9	-1	13 Exp2F
824	175	4.7	4.6	-0.23	0.12	0.7	-2	0.8	-2	14 Exp2V
836	175	4.8	4.7	-0.39	0.12	1.0	0	0.9	0	15 Exp2C
884	178	5.0	4.9	-0.84	0.12	0.8	-1	0.8	-1	16 DisF
827	178	4.6	4.5	-0.07	0.12	0.7	-2	0.7	-2	17 DisG
873	178	4.9	4.8	-0.69	0.12	1.6	4	1.6	4	18 DisI
833	178	4.7	4.6	-0.15	0.12	0.6	-4	0.6	-3	19 CommEf
989	178	5.6	5.6	-2.33	0.12	1.5	4	1.6	3	20 Comp
814	176	4.6	4.5	-0.06	0.12	1.0	0	1.1	0	21 TDes1F
781	176	4.4	4.3	0.38	0.12	0.8	-1	0.8	-1	22 TDes1G
789	176	4.5	4.4	0.28	0.12	1.1	1	1.2	1	23 TDes1V
756	176	4.3	4.2	0.72	0.12	0.8	-2	0.8	-1	24 TNarG
787	176	4.5	4.4	0.30	0.12	0.8	-2	0.8	-1	25 TNarV
804	176	4.6	4.5	0.08	0.12	1.1	0	1.1	1	26 TNarC
797	174	4.6	4.5	0.08	0.12	1.1	0	1.1	0	27 TSumF
730	174	4.2	4.1	0.99	0.12	0.8	-2	0.7	-2	28 TSumG
730	174	4.2	4.1	0.99	0.12	1.0	0	1.0	0	29 TSumV
799	173	4.6	4.5	-0.01	0.12	1.3	2	1.4	2	30 TRPF
741	173	4.3	4.2	0.78	0.12	0.9	-1	1.0	0	31 TRPG
844	173	4.9	4.8	-0.61	0.12	1.5	4	1.5	4	32 TRPI
809	175	4.6	4.5	-0.02	0.12	0.9	0	1.0	0	33 TExpF
781	175	4.5	4.4	0.35	0.12	0.9	0	1.0	0	34 TExpV
794	175	4.5	4.4	0.18	0.12	1.3	2	1.4	2	35 TExp
843	178	4.7	4.7	-0.32	0.11	1.1	0	1.1	0	36 TInsF
802	178	4.5	4.4	0.22	0.11	1.0	0	1.0	0	37 TInsV
799	178	4.5	4.4	0.26	0.11	1.2	1	1.2	1	38 TInsC
827	178	4.6	4.6	-0.11	0.11	1.0	0	1.1	1	39 TDisF
795	178	4.5	4.4	0.31	0.11	0.6	-3	0.7	-3	40 TDisG
886	178	5.0	4.9	-0.89	0.12	1.3	2	1.3	2	41 TDisI
834	178	4.7	4.6	-0.20	0.11	0.7	-2	0.8	-1	42 TDes2F
791	177	4.5	4.4	0.31	0.11	0.6	-4	0.6	-4	43 TDes2G
811	178	4.6	4.5	0.10	0.11	0.8	-1	0.8	-1	44 TDes2V
807	178	4.5	4.4	0.15	0.11	0.6	-4	0.7	-3	45 TComm

Obsvd Score	Obsvd Count	Obsvd Average	Fair Avrge	Measure	Model S.E.	Infit MnSq	Infit Std	Outfit MnSq	Outfit Std	Nu Item
812.5	176.3	4.6	4.5	0.00	0.12	1.0	-0.4	1.0	-0.2	Mean
44.3	1.6	0.2	0.3	0.57	0.00	0.3	2.3	0.3	2.2	S.D.

RMSE 0.12 Adj S.D. 0.56 Separation 4.84 Reliability 0.96
Fixed (all same) chi-square: 1054.98 d.f.: 44 significance: .00
Random (normal) chi-square: 43.92 d.f.: 43 significance: .43

Subject index

A

access: test   1, 33–46
   Development of oral interaction sub-test 35–46
Australian Second Language Proficiency Ratings (ASLPR) 4, 44–5, 62, 68
Authenticity 6–8, 25

C

Case studies   47–9, 52–6
   Instrumental   48–9, 54–5
   Intrinsic   48–9
Conversations   7

F

FACETS   58–59, 65–79, 145–161, 164–165
   Bias analysis   58–59, 76–78, 157–161, 167
G
G-theory   19–20

I

International English Language Testing System (IELTS)   5, 35
Interviews   6, 7

M

Multi-faceted Rasch measurement   3, 42, 57–59, 65, 69, 139, 163

O

Occupational English Test   (OET) 27–8
Occupational Foreign Language Test   (OFLT) 29
Oral Proficiency Interview   (OPI) 4,7, 10, 12–27, 32, 80, 81
   Assymetry   6
Oxford-ARELS   6

P

Proficiency tests   9–10
Psychometric unidimensionality   69–74, 150–4, 163, 167

R

Recorded Oral Proficiency Examination (ROPE)   5, 16
Research
    Different approaches   49–52, 170–171
    Reliability and validity   52–5

S

Simulated Oral Proficiency Interview (SOPI)   6, 16–24, 26-32, 80–81
Speaking tests   4–6
    Direct   4–14
    Indirect   4, 6
    Semi-direct   5–11, 15–32
SPEAK test   24–25

T

Test equivalence   16, 29, 68, 76, 79, 80–81, 100–101, 117–18, 130, 145–46,
    154, 161–69
Test in English for Educational Purposes (TEEP)   6, 28
Test practicality   11–12
Test processes   3, 56, 59–60, 117–144, 166
    Rating 3, 126–27, 138–143
    Test design   3, 123–24, 126–32
    Test taking   3, 25-29, 122–24, 132–37
Test products
    Test scores   3, 15–22, 56, 58–59
    Test taker language output   3, 22–23, 30, 56, 59, 80–116, 164–65
Test of Spoken English (TSE)   5, 15–16, 24
Test reliability   10–11
Test specifications   22, 35–46
Test validity   6–11
    Concurrent   2, 9, 12–22, 30, 36, 68, 169–170
    Construct   22, 24, 31, 170
    Content   25
    Face   25–29

U

University of Cambridge Local Examinations Syndicate (UCLES)   5

Author index

A
Alderson   9, 26, 43

B
Bachman   12, 18, 21, 24, 25, 43
Benson   49
Berwick   31
Brindley   36
Brown   29

C
Cherryholmes   2, 51
Cizek   148
Clark   4, 5, 6, 7, 8, 9, 12, 13, 15, 16, 17, 26, 27
Clifford   5, 13, 16

D
Davies   43

F
Filipi   31

G
Gardner   37, 38
Goetz   52, 53
Guba   50, 51, 54, 55

H
Halliday   103, 102, 105, 106
Hamilton   43
Hamp-Lyons   29, 171
Hasan   102, 103
Hawthorne   33
Hill   124, 135
Hoejke   9, 24, 25
Howe   51
Hughes   6, 7, 10

I
Ingram   4, 12, 44

J
James   6, 11, 28, 29
Johns-Lewis   101, 102, 103, 114, 115
Johnson   2, 48, 49

K
Kenyon   17, 19, 21

L
Labov   123
Lazaraton   10, 11, 31, 169
LeCompte   52, 53
Li   17
Linacre   42, 58, 65, 145
Lincoln   51, 54, 55
Linnell   9, 24, 25
Lowe 5,   12, 13, 16
Lumley   141
Luoma   29, 30, 31
Lynch   2, 29, 50, 51, 52, 59, 122, 123, 171

M
McNamara   27, 28, 58, 69, 70, 76, 77, 139, 154, 169
Meddis   18
Merriam   2, 47, 49, 50, 54
Messick   171
Morton   31, 139
Moss   171
Murray   31

N
Neeson   31
Nunan   2, 48, 49, 50, 52, 53

O
O'Loughlin   62, 65, 68, 69, 75

P
Perrett   17
Phillips   50
Pollitt   31

R
Raffaldani   17
Ross   31

S
Sato   49
Saville   31
Savignon   43
Sheorey 15,   16
Shephard   177
Shohamy   2, 3, 5, 17, 21, 22, 23, 24, 26, 29, 32, 36, 37, 56, 59, 80, 81–100, 103, 104, 114, 115, 165, 169
Southard   15,16
Spolsky   25, 171–173
Stake   2, 48, 49, 53, 54
Stansfield   6, 16, 17, 18, 19, 20, 27
Stevenson   25, 27
Stubbs   102, 103, 112
Sunderland   149
Swinton   15

U
Underhill   8, 10, 11
Ure   101, 102, 103, 112, 113

V
van Lier   6, 7, 9, 10, 17, 169

W
Wigglesworth   31, 42, 62, 65, 68, 69, 75, 77, 78, 139
Williams   31
Willis   105
Wylie   4, 12, 44

Y
Yin   2, 47, 48, 49

Z
Zora   101, 102, 103, 114, 115